HENRY MARTYN

HENRY MARTYN

Engraved by W. Finden, from a Picture in the possession of the Rev. C. Simeon.

H. Martyn

THE LIFE AND LETTERS OF HENRY MARTYN

John Sargent, M.A.

THE BANNER OF TRUTH TRUST

THE BANNER OF TRUTH TRUST
3 Murrayfield Road, Edinburgh EH 12 6EL
P.O. Box 621, Carlisle, Pennsylvania, 17013, U.S.A.

*

First published 1819
This edition first published 1862
First Banner of Truth Trust edition 1985
ISBN 0 85151 468 5

*

Printed and bound in Great Britain by
Hazell Watson & Viney Limited,
Member of the BPCC Group,
Aylesbury, Bucks

PREFACE TO THE FIRST EDITION.

BEFORE the reader proceeds to the perusal of the following Memoir, it may be proper to inform him, that the first and second parts of it have been chiefly selected from various journals which Mr. Martyn was in the habit of keeping for his own private use, and which, beginning with the year 1803, comprehend a period of eight years. The third part is extracted from an account which he drew up of his visit to Shiraz, in Persia, in which some occasional observations on the state of his own mind and feelings are interspersed. It is termed "A Narrative" by Mr. Martyn; and it was probably his intention to have enlarged it for the use of the public had his life been spared, or perhaps to have communicated it, nearly in its original shape, to his intimate friends. From the style and manner of it, at least, it may be presumed not to have been exclusively intended, as the journals above mentioned evidently were, for his own recollection and benefit. The greater part of the last-mentioned papers were upon the point of being destroyed by the writer on his undertaking his voyage to Persia; but, happily, he was prevailed upon by the Rev. D. Corrie to confide them under a seal to his care, and by him they were trans-

mitted from India to the Rev. C. Simeon and J.
Thornton, Esq., Mr. Martyn's executors, in the year
1814. "The Narrative," which was sent by Mr. Morier
from Constantinople, came into their hands in the following year. Such are the materials from which I have
compiled the present Memoir,—throughout the whole of
which I have endeavoured, as much as possible, to let
Mr. Martyn speak for himself, and thus to exhibit a
genuine picture of his own mind.

In making a selection from a mass of such valuable
matter, it has been my anxious wish and sincere prayer,
that it might prove subservient to the interests of true
religion. One principal object with me has been, to
render it beneficial to those disinterested ministers of the
Gospel, who, "with the Bible in their hand, and their
Saviour in their hearts," devote themselves to the
great cause for which Mr. Martyn lived and died : and,
truly, if the example here delineated should excite any
of those servants of Christ to similar exertion, or if it
should animate and encourage them, amidst the multiplied difficulties of their arduous course, my labour will
receive an eminent and abundant recompense.

                                        J. S.

PREFACE TO THE TENTH EDITION.

IN *a Tenth Edition* it certainly is tardy,—at any period it probably would have been fruitless,—to attempt the counteraction of an impression not uncommon with the reader;—that the subject of this work was of a gloomy temperament, and that his religion assumed a desponding character. Late, however, as the declaration is,—ineffectual as perhaps it will be,—I am anxious to testify, from intimate personal knowledge, that this opinion is founded in complete misconception. Few persons, if any, known to me, have equalled him in the enjoyment of that "peace which passeth all understanding,"—few have possessed so animating and abiding an expectation of life and immortality. Those who are disposed to question this statement, from the strain of deep self-abasement which he perpetually adopts,—do in my judgment convert what is a substantial *proof* of the assertion, into an ill-founded *objection*. SUCH, AT ALL EVENTS, WAS THE FACT : I can appeal to many living witnesses ; they can confirm what is advanced ; they also with me can aver, that Henry Martyn was not less cheerful as a companion, than he was warm-hearted and constant as a friend.

Those who imagine that a smile scarcely ever played

upon his countenance,—that his manner was cold and
forbidding, would have been startled at hearing his hearty
laugh, which still sounds in my ears, and in seeing little
children climbing his knees, affording him a pleasure as
great as they themselves received.   That his natural
temper was more irritable than I had supposed, is plain
from the story of the knife, p. 7, which I at first dis-
believed, but have since ascertained to be true.   Of the
tenderness of his heart,—in addition to the evidences
before given, there is a touching one, p. 272, which, whilst
his "beloved Persis" was yet amongst us, could not so
well be published.   For the previous non-insertion of that
golden passage, p. 239, I have only one excuse,—the dis-
tracting richness of his voluminous journals.   Many
masses of ore, and not mere filings, are still necessarily
left behind.   I will only add that I cannot enough deplore
the unaccountable loss of the introduction to that sermon
preached by him on ship-board, on the awful subject of
eternal punishment.   The preference it expresses for other
topics of discourse,—the reluctance it avows in bringing
forward the painful one then under consideration,—the
motives it exhibits,—love and concern for those whom he
addressed,—would convince those who may have suspected
him of harshness, that if on this occasion he "used the
lancet, it was not till he had concealed it in the sponge."

In the absence of the document itself, my testimony, I
hope, to the above effect, will not be discredited.

J. S.

In an Appendix to the present volume will be found a series of seventeen letters which have appeared in no former edition of this Memoir. This series comprises all the letters addressed by Mr. Martyn to Miss Grenfell, from the period of his departure from England until the close of his life. During Miss G.'s lifetime, or while her death was yet recent, there would have been a manifest impropriety in giving publicity to such a correspondence; but when both the parties, and all their near connexions, had long since descended to the tomb, it was felt that all ground for the continuance of this privacy was taken away; and accordingly, in the large edition of all Mr. Martyn's Journals and Letters, published in the year 1837, these letters for the first time appeared. It now seems desirable, for the complete filling up of Mr. M.'s portraiture, to add these letters to the present volume. The value of his character, as an example to the Christian missionary, consists mainly in his spirit of patient self-sacrifice; and the measure and extent of this cannot be fully appreciated, without a perusal of these interesting letters.

April, 1862.

CONTENTS.

CHAPTER IV.

CHAPTER V.

CHAPTER VI.

CHAPTER VII.

CHAPTER XI.

APPENDIX.

ILLUSTRATIONS.

A MEMOIR.

CHAPTER I.

EARLY LIFE OF HENRY MARTYN.——HIS SUCCESSFUL ACADEMICAL CAREER.

It has been well observed, by one* who took a profound view of human nature, that there are three very different orbits in which great men move and shine ; and that each sphere of greatness has its respective admirers. There are those who, as heroes, fill the world with their exploits ; they are greeted by the acclamations of the multitude ; they are ennobled whilst living, and their names descend with lustre to posterity. Others there are who, by the brilliancy of their imagination or the vigour of their intellect, attain to honour of a purer and a higher kind ; the fame of these is confined to a more select number ; for all have not a discriminating sense of their merit. A third description remains, distinct from both of the former, and far more exalted than either ; whose excellence consists in a renunciation of themselves, and a compassionate love for mankind. In this order the

* Pascal.

B

Saviour of the world was pleased to appear ; and those persons obtain the highest rank in it, who, by his grace, are enabled most closely to imitate his example.

HENRY MARTYN, the subject of this Memoir, was born at Truro, in the county of Cornwall, on the 18th of February, 1781, and appears, with his family in general, to have inherited a weak constitution ; as, of many children, four only, two sons and two daughters, survived their father, Mr. John Martyn, and all of these, within a short period, followed him to the grave. Of these Henry was the third. His father was originally in a very humble situation of life, having been a labourer in the mines of Gwenap, the place of his nativity. With no education but such as a country reading-school afforded, he was compelled to engage, for his daily support, in an employment which, dreary and unhealthy as it was, offered some advantages, of which he most meritoriously availed himself. The miners, it seems, are in the habit of working and resting alternately every four hours ; and the periods of relaxation from manual labour, they frequently devote to mental improvement. In these intervals of cessation from toil, John Martyn acquired a complete knowledge of arithmetic, and also some acquaintance with mathematics ; and no sooner had he gathered these valuable and substantial fruits of persevering diligence, in a soil most unfriendly to their growth, than he was raised from a state of poverty and depression to one of comparative ease and comfort. Being admitted to the office of Mr. Daniel, a merchant of Truro, he lived there as chief clerk, very respectably, enjoying considerably more than a competency. At the grammar-school in this town, the master of which was the Rev. Cornelius Cardew, D.D., a gentleman of learning and

TRURO.

Page 2.

TRURO.

Page 2.

talents, Henry was placed by his father in Midsummer, 1788, being then between seven and eight years of age. Of his childhood, previous to this period, little or nothing can be ascertained; but those who knew him, considered him to be a boy of promising abilities.

Upon his first entering the school, Dr. Cardew observes, that "he did not fail to answer the expectations which had been formed of him : his proficiency in the classics exceeded that of most of his schoolfellows ; yet there were boys who made a more rapid progress ;—not perhaps that their abilities were superior, but their application was greater ; for he was of a lively cheerful temper, and, as I have been told by those who sat near him, appeared to be the idlest among them ; being frequently known to go up to his lesson with little or no preparation,—as if he had learned it by intuition."

In all schools there are boys, as is well known, who from natural softness of spirit, inferiority in point of bodily strength, or an unusual thirst for literary acquirements, become much secluded from the rest ; and such boys are generally exposed to the ridicule and oppression of their associates. Henry Martyn, though not at that time eminently studious, was one of this class ; he seldom joined the other boys in their pastimes, in which he was not an adept ; and he often suffered from the tyranny of those older and stronger than himself.

"Little Harry Martyn" (for by that name he usually went), says one of his earliest friends and companions, "was in a manner proverbial among his schoolfellows for a peculiar tenderness and inoffensiveness of spirit, which exposed him to the ill offices of many overbearing boys ; and as there was at times some peevishness in his manner when attacked, he was often unkindly treated. That he might receive assistance in his lessons he was placed near one of the upper boys, with whom he contracted a friendship which lasted through life, and whose imagination readily recalls the position in which he used to sit, the thankful expression of his affectionate countenance, when he happened to be helped out of some difficulty, and a thousand other little incidents of his boyish days."—— Besides assisting him in his exercises, his friend, it is added, "had often the happiness of rescuing him from the grasp of oppressors, and has never seen more feeling gratitude evinced than was shown by him on those occasions."

At this school, under the same excellent tuition, Henry remained till he was between fourteen and fifteen years of age ; at which period he was induced to offer himself as a candidate for a vacant scholarship at Corpus Christi College, Oxford. Young as he was, he went there alone, without any interest in the University, and with only a single letter to one of the tutors ; and while there, he acquitted himself so well, though strongly and ably opposed, that in the opinion of some of the Examiners he ought to have been elected. How often is the hand of God seen in frustrating our fondest designs ! Had success attended him, the whole circumstances of his after-life would have been varied ; and however his temporal interests might have been promoted, his spiritual interests would probably have sustained a proportionate loss.

It was with sensations of this kind that he himself many years afterwards reverted to this disappointment. "In the Autumn of 1795," he says, in an account prefixed to his private journal of the year 1803, "my father, at the persuasion of many of his friends, sent me to

Oxford, to be a candidate for the vacant scholarship at Corpus Christi. I entered at no college, but had rooms at Exeter College, by the interest of Mr. Cole, the sub-rector. I passed the examination, I believe, tolerably well; but was unsuccessful, having every reason to think that the decision was impartial. Had I remained, and become a member of the University at that time, as I should have done in case of success, the profligate acquaintances I had there would have introduced me to scenes of debauchery, in which I must, in all probability, from my extreme youth, have sunk for ever."

After this repulse, Henry returned home, and continued to attend Dr. Cardew's school till June, 1797. That he had made no inconsiderable progress there was evident from the very creditable examination he passed at Oxford; and in the two years subsequent to this, he must have greatly augmented his fund of classical knowledge; but it seems not to have been till after he had commenced his academical career, that his superiority of talent was fully discovered. The signal success of that friend, who had been his guide and protector at school, led him in the spring of this year to direct his views towards the University of Cambridge, which he probably preferred to that of Oxford, because he hoped there to profit by the advice and assistance to which he was already so much indebted. Whatever might be the cause of this preference, it certainly did not arise from any predilection for mathematics; for he confesses that in the autumn before he went to Cambridge, instead of the study of Euclid and Algebra, one part of the day was dedicated to his favourite employment of shooting, and the other to reading, for the most part travels, and Lord Chesterfield's Letters;—"attributing to a want of

taste for mathematics what ought to have been ascribed
to idleness ; and having his mind in a roving, dissatisfied,
restless condition, seeking his chief pleasure in reading
and in human praise."

His residence at St. John's College, where his name
had been previously entered in the summer, commenced
in the month of October, 1797 ; and it may tend to show
how little can be determined from first attempts, to
relate that Henry Martyn began his mathematical pursuits by attempting to commit the propositions of Euclid
to memory.   The endeavour may be considered as a proof
of the confidence he himself entertained in the retentive
powers of his mind ; but it certainly did not supply an
auspicious omen of future excellence.

On his introduction to the University, happily for him,
the friend of his "boyish days" became the counsellor of
his riper years ; nor was this most important act of friendship either lost upon him at the time, or obliterated from
his memory in after-life.   "During the first term," he
has recorded in his journal, "I was kept a good deal in
idleness by some of my new acquaintances, but the kind
attention of K—— was a principal means of my preservation from excess."   That his time was far from
being wholly misemployed, between October and Christmas, is evident from the place he obtained in the first
class at the public examination of his college in December ;
a circumstance which, joined to the extreme desire he
had to gratify his father, encouraged and excited him to
study with increased alacrity ; and as the fruit of this
application, at the next public examination in the
summer, he reached the second station in the first
class, a point of elevation which "flattered his pride
not a little."

The tenour of Henry Martyn's life during this and the succeeding year, would, in the eye of the world, be considered to have been amiable and commendable. He was outwardly moral; was with little exception unwearied in application ; and exhibited marks of no ordinary talent. One exception to this statement is to be found in an irritability of temper, increased, if not engendered, by the treatment he had met with at school. These ebullitions of passion had, on one occasion, nearly proved fatal to a friend,—the late excellent Mr. Cotterill;—afterwards minister of St. Paul's Church, Sheffield. . He barely escaped the point of a knife, which, thrown by the hand of Henry Martyn, most providentially missed him, and was left trembling in the wall. If from this unsubdued impetuosity of temper we pass to his avowed and fixed principles,—these, as might well be expected, evince him to have been living at this time "without God in the world." The consideration that God chiefly regards the *motives* of our actions,—a consideration so momentous, and so essential to the character of a real Christian, appears as yet never to have entered his mind ; and even when it did, as was the case at this time, it rested there as a theoretic notion, which was never meant to be reduced to practice. His own account of himself is very striking. Speaking of June, 1799, he says, "K——— (the friend alluded to before) attempted to persuade me that I ought to attend to reading, not for the praise of men, but for the glory of God. This seemed *strange* to me, but *reasonable.* I resolved, therefore, to *maintain this opinion* thenceforth ; but never designed, that I remember, that it should *affect my conduct.*" What a decisive mark this of an unrenewed mind —what an affecting proof that light may break in upon the understanding, whilst there is not so much as the dawn of it on the heart !

Providentially for Henry Martyn, he had not only the great blessing of possessing a religious friend at College, but he possessed likewise the happiness of having a sister in Cornwall, who was a Christian of a meek, heavenly, and affectionate spirit ; to whom, as well as to the rest of his relations there, he paid a visit in the summer of the year 1799, carrying with him no small degree of academical honour, though not all that he had fondly and ambitiously expected. He had lost the prize for themes in his college, and was only second again in the first class at the public examination, when he had hoped to have been first ;—a "double disappointment," to use his own words, "which nettled him to the quick." It may be well supposed, that to a sister such as we have described, her brother's spiritual welfare would be a most serious and anxious concern ; and that she often conversed with him on the subject of religion, we learn from his own declaration. " I went home this summer, and was frequently addressed by my dear sister on the subject of religion ; but the sound of the Gospel, conveyed in the admonition of a sister, was grating to my ears." The first result of her tender exhortations and earnest endeavours was very discouraging : a violent conflict took place in her brother's mind, between his conviction of the truth of what she urged, and his love of the world ; and, for the present, the latter prevailed. Yet sisters, similarly circumstanced, may learn from this case, not merely their duty, but also, from the *final* result, the success they may anticipate in the faithful discharge of it. " I think," he observes, when afterwards reviewing this period with a spirit truly broken and contrite, "I do not remember a time in which the wickedness of my heart rose to a greater height than during my stay at home. The consummate selfishness and exquisite irritability of my mind were displayed in rage, malice, and envy ; in pride, and vain glory, and contempt of all ; in the harshest language to my sister, and even to my father, if he happened to differ from my mind and will. O what an example of patience and mildness was he ! I love to think of his excellent qualities, and it is frequently the anguish of my heart, that I ever could be so base and wicked as to pain him by the slightest neglect. O my God and Father, why is not my heart *doubly* agonized at the remembrance of all my great transgressions against Thee ever since I have known Thee as such ! I left my sister and father in October, and him I saw no more. I promised my sister that I would read the Bible for myself, but on being settled at college, Newton engaged all my thoughts."

At length, however, it pleased God to convince Henry by a most affecting visitation of his providence, that there was a knowledge far more important to him than any human science ; and to lead him, whilst contemplating the heavens by the light of astronomy, to devote himself to *His* service, who having made those heavens, and having left them for man's salvation, is now again exalted to the right hand of God, as his Mediator and Advocate. The sudden and heart-rending intelligence of the death of his father was the proximate, though, doubtless, not the efficient, cause of his receiving these convictions. How poignant were his sufferings under this affliction may be seen in the account he himself has left of it ;— from whence it is evident that it was a season of not only severe but also sanctified sorrow ; a seed-time of tears, promising that harvest of holiness, peace, and joy, which succeeded it.

"At the examination at Christmas, 1799," he writes, "I was first, and the account of it pleased my father prodigiously, who, I was told, was in great health and spirits. What then was my consternation when, in January, I received from my brother an account of his death! But while I mourned the loss of an earthly parent, the angels in heaven were rejoicing at my being so soon to find an heavenly one. As I had no taste at this time for my usual studies, I took up my Bible, thinking that the consideration of religion was rather suitable to this solemn time; nevertheless I often took up other books to engage my attention, and should have continued to do so, had not K—— advised me to make this time an occasion of serious reflection. I began with the Acts, as being the most amusing; and, whilst I was entertained with the narrative, I found myself insensibly led to inquire more attentively into the doctrines of the Apostles. These corresponded nearly enough with the few notions I had received in my early youth. I believe, on the first night after, I began to pray from a precomposed form, in which I thanked God in general, for having sent Christ into the world. But though I prayed for pardon, I had little sense of my own sinfulness; nevertheless, I began to consider myself a religious man. The first time after this that I went to chapel, I saw, with some degree of surprise at my former inattention, that in the 'Magnificat' there was a great degree of joy expressed at the coming of Christ, which I thought but reasonable. K—— had lent me Doddridge's 'Rise and Progress.' The first part of this I could not bear to read, because it appeared to make religion consist too much in humiliation: and my proud and wicked heart would not bear to be brought down into the dust. And K——, to whom I mentioned the gloom which I felt, after reading the first part of Doddridge, reprobated it strongly. Alas! did he think that we can go along the way that leadeth unto life, without entering in at the 'strait gate?'"

It was not long after Henry had been called to endure this gracious, though grievous, chastening from above, that the public exercises commenced in the University; and although his greatest stimulus to exertion was removed by the loss of his father, whom it had been his most anxious desire to please, he again devoted himself to his mathematical studies with unwearied diligence. That spiritual danger exists in an intense application of the mind to these studies, he was so deeply sensible at a later period of his life, as, on a review of this particular time, most gratefully to acknowledge, that "the mercy of God prevented the extinction of that spark of grace which His Spirit had kindled." At the moment of his exposure to this peril he was less conscious of it; but we may perceive, from the following letter to his youngest sister, that he was not wholly devoid of circumspection on this head. Having shortly, and with much simplicity, announced that his name stood first upon the list at the college examination of the summer of the year 1800, he thus expresses himself:—"What a blessing it is for me that I have such a sister as you, my dear S——, who have been so instrumental in keeping me in the right way. When I consider how little human assistance you have had, and the great knowledge to which you have attained on the subject of religion—especially observing the extreme ignorance of the most wise and learned of this world—I think this is itself a proof of the wonderful influence of the Holy Ghost on the minds of well-disposed persons. It is certainly by the Spirit alone that we can have the will, or power, or knowledge, or confidence to pray ; and by Him alone we come unto the Father through Jesus Christ. ' Through Him we both have access by one Spirit unto the Father.' How I rejoice to find that we disagreed only about words ! I did not doubt, as you suppose, at all about that joy which true believers feel. Can there be any one subject any one source of cheerfulness and joy, to be at all compared with the heavenly serenity and comfort which such a person must find, in holding communion with his God and Saviour in prayer,—in addressing God as his Father, and, more than all, in the transporting hope of being preserved unto everlasting life, and of singing praises to his Redeemer when time shall be no more ? Oh ! I do indeed feel this state of mind at times ; but at other times I feel quite humbled at finding myself so cold and hard-hearted. That reluctance to prayer, that unwillingness to come unto God, who is the fountain of all good, when reason and experience tell us that with Him only true pleasure is to be found, seem to be owing to Satanic influence. Though I think my employment in life gives me peculiar advantages, in some respects, with regard to religious knowledge ; yet, with regard to having a practical sense of things on the mind, it is by far the worst of any. For the labourer as he drives on his plough, and the weaver as he works at his loom, may have his thoughts entirely disengaged from his work, and may think with advantage upon any religious subject. But the nature of *our* studies require such a deep abstraction of the mind from all other things, as to render it completely incapable of anything else, and that during many hours of the day. With respect to the dealings of the Almighty with me, you have heard in general the chief of my account; as I am brought to a sense of things gradually, there is nothing peculiarly striking in it to particularize. After the death of our father, you know I was extremely low-spirited; and, like most other people, began to consider seriously, without any particular determination, that invisible world to which he was gone, and to which I must one day go. Yet I still read the Bible unenlightened; and said a prayer or two, rather through terror of a superior power than from any other cause. Soon, however, I began to attend more diligently to the words of our Saviour in the New Testament, and to devour them with delight;—when the offers of mercy and forgiveness were made so freely, I supplicated to be made partaker of the covenant of grace with eagerness and hope;—and thanks be to the ever-blessed Trinity, for not leaving me without comfort. Throughout the whole, however, even when the light of Divine truth was beginning to dawn on my mind, I was not under that great terror of future punishment, which I now see plainly I had every reason to feel: I now look back upon that course of wickedness which, like a gulph of destruction, yawned to swallow me up, with a trembling delight, mixed with shame at having lived so long in ignorance, error, and blindness. I could say much more, my dear S——, but I have no more room. I have only to express my acquiescence in *most* of your opinions, and to join with you in gratitude to God for His mercies to us : may He preserve you and me and all of us to the day of the Lord !"

How cheering to his sister must it have been to receive at a moment of deep sorrow such a communication as this, indicating a state of mind not thoroughly instructed, indeed, in the mystery of faith, but fully alive to the

supreme importance of religion. How salutary to his
own mind to have possessed so near a relation to whom
he could thus freely open the workings of his heart !
But the chief cause, under God, of his stability, at this
season, in those religious principles which by Divine
grace he had adopted, was evidently that constant
attendance which he now commenced on the ministry of
the Rev. Charles Simeon, at Trinity Church, in Cambridge ; under whose truly pastoral instructions, he himself declares that he " gradually acquired more knowledge
in Divine things."

In the retrospect which Henry afterwards took of this
part of his life, he seems sometimes ready to suspect
a want of growth, and almost a want of vitality in his
religion ; but though there may have been some ground
for the former of these suspicions, there certainly was
none, whatever his humility may have suggested, for the
latter. " I can only account," he says, " for my being
stationary so long, by the intenseness with which I pursued my studies, in which I was so absorbed, that the
time I gave to them seemed not to be a portion of
my existence. That in which I now see I was lament-
ably deficient, was a humble and contrite spirit, through
which I should have perceived more clearly the excellency of Christ. The eagerness, too, with which I looked
forward to the approaching examination for degrees, too
clearly betrayed a heart not dead to the world."

That a public examination for a degree in the University must be a time of painful solicitude to those about
to pass through it, is obvious ;—especially when great
expectations have been raised, and worldly prospects are
likely to be seriously affected by the event. From Henry
Martyn much was expected ; and had he altogether failed,

his temporal interests would have materially suffered. Nor was he naturally insensible to those perturbations which are apt to arise in a youthful and ambitious breast. It happened, however (as he was frequently known to assert), that upon entering the Senate House,—in which a larger than the usual proportion of able young men were his competitors,—his mind was singularly composed and tranquillized by the recollection of a sermon which he had heard not long before, on the text—"Seekest thou great things for thyself; seek them not, saith the Lord." He thus became divested of that extreme anxiety about success, which by harassing his spirit, must have impeded the free exercise of his powers. His decided superiority in mathematics therefore soon appeared; and the highest academical honour, that of "Senior Wrangler," was awarded to him, in January, 1801, at which period he had not completed the twentieth year of his age. Nor is it any disparagement to that honour, or to those who conferred it on him, to record that it was attended in this instance with that sense of disappointment and dissatisfaction to which all earthly blessings are subject. His description of his own feelings on this occasion is very remarkable—"I obtained my highest wishes, but was surprised to find that I had grasped a shadow." So impossible is it for earthly distinctions, even though awarded for successful exertions of the intellect, to fill and satisfy the mind, especially after it has tasted "the good word of God, and the powers of the world to come." So certain is it, that he who drinks of the water of the wells of *this* life must thirst again; and that it is the water which springs up to *everlasting* life which alone affords never-failing refreshment.

CHAPTER II.

HAVING thus attained that station of remarkable merit and eminence, upon which his eye from the first had been fixed, and for which he had toiled with such astonishing diligence as to be designated in his college as "the man who had not lost an hour," and having received likewise the first of two prizes given annually to the best proficients in mathematics amongst those bachelors who have just taken their degree—in the month of March, Henry again visited Cornwall, where amidst the joyful greetings and congratulations of all his friends, his youngest sister was alone dejected; not witnessing in him that progress in Christian knowledge which she had been fondly led to anticipate.

Nor ought we to attribute this wholly to that ardency of affection, which might dispose her to indulge in sanguine and somewhat unreasonable expectations. Those who know what human nature is, even after it has been renewed by the Spirit of God, will not deny that it is more than possible that her brother's zeal might have somewhat relaxed in the bright sunshine of academical honour; and certain it is that his standard of duty, though superior to that of the world, was at this time far from reaching that degree of elevation which it afterwards attained. Who can wonder, then, that a person tremblingly alive to his best interests, should not be wholly free from apprehension, and should be continually urging on his conscience the solemn sanctions of the Gospel, entreating him to *aim at* nothing less than Christian perfection ?

Returning to Cambridge in the summer of this year, he passed the season of vacation most profitably; constrained, happily, to be *much alone*, he employed his solitary hours in frequent communion with his own heart, and with that gracious Lord who once blessed Isaac and Nathanael in their secret devotions, and who did not withhold a blessing from his. " God," he observes, " was pleased to bless the solitude and retirement I enjoyed this summer, to my improvement ; and not until then had I ever experienced any real pleasure in religion. I was more convinced of sin than ever, more earnest in fleeing to Jesus for refuge, and more desirous of the renewal of my nature."

It was during this vacation also that an intimate acquaintance commenced, as much distinguished by a truly parental regard on the one hand, as it was by a grateful, reverential, and filial affection on the other. Having long listened with no small degree of pleasure and profit to Mr. Simeon, as a preacher, Henry now began to enjoy the happiness of an admission to the most friendly and unreserved intercourse with him, and was in the habit of soliciting and receiving, on all important occasions, his counsel and encouragement. By Mr. Simeon's kindness it was that he was now made known to several young men, with some of whom he formed the most enduring of all attachments—a Christian friendship ; and it was from his conversation and example also, that he imbibed his first impressions of the transcendent excellence of the Christian ministry ; from which it was but a short step to resolve upon devoting himself to that sacred calling:—for until now he had an intention of applying to the law, "chiefly," he confesses, "because he could not consent to be poor for Christ's sake."

The great advancement which he had made in genuine piety at this period, from intercourse with real Christians, and, above all, from secret communion with his God, is discernible in the following extracts from two letters—the first dated September 15, 1801, and addressed to his earliest friend; the second written a few days afterwards, to his youngest sister. "That you may be enabled to do the will of your heavenly Father, shall be, you may be assured, my constant prayer at the throne of grace; and this, as well from the desire of promoting the edification of Christ's body upon earth, as from motives of private gratitude. You have been the instrument in the hands of Providence of bringing me to a serious sense of things: for at the time of my father's death, I was using such methods of alleviating my sorrow, as I almost shudder to recollect. But, blessed be God, I have now experienced that Christ is 'the power of God, and the wisdom of God.' What a blessing is the Gospel! No heart can conceive its excellency, but that which has been renewed by Divine grace."

"I have lately," he writes in the second letter, "been witness to a scene of distress. P——, in this town, with whom I have been a little acquainted, and who had lived to the full extent of his income, is now dying, and his family will be left perfectly destitute. I called yesterday to know whether he was still alive, and found his wife in a greater agony than you can conceive. She was wringing her hands, and crying out to me, 'Oh, pray for his soul!' and then again recollecting her own helpless condition, and telling me of her wretchedness in being turned out upon the world without house or home. It was in vain to point to heaven; the heart, distracted and overwhelmed with worldly sorrow, finds it hard to look to God. Since writing this, I have been to call on the daughters of P——, who had removed to another house, because, from the violence of their grief, they incommoded the sick man. Thither I went to visit them, with my head and heart full of the subject I was come upon; and was surprised to find them cheerful, and thunderstruck to see a gownsman reading a play to them. A play! when their father was lying in the agonies of death. What a species of consolation! I rebuked him so sharply, and, I am afraid, so intemperately, that a quarrel will perhaps ensue.

"But it is time that I should take some notice of your letter. When we consider the misery and darkness of the unregenerate world, oh, with how much reason should we burst out into thanksgiving to God, who has called us in his mercy through Christ Jesus! What are we, that we should thus be made objects of distinguishing grace! Who, then, that reflects upon the rock from which he was hewn, but must rejoice to give himself entirely and without reserve to God, to be sanctified by his Spirit? The soul that has truly experienced the love of God will not stay meanly inquiring how much he shall do, and thus limit his service, but will be earnestly seeking more and more to know the will of our heavenly Father, that he may be enabled to do it. Oh may we be both thus minded! May we experience Christ to be our all in all, not only as our Redeemer, but also as the fountain of grace! Those passages of the Word of God which you have quoted on this head, are indeed awakening. May they teach us to breathe after holiness, to be more and more dead to the world, and alive unto God, through Jesus Christ! We are lights in the world; how needful then that our tempers and lives should manifest our high and heavenly calling. Let us, as we do, provoke one another to good works, not doubting that God will bless our feeble endeavours to his glory.

"I have to bless Him for another mercy I have received, in addition to the multitude of which I am so unworthy, in his having given me a friend indeed, one who has made much about the same advances in religion as myself. We took our degrees together, but Mr. Simeon introduced us to each other. I do not wonder much at the backwardness you complain of before ——, having never been in much company. But the Christian heart is ever overflowing with goodwill to the rest of mankind; and this temper will produce the truest politeness, of which the affected grimace of ungodly men is but the shadow. Besides, the confusion felt in company arises in general from vanity; therefore, when this is removed, why should we fear to speak before the whole world?

"The gownsman I mentioned, so far from being offended, has been thanking me for what I said, and is so seriously impressed with the awful circumstances of death, that I am in hopes it may be the foundation of a lasting change."

It will be highly pleasing to the reader to know, that the anticipation with which the above letter concludes was verified. Mr. Martyn had afterwards the happiness of labouring in India together with that very person who had been reproved by him, and who, from the Divine blessing accompanying that reproof, was then first led to appreciate the value of the Gospel.

From this time to that of proposing himself for admission to a fellowship in his college, Mr. Martyn's

ST. JOHN'S COLLEGE, CAMBRIDGE.

Page 21.

engagements consisted chiefly in instructing some pupils, and in preparing himself for the examination, which was to take place previous to the election in the month of March, 1802,—when he was chosen fellow of St. John's. Soon after obtaining which situation, as honourable to the Society in the appointment, as it was gratifying to himself, he employed some of his leisure hours, as he expresses it, in writing for one of the prizes which are given to those who have been last admitted Bachelors of Arts: and though there were men of great classical celebrity among those who contested the palm with him, the *first* prize was assigned to him for the best Latin prose composition;—a distinction the more remarkable, as, from his entrance into the University, he had directed an unceasing and almost undivided attention to Mathematics. Having thus added another honour to those for which he had been before so signally distinguished, Mr. Martyn departed from Cambridge on a visit to his relations in Cornwall;—making a circuit on foot through Wenlock, Liverpool, and the vale of Llangollen. Of this tour (on which he was first attended by one of his friends) he has left a Journal, briefly and hastily written, from which a few extracts illustrative of his character may prove not uninteresting.

"July 9, 1802.—We walked into Wenlock, along a most romantic road. My mind during these three days has been less distracted than I expected; and I have had, at times, a very cheering sense of the presence of my God.

"July 17.—I went on board a little sloop, and began to beat down the Mersey. The Mersey is here more than four miles broad, and the wind now increasing almost to a storm, the ship was a scene of confusion. One wave broke over us, and wetted me completely through. I think there was some danger, but the composure I felt did not arise, I fear, so much from a sense of my acceptance with God, as from thinking the danger not to be great. Still I had sufficiently near views of death to be uneasy on considering how slothful I had been in doing the Lord's work, and what little meetness I possessed for the kingdom of glory. Learn then, O my soul, to be always ready for the coming of the Lord; that no disquieting fear may arise to perplex thee in that awful hour.

"July 23.—Holywell. Found myself very low and melancholy. If this arises from solitude, I have little pleasure to expect from my future tour. I deserve to be miserable, and wish that I may be so, whenever I seek my pleasure in anything but God.

"July 25.—Carewys. I did not go to church this morning, as the service was in Welch; but went through the church service at home. In the evening read Isaiah.

"July 29.—Aber. Walked two miles into the country to see a waterfall. I followed the course of the stream, which soon brought me to it. The water makes three successive falls;—the last appeared to be about seventy feet. While lingering about here, I was put into great terror by some huge stones rolling down the hill behind me. They were thrown down by some persons above, who could not approach near enough to the precipice to see me below. The slipperiness of the rocks, on which the spring is continually falling, added to my danger.

"The beautiful and retired situation of the inn at Aber, which commands an extensive view of the sea, made me unwilling to leave the house. However, I set off at eleven, and paced leisurely to Bangor. It was a remarkably clear day. The sun shone on every object around me, and the sea breeze tempered the air. I felt happy at the sight, and could not help being struck with the beauty of the creation and the goodness of the God of nature.

"July 31.—Bethgelert. The descent after ascending Snowdon, was easy enough, but I cannot describe the horror of the ascent. The deep darkness of the night, the howling of the wind in the chasms of the rocks, the violence of the rain, and the sullen silence of the guide, who was sometimes so far back that I could hardly see him, all conspired to make the whole appear a dream.

"— Pont Aberglaslin. I met a poor Welch pedlar, with a bundle of hats on his back, who, on my inquiring the distance to Tan-y-Bwlch, told me he was going thither. He went by the old road, which is two miles nearer. It passes over the most dreary, uncultivated hills I ever saw, where there is scarcely any mark of human industry. The road in most places is overgrown with grass. The poor man had walked from Carnarvon that day, with an enormous bundle ; and pointed with a sorrowful look to his head ; and indeed he did look very ill ; he was however very cheerful : what a difference between this man's temper and my own ! The difference was humbling to myself :—when shall I learn 'in whatsoever state I am, therewith to be content ?'

"August 5.—My walk for ten miles was similar to that of the preceding evening, only still more beautiful, for the Dovey widened continually, and the opposite hills were covered with wood : at last the river fell into the sea, and the view was then fine indeed ; the weather was serene, and the sea unruffled. I felt little fatigue ; and my thoughts were turned towards God. But if I cannot be thankful to Him, and sensible of his presence, in seasons of fatigue as well as in periods of enjoyment, how can I distinguish the working of the Spirit from the ebullitions of animal joy."

It is in scenes and seasons of solitude and relaxation, such as those here described, that the true bias of the mind is apt to discover itself; in which point of view the above account is important; for, short as it is, it evinces an habitual devotedness to the fear of God, and great spirituality in the affections.

This tour terminated in bringing Mr. Martyn to the bosom of his family; and days more delightful than those which he then spent, he never saw in this world. The affectionate reception he met with from his friends; the pious conversation he held with his sister on the things dearest to his heart; his sacred retirements; and the happy necessity imposed upon him of almost exclusively studying the word of God,—all conspired to promote his felicity. These hours left for a long time "a fragrancy upon his mind, and the remembrance of them was sweet."

"As my sister and myself," he remarks, "were improved in our attainments, we tasted much agreeable intercourse. I did not stay much at Truro, on account of my brother's family of children; but at Woodbury, with my brother in-law, I passed some of the sweetest moments of my life. The deep solitude of the place favoured meditation; and the romantic scenery around supplied great external sources of pleasure. For want of other books, I was obliged to read my Bible almost exclusively; and from this I derived great spirituality of mind, compared with what I had known before."

In the beginning of October, 1802, all these tranquil

and domestic joys were exchanged for the severer engagements of the University; and the conclusion of this year
constituted a memorable era in Mr. Martyn's life. We
have already seen him becoming the servant of Christ,
dedicating himself to the ministry of the Gospel, ex-
periencing the consolations of real religion, exhibiting its
genuine fruits; we are now to behold him in a yet higher
character, and giving the most exalted proofs of faith and
love.

God, who has appointed different orders and degrees in
his Church, and who assigns to all the members of it
their respective stations, was at this time pleased, by the
almighty and gracious influence of his Spirit, to call the
subject of this Memoir to a work demanding the most
painful sacrifices and the most arduous exertions,—that
of a Christian Missionary. The immediate cause of his
determination to undertake this office, was hearing a
remark from Mr. Simeon on the benefit which had
resulted from the services of a *single* Missionary* in
India; his attention was thus arrested, and his thoughts
occupied with the vast importance of the subject. Soon
after this, perusing the Life of David Brainerd, who
preached with apostolical zeal and success to the North
American Indians, and who finished a course of self-
denying labours for his Redeemer, with unspeakable joy,
at the early age of thirty-two, his soul was filled with a
holy emulation of that extraordinary man, and, after
deep consideration and fervent prayer, he was at
length fixed in a resolution to imitate his example. Nor
let it be conceived that he could adopt this resolution
without the severest conflict in his mind, for he was endued with the truest sensibility of heart, and was sus-

* Dr. Carey.

ceptible of the warmest and tenderest attachments. No one could exceed him in love for his country, or in affection for his friends; and few could surpass him in an exquisite relish for the various and refined enjoyments of a social and literary life. How then could it fail of being a moment of extreme anguish when he came to the deliberate resolution of leaving for ever all he held dear upon earth? But he was fully satisfied that the glory of that Saviour who loved him, and gave Himself for him, would be promoted by his going forth to preach to the heathen; —he considered their pitiable and perilous condition; he thought on the value of their immortal souls; he remembered the last solemn injunction of his Lord, "Go and teach all nations, baptizing them in the name of the Father, and of the Son, and of the Holy Ghost"—an injunction never revoked, and commensurate with that most encouraging promise, "Lo, I am with you alway, even unto the end of the world." Actuated by these motives, he offered himself in the capacity of a Missionary to the Society for Missions to Africa and the East; * and from that time stood prepared, with a child-like simplicity of spirit, and an unshaken constancy of soul, to go to any part of the world, whither it might be deemed expedient to send him.

The following letter to his youngest sister, written not long after the adoption of a resolution so self-denying in its character, and more particularly some passages extracted from his private Journal, will strikingly exhibit the varied exercises of his mind at this interesting and most trying juncture. From these it will be seen that he

* It is now called "The Church Missionary Society for Africa and the East," and eminently deserves the cordial support of every member of the Church of England.

steadily contemplated the sacrifices he must make, and the difficulties he might encounter ;—that though sometimes cast down, he was yet upheld in the prospect of his great work by Him who had called him to it ;—that his notions of the character of a missionary were elevated—his supplications for grace and mercy incessant—his examinations of his own heart, deep, and sober, and searching ;—in one word, that he was a man of God, eminently endued with "the spirit of love, and of power, and of a sound mind."

"I received your letter yesterday, and thank God for the concern you manifest for my spiritual welfare. O that we may love each other more and more in the Lord ! The passages you bring from the Word of God were appropriate to my case, particularly those from the first Epistle of St. Peter, and from that to the Ephesians ; though I do not seem to have given you a right view of my state. The dejection I sometimes labour under seems not to arise from doubts of my acceptance with God, though it tends to produce them ; nor from desponding views of my own backwardness in the Divine life, for I am more prone to self-dependance and conceit ; but from the prospect of the *difficulties I have to encounter in the whole of my future life*. The thought that I must be unceasingly employed in the same kind of work, amongst poor ignorant people, is what my proud spirit revolts at. To be obliged to submit to a thousand uncomfortable things that must happen to me, whether as a minister or a missionary, is what the flesh cannot endure. At these times I feel neither love to God nor love to man, and in proportion as these graces of the Spirit languish, my besetting sins—pride, and discontent, and unwillingness for every duty, make me miserable.

" You will best enter into my views by considering those texts which serve to recal me to a right aspect of things. I have not that coldness in prayer you would expect, but generally find myself strengthened in faith, and humility, and love after it ; but the impression is so short. I am at this time enabled to give myself, body, soul, and spirit, to God, and perceive it to be my most reasonable service. How it may be when the trial comes, I know not, yet I will trust and not be afraid. In order to *do* his will cheerfully, I want love for the souls of men ; to *suffer* it, I want humility : let these be the subjects of your supplications for me. I am thankful to God that you are so free from anxiety and care ; we cannot but with praise acknowledge his goodness. What does it signify whether we be rich or poor, if we are sons of God ? How unconscious are they of their real greatness, and they will be so till they find themselves in glory ! When we contemplate our everlasting inheritance, it seems too good to be true ; yet it is no more than is due to the kindred of 'God manifest in the flesh.'

" A journey I took into Norfolk last week seems to have contributed greatly to my health. The attention and admiration shown me are great and very dangerous. The praises of men do not now, indeed, flatter my vanity as they formerly did ; I rather feel pain, through anticipation of their consequences : but they tend to produce, imperceptibly, a self-esteem and hardness of heart. How awful and awakening a consideration is it, that God judgeth not as man judgeth ! Our character before Him is precisely as it was, before or after any change of external circumstances. Men may applaud or revile, and make a man think differently of himself, but *He* judgeth of a man according to his secret walk. How difficult is the work of self-examination! Even to state to you, imperfectly, my own mind, I found to be no easy matter. Nay, St. Paul says, 'I judge not mine own self, for He that judgeth me is the Lord.' That is, though he was not conscious of any allowed sin, yet he was not thereby justified, for God might perceive something of which he was not aware. How needful then the prayer of the Psalmist, 'Search me, O God, and try my heart, and see if there be any evil way in me.' May God be with you, and bless you, and uphold you with the right hand of His righteousness; and let us seek to love, for 'he that dwelleth in love dwelleth in God, for God is love.'"

In a journal replete with sentiments of most ardent piety, we meet with the following reflections, recorded in the interval between the latter end of the year 1802, the time when he first resolved to serve Christ as a Missionary, and the autumn of the year 1803, when he was admitted into Holy Orders.

But let us hear his reasons for keeping such a record of the state of his mind:—"I am convinced that Christian experience is not a delusion; whether mine is so or not will be seen at the last day; and my object in making this Journal, is to accustom myself to self-examination, and to give my experience a visible form, so as to leave a stronger impression on the memory, and thus to improve my soul in holiness; for the review of such a lasting testimony will serve the double purpose of conviction and consolation."

Divided as Christians are in judgment respecting the general utility of a religious diary, there can be but one opinion amongst them respecting the uncommon excellence of the following observations:—

"Since I have endeavoured to divest myself of every consideration independent of religion, I see the difficulty of maintaining a liveliness in devotion for any considerable time together; nevertheless, as I shall have to pass the greater part of my future life, after leaving England, with no other source of happiness than reading, meditation, and prayer, I think it right to be gradually mortifying myself to every species of worldly pleasure."—"In all my past life I have fixed on some desirable ends, at different distances, the attainment of which was to furnish me with happiness. But now, in seasons of unbelief, nothing seems to lie before me but one vast uninteresting wilderness, and heaven appearing but dimly at the end. Oh, how does this show the necessity of living by faith ! What a shame that I cannot make the doing of God's will my ever-delightful object; and the prize of my high calling the mark after which I press ! "

"I was under some disquiet at the prospect of my future work, encompassed, as it appeared, with difficulties; but I trusted I was under the guidance of Infinite Wisdom, and on that I could rest. Mr. Johnson, who had returned from a mission, observed that the crosses to be endured were far greater than could be conceived; but 'none of these things move me, neither count I my life dear unto me, so that I might finish my course with joy.' I had some disheartening thoughts at night, on the prospect of being stripped of every earthly comfort; but who is it that maketh my comforts to be a source of enjoyment? Cannot the same hand make cold, and hunger, and nakedness, and peril, to be a train of ministering angels conducting me to glory?"—"O my soul, compare thyself with St. Paul, and with the example and precepts of the Lord Jesus Christ! Was it not his meat and drink to do the will of his heavenly Father?"

"Finished the account of Dr. Vanderkemp, and longed

to be sent to China. But I may reasonably doubt the reality of every gracious affection; they are so like the morning cloud, and transient as the early dew. If I had the true love of souls, I should long and labour for those around me, and afterwards for the conversion of the heathen."

"I had distressing thoughts about the little prospect of happiness in my future life. Though God has not designed man to be a solitary being, yet surely the child of God would delight to pour out his soul for whole days together before God. Stir up my soul to lay hold of Thee, and remove from me the cloud of ignorance and sin that hides from me the glory of Jehovah; the excellency of my God." "I found Butler's 'Analogy' useful in encouraging me to self-denial, by the representation ne gives of this life, as a state of discipline for a better." "Since adopting the Gospel as the ground of my hope and the rule of my life, I feel the force of the argument drawn from its exalted morality. In so large a work as the Bible, produced by so many writers, in such different ages, never to meet with anything puerile or inconsistent with their own views of the Deity, is a circumstance unparalleled in any other book."—"Respecting what is called the experience of Christians, it is certain that we have no reason, from the mere contemplation of the operations of our own minds, to ascribe them to an extrinsic agent, because they arise from their proper causes, and are directed to their proper ends. The truth or falsehood of pretences to the experience of Divine agency, must depend on the truth or falsehood of Scripture; that warrants us sufficiently,—for it informs us that it is 'God that worketh in us, both to will and to do, of his good pleasure;' which passage, while it asserts the reality of God's influence, points out also the manner of his acting, for He works in us to will before He works in us to do. This effectually guards against fanaticism, for no one will pretend that he can ever put his finger on those mysterious springs which move the will, or knows what they be ; and therefore he cannot say, *now* God is exerting his influence. He may reasonably, indeed, and ought to, ascribe every good thought to God, but still every good thing in him is but the effect of something preceding his first perception, therefore is posterior to the moving cause, which must hence be for ever concealed from the immediate knowledge of man."—" H—— came, and we resumed our exercises of reading and prayer. Though it be true that the more strict our obedience is, the more evidently does the imperfection of it appear, yet I think it reasonable to be thankful that I have received grace to stir one single step this day towards the kingdom of heaven."—" After my prayers, my mind seems touched with humility and love, but the impression decays so soon ! Resolved for the future to use more watchfulness in reading and prayer."—" My prayers have been frequent of late, but I cannot realize the presence of the Almighty God : I have not enjoyed communion with Him, or else there would not be such strangeness in my heart towards the world to come."— " In my walk out, and during the remainder of the day, the sense of my own weakness and worthlessness called me to watchfulness, and dependance on the grace of Christ."—" My soul was rather benumbed than humble and contrite ; tired with watchfulness, though so short and so feeble."—" Sudden flashes of faint affection to-day, which raised self-satisfaction, but no abiding humilia- tion."—" Talked with much contemptuous severity about conformity to the world; alas! all that is done in this way had better be left undone."—"This was a day when I could only by transient glimpses perceive that all things were 'loss, for the excellency of the knowledge of Christ Jesus my Lord.'"

"I am not conscious of any particular backsliding from God; I think my prayers have been more earnest; yet the views of my own heart have produced, not humility, but discontent; I suppose because they are grating to pride."—"What is the state of my own soul before God? I believe that it is right in principle: I desire no other portion but God: but I pass too many hours as if there were no God at all. I live far below the hope, comfort, and holiness of the Gospel: but be not slothful, O my soul;—look unto Jesus, the author and finisher of thy faith. For whom was grace intended, if not for me? Are not the promises made to me? Is not thy Maker in earnest, when He declareth that He willeth my sanctification, and hath laid help on One that is mighty? I will therefore have no confidence in the flesh, but will rejoice in the Lord, and the joy of the Lord shall be my strength. May I receive from above a pure, a humble, a benevolent, a heavenly mind!"

"Rose at half-past five, and walked a little before chapel hour, in a happy frame of mind. Endeavoured to maintain affectionate thoughts of God as my Father, on awaking in the morning. Setting a watch over my thoughts, and endeavouring to make them humble and devout, I find to be an excellent preparation for prayer, and for a right spirit during the day. I was in a happy frame most of the day: towards the evening, from seeking to maintain this right state by my own strength, instead of giving it permanency by faith in Jesus, I grew tired and very insensible to most things. At chapel the sacred melody wafted my soul to heaven; the blessedness of heaven appeared so sweet, that the very possibility of losing it appeared terrible, and raised a little disquiet with my joy. After all, I had rather live in a humble and dependent spirit; for then, perceiving underneath me the everlasting arms, I can enjoy my security."— "Amid the joyous affections of this day, I quickly forgot my own worthlessness and helplessness, and thus, looking off from Jesus, found myself standing on slippery ground. But oh! the happiness of that state, where pride shall never intrude, to make our joys an occasion of sorrow."

"Rose at six, and passed the morning in great tranquillity. Learnt by heart some of the first three chapters of Revelation. This is to me the most searching and alarming part of the Bible; yet now with humble hope I trusted that the censures of my Lord did not belong to me: except that those words, Rev. ii. 3, 'For my name's sake thou hast laboured, and hast not fainted,' were far too high a testimony for me to think of appropriating to myself; nevertheless I besought the Lord, that whatever I had been, I might now be perfect and complete in all the will of God."—"Men frequently admire me, and I am pleased; but I abhor the pleasure I feel; oh! did they but know that my root is rottenness!"—"Heard Professor Farish preach at Trinity Church, on Luke xii. 4, 5, and was deeply impressed with the reasonableness and necessity of the fear of God. Felt it to be a light matter to be judged of man's judgment; why have I not awful apprehensions of the glorious Being at all times? The particular promise—'Him that overcometh will I make a pillar in the temple of my God, and he shall go no more out'—dwelt a long time in my mind, and diffused an affectionate reverence of God."—"I see a great work before me now, namely, the subduing and mortifying of my perverted will. What am I that I should *dare* to do my own will, even if I were not a sinner; but now, how plain, how reasonable, to have the love of Christ constraining me to be his faithful, willing servant, cheerfully taking up the cross He shall appoint me."—" Read some of Amos, with Lowth. The reading of the Prophets is to me one of the most delightful employments. One cannot but be charmed with the beauty of the imagery, while they never fail to inspire me with awful thoughts of God and of his hatred of sin. The reading of Baxter's ' Saint's Rest ' determined me to live more in heavenly meditation."—" Walked by moonlight, and found it a sweet relief to my mind to think of God and consider my ways before Him. I was strongly impressed with the vanity of the world, and could not help wondering at the imperceptible operation of grace, which had enabled me to resign the expectation of happiness from it."—" How frequently has my heart been refreshed by the descriptions given in the Scriptures of the future glory of the Church, and the happiness of man hereafter."—" I felt the force of Baxter's observation, that if an angel had appointed to meet me, I should be full of awe ;—how much more when I am about to meet God."—" In my usual prayer at noon, besought God to give me a heart to do His will."—" For poor —— I interceded most earnestly, even with tears."

That one thus eminently watchful and holy, who "counted all things but loss for the excellency of the knowledge of Christ Jesus his Lord," should speak of himself in the strongest terms of self-condemnation, will appear incongruous to those only who forget that the

prophet who uttered in the presence of Jehovah the
words of submissive devotion, " Here am I, send me," exclaimed at the same time, in the lowly language of contrition, " Woe is me, for I am undone, for I am a man of
unclean lips ; " and that it was when the Laodiceans ceased
to know that they were "wretched, and miserable, and
poor, and blind, and naked," that they became defective
in zeal for the glory of their Saviour.   Whoever considers
that tenderness of conscience is found always in an exact
proportion to fervent desires after an entire conformity to
the Divine image, will be prepared to expect, and pleased
to peruse, such humble confessions and sacred aspirations
as Mr. Martyn's, which seem to bring us back to the days
of Ephrem the Syrian and St. Augustine.   " The essence
of Evangelical humiliation," observes a celebrated writer*
on the religious affections, " consists in such humility as
becomes a creature under a dispensation of grace ; consisting in a mean esteem of himself, as nothing, and as
altogether contemptible and odious, attended with a mortification of a disposition to exalt himself, and a free
renunciation of his own glory.   He that has much grace
apprehends, much more than others, that great height to
which his love ought to ascend, and he sees better than
others how little a way he has risen towards that height,
and, therefore, estimating his love by the whole height of
his duty, it appears astonishingly little and low in his
eyes.   It most demonstratively appears that true grace
is of that nature, that the more a person has of it, with
remaining corruption, the less does his goodness and holiness appear, in proportion, not only to his *past* deformity,
but to his *present* deformity, in the sin that now appears
in his heart, and in the abominable defects of his highest

* Jonathan Edwards.

affections and brightest experience." What better comment can be found on these profoundly scriptural remarks of a Divine who stood singularly high in Mr. Martyn's estimation, than the self-abasing acknowledgments which follow?

"What a sink of corruption is the heart! and yet I can go from day to day in self-seeking and self-pleasing! Lord! show me myself as nothing but wounds and bruises and putrefying sores, and teach me to live by faith on Christ my all."—"I fear that the exemption from assaults, either external or internal, is either in itself a bad symptom of self-ignorance, or leads to pride and self-seeking. Reveal to me the evil of my heart, O thou heart-searching God."

"I feel a sad strangeness between God and my soul, following from careless, unbelieving prayer; I am afraid the work of grace is but shallow. I pray, but look not for an answer from above: but while I consider, at the times of prayer, every grace as coming from God, yet, in the general tenor of my course, I seem to lay the greater stress on my own endeavours, heedless of the strength of Christ."—"How much better is it to have a peaceful sense of my own wretchedness, and a humble waiting upon God for sanctifying grace, than to talk much, and appear to be somebody in religion!"

"O my God! who seest me write, and recordest in the book of thy remembrance more faithfully my sins and backslidings, bring down my soul to repent in dust and ashes for my waste of time, carnal complacency, and self-sufficiency. I would desire to devote myself anew to Thee in Christ; though I fear I hardly know what it means, so great, in reality, is my ignorance of myself."

"Short and superficial in prayer this morning, and *there* undoubtedly is the evil. Read Lowth; learnt the fifteenth of John; and endeavoured faintly to be drawing nigh unto God. Read ' Brainerd's Journal' in the afternoon. At Mr. Simeon's church this evening my mind was wandering and stupid. His sermon was very impressive, on Rev. iii. 2. Thanks to God, that though my graces are declining, and my corruptions increasing, I am not unwilling to be reclaimed. For with all this evil in my heart, I would not, could not, choose any other than God for my portion."—"At dear Mr. Simeon's rooms I perceived that I had given him pain by inattention to his kind instructions. Base wretch that I am, that by carelessness and unmortified pride I should thus ungratefully repay his unexampled kindness. But if the sense of ingratitude to man be thus painful, what ought I not to feel in reference to God, that good and holy Being, whose sparing mercy keeps me out of hell, though I daily dishonour Christ, and grieve His Holy Spirit! But, O my soul! it is awful to trifle in religion. Confession is not repentance, neither is the knowledge of sin contrition."—"Hearing I was to meet two men who were not serious, I felt pride, contempt, and discontent to be the torment of my heart."—"Condemned myself for not exerting myself in doing good to man, by visiting the sick, &c. Certainly every grace must be in exercise, if we would enjoy the communion of the perfect God. 'I am the Almighty God, walk before me, and be thou perfect.' Every wheel of the chariot must be in motion to gain the race."

"I found a want of the presence of God, arising from a fear of having acted against the suggestion of conscience, in indulging myself in reading the amusing account of Dr. Vanderkemp, instead of applying to the severer duties of the morning. God be merciful to me a sinner ! "

"Was in a composed state, but security led to pride. On my looking up to God, for pardon of it and for deliverance from it, I feel overwhelmed with grief. How fast does pride ripen the soul for hell ! "—" Retained the manna of past experience till it putrefied in my hand."— " How utterly forgetful have I been this day of the need of Christ's grace, of my own poverty and vileness ! Let me then remember that all apparent joy in God, without humility, is a mere delusion of Satan."—"This is my birth-day, and I am ashamed to review the past : Lord Jesus, watch over me in the deceitful calm ! Let me beware of the lethargy, lest it terminate in death. I de- sire this day to renew my vows to the Lord, and oh that every succeeding year of my life may be more devoted to His glory than the last ! "

" I thought that my fretfulness, and other marks of an unsubdued spirit, arose from a sense of my corruption, and a secret dependance on my own powers for a cure. Were I to bring the maladies of my soul to the great Physician, in simple reliance on His grace, I should, with many other benefits, receive a cure of that bane of my peace, disappointed arrogance, which proudly seeks for good where it can never be found. In every disease of the soul, let me charge myself with the blame, and Christ with the cure of it ; so shall I be humbled and Christ glorified."—" I do not doubt but that I belong to God, yet I am afraid to rejoice in that relation. I do not live in the sense of my own helplessness, and therefore do not perceive that my security is not in myself, but in Jesus Christ, the same yesterday, to-day, and for ever."—" I found that the omission of my journal has been attended with bad effects. O wretched man that I am! If God's Word did not unequivocally declare the desperate wickedness of the heart, I should sink down in despair. Nothing but infinite grace can save me. But that which most grieves me, is that I am not more humbled at the contemplation of myself."

"When I look back on every day, I may say I have lost it. So much time mis-spent, so many opportunities lost of doing good, by spreading the knowledge of the truth by conversation or by example; so little zeal for God, or love to man; so much vanity, and levity, and pride, and selfishness, that I may well tremble at the world of iniquity within. If ever I am saved, it must be by grace. May God give me a humble, contrite, childlike, affectionate spirit, and a willingness to forego my ease continually in his service."

"What is my journal but a transcript of my follies? what else is the usual state of my mind but weakness, vanity, and sin? O that I could meditate constantly upon Divine things; that the world and its poor concerns might no more distract my heart from God! But how little do I know or experience of the power of Christ! Truly I find my proneness to sin, and that generally prevailing ignorance of my mind by which all motives to diligence and love are made to disappear, to be my misery. Now, therefore, I desire to become a fool, that I may be wise: 'the meek will he guide in judgment.'"

"I felt humbled at the remembrance of mis-spent hours, and while this frame of mind continued, all the powers of my soul were perceptibly refreshed. The last three chapters of St. John were peculiarly sweet, and I

longed to love. Mr. Simeon preached on John xv. 12 :
'This is my commandment, that ye love one another, as
I have loved you.' I saw my utter want of such a love
as he described : so disinterested, sympathizing, bene-
ficent, and self-denying. Resolved to make the acquisition
of it the daily subject of my future endeavours."—"1
cared not what was the state of pleasure or pain in my
heart, so that I knew its depth of iniquity, and could be
poor and contrite in spirit ; but it is hard and stubborn
and ignorant."—"Pride shows itself every hour of every
day ; what long and undisturbed possession does self-
complacency hold of my heart ! What plans, and dreams,
and visions of futurity fill my imagination, in which self
is the prominent object."—"In my intercourse with some
of my dear friends, the workings of pride were but too
plainly marked in my outward demeanour; on looking
up to God for pardon for it, and deliverance from it,
I felt overwhelmed with guilt. I was unwilling to
resume my studies, while so much seemed to remain to be
done in my own heart. Read Hopkins's Sermon on true
Happiness, and analyzed it. The obedience required
in it terrified me at first, but afterwards I could adore
God that He had required me to be perfectly holy. I
thought that I could cheerfully do his will, though
the world, the flesh, and the devil should rise up
against me; I desired to be filled with the fruits
of righteousness; particularly with humility and love
for the poor of Christ's flock."

"Drew near to the Lord in prayer, but was rather
elevated than humbled afterwards. At Mr. Simeon's
was deeply impressed with his sermon on Eccles. viii.
11. It was a complete picture of the human heart;
and when he came to say, that they sinned habitually,

deliberately, and without remorse, I could scarcely
believe I was so vile a wretch as I then saw myself
to be. It was a most solemn discourse."—"The less
we do, the more we value it; how poor, how mean
and pitiful would many even of present Christians
esteem my life! Dear Saviour, I desire to be no
more lukewarm, but to walk nigh to God, to be dead
to the world, and longing for the coming of Christ."

"I read Hebrew, and the Greek of the Epistle to
the Hebrews. This Epistle is not only not most uninteresting, as it formerly was, but is now the sweetest
portion of the Holy Scripture I know; partly, I suppose,
because I can look up to Jesus as my High Priest, though
I may very often doubt whether I am interested in Him.
Yet O how free is his love to the chief of sinners!"
—"How many of my days are lost, if their worth is
to be measured by the standard of prevailing heavenly-
mindedness! I want, above all things, a willingness
to be despised. What but the humbling influence of
the Spirit, showing me my vileness and desperate
wickedness, can ever produce such an habitual temper!

"Mr. Simeon's sermon this evening on 2 Chron. xxxii.
31, discovered to me my corruption and vileness more
than any sermon I had ever heard."—"Oh that I had
a more piercing sense of the Divine presence! How much
sin in the purest services! If I were sitting in heavenly
places with Christ, or rather with my thoughts habitually
there, how would every duty, but especially this of social
prayer, become easy. Memoria tua sancta, et dulcedo tua
beatissima possideat animam meam, atque in invisibilium
amorem rapiat illam."

"This day was set apart for a public fast. I prayed
rather more than two hours, chiefly with confession of my

own sins, those of my family, and of the Church : alas! so much was required to be said on the first head, that I should have been at no loss to have dwelt upon it the whole day."—" Suffered sleepiness to prevent my reading to my servant : it is hurtful to my conscience to let slight excuses prevail for an omission of duty."—" O what cause for shame and self-abhorrence arises from the review of every day :—in morning prayer, as usual of late, my soul longed to leave its corruptions, to think of Christ and live by Him. I laboured to represent to myself powerful considerations, to stir up my slothful heart to activity, particularly that which respects giving instruction to, and praying with people. I set before myself the infinite mercy of being out of hell,—of being *permitted* to do the will of God,—of the love of Christ, which was so disinterested,—how He passed his life in going about doing good,—how those men who were truly great, the blessed Apostles, did the same,—how the holy angels would delight to be employed on errands of mercy. A ray of light seems to break upon my mind for a moment, and discovers the folly and ignorance of this sinful heart; but it quickly returns to its former hardness. My will is to sit all day reading, not making any effort to think, but letting the book fill the mind with a succession of notions: and when the time comes for reading the Scriptures and praying, then it recoils. When an opportunity offers of speaking for the good of others, or assisting a poor person, then it makes a thousand foolish excuses. It would rather go on wrapt in self, and leave the world to perish. Ah! what a heart is mine! The indistinctness of my view of its desperate wickedness is terrible to me; that is, when I am capable of feeling any terror. But now, my soul! rise from earth

and hell ;—shall Satan lead me captive at his will, when
Christ ever liveth to make intercession for the vilest
worm? O Thou! whose I am by creation, preservation,
redemption, no longer my own, but His who lived and
died and rose again, once more would I resign this body
and soul, mean and worthless as they are, to the blessed
disposal of thy holy will! May I have a heart to love
God and his people, the flesh being crucified! May grace
abound, where sin has abounded much! May I cheerfully and joyfully resign my ease and life in the service of
Jesus, to whom I owe so much! May it be sweet to me
to proclaim to sinners like myself the blessed efficacy of
my Saviour's blood! May He make me faithful unto
death! The greatest enemy I dread is the pride of my
own heart. Through pride reigning I should forget to
know a broken spirit: then would come in unbelief,—
weakness,—apostasy."—" If it is a mercy that I am out
of hell, what account should I make of the glorious work
of the ministry, to which I am to be called, who am not
worthy to be trodden under foot of men ? "

Thus having attained to a degree of self-knowledge and
spirituality equally rare, and being thoroughly instructed
how "he ought to behave himself in the Church of God,—
the Church of the living God,—the pillar and ground of
the truth," Mr. Martyn prepared for the solemn rite of
his ordination, which was administered at Ely on Sunday,
Oct. 22, 1803. "Blessed is the man whom thou choosest,
and causest to approach unto Thee, that he may dwell in
thy courts." (Psalm lxv. 4.) This blessing surely rested in
an eminent degree on Mr. Martyn; for what a contrast
does his approach to the altar on this occasion exhibit to
that of those, who presumptuously intrude into the sacred
office, "seeking their own things and not the things of

Jesus Christ." Truly might *he* affirm, that he was "inwardly moved by the Holy Ghost, to take upon him that office and ministration, to serve God by promoting his glory, and edifying his people;" and truly did he resolve to "give himself continually to prayer and to the ministry of the word." Yet his self-abasement was as usual conspicuous; and he bewailed having presented himself for admission into the ministry of the Lord Jesus "in so much ignorance and unholiness;" and at the same time poured out his prayer, that he might have "grace to fulfil those promises which he had made before God and his people." The awful weight of ordination vows was impressed on no one's mind more deeply than on his;— the thought of his responsibility would have overwhelmed him, had he not been supported by remembering that the treasure of the Gospel was placed "in earthen vessels, that the excellency of the power might be of God and not of man." That which was the comfort of Polycarp as a Bishop, was his consolation as a Deacon,—that he who was constituted an *overseer* of the Church, was himself *overlooked* by Jesus Christ,—and that in the discharge of his office as pastor of the flock, he was ever under the gracious superintendence of that great and good Shepherd who "laid down his life for the sheep."

A circumstance which occurred at this time shows how seriously his mind was affected. From a constitutional delicacy and reserve, no one had naturally a greater reluctance than Mr. Martyn to obtrude himself on the notice of others in the way of admonition: it was a task from which his feelings recoiled. Observing, however, with pain and sorrow, one of the candidates for ordination in an apparently careless and unconcerned state, he took an opportunity, though the party was not per-

sonally known to him, of admonishing him privately on
the subject : and in what a strain *such a man* would
speak at *such a moment,* may more easily be conceived
than expressed. A deep conviction of the necessity of
reproving others, and not suffering sin to remain in them,
often induced Mr. Martyn to do violence to the retiring
tenderness of his disposition. He felt reproof to be " a
duty of unlimited extent and almost insuperable
difficulty"—but, said he, "the way to know when to
address men, and when to abstain, *is to love ;*"—and, as
love is most genuine when the heart is most abased, he
resolved "not to reprove others, where he could conscien-
tiously be silent, except he experienced at the time a
peculiar contrition of spirit."

CHAPTER III.

COMMENCEMENT OF HIS MINISTERIAL LABOURS—COLLEGIATE
DUTIES—APPLIES FOR A CHAPLAINSHIP UNDER THE
EAST INDIA COMPANY—VISITS CORNWALL—HIS SUF-
FERINGS ON LEAVING ENGLAND.

THE exercise of his pastoral function Mr. Martyn commenced as curate of the Rev. C. Simeon, in the Church
of the Holy Trinity in Cambridge : undertaking likewise
the charge of the parish of Lolworth, a small village at
no great distance from the University.   There it was, on
the Sunday after his ordination, that he preached his first
sermon, on the following words : " If a man die, shall he
live again ? all the days of my appointed time will I
wait, till my change come." (Job xiv. 14.) After delivering his second sermon at this place, on the succeeding
Sunday, an incident occurred on his way home, which he
recorded in his Journal, and which could not well be
effaced from his remembrance.   An old man, who had
been one of his auditors, walked by the side of his horse
for a considerable time, warning him to reflect, that if any
souls perished through his negligence, their blood would
be required at his hand.   He exhorted him to show his
hearers that they were perishing sinners; to be much
engaged in secret prayer; and to labour after an entire
departure from himself to Christ.   " From what he said
on the last head (observes Mr. Martyn,) it was clear
that I had but little experience ; but I lifted up my

heart afterwards to the Lord, that I might be fully instructed in righteousness." So meekly and thankfully did this young minister listen to the affectionate counsel of an old disciple.

On Thursday, November 10, he preached for the first time at Trinity Church, to a numerous and earnestly attentive congregation, upon part of that address of Jesus to the woman of Samaria: "If thou knewest the gift of God, and who it is that saith unto thee, Give me to drink, thou wouldest have asked of him, and he would have given thee living water," John iv. 10: when it was his fervent desire and prayer to enter fully into the solemn spirit of those well-known lines,—

> "I'd preach as though I ne'er should preach again;
> I'd preach as dying unto dying men."

Nor could words characterize more justly the usual strain of his preaching; for whether the congregation he addressed were great or small, learned and refined, or poor and ignorant, he spake as one who had a message to them from God, and who was impressed with the consideration, that both he and they must shortly stand before the Judge of quick and dead.

The burdens and difficulties of his sacred employments lay heavily at first on Mr. Martyn's mind, and considerably depressed his spirits; but he endeavoured,—he writes in a letter to his earliest friend,—to keep in view "the unreasonableness of his discontent (who was a brand plucked out of the fire), and the glorious blessedness of the ministerial work." At times, he confesses, he was tried with a "sinful dislike of his parochial duty"—and seemed frequently "as a stone speaking to stones"—and he laments that "want of private devotional reading, and shortness of prayer, through incessant sermon-making, had produced much strangeness between God and his soul."—"Every time," he remarked, "that I open the Scriptures, my thoughts are about a sermon or exposition, so that even in private I seemed to be reading in public." Young ministers, those especially who are placed in extensive spheres of action,—are not ignorant of the temptations of which Mr. Martyn here complains ;—and to them it must be a consolation to be assured, that the same trials were not unknown to one of the most devoted and most faithful of their brethren.

Added to those duties which had now become his peculiar care, and in which, notwithstanding some momentary depressions, he continued stedfast and un-movable, always abounding in his work,—an office of another kind devolved on him towards the close of the year 1803; that of one of the public examiners in his college : and if it were too much to say, that an examination in the classics at St. John's has rarely been conducted more to the credit of the society, or to the advantage of the students, or to the honour of the examiner ; certainly it would not be presuming too far to aver, that never since the foundation of the college has one been held in a more Christian spirit, and in a more strict accordance with that extensive apostolical injunction—"Whatsoever ye do, in word or deed, do all in the name of the Lord Jesus." The vigilance with which Mr. Martyn prepared for this duty, and the humility with which he speaks of himself when engaged in the execution of it, show that his Christianity was of the highest proof.

"I read Mitford's History of Greece, as I am to be classical examiner. To keep my thoughts from wandering away to take pleasure in these studies, required more watchfulness and earnestness in prayer than I can account for. But earnest ejaculation was effectual to make me return to the Word of God with some delight. 'The carnal mind is enmity against God,'—and so I find it. I was obliged to reason with myself and to force open my eyes that I might see the excellency of divine things. Did I delight in reading the retreat of the ten thousand Greeks; and shall not my soul glory in the knowledge of God, who created the Greeks, and the vast countries over which they passed? I examined in Butler's Analogy, and in Xenophon; how much pride and ostentatious display of learning was visible in my conduct!—how that detestable spirit follows me, whatever I do."

It was customary with Mr. Martyn, at the commencement of a new year, to take a solemn review of the time past, and to contemplate his future prospects. In the review of his Journal of the year 1803, he judged that he had dedicated too much time to *public* ministrations, and too little to *private* communion with God. Yet he trusted that he had grown in grace, inasmuch as the bent of his desires was towards God, more than when he first thought of becoming a Missionary. "In heavenly contemplation and abstraction of mind," he adds, "my attainments have fallen far short of my expectation; but in a sense of my own worthlessness and guilt, and in a consequent subjugation of the will, and in a disposition for labour and active exertion, I am inclined to think myself gaining ground. My soul approves thoroughly the life of God, and my one only desire is to be entirely devoted to Him; and oh may I live very near to Him in the ensuing year, and follow the steps of Christ and his holy saints. I have resigned, in profession, the riches, the honours, and the comforts of this world; and I think also it is a resignation of the heart." Then after having set apart a day for fasting and prayer, he besought God "for understanding and strength, to fit him for a long life of warfare and constant self-denial; and that he might see clearly why he was placed here, how short the time was, and how excellent to labour for souls; and, above all, to feel his desert of hell." He prayed also for grace, to "enlighten him in the dark seasons of trouble and desponding faith; that he might not shrink from cold and hunger, and painful labour, but might follow the Lamb whithersoever he went." His soul longed for perfection; but he "feared that he had not yet learned the *secret of happiness,*—a poor and contrite spirit."

In the early part of the year 1804, Mr. Martyn's expectations of becoming a Missionary were considerably damped by the very trying event of his losing all his slender patrimony; a loss rendered more severe to him by the circumstance of his younger sister being involved in the same calamity. His designs of leaving England were, in consequence of this disaster, likely to be frustrated: for his pecuniary resources were cut off, and it appeared to him scarcely justifiable to leave his sister in actual distress, when his presence in England might alleviate or remove it. In order, therefore, that he might consult some of his friends in this emergency, at the end of June he left Cambridge for London.

The situation of a Chaplain to the East India Company had long appeared to many of those who took a lively interest in him and his work, to be peculiarly eligible, as

offering singular facilities for Missionary exertions among
millions of Idolaters. The pecuniary advantages of the
appointment were at first wholly out of their contemplation; and for himself, when it was intimated to him
that there was some expectation of his leaving England in
the capacity of Chaplain to the East India Company—his
private Journal contains this remarkable reflection.--
" *The prospect of this world's happiness gave me rather
pain than pleasure, which convinced me that I had been
running away from the world rather than overcoming it.*"
That unexpected change which had now taken place in
Mr. Martyn's circumstances, caused an increased anxiety
amongst his friends to procure, if possible, the appointment which before they had deemed so desirable; and
they were not without hopes of seeing the Mission Church
at Calcutta placed under his pastoral superintendence.
Insuperable obstacles, however, interfered with this
arrangement, and "a veil was thus cast over his
future proceedings."

The patience which Mr. Martyn manifested under this
disappointment was as edifying and extraordinary, as the
watchfulness which he exercised over his mind during his
visit to London, lest scenes so different from those at
Cambridge, should prove to him a source of distraction
and dissipation. He speaks at this time of returning on
one occasion to his room, after having been much abroad
and making many visits, "unable to remain in an unholy
dissipated state, and seeking God earnestly in prayer."
Whilst waiting at the India House, he employed that
time—"for which," he says, "he would have given anything at Cambridge," in private ejaculatory prayer, and
in repeating passages from the Word of God;—and yet,
though he ever aimed at an entire abstraction from the

vanities of the world, he hesitated not to allow himself
the full enjoyment of rational and refined gratifications :
his observations on this head are well worth recording :
" Since I have known God in a saving manner," he
remarks, " painting, poetry, and music, have had charms
unknown to me before. I have received what I suppose
is a taste for them; for religion has refined my mind, and
made it susceptible of impressions from the sublime and
beautiful. Oh how religion secures the heightened enjoyment of those pleasures which keep so many from God, by
their becoming a source of pride !"

Unable at present to discern the cloud which should
conduct him on his way, Mr. Martyn resumed his ministerial functions at Cambridge with ardour, but with a
heavy heart. The affairs of his family, affecting, as they
did, his own destination as well as his sister's happiness,
were no light pressure upon his spirits; in any other point
of view they would scarcely have raised a sigh, and certainly would not greatly have disturbed his composure.
But when " most oppressed," he was enabled to find
comfort in reflecting, that " even such a condition was
infinitely preferable to that of those, whose minds were
discontented in the pursuit of dangerous trifles."

The words of the wise man, that " the day of death is
better than the day of one's birth," can apply only to
those who practically discern in the light of the Scriptures
the great end of their existence. This subject was ever
in Mr. Martyn's contemplation ; and that he might more
closely consider the object for which he was created, he
never failed in making a particular commemoration of the
anniversary of his birth. " Twenty-three years have
elapsed," (he wrote on the 18th of February, 1804,)
"since I saw the light—only four of which have been

professedly given to God;—much has been left undone; much remains to be done as a Christian and minister; yet my past experience of the long-suffering of God, leaves me no doubt of being carried on all the way. I feel that my heart is wholly for heaven, and the world mainly behind my back. Praised be the Lord for his mercy and patience! The number of my days is fixed in his purpose:—Oh may I 'glorify Him on earth, and finish the work he has given me to do.'"

That his heart was "wholly for heaven," is evinced by the following reflection on a conversation in the hall of St. John's. "At dinner they were talking of stones falling from the moon. My imagination began to ascend among the shining worlds hung in the midst of space, and to glance from one to another; and my heart bounded at the thought that I was going a much surer way to behold the glories of the Creator hereafter, than by giving up my time to speculations about them."

In the interval which passed between the months of February and June, he was found earnestly labouring in the service of his Divine Master. He preached animating and awakening discourses; he excited societies of private Christians to "watch, quit themselves as men, and be strong;" he visited many of the poor, the afflicted, and the dying; he warned numbers of the careless and profligate;—in a word, he did the work of an Evangelist. Often did he redeem time from study, from recreation, and from the intercourse of friends, that, like his Redeemer, he might enter the abodes of misery, either to arouse the unthinking slumberer, or to administer consolation to the dejected penitent. Many an hour did he pass in an hospital or an almshouse; and often, after a day of labour and fatigue, when wearied almost to the extremity of endurance, he would read and pray with the servant, who had the care of his rooms ; thus making it his meat and drink, his rest as well as his labour, to do the will of his Heavenly Father, in conformity to the example of Christ.

> " His care was fixed,
> To fill his odorous lamp with deeds of light,
> And hope that reaps not shame."

The delight he experienced on hearing that benefit resulted from his exertions, proved to him an ample recompence for every sacrifice of time, comfort, or convenience ; and it was equalled only by the humility with which he received such cheering intelligence. " I was encouraged " (he observes, on receiving a communication of this nature) " and refreshed beyond description, and I could only cheerfully and gratefully offer up myself to God's service ; but it was, at the same time, a check to my pride to reflect that, though God might in His sovereignty bless His Word by my mouth, I was not, on that account, the less sinful in my ministrations." On another occasion, with touching simplicity and true lowliness, he writes, after meeting some of his flock in the way so strongly and ably recommended by Archbishop Sumner, —" I spoke for twenty minutes on ' Thy will be done on earth, as it is in heaven.' When shall I pour out of a full heart these blessed and Divine truths which drop from these lips of clay ! An old woman, at the conclusion, said, ' The Lord Almighty bless you ! ' This unexpected benediction encouraged me much."

The incalculable value of habits of self-denial seems never to have been more deeply impressed upon the mind of Mr. Martyn than at this time. " A despicable in-

dulgence in lying in bed," he says, "gave me such a view
of the softness of my character, that I resolved, on my
knees, to live a life of more self-denial; the tone and
vigour of my mind rose rapidly : all those duties from
which I usually shrink, seemed recreations. I collected
all the passages from the Four Gospels that had any
reference to this subject ; it is one on which I need to
preach to myself, and mean to preach to others. Whenever I can say, ' Thy will be done,' ' Teach me to do thy
will, O God, for thou art my God,' it is like throwing
ballast out of an air-balloon ; my soul ascends immediately, and light and happiness shine around me." Such
was his thirst after this Christian temper! such his enjoyment of its blessedness !

At the beginning of the present year, Mr. Martyn was
apprehensive, as we have seen, of having bestowed too
much time on public duties, and too little on those which
are private and personal. He was fully persuaded that,
in order to take heed effectually to his ministry, he must,
in obedience to the apostolic injunction, "take heed"
primarily " to himself ; " and this, in fact, was his settled
course and practice. He would sometimes set apart
seasons for humiliation and prayer, and would frequently
spend whole evenings in devotion. Of the Bible he could
ever affirm, " Thy word is very pure, therefore thy servant
loveth it." "The word of Christ dwelt richly in him in
all wisdom." Large portions of it did he commit to
memory ; repeating them during his solitary walks, at
those times when he was not expressly meditating on
some scriptural subject, which was his general custom ;
and so deep was his veneration for the Word of God, that
when a suspicion arose in his mind, that any other book
he might be studying was about to gain an undue influence

over his affections, he instantly laid it aside, nor would he resume it till he had felt and realized the paramount excellence of the Divine oracles : he could not rest satisfied till all those lesser lights which were beginning to dazzle him, had disappeared before the effulgence of the Scriptures.

How much he loved secret prayer, and how vigilantly he engaged in the exercise of it, may be seen in the subjoined remarks on that subject :—

"I felt the need of setting apart a day for the restoration of my soul by solemn prayer. My views of eternity are become dim and transient. I could live for ever in prayer, if I could always speak to God. I sought to pause, and to consider what I wanted, and to look up with fear and faith, and I found the benefit ; for my soul was soon composed to that devout sobriety, which I knew, by its sweetness, to be its proper frame. I was engaged in prayer, in the manner I like—*deep seriousness;* at the end of it, I felt great fear of forgetting the presence of God, and of leaving Him as soon as I should leave the posture of devotion. I was led through the mists of unbelief, and spake to God as one that was true ; and rejoiced exceedingly that He was holy and faithful. I endeavoured to consider myself as being alone on the earth with Him, and that greatly promoted my approach to His presence. My prayer for a meek and holy sobriety was granted. Oh how sweet the dawn of heaven !"

Nor was Mr. Martyn less diligent and fervent in the yet higher branch of Christian worship—thanksgiving. "Let me praise God," he would say, "for having turned me from a life of woe to the enjoyment of peace and hope. The work is real. I can no more doubt it than I can doubt my existence. The whole current of my desires is altered; I am walking quite another way, though I am incessantly stumbling in that way." "I had a most blessed view of God and Divine things. Oh how great is His excellency! I find my heart pained for want of words to praise Him according to His excellent greatness. I looked forward to complete conformity to Him, as the great end of my existence, and my assurance was full. I said, almost with tears, 'Who shall separate us from the love of Christ?'"

It has been well observed,* that "we may judge, by our regard for the Sabbath, whether eternity will be *forced upon us.*" The application of this rule, as it respects Mr. Martyn, will discover a singular meetness in him for the inheritance of the saints in light. His Sabbaths were Sabbaths indeed; the antepast, often, of that rest which is everlasting.

Let us hear his own description of his happiness at some of those sacred times :—" Before setting out to go to Lolworth, I endeavoured to cast away all those contemptible prejudices and dislikes which I often feel, and on the road experienced a sweet sense of the Divine presence, and happy meditation on God and His truths. I was thinking of the love of Christ, and of His unparalleled humility, and that to Him belonged all the glory, as having truly merited it. I felt quite devoted to God, and assured of His love. I did not doubt of having been apprehended by Christ (for the purpose, I hope, of preaching His Gospel), and, during the service, my heart was full of love and joy." "At church, this morning, my heart was overflowing with love and joy.

---

* Adams's " Private Thoughts."

During the sermon, which was an exhortation to diligence, a sense of my unprofitableness depressed me. But, in my ride to Lolworth, I enjoyed sweet delight; every breeze seemed to breathe love into my heart; and, while I surveyed the landscape, I looked forward to the days when all nations should come to the mountain of the Lord's house."

By those who forget the history of our Lord's life, it might be conceived, that one so blameless and harmless as Mr. Martyn—so poor in spirit, and pure in heart—would pass on his way, unassailed by calumny or unkindness. But those who draw their anticipations from the Scripture, will not "marvel" that he should be called to endure unjust insinuations and aspersions, when his whole life was devoted to the welfare of his fellow-creatures. Yet, "when reviled he reviled not again, but committed himself to him that judgeth righteously." "Is not this sweet, O my soul," he exclaimed, under a trial of this kind, "to have a holy God to appeal to and converse with, though all the world should turn their backs!" And it should be remarked here, that his patience, under the severe and unmerited censures of others, was not that which is sometimes mistaken for it—the indifference of apathy, or the superciliousness of contempt; the one was as abhorrent to his nature as the other was to the principles of his religion. Censorious tongues were to him, as they were to David,—"Spears and arrows, and sharp swords." So far from being callous to any attempts to wound his character and his peace, he acknowledges that obloquy was a trying exercise of his Christian temper, and he considered the dispensation as "wholesome," because, "to be despised by men affected him very deeply." But "the name of the Lord is a strong tower;

the righteous runneth into it, and is safe." "Conscious," said he, "that I did not deserve the censures that were cast upon me, I committed myself to God; and in Him may I abide, till the indignation be overpast!"

Those, however, who maligned and traduced Mr. Martyn's character, wounded his spirit far less than those who either scoffed at his high and self-denying designs of usefulness, or, from worldly motives, discouraged him from attempting their accomplishment. No one could be more ready than he to consider the fittest means for compassing the ends he had in view, and to weigh beforehand the difficulties attending the life of a missionary, however favoured by external circumstances. But objections of a contemptuous kind, or those arguments which founded themselves on an ignorance of the very spirit of the Gospel, painfully affected his mind. His reflections, after a long discourse with a person who had addressed him with the kindest intentions, but with a judgment unenlightened by that wisdom which is from above, are worth preserving:—" All our conversation on the subject of religion ended in nothing. He was convinced that he was right, and all the texts I produced were, according to him, *applicable only to the times of the Apostles.* How am I constrained to adore God's sovereign mercy! My soul, dost thou not esteem all things but dung and dross for the excellency of the knowledge of Christ Jesus my Lord? Yea, did not gratitude constrain me—did not duty and fear of destruction—yet surely the excellency of the service of Christ would constrain me to lay down a thousand lives in the prosecution of it." When called to encounter the ridicule of those who, not knowing the hope of Christ's calling, nor the riches of the glory of his inheritance in the saints, nor the exceed-

ing greatness of his power towards those who believe,
despised all labours of love amongst the heathen as wild
and visionary; the Lord helped him to maintain his
ground and to bear his testimony. "With my Bible in
my hand, and Christ at my right hand," said he, "I can
do all things: what though the whole world believe not,
God abideth true, and my hope in Him shall be stedfast."

In the latter part of the spring of this year he had the
singular satisfaction of being introduced to a personal
acquaintance with one of a kindred spirit with himself,—
the late Henry Kirke White. Rare genius, and, above
all, sterling piety, could not fail of being greatly admired
and highly prized by Mr. Martyn; he consequently took
the liveliest interest in behalf of that extraordinary young
man; and used his utmost endeavours to facilitate his
entrance upon that course at college, which afterwards
proved so brilliant, though so transient.

The duties of a public examiner in St. John's were
now, in the month of June, for the second time consigned
to Mr. Martyn: the subjects for examination being, one
of them from the Classics, the other, Locke's "Treatise
on the Understanding." To those who embark in metaphysical disquisitions it will serve as a matter of caution,—
and to those who are harassed with distressing thoughts,
it may administer consolation,—to recite in Mr. Martyn's
own words, the exquisite mental sufferings he endured,
after allowing his mind a range of too unlimited a nature
in these abstract questions. "My soul," he writes, "was
filled with greater misery and horror than I ever before
experienced. I know not how to describe my feelings,
or how I got into them; *but it was after metaphysical
inquiries into the nature and end of my being, and in
what consists the happiness of my soul.* I was afraid to

leave off praying, and went to bed earnestly recommending my soul to Christ." "I tremble," said he, on the succeeding day, "to enter on these inquiries, lest my beclouded reason should lead me to the brink of hell. But I know by experience that the spirit of submission, and a sense of the authority of God, is the only state in which I can ever be happy; and precisely in proportion as I depart from that state of things, I am unhappy. And so strong is this sentiment, that were it not my hope that I should one day *wholly submit to God and descend to my right place,* I would not wish to exist another moment. My trust is, that God will, according to the riches of his grace in Christ Jesus, enable a poor worm, who groans under pride, to advance steadily and humbly to his end, and preserve him from those dreadful thoughts which almost overwhelm the soul." Thus, when in danger of being "spoiled by philosophy," was his soul "upheld by the free Spirit of a faithful God."

It now appeared to be past a doubt that Mr. Martyn would succeed in obtaining a chaplainship in the service of the East India Company; and that in the ensuing spring he would be summoned to leave the shores of his native country for ever. In July, therefore, he revisited those scenes which were endeared to him by numberless early associations, and enlivened by the presence of many whom he admired and loved. And here it is due to the full illustration of his Christian character to mention, that it was not merely the ties of family or friendship which bound him to Cornwall; others there were of a tenderer, if not stronger kind: for he had conceived a deeply-fixed attachment for one, of whom less ought not, and more cannot be said, than that she was worthy of him: an attachment which,—whether he thought, as he afterwards did, that it should be encouraged, or as he now did, that, from peculiar circumstances, it ought to be repressed,—equally exhibits him as a man of God, whose affections were set upon things above, and not on things on the earth.

As this was the first time he had been in Cornwall since his ordination, and the last time he expected ever to visit it, he was extremely anxious to testify the grace of God in his public ministry, whenever he had an opportunity. Such, however, was the prejudice excited against his religious principles, that his labours were almost entirely confined to two churches under the care of his brother-in-law. There he frequently preached, and there both his sisters heard him, the youngest with much delight, the eldest with a most gratifying appearance of having been seriously impressed by what fell from his lips. "I found," said he, "that she had been deeply affected, and from her conversation I received great satisfaction: in the evening, I walked by the water-side till late, having my heart full of praise to God for having given me such hopes of my sister."

To the churches where he preached, the common people crowded in numbers. At Kenwyn,—where he addressed them from 2 Cor. v. 20, 21, "Now then we are ambassadors for Christ, as though God did beseech you by us; we pray you in Christ's stead, be ye reconciled to God. For He hath made Him to be sin for us, who knew no sin, that we might be made the righteousness of God in Him,"—the church was so full that many were compelled to stand on the outside, and many obliged to go away. How acceptable he was to those who loved and valued the Gospel, may be easily conceived; yet such was his vigilance of mind and tenderness of conscience, that "their commendations occasioned him some *pain*," inasmuch as "they tended to fan the flame of vanity." The Christian, especially the Christian minister, has to pass through good report and evil report;—and praise is a severer test of the strength of his principles than dispraise. Mr. Martyn ever found it so; and he experienced himself, as well as exemplified to others, the truth of those words of wisdom,—"as the fining-pot for silver, and the furnace for gold, so is a man to his praise." (Prov. xxvii. 21.)

In the private and more retired duties of his calling, he was now, as usual, most unremitting in his attention: these, in fact, were to him the most delightful parts of his vocation. Happier would he have esteemed it, as far as his personal feelings were concerned, to kneel, as he did frequently with his youngest sister, beside the beds of the sick and dying, than to have had the largest churches in his native county thronged with multitudes attentive to hear him: he was of the spirit of that Redeemer, who sought to be hid whilst He went about doing good.

His habits of reading and prayer, and particularly those of Divine meditation, were in no degree relaxed during his visit, and the less so, because he acknowledged that "he felt an increased difficulty of living in communion with God, where so many remembered him a different character." The solitude of the spot where he resided was happily fitted for contemplation. "The scene," he wrote, in a letter to a friend from Lamorran, "is such as is frequently to be met with in this part of Cornwall. Below the house is an arm of the sea, flowing between the hills, which are covered with wood. By the side of this water I walk in general in the evening, out of the reach of all sound but the rippling of the waves and the whistling of the curlew." In these pensive and solitary walks, the great sacrifices he was about to make could not but force themselves frequently upon his mind, and raise the silent and involuntary sigh : but we may be well assured that "in the multitude of the thoughts which he had in his heart, God's comforts refreshed his soul."

At length, after having withstood in Cornwall, as well as at Cambridge, the arguments of those who "at all events would have detained him in England," arguments of which he confesses that "some were not without weight," he prepared to leave that part of his native country which was peculiarly dear to his feeling and affectionate heart.

The separations of Christians from each other, in this world of mutability, afflictive as they ever must be, have their peculiar alleviations : they know that Christ "fills all things ; "—and they have the blissful expectation of an endless reunion in that world of glory whither they are hastening.

Mr. Martyn, with respect to several from whom he was now to part, could fully indulge in these animated anticipations : but he could not as it respected all. The following is a mournful record of a final interview, overclouded by the gloom of an almost hopeless sorrow :—
"M——— rode with me part of the way, but kept the conversation on general subjects. If I brought him by force to religion, he spoke with the most astonishing apathy on the subject. His cold, deliberate superiority to everything but argument, convinced me not merely that he was not only fully convinced, as he said, but that he

was rooted in infidelity. Nothing remained for me but to
pray for him. Though he parted from me probably to see
me no more, he said nothing that could betray the existence of any passions in him. O cursed infidelity, that
freezes the heart's blood here, as well as destroys the soul
hereafter! I could only adore the sovereign grace of
God, which distinguished me from him, though everything was alike in us. We have been intimate from our
infancy; and have had the same plans and pursuits, and
nearly the same condition: but the one is taken and the
other is left. I, through mercy, find my only joy and
delight in the knowledge of Christ; and he in denying
the truth of religion altogether."

By another farewell, which he has also depicted, he
could not be otherwise than very deeply affected : but the
sorrow was of a character very dissimilar to the last :—
"Rode before E——, with L——, to an old man five
miles off. Our conversation was such as becometh saints,
but it was too pleasant for me. I sighed at the thought
of losing their company. When we arrived, the old man
was out, but his sister, a blind woman of seventy, was
confined to her bed, without any comfortable hope.
L—— and myself said everything we could to cheer her,
and then I prayed. When the old man arrived, we
formed a little circle before the door, under the trees, and
he conversed with his young hearers concerning the things
of God. I then read Psalm lxxxiv. Our ride home was
delightful, our hearts being all devoutly disposed; only
mine was unhappy. Parted with L—— for ever in this
life, with a sort of uncertain pain, which I knew would
increase to greater violence."

These forebodings were but too soon realized. On the
evening of that day, and for many succeeding days, his

mental agony was extreme ;—yet he could speak to God, as one who knew the great conflict within him : he was convinced, that as God willed his happiness, he was providing for it eventually by that bitter separation : he resolved through grace to be his, though it should be through much tribulation : he experienced sweetly and solemnly the excellence of serving Him faithfully, and of following Christ and his apostles : he meditated with great joy on the end of this world, and enjoyed the thought of walking, as he now does, with her from whom he was then removed, in the realms of glory.

But Mr. Martyn had not filled up the measure of his sufferings, having not yet bid adieu to his sisters. With the eldest he spent one melancholy evening in exhorting her for the last time, and endeavouring to comfort her ; and on the succeeding day he took leave of the youngest : "they parted as if to meet no more," and, overwhelmed with inexpressible grief, could find no consolation but in mutually commending each other to the grace of God in prayer.

Then, turning his back, like Abraham of old, on his kindred and his country, and "looking for that city which hath foundations, whose builder and maker is God "—Mr. Martyn departed from Cornwall.

At Plymouth, whither he proceeded, he passed a Sabbath in a heavenly serenity of spirit, and in the full exercise of that faith which is "the substance of things hoped for, the evidence of things not seen." There he preached twice : on Dan. v. 22, 23, "And thou, his son, O Belshazzar, hast not humbled thy heart, though thou knewest all this : but hast lifted up thyself against the Lord of heaven ; and they have brought the vessels of his house before thee, and thou, and thy lords, thy wives, and

thy concubines, have drunk wine in them : and thou hast
praised the gods of silver and gold, of brass, iron, wood,
and stone, which see not, nor hear, nor know : and the
God in whose hand thy breath is, and whose are all thy
ways, hast thou not glorified ; " and on Rev. xxii. 17,
"And the Spirit and the bride say, Come. And let him
that heareth say, Come. And let him that is athirst
come : and whosoever will, let him take of the water of
life freely." "His soul longed," he said, "for the eternal
world, and he could see nothing on earth for which he
would wish to live another hour." At this place an incident occurred indicative as well of his extraordinary
humility, as of that extreme temerity of judgment, in
which those who make a loud, though in the main a
genuine, profession of religion, are too apt to indulge.
Having expounded the Scriptures, and prayed with many
who assembled to listen to his parting words, he discovered
that there were some present who ventured to *express a
doubt of the reality of his religion.* One person in particular openly avowed his apprehensions concerning him ;
—so that his heart was wounded : yet, observed this
meek and lowly man of God, "I was thankful to God for
admonishing me, and my gratitude to the man was, I
think, unfeigned." Such was his recorded comment at
the time ; and it is noted afterwards in his journal, that
this very person was especially remembered by him in
his prayers.

From Plymouth, where his sorrow was painfully renewed, by being separated from a family nearly related
and greatly endeared to him, he proceeded to London ;
during which journey he sought, according to his settled
custom, to render his conversation profitable to his fellow-
travellers : and in one instance on this occasion, his

attempts were not, it may be hoped, unattended with success. He had for his companion a young French officer on his parole—a Protestant, who had been accustomed, he found, to attend to morning and evening prayer, and to read his Bible, which he had unfortunately lost when he was taken prisoner. But his views of the Gospel appearing to Mr. Martyn very defective, he explained to him "his state by nature; his condemnation by the law; the necessity of regeneration; and of free salvation by Christ; and the promise of the Spirit." The young man paid much attention to these admonitions, and expressed great affection for his adviser; who afterwards presented him with a French Testament, and corresponded with him on those important topics which he had set before him.

Change of place and circumstances did not prevent Mr. Martyn from communing with that Lord and Saviour who is everywhere, and who was with him whithersoever he went. On his journey, when leaving Bath early in the morning, "he found his soul ascending unto God with Divine sweetness. Nothing seemed desirable but to glorify Him: all creatures were as nothing." Towards the evening, as they drew near London, he was delightfully engaged in meditation on the latter part of the second chapter of the Epistle to the Ephesians, " contemplating the building as it was rising, and as it would be when finished." "O the transcendent glory!" said he, "of this temple of souls, lively stones, perfect in all its parts, the purchase and the work of God."

On the 18th of September we find Mr. Martyn again quietly settled at Cambridge, from whence his youngest sister received a letter from him, of which the following

is an extract ; and so excellent, surely, is the spirit which
pervades it, that tears of thankfulness for possessing such
a brother must have mingled themselves with those which
she could not but shed abundantly on account of his
departure.

"We should consider it as a sign for good, my dearest
S——, when the Lord reveals to us the almost desperate
corruption of our hearts. For, if He causes us to groan
under it as an insupportable burden, He will, we may
hope, in his own time, give us deliverance. The pride
which I see dwelling in my own heart, producing there
the most obstinate hardness, I can truly say my soul
abhors. I see it to be unreasonable, I feel it to be tormenting. When I sometimes offer up supplications, with
strong crying to God, to bring down my spirit unto the
dust, I endeavour calmly to contemplate the infinite
majesty of the most high God, and my own meanness and
wickedness. Or else I quietly tell the Lord, who knows
the heart, that I would give him all the glory of everything, if I could. But the most effectual way I have ever
found, is to lead away my thoughts from myself and my
own concerns, by praying for all my friends ; for the
Church, the world, the nation ; and, especially by beseeching that God would glorify his own great name, by con-
verting all nations to the obedience of faith ; also by
praying that he would put more abundant honour on those
Christians whom He seems to have honoured especially,
and whom we see to be manifestly our superiors. This is
at least a positive act of humility, and it is certain that
not only will a good principle produce a good act, but the
act will increase the principle. But even after doing all
this, there will often arise a certain self-complacency which
has need to be checked ; and in conversation with Chris-

tian friends, we should be careful, I think, how self is introduced. Unless we think that good will be done, self should be kept in the back-ground and mortified. We are bound to be servants of all, ministering to their pleasure as far as will be to their profit. We are to 'look not at our own things, but at the things of others.' Be assured, my dear S——, that, night and day, making mention of you in my prayers, I desire of God to give you to see the depth of pride and iniquity in your heart, yet not to be discouraged at the sight of it : that you may perceive yourself deserving to be cast out with abhorrence from God's presence ; and then may walk in continual poverty of spirit, and the simplicity of a little child. Pray, too, that I may know something of humility. Blessed grace ! how it smooths the furrows of care, and gilds the dark paths of life ! It will make us kind, tender-hearted, affable, and enable us to do more for God and the Gospel, than the most fervent zeal without it.

"I am here without a companion ; at first the change from the agreeable society in Cornwall, as also from that which I enjoyed at Plymouth, was very irksome ; but it is good for me ! "

His journal at this period contains many observations accordant with the last sentence in this letter : his mind naturally often recurred with fond and mournful recollections to Cornwall. But he endeavoured to check such thoughts, as savouring "too much of earthliness and discontent ! "—knowing that "he ought to be happy wherever God had placed him ;" and "being sure that the exchange he was soon to make, of college for a stormy ocean and the burning plains of India, would not be very pleasant to the flesh."

The happiness Mr. Martyn enjoyed in prosecuting his ministerial vocation, received at this time a wonderful increase : whilst *suffering* the will of God with the meek resignation of faith, he was enabled to *do* it with all the delightful fervency of love. "Blessed be God," he found reason to say, with exceeding joy and gratitude, " *I feel myself to be his minister.* This thought, which I can hardly describe, came, in the morning, after reading Brainerd. I wish for no service but the service of God; to labour for souls on earth, and to do his will in heaven." As far as the external duties of his office were concerned, only this variation occurred;—he became extremely diligent in the humble but most important work of catechising children; giving sometimes a great part of his evenings to the task, and leaving the society he most valued for the sake of it. He determined likewise upon preaching more frequently extempore; (for he had already at times adopted the practice) partly from thinking it, upon the whole, more profitable to himself as well as to the congregation; and partly from the desire of devoting the time spent in writing sermons to other purposes. He by no means, however, renounced these compositions. On the contrary, he enjoined it upon himself, as a rule, never to pass a week without writing a sermon.

In visiting his flock, and thus "preaching from house to house," Mr. Martyn's perseverance kept pace with the heightened pleasure and satisfaction he experienced in his Divine calling: happy, however, as he was in this work of labour and love, the sympathies of his heart were painfully and powerfully called forth by many a scene of extreme misery, and his holy sensibilities were yet more acutely excited by the vice and profligacy he perpetually witnessed. The following are some of several scenes of wretchedness with which he was conversant:—"In prayer I found my soul composed to a blessed and serious view of eternity. Visited the hospital, and read the 11th chapter of John there, with a poor man, in whose room at the workhouse I was struck with the misery that presented itself. He was lying, in his clothes and hat, upon the bed dying; his wife was cleaning the room as if nothing was the matter; and on the threshold was the daughter, about thirty years old, who had been delirious thirteen years. Her mother said that the poor creature sometimes talked of religion : so I asked her, several times before I could arrest her attention, who came into the world to save sinners? After several wild looks, she hastily answered, 'Christ,' and then talked on as before. The dying man was almost insensible to anything I could say. He had formerly been a respectable innkeeper in the town; but the extravagance of a son brought him to poverty, and his daughter, who foresaw it, to insanity."—"In the afternoon I enjoyed solemn thoughts in prayer, and visited several people; amongst them one poor penitent, with whom I had prayed the day before. The desires she expressed amidst her tears were, that God would change her heart, and forgive her, and take her to his mercy. If it was his will, she wished to leave this world. But what if she should live? I asked her : she said she could not say she should not sin, as she was constantly liable ; but rather than return to her former ways, she would be cut in pieces. I was much affected with pity, and preached the Gospel of peace with great delight to her." At another time, when a friend had given him a lamentable account of the gross misconduct of a woman who had made a profession of religion; "the consideration," he remarked, "quite swallowed up my other thoughts, and brought me to a tender grief and godly sorrow. I went to church, ruminating on it, and could almost say, 'Rivers of waters run down mine eyes, because men keep not thy law.' O that I could feel more sensibly the dishonour done to God, and to his Christ, and to his Gospel, and the ruin she is bringing on her own soul." And on hearing, the same day, of the death of one whom he had remembered in innocence, and in the bloom of health and beauty, and who died after a very short career of vice, the account was too much for him, "My heart," said he, "was ready to burst. When I thought of the man who had seduced her; and then of many in the university, who had behaved with extraordinary effrontery at church, my soul groaned within me. Oh, my God, it is enough; hasten, O hasten the day when I shall leave the world to come to Thee; when I shall no more be vexed, and astonished, and pained, at the universal wickedness of this lost earth. But here would I abide my time; and spend and be spent for the salvation of any poor soul; and lie down at the feet of sinners, and beseech them not to plunge into an eternity of torment."

How "honourable," and what a delight the Sabbath was to Mr. Martyn we have already seen; it might be called with him "a kind of transfiguration-day, when his garments shone with peculiar lustre." * Can it be deemed irrelevant, then, to advert again to the state of his mind, as delineated by himself, during some of those sacred seasons at this period?

Sept. 30.—"My mind, this morning, easily ascended to God in peaceful solemnity. I succeeded in finding

* Gilpin's Monument of Parental Affection.

access to God, and being alone with Him. Could I but enjoy this life of faith more steadily, how much should I 'grow in grace,' and be renewed in the spirit of my mind. At such seasons of fellowship with the Father and his Son Jesus Christ, when the world, and self, and eternity, are nearly in their right places, not only are my views of duty clear and comprehensive, but the proper motives have a more constraining influence."

Oct. 28.—"This has been in general a happy day. In the morning, through grace, I was enabled by prayer to maintain a calm recollection of myself, and, what was better, of the presence of my dear Redeemer. From the church I walked to our garden, where I was above an hour, I trust, with Christ, speaking to Him chiefly of my future life in his service. I determined on entire devotedness, though with trembling ; for the flesh dreads crucifixion. But should I fear pain, when Christ was so agonized for me ? No, come what will, I am determined, through God, to be a fellow-worker with Christ. I recollected with comfort, that I was speaking to the great Creator, who can make such a poor weak worm as myself 'more than conqueror.' At church I found by the attention of the people that the fervour of my spirit yesterday had been conveyed into my sermon. I came to my rooms, rejoicing to be alone again, and to hold communion with God."

Dec. 9.—"This has been in general a sweet and blessed day—a foretaste of my eternal Sabbath. Preached on the Third Commandment : in the afternoon, on the Tenth. Rode back to Cambridge, feeling quite willing to go anywhere or suffer anything for God. Preached in Trinity Church on Ezek. xxxiii. 11. 'Say unto them, As I live, saith the Lord God, I have no pleasure in the death of the wicked : but that the wicked turn from his way and live : turn ye, turn ye from your evil ways ; for why will ye die, O house of Israel ?' It was pleasant to me to think of being alone again with God."

The year 1804 closed with Mr. Martyn's being a third time selected as one of the examiners in St. John's, in fulfilling which office, he speaks of his "soul drawing near to God, whilst in the Hall; and of a sacred impression being upon his mind during the examination."—"Several of the poetical images in Virgil," in which he had been examining, "especially those taken from nature, together with the sight of the moon rising over the venerable wall, and sending its light through the painted glass, turned away his thoughts from present things, and raised them to God. His soul was stirred up to renewed resolutions to live a life of entire independence of earthly comforts ; though he felt that the flesh was very weak."

The last day of the year found him "rejoicing at the lapse of time, but sorrowing at his unprofitableness." "So closes," he remarks, "the easy part of my life ; enriched by every earthly comfort, and caressed by friends, I may scarcely be said to have experienced trouble ; but now, farewell ease, if I might presume to conjecture. O Lord, into Thy hands I commit my spirit ! Thou hast redeemed me, Thou God of truth ! May I be saved by Thy grace, and be sanctified to do Thy will, now, and to all eternity, through Jesus Christ." His reflections on the following day, the first of that year which was his last in England, carry with them a peculiar interest, as well from their intrinsic excellence, as from the circumstances under which they were indited.

Jan. 1, 1805.—"Hitherto hath the Lord helped me. It is now about five years since God stopped me in the career of worldliness, and turned me from the paths of sin ; three years and a-half since I turned to the Lord with all my heart ; and a little more than two years since He enabled me to devote myself to his service as a missionary. My progress of late has become slower than it had been ; yet I can truly say, that in the course of this time, every successive year, every successive week, has been happier than the former. From many dangerous snares hath the Lord preserved me ; in spite of all my inward rebellion He hath carried on his work in my heart ; and in spite of all my unbelieving fears, he hath given me a hope full of immortality ; 'he hath set my foot on a rock, and established my goings, and hath put a new song in my mouth, even praises to my God.' It is the beginning of a critical year to me : yet I feel little apprehension. The same grace and long-suffering, the same wisdom and power, that have brought me so far, will bring me on, though it be through fire and water, to a goodly heritage. I see no business in life but the work of Christ, neither do I desire any employment to all eternity but his service. I am a sinner saved by grace. Every day's experience convinces me of this truth. My daily sins and constant corruption leave me no hope but that which is founded on God's mercy in Christ. His Spirit, I trust, is imparted, and is renewing my nature ; as I desire much, though I have attained but little. Now to God, the Father, Son, and Holy Ghost, would I solemnly renew my self-dedication, to be his servant for ever."

Towards the end of January, a sudden summons to leave England in ten days caused some perturbation in Mr. Martyn's spirits. Short, however, as the notice was, he would instantly have complied with it, had he been in Priest's orders, which legally he could not be till the

18th of February, when he completed his twenty-fourth year.

The solemn and most impressive rite of admission to the functions and privileges of a Presbyter of the Church of England, was administered to him, who had well "performed the office of a Deacon," at St. James's Chapel, London, in the month of March; after which he received the degree of Bachelor of Divinity, conferred upon him by mandate from the University; when nothing remained to detain him any longer at Cambridge.

At the thoughts of his departure he confesses that the flesh betrayed its weakness, but he did not regret having resigned the world; life he knew was but a short journey —a little day; and then, if faithful unto death, his gracious reward would begin. Happily for him, such was the Divine goodness and mercy, that he was, at this moment, more than ever persuaded of his being truly called of God to preach the Gospel to the heathen. "I rejoice to say (he wrote to his youngest sister) that I never had so clear a conviction of my call as at present, as far as respects the inward impression. Never did I see so much the exceeding excellency, and glory, and sweetness of the work, nor had so much the favourable testimony of my own conscience, nor perceived so plainly the smile of God. I am constrained to say, What am I, or what is my father's house, that I should be made willing —what am I that I should be so happy, so honoured?" In his journal, likewise, he expresses himself to the same effect :—"I felt more persuaded of my call than ever; there was scarcely the shadow of a doubt left; rejoice, O my soul, thou shalt be the servant of God in this life, and in the next, for all the boundless ages of eternity."

A remarkable spirit of supplication, likewise, was in

this hour of need poured out upon him; and the sure word of prophecy, predicting the glory of the latter times, was as the dawning of the day and the rising of the day-star in his heart. "I could not," he remarks, "help reflecting on the almost supernatural fervour and deep devotion which came upon me, whilst I declared that I had rightfully no other business each day but to do God's work as a servant, constantly regarding his pleasure." "My thoughts were full of what God would do for his own glory, in the conversion of multitudes to Himself in the latter day. I did not wish to think about myself in any respect, but found it a precious privilege to stand by, a silent admirer of God's doings."

To be removed for ever from many dear friends, and from a congregation who "esteemed him very highly in love for his work's sake," would have greatly afflicted one of far less affection than that which animated the breast of Mr. Martyn. As for him, his sufferings on this occasion were most severe. Those of his flock, likewise, were no less so: they would willingly have renewed the touching scene once beheld at Miletus, "sorrowing as they did for the words that he spake, that they should see his face no more." One old man—to adduce no other instance of their undissembled regard and poignant regret —could not refrain from coming to him, that he might commend him solemnly to God in prayer. And when he delivered his farewell discourse in Trinity Church, on these words (2 Sam. vii. 27, 29), "For thou, O Lord of Hosts, God of Israel, hast revealed to thy servant, saying, I will build thee an house; therefore hath thy servant found in his heart to pray this prayer unto thee. And now, O Lord God, thou art that God, and thy word be true, and thou hast promised this goodness unto thy servant : therefore now let it please thee to bless the house of thy servant, that it may continue for ever before thee : for thou, O Lord God, hast spoken it : and with thy blessing let the house of thy servant be blessed for ever ; " the whole assembly was dissolved in grief, thus testifying by their tears that their attachment to him was equalled only by their admiration of his character.

On the 3d of April, the day after he had preached his valedictory sermon, Mr. Martyn quitted for ever the place which had been "the dear abode of his youth,"—in which he had obtained no moderate portion of honour and reputation, and in which, had he deemed it right to remain, he might have acquired that ample share of emolument which talents such as his never fail to secure. At such a moment he would have been glad to have been left to uninterrupted meditation ; but many young students happened to accompany him on his journey, and he thought it his duty to enter into religious conversation with them for their benefit. "At intervals, however," said he, "I meditated and prayed,—the coldness and ingratitude of my wicked heart made me feel loathsome to myself ; and I longed but for one thing, which was, to be delivered from all my iniquity."

The day after his arrival in London, other natural feelings were called into exercise ; feelings which it is the design of the Gospel to moderate but not to suppress. Some hymns sung in the evening worship of the family into which he was most hospitably received, recalling Cambridge to his remembrance, affected him even to tears ; and as he dwelt with melancholy pleasure on its past delights, all his dear Christian friends in it seemed doubly interesting.

During the two months Mr. Martyn was resident in

London, he considered that he could not better employ his time than by devoting it to the attainment of the Hindostanee language; and having the advantage of being assisted by a gentleman eminently competent to direct him,* he was incessant in his endeavours to obtain that necessary qualification for an Indian missionary. In order, also, that he might correct some defects in his speech, he at the same time deemed it incumbent on him to attend several lectures on pronunciation : for nothing did he disdain which, tending to make his ministry more acceptable, might conduce to the glory of God. In the delivery of the great message committed to him as an ambassador of Christ, he was at this time by no means remiss. During the short period of his abode in London he often preached ; occupying the pulpit, principally, at St. John's Chapel, Bedford-row, then under the care of the Rev. Richard Cecil, from whose holy example and faithful advice Mr. Martyn conceived himself to have derived the most substantial and lasting benefit. Nor was he without another high gratification and privilege,—that of being introduced to the aged and venerable Mr. Newton, who, expecting soon to be " gathered to his people," rejoiced to give this young minister, about to proceed on his sublime embassy of love, his paternal counsel and benediction.

An intercourse with such men as Mr. Newton and Mr. Cecil was more than a compensation to Mr. Martyn for his detention in London, and for the uneasiness of that period of uncertainty and delay, which is almost as oppressive to the spirit as the moment of actual departure. But if he received unmingled satisfaction

* Mr. Gilchrist.

and abiding profit from the conversation he enjoyed with those eminent Christians, there were others with whom he conferred, who, "seeming to be somewhat, in conference added nothing to him," but, on the contrary, occasioned him no small measure of disquietude Once, indeed, these very persons were in the habit of manifesting great cordiality towards him; but now they began to slight him, and in his presence were continually raising disparaging comparisons between him and certain preachers, whose theological sentiments, if not erroneous, were at least far too exclusive; and whose strain of doctrine, in Mr. Martyn's judgment, was more calculated to produce ill-grounded confidence, than righteousness and true holiness. Interviews of this kind he endured than rather enjoyed : they are to be ranked amongst his trials, and not placed on the side of his comforts.

The subject of his union, likewise, with that excellent person (lately consigned to her grave), on whom his affections were so unalterably fixed, became at this time a matter of consideration and discussion amongst some of his more intimate friends ; and their difference of opinion respecting the propriety of the measure, should it ever be practicable, caused no small tumult and anguish in his heart.

On the other hand, there were two events, the prospect of which was of the most cheering complexion; the one, the satisfactory marriage of his youngest sister; the other, a hope of being soon followed to India by two of his friends, who, strengthened, if not excited by his example, declared their willingness to go forth and labour with him in that distant vineyard.

But as it may administer much profitable as well as encouraging matter for reflection, to those who may hereafter tread in the footsteps of Mr. Martyn, his journal shall speak for him at some length during the interval between his quitting Cambridge and preparing to sail from England.

April 10.—"Walked out to buy books, and strove to be diligent in thinking of my subject.* When I got into the spirit of it, Christ appeared at times inexpressibly precious to me."

April 14.—Sunday.—"I felt very unconcerned about men's opinions, both before and after sermon. Before it, I could solemnly appeal to God, and found comfort and pleasure in doing so,—that I desired his glory alone,—that I detested the thought of seeking my own praise, or taking pleasure in hearing it. The rest of the evening I continued in a very ardent frame; but, in private, I was taught by former experience to labour after a calm and sober devotedness to God, and that my fervour might show itself in a steady course of action. My soul felt growing in holiness nigh unto the blessed God, with my understanding, will, and affections turned towards Him. Surely many of the children of God have been praying for me to-day. May the Lord return their prayers tenfold into their own bosoms."

April 15.—"Oh, may God confirm my feeble resolutions! What have I to do but to labour, and pray, and fast, and watch, for the salvation of my own soul and those of the heathen world. Ten thousand times more than ever do I feel devoted to that precious work. Oh, gladly shall this base blood be shed, every drop of it, if India can but be benefited in one of her children;—if but one of those children of God Almighty might be brought home to his duty."

* The subject he had chosen in the morning for meditation.

April 16.—"How careful should I and all be, in our ministry, not to break the bruised reed! Alas! do I think that a schoolboy, a raw academic, should be likely to lead the hearts of men?—what a knowledge of men, and acquaintance with the Scriptures, what communion with God, and study of my own heart, ought to prepare me for the awful work of a messenger from God on the business of the soul."

April 22.—"I do not wish for any heaven upon earth besides that of preaching the precious Gospel of Jesus Christ to immortal souls. May these weak desires increase and strengthen with every difficulty."

April 27.—"My constant unprofitableness seemed to bar my approach to God. But I considered that for all that was past, the blood of Christ would atone : and that for the future, God would that moment give me grace to perform my duty."

May 7.—"Went in the evening to hear ——. He was on the same subject as usual, but without variety. I confess I was dissatisfied; not only because I could fix on nothing that could edify me, but because I could not but think that there was nothing to offend or detect carnal professors."

May 9.—"O my soul, when wilt thou live consistently? When shall I walk steadily with God? When shall I hold heaven constantly in view! How time glides away,—how is death approaching,—how soon must I give up my account,—how are souls perishing,—how does their blood call out to us to labour, and watch, and pray for those that remain."

May 16.—"I went down with Captain —— to Deptford : passing through an inn which was close to the water-side, I came at once, to my great surprise, close to the Indiaman, before I was aware of it. The sudden sight of water and of the ship affected me almost to tears. My emotions were mixed—partly of joy, and partly of trembling apprehension of my being now so soon to go away."

May 18.—"Happening to look over some of my farewell sermons at Cambridge, I was affected to tears."

May 22.—"Heard Mr. Crowther preach. At first I could not enter into those humiliating views which I knew I ought to have: but by stirring up myself to attend, and to mix faith with what he said, and by turning every sentence into a petition, I got great good in my soul."

"May 24.—"I felt more than I ever had done, the shame attending poverty; nothing but the remembrance that I was not to blame supported me: whatever comes to me in the way of providence is and must be for my good. Dined at ——, where I could plainly see I was scarcely a welcome guest: the neglect of me was too plain to be unnoticed. The weakness of my human nature would have expressed itself, had I not looked up to God, and prayed for a sense of my desert of the scorn of men. The conversation amongst these high professors was of course about ——. One said to me, '*His* sermons are not *fine* and *eloquent*, but *spiritual*;'—alluding to the first of mine which he had heard."

May 30.—"Read Brainerd. I feel my heart knit to this dear man, and really rejoice to think of meeting him in heaven."

June 1.—"Memory has been at work to unnerve my soul: but reason, and honour, and love to Christ and souls shall prevail. Amen. God help me."

June 2.—Whitsunday.—"My dear Redeemer is a fountain of life to my soul. With resignation and peace can I look forward to a life of labour and entire seclusion from earthly comforts, while Jesus thus stands near me, changing me into his own image."

June 6.—" God's interference in supporting me continually, appears to me like a miracle."

June 7.—" I have not felt such heart rending pain since I parted with L—— in Cornwall. But the Lord brought me to consider the folly and wickedness of all this. I could not help saying,—Go, Hindoos,—go on in your misery,—let Satan still reign over you; for he that was appointed to labour among you is consulting his ease. No, thought I, earth and hell shall never keep me back from my work. I am 'cast down, but not destroyed.' I began to consider why I was so uneasy,—'Cast thy care upon Him, for He careth for you.' 'In everything by prayer and supplication, with thanksgiving, let your requests be made known unto God;'—these promises were sweetly fulfilled, before long, to me."

June 8.—" My heart was sometimes ready to break with agony. At other times, I was visited by a few moments of sublime and enraptured joy. Such is the conflict. Why have my friends mentioned this subject? It has torn open old wounds, and I am again bleeding."

June 13.—" Had I a more tender sense of mercy, I should have delighted to write on the subject I had chosen. Yet it is very sweet to be desiring such a state. I would wish, like Mary, to lie weeping at the feet of Jesus."

June 15.—" Shed tears to-night at the thoughts of my departure. I thought of the roaring seas, which would soon be rolling between me and all that is dear to me on earth."

June 23.—" The grief of the Miss C——s, at the departure of their brother for India, called forth some of my natural feelings. Had I been going from necessity, it would almost break my heart. But I go, from choice, into a part of the vineyard where my dearest friend will be present. On the subject of the mission, I seemed assisted to unfold my heart unto the Lord, and to pray for his mighty protection in the fiery trial which is about to try me."

June 25.—"I heard something about Schwartz to-day, which struck me much—his simple mode of living."

June 28.—"Was much struck and affected with the words of a Hottentot woman, quoted in Mr. Biddulph's sermon. How happy and honoured am I, in being *suffered* to be a Missionary."

July 4.—"Mr. Cecil showed me a letter in Schwartz's own handwriting.* Its contents were of a very experimental nature,—applicable to my case. The life of faith in Jesus is what I want. My soul might almost burst with astonishment at its own wickedness! but, at the same time, trusting to mercy, rise and go, and try to make men happy. The Lord go with me! Let my right hand forget her cunning, if I remember not Jerusalem above my chief joy."

After delivering a sermon to the congregation at St. John's, upon Acts xx. 32, "And now, brethren, I commend you to God, and to the word of his grace, which is

---

* It is in vain to wish that very large extracts from Mr. Schwartz's correspondence with the Society for Promoting Christian Knowledge were published: much of which would doubtless be found "applicable to the case" of Christians in general, and of Ministers and Missionaries in particular. It is said, that the whole is either *lost* or *burnt*.

able to build you up, and to give you an inheritance among all them that are sanctified," on the 8th of July, Mr. Martyn left London for Portsmouth : and such was the acuteness of his feelings during this journey, that he fainted and fell into a convulsion-fit, at the inn at which he slept on the road,—a painful intimation to those friends who were with him of the poignancy of that grief which he endeavoured as much as possible to repress and conceal. The next morning, however, he was sufficiently recovered to proceed, and was much refreshed in his spirit at the sight of many of his brethren, at Portsmouth, who had come (several from a considerable distance) that they might affectionately accompany him to the ship. Among these was one whose presence afforded him an unexpected happiness. "To be obliged to give up all hopes of your accompanying me to Portsmouth" (he had written a short time before to Mr. Simeon) "is a greater disappointment than I can well describe. Having been led to expect it, I seem to experience a painful privation. However, you will not now have the pain of observing in your brother a conversation and spirit unsuitable to the important work on which he is going. Yet, this I believe, that though I have little affection towards heavenly things, I have less towards everything earthly." From Mr. Simeon he learnt, to his exceeding comfort, that his flock at Cambridge intended, on the day of his departure, as far as it could be ascertained, to give themselves to fasting and prayer ; and at his hands he received, with peculiar gratification, a silver compass, sent by them as a memorial of their unfeigned affection ; for which the following letter expressed his acknowledgments :—

Portsmouth, July 11, 1805.

"My dearest Brethren,

"I write in great haste to thank you most affectionately for the token of your love, which our dear brother and minister has given me from you. Oh may my God richly recompense you for your great affection! May He reward your prayers for me, by pouring tenfold blessings into your own bosoms! May He bless you with all spiritual blessings in Christ Jesus! At the command of God, as I believe, I shall, in a few hours, embark for those regions where your little present may be of use to me, in guiding my way through the trackless desert. I pray that the word of God, which is your compass, may, through the Spirit, direct your path through the wilderness of this world, and bring you in safety to the 'better country' above. I beg your prayers, and assure you of mine. Remember me sometimes at your social meetings, and particularly at that which you hold on the Sabbath morning. Pray not only for my sinful soul,—that I may be kept faithful unto death;—but also especially for the souls of the poor Heathen. Whether I live or die, let Christ be magnified by the ingathering of multitudes to Himself. I have many trials awaiting me, and so have you; but that covenant of grace in which we are interested, provides for the weakest, and secures our everlasting welfare.—Farewell, dear Brethren! May God long continue to you the invaluable labours of your beloved minister; and may you, with the blessing of his ministry, grow, day by day, in all spirituality and humility of mind; till God, in His mercy, shall call you, each in his own time, to the eternal enjoyment of His glory."

The few days Mr. Martyn remained at Portsmouth,

were spent in conversing with his brethren on the things pertaining to the kingdom of God; and in social supplication and thanksgiving. His prayer, on the day he expected finally to quit the shores of England, will not easily be forgotten by those who 'bowed their knees together with him to the God and Father of our Lord Jesus Christ:' it ascended to the 'lofty One' from the lowest depths of humiliation, and breathed the most entire devotedness of body, soul, and spirit to his service. His whole demeanour, indeed, could not fail of tenderly affecting, as well as indelibly impressing, their hearts and minds.—One of those then present, who little thought that the task he now so inadequately attempts to execute would ever be assigned him, well remembers his own sensations on that most trying and yet triumphant occasion; and how completely every thought within him was absorbed in admiration of the astonishing grace bestowed on his friend, and in bitter regret at being deprived of his society. Nor let it be surmised that the fondness of friendship has exaggerated the sacrifices Mr. Martyn was then enduring. A chaplainship in the East India service presents to many, advantages highly valued and eagerly sought;—but considered as a pecuniary provision, it could have no attractions to Mr. Martyn. To him a curacy in Cornwall would have been far preferable; and at Cambridge, such was his academic fame, that ample emolument was certain. In our estimate, too, of his privations, we should remember, that whilst motives not to be disparaged, carried many with him, far from the happy land of their nativity;—the principles which actuated him were *purely spiritual*. They also had hopes of a return; their eyes might one day sparkle with joy on the shores where then they were suffused with sorrow. Mr. Martyn had no such anticipations; before him the horizon was dark around,—not a streak of light was visible. He went forth to preach the gospel to the heathen, and it was his fixed resolution to live and die amongst them. When he left England, he left it wholly for Christ's sake, and he left it for ever.

On the 17th of July, 1805, the Union East Indiaman, which was to convey Mr. Martyn to Calcutta, sailed from Portsmouth in company with a large fleet, under the command of Captain Byng; and two days afterwards came to an anchor in the port of Falmouth. An extract of a letter written from this place to Mr. Simeon, feelingly depicts Mr. Martyn's sensations, when, on awaking on the morning of the 17th, it rushed upon his mind, that his voyage was really commenced :—" It was a very painful moment to me when I awoke, on the morning after you left us, and found the fleet actually sailing down the channel. Though it was what I had actually been looking forward to so long, yet the consideration of being parted for ever from my friends, almost overcame me. My feelings were those of a man who should suddenly be told, that every friend he had in the world was dead. It was only by prayer for them that I could be comforted; and this was indeed a refreshment to my soul, because by meeting them at the throne of grace, I seemed to be again in their society."

The arrival of the fleet at Falmouth was an event wholly unforeseen by Mr. Martyn, who was somewhat agitated " at the singularity of the providence of God, in thus leading him once more into the bosom of all his friends." " May the Lord," said he, " glorify himself in this and in every other dispensation ! "—How trying this dispensation was to him, it will not require many quotations from his journal to demonstrate. From these it will be evident, that delightful as it was to him once more to land upon the shores where he had sported gaily in his infancy, and meditated divinely in maturer age, it would have been far happier for him had a storm in the night hurried him past his beloved Cornwall. But God, who doeth all things well, manifestly intended to strengthen his faith, by putting it to a severe exercise. *

July 29.—" I was much engaged, at intervals, in learning the hymn ' The God of Abraham praise.' As often as I could use the language of it with any truth, my heart was a little at ease.

> ' The God of Abraham praise,
>   At whose supreme command
> From earth I rise, and seek the joys
>   At his right hand.
>
> I all on earth forsake,
>   Its wisdom, fame, and power;
> And Him my only portion make,
>   My shield and tower.'

" There was something peculiarly solemn and affecting to me in this hymn, and particularly at this time. The truth of the sentiments I knew well enough. But alas! I felt that the state of mind expressed in it was above mine at the time; and I felt loth to forsake all on earth."

" Not being able to reach the ship, I slept at a little public house on the road, where I lay down in the most acute mental misery; and rose the next morning disturbed and unrefreshed. The morning was beautifully serene, but on account of the tempest within, that very circum-

* We here commence, in the Appendix, a series of letters to Miss Grenfell, which are now, for the first time, added to this Memoir. (See Appendix I.)

stance was disgusting to me. A dark and stormy day would have been more in unison with my feelings."

"I went on board in extreme anguish, and found an opportunity in the sloop by which I passed to the ship, to cry, with brokenness of spirit, to the Lord. The words, 'Why sayest thou, O Jacob, and speakest, O Israel, My way is hid from the Lord, and my judgment is passed over from my God;' were brought to my mind with such force, that I burst into a flood of tears; and felt much relieved in my soul, by the thought that God was thus compassionate, and the blessed Lord Jesus a merciful and compassionate High Priest, who condescended to sympathize with me. In the afternoon, it pleased God to give me a holy and blessed season in prayer, in which my soul recovered much of its wonted peace." Thus did God, in answer to prayer, in some measure refresh his soul. An attempt, also, which he made to comfort another person in the ship with him, served to invigorate his own drooping spirit. "They stood together," as he represents it, "looking anxiously at the raging sea, and sighed to think of the happy societies of God's people, who (as it was the Sabbath-day) were then joining in sweet communion in public worship. But the topics of conversation which Mr. Martyn endeavoured to bring before his disconsolate companion, had a happy re-action on his own mind: whilst cheering him, he was cheered himself:— "the blessed Spirit of God applied the blood of Jesus to cleanse away his sin, and restore him to comfort:" and at night he could commit himself to rest, "tossed," as he expresses it "by the roaring surge, but composed and peaceful with the everlasting arms underneath him."

During his detention for about three weeks at Falmouth, he preached several times in the ship, as well as on shore : and amongst other texts, he addressed his hearers from that most appropriate one, "Jesus came and spake unto them, saying, All power is given unto me, in heaven and on earth. Go ye, therefore, and teach all nations, baptizing them in the name of the Father, and of the Son, and of the Holy Ghost : Teaching them to observe all things whatsoever I have commanded you : and lo ! I am with you alway, even unto the end of the world. Amen." (Matt. xxviii. 18, 20.) A sermon from Mr. Martyn on those words of Scripture was well calculated to produce a powerful effect on the minds of his audience : for what more striking comment upon the passage could there be, than the very circumstance of his appearance amongst them, upon his apostolical labour of love.

On the 10th of August, the signal was made for the ships to sail, at which time, having been deceived by the information communicated to him concerning the continuance of the fleet in port, Mr. Martyn was absent, at the distance of twenty miles in the country. The express announcing this mistake, was like a thunderstroke to him ; but by making all possible dispatch, he contrived to reach the Union just in time. That ship, as if by the appointment of Providence, had met with an accident in clearing out of the harbour, which impeded her progress, whilst almost all the others were under weigh. The commander, as he passed, expressed his displeasure at her delay; but Mr. Martyn discovered the high and gracious hand of God in this event, and "blessed Him for having thus saved his poor creature from shame and trouble." "So delusive," to adopt his own reflections, "are schemes of pleasure ! At nine in the morning, I was sitting at ease with the person dearest to me upon earth, intending to go out with her afterwards to see different views ; to visit some persons with her, and preach on the morrow; four hours only elapsed, and I was under sail from England." *

The anxiety Mr. Martyn had felt to reach his ship, and the joy he experienced at having effected his object, for a time absorbed other and more sorrowful considerations: but when left a little at leisure, his spirits, as he acknowledges, began to sink. "He seemed backward, also, to draw near to God; and though, when he did so, he found relief, he was still slow to flee to the refuge of his weary soul."

Unhappily for him, during the whole of the 10th, and for the greater part of the succeeding day, Cornwall was still in sight: and who is there, endued with the sensibilities of our common nature, but must have been subjected to the most painful emotions, whilst slowly passing for the last time along a coast, where every object which caught the eye,—every headland,—every building,— every wood, served to remind him of endearments that were passed, and of pleasures never to be renewed?

That Apostle who professed that he was 'ready, not to be bound only, but even to die at Jerusalem, for the name of the Lord Jesus,' exclaimed also, —"What mean ye to weep, and to break my heart?" And he, too, when sailing to Rome along the 'sea of Cilicia,' may well be supposed to have looked mournfully towards the region of his nativity, and to have thought with pain on Tarsus. But Mr. Martyn's own hand shall pourtray his feelings:—

Sunday, August 11.—"I rose dejected, and extremely weak in body. After simply crying to God for mercy and assistance, I preached on Heb. ix. 16:—'But now

* See Appendix II.

they desire a better country, that is, an heavenly: wherefore God is not ashamed to be called their God, for he
hath prepared for them a city.' On repeating the text
a second time, I could scarcely refrain from bursting into
tears. For the Mount and St. Hilary spire and trees
were just discernible by the naked eye at the time I
began my sermon, by saying, 'that now the shores of
England were receding fast from our view, and that we
had taken a long, and to many of us, an everlasting
farewell,' &c. We had made little way during the night,
and in the morning I was pleased to find that we were
in Mount's Bay, midway between the Land's-End and the
Lizard; and I was often with my glass, recalling those
beloved scenes, till after tea, when, on ascending the
poop, I found that they had disappeared; but this did
not prevent my praying for all on shore. Amidst the
extreme gloom of my mind this day, I found great pleasure, at seasons of prayer, in interceding earnestly for my
beloved friends all over England."

The dejection of mind of which Mr. Martyn here
speaks, and which returned the next day with an overpowering influence, was evidently combined with, and
augmented by, much bodily infirmity, and, no doubt,
would have been alleviated by the sympathizing intercourse of a companion in tribulation, and in the kingdom
and patience of Jesus Christ. The original injunction
given to the seventy, was given by Him who knew what
was in man, and who therefore sent them "*two and two*
before his face into every city," for "two are better than
one, because they have a good reward for their labour;
for if they fall, the one will lift up his fellow; but woe to
him that is alone when he falleth, for he hath not another
to help him up." (Eccles. iv. 9, 10.)

VIEW NEAR MARAZION.

Page 96.

" England had disappeared, and, with it, all my peace."
"The pains of memory were all I felt. Would I go
back? Oh no; but how can I be supported? My faith
fails. I find, by experience, that I am weak as water.
Oh, my dear friends in England! when we spoke with
exultation of the Mission to the heathen, whilst in the
midst of health, and joy, and hope, what an imperfect
idea did we form of the sufferings by which it must be
accomplished."

Such were the complainings of his spirit, overwhelmed
within him. Yet there were moments when he could
"realize the realms of glory," and when "all earthly
things died away in insignificance."

On the 14th of August, the fleet came to an anchor in
the Cove of Cork, and there, in a spiritual sense, Mr.
Martyn found that "haven where he would be;" there
he discovered that "heaviness may endure for a night,
but joy cometh in the morning," and he who before had
felt "poor and needy, with his heart wounded within
him," could then say, "I will greatly praise the Lord
with my mouth;" "thanks be to God, which causeth
us always to triumph in Christ." (2 Cor. ii. 14.)
"After a long and blessed season in prayer, I felt,"
he says, "the spirit of adoption drawing me very near
to God, and giving me the full assurance of his love.
My fervent prayer was that I might be more deeply and
habitually convinced of his unchanging, everlasting love,
and that my whole soul might be altogether in Christ.
I scarcely knew how to express the desires of my
heart. I wanted to be all in Christ, and to have
Christ for my 'all in all,'—to be encircled in his
everlasting arms, and to be swallowed up altogether
in his fulness. I wished for no created good, or for

men to know my experience; but to be one with
Thee, and live for Thee, O God, my Saviour and
Lord. Oh, may it be my constant care to live free
from the spirit of bondage, at all times having access to
the Father. This I feel should be the state of the Christian: perfect reconciliation with God, and a perfect
appropriation of Him in all his endearing attributes,
according to all that He has promised: it is this that
shall bear me safely through the storm." What is this,
but the happiness intended by the Psalmist, when he
breaks forth in those words of sublimity and rapture:
"Blessed are the people which know the joyful sound;—
they shall walk, O Lord, in the light of thy countenance:
in thy name shall they rejoice all the day, and in thy
righteousness shall they be exalted." (Psalm lxxxix.
15, 16.)

At Cork, Mr. Martyn endeavoured to procure admission to a pulpit in the city, as well as to preach to the
convicts going out with the fleet to Botany Bay, but was
unsuccessful in both these attempts. On board his own
ship he regularly read prayers, and preached once every
Sabbath, lamenting that the captain would not permit the
performance of more than one service. This being the
case, his usefulness in the ship depended much, he conceived, on his private ministrations. Scarcely a day,
therefore, passed without his going between the decks;
where, after assembling all who were willing to attend, he
read to them some religious book, upon which he commented as he went on. "Some attended fixedly,—others
are looking another way,—some women are employed
about their children, attending for a little while, and
then heedless; some rising up and going away,—others
taking their place; and numbers, especially of those who

have been upon watch, strewed all along upon the deck fast asleep,—one or two from the upper decks looking down and listening;"—such is the picture he draws of his congregation below. The situation of things above, when he performed his weekly duty on the Sabbath, was not, according to his own statement, more encouraging. There, the opposition of some, and the inattention of others, put his meekness and patience very strongly to the test. "The passengers," as he describes it, "were inattentive,—the officers, many of them, sat drinking, so that he could overhear their noise—and the captain was with them. His own soul was serious, and undisturbed by the irreverence of the hearers, and he thought that he could have poured it out in prayer without restraint, in defiance of their scornful gaze."—"How melancholy and humiliating," he could not help adding, "is this mode of public ordinances on ship-board, compared with the respect and joy with which multitudes come up to hear my brethren on shore! but this prepares me for preaching amongst the heedless Gentiles."

CHAPTER IV.

ON the 31st of August, after having been detained above
a fortnight in the Cove of Cork, the fleet, consisting of
fifty transports, five men-of-war, and the Indiamen, put
to sea; and now again Mr. Martyn suffered much both in
body and mind; he became languid and feverish; his nights
were sleepless; and his mental conflict was extremely
sharp. "My anguish at times," he says, "was inexpressible, when I awoke from my disturbed dreams,
to find myself actually on my way, with a long sea
rolling between me and all I held dear in this life." "To
describe the variety of perplexing, heart-rending, agonizing
thoughts which passed through my mind, and which,
united with the weakness and langour of my body, served
to depress me into the depths of misery, would be impossible. The bodily suffering would be nothing, did
not Satan improve his advantage in representing the
happiness and ease of the life I had left. However, God
did not leave me quite alone, poor and miserable as I
was. I was helped to recollect several things in Scripture
which encouraged me to hold on. Such as 'If we suffer
with him, we shall also reign with him;' the examples,
likewise, of Moses, Abraham, and St. Paul; of our blessed
Lord himself, and of his saints at the present moment. I

repeated the farewell discourse of St. Paul, and endeavoured to think how he would act in my situation. I thought of all God's people looking out after me with expectation—following me with their wishes and prayers. I thought of the holy angels, some of whom, perhaps, were guarding me on my way; and of God, and of Christ, approving my course and mission. 'Who will go for me? Here am I—send me.' I thought of the millions of precious souls that now and in future ages might be benefited." By such considerations as these; by prayer; by reciting Scripture; by praying over it; by casting himself simply upon Christ; and by looking upon pain and suffering as his daily portion (which thought wonderfully served to tranquillize his mind), Mr. Martyn was carried through a season of great tribulation, in which he might almost have adopted the words of the Psalmist, "Thou hast laid me in the lowest pit, in darkness, in the deeps. Thine indignation lieth hard upon me, and thou hast afflicted me with all thy waves." (Ps. lxxxviii. 6, 7.) But it is an inspired declaration, that "they that *wait* on the Lord shall *renew* their strength : they shall mount up with wings as eagles, they shall run and not be weary; they shall walk and not faint :" nor was it long before he could affix his seal to the truth of this testimony. "In prayer," he says, shortly after this, "I soon launched sweetly into eternity, and found joy unspeakable in thinking of my future rest, and of the boundless love and joy I should ever taste in Christ's beloved presence hereafter. I found no difficulty in stirring myself up to the contemplation of heaven; my soul through grace realized it, and I delighted to dwell by faith on those blissful scenes."

Shortly after the fleet had sailed from Ireland, a

tremendous storm arose ; and though it was the first that Mr. Martyn had ever witnessed, his mind was kept, during a night of general anxiety and consternation, in perfect peace. "He lay, endeavouring to realize his speedy appearance before God in judgment; not indeed without sorrowful convictions of his sinfulness, and supplications for mercy in the name of Jesus, but with a full confidence in the willingness of God to receive him ; and a desire to depart." But he was chiefly led "to think of the many poor souls in the ship, and to pray that they might have a longer time for repentance, and that the terrors of that night might be of lasting benefit." In the morning, when the vessel was going under bare poles, the sea covered with so thick a mist from the spray and rain, that nothing could be seen but the tops of the nearest waves, which seemed to be running over the windward side of the ship, he seized the opportunity of pointing out the way of salvation to one of the passengers, who appeared much terrified ; and most willingly, had circumstances permitted, would he have preached to the whole ship's company, warning them to "flee from the wrath to come, and to lay hold on eternal life." The Sunday following, he read the thanksgiving prayer after a storm.

Mr. Martyn's voyage before this alarming tempest had been far from expeditious. Seven wearisome weeks had he passed, without having proceeded farther than the latitude of the Lizard. The wind now began to carry him forward, and about the end of the month of September he reached Madeira.

His journal, during the interval between the subsiding of the storm and his arrival at Porto Santo, contains these admirable reflections :—

Sept. 9.—" My chief concern was, that this season of

peace might be improved : when the Lord gave David rest from all his enemies round about, then he began to think of building a temple to the Lord. Passed many sweet hours of the evening in reading ; found a rich feast in reading Hooker's Sermons : the doctrines of grace are a cordial to me. We are now in latitude 46° long. 12°. The sea on which I am looking from the port-hole is comparatively smooth, yet it exhibits the moonbeams only in broken reflections. It is thus an emblem of my heart : no longer tossed with tempestuous passions, it has subsided a little ; but still the mild beams of the Spirit fall on an undulating surface ; but the time of perfect rest approaches."

Sept. 10.—" Endeavoured to consider what should be my study and preparation for the mission ; but could devise no particular plan, but to search the Scriptures. What are God's promises respecting the spread of the Gospel, and the means by which it shall be accomplished ? Long seasons of prayer in behalf of the heathen, I am sure, are necessary. (Isaiah lxii.) I began Isaiah, and learnt by heart the promises scattered through the first twelve chapters, hoping that they may prove profitable matter for meditation as well as prayer. Read the 'Pilgrim's Progress' below, amidst the greatest noise and interruption. Notwithstanding the clamour, I felt as if I could preach to a million of noisy persons with unconquerable boldness. We have been becalmed the whole day. I fear my soul has been much in the same state ; but I would not that it should be so any longer."

Sept. 13.—" In my walk, my attention was engaged by the appearance of mutiny amongst the men. Last night, the ship's crew and the soldiers refused their allowance, and this morning, when they piped to dinner, they gave three cheers. After some time, a seaman was fixed on as the ringleader; and from his behaviour, I was not sorry to hear the captain order him to be put in irons. As it was a sorrowful and humiliating thing to me, I retired to pray for them and myself. In the afternoon I read as usual, and found two occasions of speaking in reference to the mutinous murmurs."

Sept. 14.—"Found great pleasure and profit in 'Milner's Church History.' I love to converse, as it were, with those holy bishops and martyrs, with whom I hope, through grace, to spend a happy eternity."

Sept. 15.—Sunday.—"'He that testifieth these things saith, Behold, I come quickly! Amen. Even so; come quickly, Lord Jesus!' Happy John! though shut out from society and the ordinances of grace, happy wast thou in thy solitude, when by it thou wast induced thus gladly to welcome the Lord's words, and repeat them with a prayer. Read and preached on Acts xiii. 38, 39. In the latter part, when I was led to speak, without preparation, on the all-sufficiency of Christ to save sinners, who came to Him with all their sins without delay, I was carried away with a Divine aid, to speak with freedom and energy; my soul was refreshed, and I retired, seeing reason to be thankful. The weather was fair and calm, inviting the mind to tranquillity and praise: the ship just moved on the face of the troubled ocean. I went below, in hopes of reading Baxter's 'Call to the Unconverted;' but there was no getting down, as they were taking out water: so I sat with the seamen on the gundeck. As I walked in the evening at sunset, I thought with pleasure, ' But a few more suns, and I shall be where my sun shall no more go down.' Read Isaiah the rest of the evening, sometimes happy, but at other times tired, and desiring to take up some other religious book; but I saw it an important duty to check this slighting of the Word of God."

Sept. 16.—"Two things were much on my mind this morning in prayer: the necessity of entering more deeply into my own heart, and labouring after humiliation, and, for that reason, setting apart times for fasting; as also to devote times for solemn prayer for fitness in the ministry, especially love for souls, and for the effusion of the Spirit on heathen lands, according to God's command.

"M——, coming in, said, that many had become more hostile than ever, saying, they should come up to prayers, because they believed I was sincere, but not to the sermon, as I did nothing but preach about hell. I hope this portends good. Prevented reading below, from the same cause as on Sunday."

Sept. 17.—"It began to blow hard again. The calmness and pleasure with which I contemplated death made me rather fear that I did not fear it enough. Read below with the soldiers."

Sept. 18.—"Rose ill, and continued so all the day. Tried to encourage myself in the Lord. Looking at the sea, my soul was enabled to rejoice in the great Maker of it as my God."

Sept. 19.—"Was assisted this morning to pray for two hours, principally in regard to God's promises respecting the spread of the Gospel. Read Hindostanee and 'Milner.' Found the men forbidden to go below; so I know not how they are to be instructed. May the Lord open a way! The weather is calm and sultry; my frame relaxed to a painful degree. I am led to seek a quiet, meek submission to everything that shall befal me. Oh this blessed frame! Would that it may contnue. I feel it to be the right disposition of a creature—approving of everything, because it is God's doing."

Sept. 20.—"My soul was blessed with a sacred and holy reverence in the work of God this morning; it was the sentiment of serious love, such as I should always wish to maintain. To behold God in his glory, and worship Him for what He is in Himself, I believe is the bliss of heaven. Exercised myself in Hindostanee. Read the 'Pilgrim's Progress' to a few below deck. Continued to delight in the prospect of preaching in India. The example of the Christians of the early ages has been a source of sweet reflection to me frequently to-day. The holy love and devout meditations of Augustine and Ambrose I delight to think of."

Sept. 21.—"I seemed uneasy at the thoughts of calling forth the hatred of the people to-morrow, by preaching to them unpleasant truths."

Sept. 22.—Sunday.—"Was more tried by the fear of man, than I ever have been since God has called me to the ministry. The threats and opposition of these men made me unwilling to set before them the truths which they hated; yet I had no species of hesitation about doing it. They had let me know that if I would preach a sermon like one of Blair's, they should be glad to hear it; but they would not attend, if so much of hell was preached. This morning, again, Capt. —— said, 'Mr. Martyn must not damn us to-day, or none will come again.' I was a little disturbed; but Luke x., and, above all, our Lord's last address to his disciples (John xiv. 16), strengthened me, and I took for my text Psalm ix. 17, 'The wicked shall be turned into hell, and all the nations that forget God.' The officers were all behind my back, in order to have an opportunity of retiring, in case of dislike. B—— attended the whole time. H——, as soon as he heard the text, went back, and said he would hear no more about hell ; so he employed himself in feeding the geese. S—— said, I had shut him up in hell, and the universal cry was, 'We are all to be damned.' However, God, I trust, blessed the sermon to the good of many. Some of the cadets, and many of the soldiers, were in tears. I felt an ardour and vehemence, in some parts, which are unusual with me. After service, walked the deck with Mrs. ——. She spoke with so much simplicity and amiable humility, that I was full of joy and adoration to God, for a sheep brought home to his fold. In the afternoon went below, intending to read to them at the hatchway; but there was not one of them, so I could get nothing to do among the poor soldiers."

Sept. 23.—"We are just to the south of all Europe, and I bid adieu to it for ever, without a wish of ever revisiting it, and still less with any desire of taking up my rest in the strange land to which I am going. Ah, no ; farewell, perishing world ! 'To me to live' shall be 'Christ.' I have nothing to do here, but to labour as a stranger, and, by secret prayer and outward exertion, do as much as possible for the Church of Christ, and my own soul, till my eyes close in death, and my soul wings its way to a brighter world. Strengthen me, O God, my Saviour ; that, whether living or dying, I may be Thine."

Sept. 24.—"The determination, with which I went to bed last night, of devoting this day to prayer and fasting, I was enabled to put into execution."

Sept. 25.—"Most of the morning employed in Hindoostanee. Read the 'Pilgrim's Progress' and

'Baxter' below.   Had a long conversation with one of
the Lascars."

Sept. 27.—"The oaths I heard on deck moved my
indignation, but I recollected the words of the Macedonian
in the dream, 'Come over and help us.'   Probably there
was no one in Macedon that felt his need of help ; but
the Holy Spirit put it in this engaging way, because
they did request as much by their silent misery.   So I
thought that every oath they swore was a call on me to
help them.   In the afternoon I was told that I could
not go below, as there had been fires lighted to air
the deck.   Went in a boat, by way of changing the
scene, to the Sarah Christiana, about three miles off.
It was a novel thing to be in a little boat, in the
midst of the great ocean.   The nearest mainland,
Africa, was three hundred and fifty miles distant.   I
reflected, without pain, that England was eleven hundred
miles off."

Sept. 28.—"My thoughts were much engaged, as well
as those about me, with the prospect of going on shore.
They were doing nothing else for hours, but looking out
with their glasses for land.   After dinner, on coming out,
I saw the majestic heights of Porto Santo, distant about
five or six leagues.   Again I was disappointed of going
below, from the same cause as before.   Was diverted from
my proper work by looking at a Portuguese grammar.
So astonishing is the weakness of my heart, that every
trifle has power to draw me from that communion with
God which my better will chooses as my best and beloved portion.   Oh, for the steady 'abiding under the
shadow of the Almighty;' and as the days pass on, and
bring me nearer to the end of the things which are seen,

so let me be more and more quickened, to be ready for the unseen world.

> " ' By faith I see the land
> With peace and plenty blest;
> A land of sacred liberty
> And endless rest.' "

Mr. Martyn's diligence in his humble and despised ministrations amongst the soldiers in the ship with him, will not have escaped the attention of those who have read the above extracts. It will have been remarked, that there were not many days in which he remitted this work. Nor was his labour confined to the soldiers; their officers were addressed by him with equal earnestness, on every fair and favourable opportunity. With some he had frequent religious conversations. The cadets, also, he endeavoured to "allure to brighter worlds;" and to show that he had also their welfare in this world at heart, he offered gratuitously to instruct in mathematics as many as chose to come to him; an offer which several accepted: and as if this were not enough to occupy his time, he undertook also to read French with another passenger, who was desirous of improvement in that language. He was willing to "become all things to all men, that he might by all means gain some." How far it were wise in him to preach upon the awful subject of eternal misery, immediately after an injunction to abstain from such a topic, is a question which may admit of a diversity of sentiment. Certain, however, it is, that men may be told, "even weeping, that their end is destruction;" and the temper by which Mr. Martyn was invariably characterized, leaves no room to doubt that his conduct in this instance was influenced

by an imperious sense of duty, and by the tender over-
flowings of love.

The sight of a foreign land, where superstition held
her dark and undisputed sway, naturally excited a new
train of sensations in Mr. Martyn's mind, which he thus
communicated from Funchal, to a near relation at Falmouth :—" Yesterday morning we came to an anchor at
this place. The craggy mountains at the foot of which
Funchal is situated, make a most grand and picturesque
appearance. On entering the town, I was struck with
the conviction of being in a foreign country. Everything was different ;—the houses, even the poorest, all
regular and stately,—everywhere groves of orange and
lemon trees,—the countenances, and dress, and manners
of the people different from those I had been used to,—
black-skirted Catholic priests, and nun-like women, with
beads and a crucifix, passing in all directions. How
would St. Paul have sighed in passing through this
town, so wholly given up to idolatry! I went to the
great church, where they were performing high mass,
and was perfectly dazzled with the golden splendour
of the place. But all the external aids of devotion lost
their usual effect upon me, while I contemplated the
endless multitude of mountebank tricks the priests were
exhibiting. Is it possible, thought I, that this should
be a Christian Church! There was no appearance of
attention, excepting in one poor African woman, who
was crossing herself repeatedly, with the utmost expression of contrition in her countenance. Perhaps,
said I to her in my mind, we shall meet in heaven."

After remaining four days at Funchal, the fleet put to
sea, information having been previously imparted to the
army that their object was the capture of the Cape of

Good Hope, and that accordingly they might expect, ere long, to meet an enemy on the field of battle.

Intelligence of this nature served to quicken that activity and zeal which in Mr. Martyn had not hitherto been either slugglish or supine. He was therefore perpetually visiting, or attempting to visit, that part of his flock which was so soon to be exposed to the perils of warfare. " I entreated them even with tears," said he, " out of fervent love for their souls, and I could have poured away my life to have persuaded them to return to God." By a sentence in Milner's Church History, " To believe, to suffer, and to love, was the primitive taste," he states that his mind, at this time, was very deeply impressed; observing that "no uninspired sentence ever affected him so much." It was, in fact, an epitome of his own life, conversation, and spirit: a lively exemplification of which is to be found in the manner in which, during this part of the voyage, he strove against an extreme and oppressive languor of body, which tended to impede his present labours, and threatened to impair his future efficiency,—"The extreme weakness and languor of my body made me fear I should never be used as a preacher in India. But what," said he, "means this anxiety? Is it not of God that I am led into outward difficulties, that my faith may be tried? Suppose you are obliged to return, or that you never see India, but wither and die here, what is that to you? Do the will of God where you are, and leave the rest to Him." " I found great satisfaction in reflecting that my hourly wisdom was not to repine or to look for a change, but to consider what is my duty in existing circumstances, and then to do it, in dependence upon grace." So deeply was his soul imbued with the "primitive taste," and

so entirely did it accord with that wise maxim of such
universal but difficult application

" Tu tua fac cures—cætera mitte Deo."

The voyage from Porto Santo to St. Salvador was
accomplished in little more than five weeks ; during which
the special providence of God watched over Mr. Martyn
and those who sailed with him.   Soon after crossing the
line, on the 30th of October, the Union, in which he
sailed, passed in the night within a very short distance of
a dangerous reef of rocks, which proved destructive to
two other vessels.   The reef lay exactly across the track
of the Union, and had not the second mate, who was on
watch, called up the captain and first mate as soon as
danger was discovered, they would inevitably have been
wrecked : their escape was considered to be almost mira-
culous.   Pieces of the ships that were dashed against the
rocks floated by them, and many of those who had been
cast on the reef were seen making signals for assistance.
The anxiety on board the Union respecting these unhappy
persons was intense : happily they were all saved, with
the exception of three officers, one of whom lost his life
in endeavouring to secure a large sum of money ; leaving
the vessel too soon, he sunk to rise no more ; and, as it
was supposed, was devoured by the sharks which surrounded the ships in great numbers.   Nor was this the
only peril which the Union escaped ; on the coast of South
America she incurred a similar risk.   "O how sweet,"
remarked Mr. Martyn, "to perceive such repeated instances of God's guardian care ! "   During this part of
the voyage, the novel sight of the flying-fish beginning to
attract attention, Mr. Martyn's mind, ever fertile in topics
of humiliation, could discover "a resemblance to his own

soul in these poor little creatures; who rose to a little height; and then, in a minute or two, when their fins were dry, dropped into the waves." Others, doubtless, would have chosen for him a far different similitude, and would have sought it rather in the eagle soaring into the fields of light, or in the dove of the poet.

" When at length she springs
To smoother flight, and shoots upon her wings."—DRYDFN.

"I find (Mr. Martyn wrote, on his arrival at St. Salvador, to a friend in England) that neither distance nor time can separate the hearts which are united in the fellowship of the Gospel, as well as by mutual esteem. Mere earthly affections are weakened by time and absence ; but Christian love grows stronger as the day of salvation approaches. Already a watery waste of four thousand miles lies between me and England : but because I have you in my heart, and make mention of you without ceasing in my prayers, you seem yet scarcely out of sight."

To another friend he wrote :—

" Though a long sea is rolling already betwixt us, yet I scarcely seem to have lost sight of you, or of my dear friends at Cambridge. The hymns we sing, being chiefly taken from your collection, daily bring to my remembrance the happy days when I went with the multitude to the house of God, with the voice of joy and praise. Those seasons are gone by ; but I comfort myself with thinking that they will quickly be renewed in a better country, when we come to dwell together in the mansions of our Father's house."

The description of St. Salvador, and the events connected with Mr. Martyn's stay there, are recorded at some length.

Nov. 12.—"The coast was beautiful, with much romantic scenery. The town exactly resembled Funchal, but was rather more cheerful. The objects in the street were strong negro men-slaves, carrying very heavy casks on a pole, with a sort of unpleasant note ;—negro-women carrying fish, fruit, &c. ;—a few palanquins, which are drawn by two mules. The things exposed to sale were turtles, bananas, oranges, limes, papaws, water-melons, tamarinds, fustic-wood. I walked up the hill in order to get into the country, and observed a man standing by the way-side, holding out, for the people's salutation, a silver embossed piece of plate, of a small oval size, and repeating some words about St. Antonio. Some kissed it ; others took off their hats ; but the man himself seemed to ridicule their folly. They were performing mass in one church ; it was not so splendid as that of Madeira ; many of the priests were negroes. I soon reached the suburbs, on the outside of which was a battery, which commanded a view of the whole bay, and repeated the hymn, 'O'er the gloomy hills of darkness.' What happy missionary shall be sent to bear the name of Christ to these western regions ! When shall this beautiful country be delivered from idolatry and spurious Christianity ! Crosses there are in abundance ; but when shall the doctrine of the cross be held up ! I continued my walk in quest of a wood, or some trees where I might sit down ; but all was appropriated : no tree was to be approached except through an enclosure. At last I came to a magnificent porch, before a garden-gate, which was open ; I walked in, but finding the vista led straight to the house, I turned to the right, and found myself in a grove of cocoa-nut trees, orange-trees, and several strange fruit-trees; under them was nothing but rose-trees, but no verdure on the ground : oranges were strewed like apples in an orchard. Perceiving that I was observed by the slaves, I came up to the house, and was directed by them to an old man, sitting under a tree, apparently insensible from illness. I spoke to him in French and in English, but he took no notice. Presently a young man and a young lady appeared, to whom I spoke in French, and was very politely desired to sit down at a little table, which was standing under a large space before the house like a verandah. They then brought me oranges, and a small red acid fruit, the name of which I asked, but cannot recollect. The young man sat opposite, conversing about Cambridge; he had been educated in a Portuguese University. Almost immediately, on finding I was of Cambridge, he invited me to come when I liked to his house. A slave, after bringing the fruit, was sent to gather three roses for me ; the master then walked with me round the garden, and showed me, among the rest, the coffee-plant. When I left him he repeated his invitation. Thus did the Lord give his servant favour in the eyes of Antonio Joseph Corrè."

Nov. 13.—"This morning there was a great storm of thunder, lightning, and rain, which awoke me. I got up and prayed. Oh! when the last great thunder echoes from pole to pole, I shall be in earnest, if not before."

Nov. 14.—"Senor Antonio received me with the same cordiality ; he begged me to dine with him. I was curious and attentive to observe the difference between the Portuguese manners and ours: there were but two plates laid on the table, and the dinner consisted of a great number of small mixed dishes, following one another in quick succession; but none of them very palatable. In the cool of the evening we walked out to see his plantation; here everything possessed the charm of novelty. The grounds included two hills, and a valley between them. The hills were covered with cocoa-nut trees, bananas, mangoes, orange and lemon trees, olives, coffee, chocolate, and cotton-plants, &c. In the valley was a large plantation of a shrub or tree, bearing a cluster of small berries, which he desired me to taste; I did, and found it was pepper. It had lately been introduced from Batavia, and answered very well. It grows on a stem about the thickness of a finger, to the height of about seven feet, and is supported by a stick, which, at that height, has another across it for the branches to spread upon. Slaves were walking about the grounds, watering the trees and turning up the earth; the soil appeared very dry and loose. At night I returned to the ship in one of the country boats, which are canoes made of a tree hollowed out, and paddled by three men."

Nov. 18.—"Went ashore at six o'clock, and found that Senor Antonio had been waiting for me two hours. It being too late to go into the country, I stayed at his house till dinner. He kept me too much in his company, but I found intervals for retirement. In a cool and shady part of the garden, near some water, I sat and sang, 'O'er the gloomy hills of darkness.' I could read and pray aloud, as there was no fear of any one understanding me. In the afternoon, we went in a palanquin to visit his father. Reading the eighty-fourth Psalm, 'Oh, how amiable are thy tabernacles,' this morning in the shade,— the day when I read it last under the trees with L——, was brought forcibly to my remembrance, and produced some degree of melancholy. Of this I was thinking all the way I was carried; and the train of reflections into which I was led, drew off my attention from the present scene. We visited in our way a monastery of Carmelites; in the church belonging to it my friend Antonio knelt some time, and crossed himself: I was surprised, but said nothing. At his father's house I was described to them as one who knew everything,—Arabic, Persian, Greek, &c. ; and all stared at me as if I had dropped from the skies. The father, Senor Dominigo, spoke a little Latin. A priest came in, and as it was the first time I had been in company with one, I spoke to him in Latin, but he blushed, and said that he did not speak it. I was very sorry I had undesignedly put him to pain. Had a great deal of conversation with Antonio afterwards, on England and on religion. He had formed such an idea of England, that he had resolved to send his son to be educated there. A slave in my bed-room washed my feet. I was struck with the degree of abasement expressed in the act, and as he held the foot in the towel, with his head bowed down towards it, I remembered the condescension of the blessed Lord. May I have grace to follow such humility!"

Nov. 19.—" Early after breakfast went in a palanquin to Senor Dominigo's, and from thence with him two or three miles into the country: at intervals I got out and walked. I was gratified with the sight of what I wanted to see; namely, some part of the country in its original state, covered with wood; it was hilly, but not mountainous. The luxuriance was so rank, that the whole space, even to the tops of the trees, was filled with long stringy shrubs and weeds, so as to make them impervious and opaque. The road was made by cutting away the earth on the side of the hill, so that there were woods above and below us. The object of our walk was to see a pepper plantation, made in a valley, on a perfect level. The symmetry of the trees was what charmed my Portuguese friend; but to me, who was seeking the wild features of America, it was just what I did not want. The person who showed us the grounds was one who had been a major in the Portuguese army, and had retired on a pension. The border consisted of pine-apples, planted between each tree; the interior was set with lemon-trees, here and there, between the pepper-plants. We were shown the root of the Mandioc, called by us Tapioca, it was like a large horse-radish; the mill for grinding it was extremely simple; a horizontal wheel, turned by horses, put in motion a vertical one; on the circumference of which was a thin brazen plate, furnished on the inside like a nutmeg-grater; a slave held the root to the wheel, which grated it away, and threw it in the form of a moist paste into a receptacle below; it is then dried in pans, and used as a farina with meat. At Senor Antonio's, a plate of tapioca was attached to each of our plates. Some of the pepper was nearly ripe, and of a reddish appearance; when gathered, which it is in April, it is dried in the sun. In our way to the old major's house, we came to a small church on an eminence, on a plot of ground surrounded by a wall, which was for the purpose of burying the dead from a neighbouring hospital, erected for those afflicted with a cutaneous disorder called a morphee. What this is I could not learn, as I saw none of the patients. The major had apartments at the hospital, of which he was inspector. In the church all three knelt and crossed themselves as usual. I said nothing; but upon this a conversation began among them, chiefly from Senor Antonio's mentioning to them my objection. The major spoke with a vehemence which would have become a better cause : Antonio acted as interpreter. By constant appeal to the Scriptures, on every subject, I gave immediate answers. The old man concluded the conversation by saying, that he was sure I read the Scriptures, and therefore would embrace me, which he did after the manner of the country. Senor Antonio told me plainly, at last, what I had long been expecting to hear, that the prejudices of education were strong, and operated to keep his father bigoted; but that, for himself, he had nothing to do with saints; in secret he adored God alone. I could have wished more; it was the confession rather of a liberal than a religious mind. Soon after, there was a procession of priests carrying the sacrament to the house of a person just departing ; they both knelt, and continued till it had past. Senor Antonio said, that he 'conformed to the custom of the country in trifles.' I thought of Naaman and his god Rimmon. I did not, however, think it right to push the matter too suddenly ; but told him, in general, how the English reformers were led to prison and to flames, rather than conform; and that, if I had been born a Portuguese, I would rather be imprisoned and burnt, than conform to idolatry. At the same time I talked to him of the doctrine of the 'new birth,' &c., but he did not seem to pay much attention. Senor Dominigo asked me if the soldiers had a minister to attend them in their dying moments, to instruct and to administer consolation. For the first time I felt that I had the worst of the argument, and hardly knew what to say to explain such neglect among the Protestants. He shrugged up his shoulders with horror at such a religion. We were then shown the hospital erected by the Prince of Portugal: it was a noble building, far superior to that at Haslar. In the garden, each person, alternately, gathered a sprig or fragrant leaf for me. The person who showed it to us, was a chevalier of some order. In the chapel Senor Antonio knelt; but always looked on me smiling, and said, ' c'est le coutume du pays.' I left him in order to get on board; but finding, as I went along, a chapel open, I went in to see the pictures; all of which contained, as a prominent figure, a friar of some order. In one, some people in flames were laying hold of the twisted rope which was pendant from his waist; how apt the image, if Jesus Christ were in the room of the friar! At this time a friar, dressed identically as the one in the picture, moved slowly along; I followed him through the cloisters, and addressed him in Latin. He was a little surprised; but replied. He told me that the chapel belonged to a monastery of Franciscan friars. In a cloister which led round the second floor of the building, he stopped; and by this time we were able to understand each other exceedingly well. I then asked him to prove from Scripture the doctrine of purgatory, of image-worship, the supremacy of the Pope, and transubstantiation. His arguments were exceedingly weak, and the Lord furnished me with an answer to them all. During our conversation, two or three more friars assembled round, and joined in the dispute. I confuted all their errors as plainly as possible, from the word of God, and they had nothing to reply, but did not seem disconcerted. A whole troop of others, passing in procession in the opposite cloister below, beckoned to them to retire; which they did, taking me along with them to a cell,—two before and one on each side. As we passed along the passage, one asked me whether I was a Christian. When we had all reached the cell, and sat down, I asked for a Bible, and

the dispute was renewed. I found that they considered
their errors as not tenable on Scripture ground; and
appealed to the authority of the church. I told them
that this church was, by their confession, acting against
the law of God: and was therefore not the church of
God: I also referred them to the last words in the
Revelation. They seemed most surprised at my knowledge of Scripture. When they were silent, and had
nothing to say, I was afraid the business would end here
without good; and so I said,—'You who profess to teach
the way of truth, how can you dare, before God, to let
the people go on in idolatrous practices, which you know
to be contrary to the word of God?' They looked very
grave. The one who spoke French, and also the best
Latin, grew very angry during their dispute; and talked
of the Scripturarum interpretes—pii sapientissimique viri
Augustinus, Bernardus, &c.: But, said I, 'they were
not inspired.' 'Yes,' he said. But here he was corrected by the rest. As this man seemed in earnest (the
rest were sometimes grave, and sometimes laughing), I
asked him why he had assumed the cowl of a friar;—he
answered, 'ut me abstraherem à vanitate rerum munda-
narum et meipsum sanctum faciam ad gloriam Dei.' He
spoke with great impression and earnestness, and seemed
the most sincere of any. They were acquainted with
logic, and argued according to rule. He began by saying,
'nullam salutem esse extra ecclesiam Catholicam, axioma
est;' 'Concedo,' said I,—'sed extra Romanam salus
esse potest.'—'Minime,' they all cried out. 'Quare,'
said I, 'proba,' but they could not. At last I went
away, as the sun had set, and they all attended me
through the long dark passages. I almost trembled at
the situation and company I was in, but they were ex-

ceedingly polite, and begged to know when I was coming ashore again, that they might expect me. I had stayed so long, that after waiting for hours at the different quays, no boat returned ; and I was obliged to return to Senor Antonio's, from whom I received an affectionate welcome. His wife and slaves, who seemed to be admitted to the utmost familiarity, delighted to stand around me, and teach me the Portuguese names of things."

Nov. 21.—"Went on shore and breakfasted with Senor Antonio. After dinner, while he slept, I had some time for reading, &c. In the evening, he and his wife and a female slave played at cards. I sat at the table, learning Hindostanee roots."

Nov. 23.—"In the afternoon took leave of my kind friends, Senor and Senora Corrè. They and the rest came out to the garden gate, and continued looking till the winding of the road hid me from their sight. The poor slave Raymond, who had attended me and carried my things, burst into a flood of tears as we left the door ; and when I parted from him he was going to kiss my feet ; but I shook hands with him, much affected by such extraordinary kindness in people to whom I had been a total stranger till within a few days. What shall I render unto the Lord for all his mercies ? In my way to the quay I met a young friar of the order of St. Augustine. He understood me enough to conduct me part of the way to the convent of the Franciscans, till he met with a young priest, to whom he consigned me. With him I had a dispute in Latin. When I said that in no part of Scripture was it commanded to worship the Virgin, he coloured, and said in a low tone, ' Verum est.' At the monastery I met with my old friends, the same four friars. After regaling me with sweetmeats, they renewed the dispute. We parted with mutual lamentations over one another; I telling them they were in an awful error; they smiling at my obstinacy, and mourning over my lost condition. I went away in no small dejection, that the Gospel should have so little effect, or rather none at all. This was by no means diminished when I came to the boat. It was the commemoration of the Hegira; and our Mohammedan rowers, dressed in white, were singing hymns, all the way, to the honour of Mahomet. Here was another abomination. B——— sat beside me, and we had a long conversation, and for some time went on very well. I cleared away error, as I thought, very fast; and when the time was come, I stated in a few words the Gospel. The reply was, that 'I was not speaking to the purpose; that, for his part, he could not see what more could be necessary than simply to tell mankind that they must be sober and honest.' I turned away, and, with a deep sigh, cried to God to interfere in behalf of his Gospel; for in the course of one hour I had seen three shocking examples of the reign and power of the devil, in the form of Popish and Mohammedan delusion, and that of the natural man. I never felt so strongly what a nothing I am. All my clear arguments are good for nothing: unless the Lord stretch out his hand I speak to stones. I felt, however, no way discouraged; but only saw the necessity of dependance on God."

After little more than a fortnight the fleet sailed; whilst many a grateful recollection filled the breast, and many a fervent prayer ascended from the heart of Mr. Martyn, in behalf of Senor and Senora Corrè: from them he had received signal kindness and hospitality; and it might not perhaps be too much to observe, that not being " forgetful to entertain strangers," they had

"entertained an angel unawares." "I have been with
my friend Antonio," said he, "as a wayfaring man that
tarrieth but for a night; yet hath the Lord put it into
his heart to send me on after a goodly sort. And now we
prosecute our voyage; a few more passages, and I shall
find myself in the scene of my ministry; a few more
changes and journeys, and I am in eternity."

As the time approached for the soldiers to take the
field, Mr. Martyn's anxiety for their eternal welfare
increased; and as a proof of it, he set apart a day for
fasting, humiliation, and intercession for them, as well as
for all who were in the ship. But he did not intercede
for them, he observed, as being himself righteous, but
chose rather to humble himself with them as a sinner,
earnestly crying to God in contrition and abasement of
soul. At this solemn juncture he began to read and
expound to his auditors the holy Scriptures exclusively;
and after some consideration respecting the propriety of
such a step, he determined not to suffer them to depart
without prayer to the Lord, as well as singing his praises.
Such a procedure, he was well aware, would put the faith
of his hearers, as well as his own, in some measure, to a
strong and severe test. *Above*, obloquy and contempt
might be expected; *below*, noise and clamour and scoffs.
He nevertheless persisted in his purpose, resolving, as the
line of duty seemed to be clear, to pursue it steadily, and
calmly to commit all consequences to God. "To kneel in
prayer," he remarked in a letter to a friend, "before a
considerable number of lookers-on, some working, others
scoffing, was a painful cross to my poor people at first.
But they received strength according to their day: and
now the song of us all is, 'Thou hast prepared a table
before me in the presence of my enemies.'"

The unhealthy state of the ship's company from dysentery at this period of the voyage was another call on Mr. Martyn's pastoral assiduity—a call to which he evinced no backwardness to attend. Often was he to be found by the beds of the sick, administering to them every temporal and spiritual comfort; till at length he was himself seized by that contagious disorder. His illness was not of long duration, but was such as to make him think seriously of death, and employ himself in the most solemn self-examination. On which occasion he had so much delight and joy in the consideration of heaven, and of his assured title to it, that he was more desirous of dying than living: not that it was any one thing that he had done, he remarks, that gave him substantial reason for thinking himself in Christ—it was rather the bent of his affections and inclinations towards God, and the taste he had for holy pleasures and holy employments, which convinced him that he was born of God.

No sooner had he recovered from this attack, than he was again at his post,—kneeling beside the hammocks of the dying. And amongst those who then required and received his faithful offices, was the captain of the ship, whose illness, though of a different kind from the prevailing one, was highly dangerous, and quickly terminated in his dissolution.

And now, as the year was drawing to a close, and the last Sabbath of it was come, Mr. Martyn addressed his hearers from 2 Pet. iii. 11 : "Seeing then that all these things shall be dissolved, what manner of persons ought ye to be, in all holy conversation and godliness;"—in reference to their having left England,—to their having passed through so many perils,—to their being, many of them, about to meet an enemy in the field,—and to the death of the captain. His own mind, which could not but be in an exceedingly serious frame, was also in a state of the purest joy and most perfect peace. "Separated," said he, "from my friends and country for ever, there is nothing to distract me from hearing 'the voice of my beloved,' and coming away from the world, and walking with Him in love, amidst the flowers that perfume the air of paradise, and the harmony of the happy, happy saints, who are singing his praise. Thus hath the Lord brought me to the conclusion of the year; and though I have broken his statutes, and not kept his commandments, yet 'He hath not utterly taken away his loving-kindness, nor suffered his truth to fail.' I thought, at the beginning of the year, that I should have been in India by this time, if I should have escaped all the dangers of the climate. These dangers are yet to come ; but I can leave all cheerfully to God. If I am weary of anything, it is of my life of sinfulness. I want a life of more devotion and holiness ; and yet am so vain as to be expecting the end without the means. I am so far from regretting that I ever came on this delightful work, that were I to choose for myself, I could scarcely find a situation more agreeable to my taste. On, therefore, let me go, and persevere steadily in this blessed undertaking ; through the grace of God dying daily in the opinions of men, and aiming, with a more single eye, at the glory of the everlasting God."

On the 2d of January, 1806, while Mr. Martyn was in the act of commending his flock to God in prayer, the high lands of the Cape became visible, at eighty miles distance ; and doubtless they were not seen without exciting the strongest emotions in many hearts : numbers were soon there to assemble, who should meet no more till all nations should be gathered before the tribunal of Christ.

On the 3d the fleet anchored, and the signal was instantly given for the soldiers to prepare to land. But how then was Mr. Martyn's holy and affectionate soul grieved to witness the dreadful levity concerning death which almost universally prevailed. "It was," said he, "a melancholy scene. I could speak to none of my people but to Corporal B—— and ——. I said also to Sergeant G——, 'It is *now* high time to be decided in religion.' He replied with a sigh. Poor Corporal B—— and the others gave me a last affecting look after they were in the boats. I retired to pray, and found delightful access to God, and freedom in prayer for the poor soldiers." The Indiamen being then ordered to get under weigh, and the men-of-war drawn up close to the shore, a landing was effected, and soon after seven the next day, as Mr. Martyn describes it, "a most tremendous fire of artillery began behind a mountain abreast of the ships. It seemed as if the mountain itself was torn by intestine convulsions. The smoke arose from a lesser eminence on the right of the hill; and, on the top of it, troops were seen marching down the further declivity. Then came such a long-drawn fire of musketry, that I could not conceive anything like it. We all shuddered at considering what a multitude of souls must be passing into eternity. The poor ladies were in a dreadful condition; every peal seemed to go through their hearts. I have just been endeavouring to do what I could to keep up their spirits. The sound is now retiring; and the enemy are seen retreating along the low ground on the right towards the town."

With the hope of being useful to the wounded and dying on the field of battle, Mr. Martyn, after this period of torturing suspense, went on shore ; and, in the following letter to Mr. Simeon, he states what he endured whilst engaged in that disinterested errand of love and mercy :—

"*Union, Table Bay, Jan.* 7, 1806.

" I embraced the opportunity of going to the wounded men, soon after my landing. A party of the company's troops were ordered to repair to the field of battle, to bring away the wounded, under the command of Major ——, whom I knew. By his permission, I attached myself to them, and marched six miles over a soft, burning sand, till we reached the fatal spot. We found several but slightly hurt, and these we left for a while, after seeing their wounds dressed by a surgeon. A little onward were three mortally wounded. One of them, on being asked 'where he was struck,' opened his shirt, and showed a wound in his left breast. The blood which he was spitting showed that he had been shot through the lungs. As I spread my great-coat over him, by the surgeon's desire, who passed on without attempting to save him, I spoke of the blessed Gospel, and besought him to look to Jesus Christ for salvation. He was surprised, but could not speak ; and I was obliged to leave him, in order to reach the troops, from whom the officers, out of regard to my safety, would not allow me to be separated. Among several others, some wounded and some dead, was Captain ——, who had been shot by a rifleman. We all stopped for a while, to gaze, in pensive silence, on his pale body : and then passed on to witness more proofs of the sin and misery of fallen man. Descending into the plain, where the main body of each army had met, I saw some of the 59th, one of whom, a corporal, who sometimes had sung with us, told me that none of the 59th were killed, and none of the officers wounded. Some farm-houses, which had been in the rear of the enemy's army, had been converted into an hospital for the wounded, whom they were bringing in from all quarters. The surgeon told me that there were already in the houses two hundred, some of whom were Dutch. A more ghastly spectacle than that which presented itself here I could not have couceived. They were ranged without and within the house, in rows, covered with gore. Indeed it was the blood, which they had not had time to wash off, that made their appearance more dreadful than the reality : for few of their wounds were mortal. The confusion was very great; and sentries and officers were so strict in their duty, that I had no fit opportunity of speaking to any of them, except a Dutch captain, with whom I conversed in French. After this, I walked out again with the surgeon to the field, and saw several of the enemy's wounded. A Hottentot, who had had his thigh broken by a ball, was lying in extreme agony, biting the dust, and uttering horrid imprecations upon the Dutch. I told him that he ought to pray for his enemies ; and after telling the poor wretched man of the Gospel, I begged him to pray to Jesus Christ. But our conversation was soon interrupted : for, in the absence of the surgeon, who had gone back for his instruments, a Highland soldier came up, and challenged me with the words, 'Who are you ?' 'An Englishman.' 'No,' said he, 'you are French,' and began to present his piece. As I saw that he was rather intoxicated, and did not know but that he might actually fire out of mere wantonness, I sprang up towards him, and told him, that if he doubted my word, he might take me as his prisoner to the English camp,—but that I certainly was an English clergyman. This pacified him, and he behaved with great respect. The surgeon, on examining the wound, said the man must die, and so left him. At length, I found an opportunity of returning, as I much wished, in order to recover from distraction of mind, and to give free scope to reflection. I lay down on the border of a clump of shrubs or bushes, with the field of battle in view; and there lifted up my soul to God. Mournful as the scene was, I yet thanked God that he had brought me to see a specimen, though a terrible one, of what men by nature are. May the remembrance of this day ever excite me to pray and labour more for the propagation of the gospel of peace. Then shall men love one another : 'Nation shall not lift up sword against nation, neither shall they learn war any more.' The Blue Mountains, which formed the boundary of the prospect to the eastward, were a cheering contrast to what was immediately before me; for there I conceived my beloved and honoured fellow-servants, companions in the kingdom and patience of Jesus Christ, * to be passing the days of their pilgrimage, far from the world, imparting the truths of the precious gospel to benighted souls. May I receive grace to be a follower of their faith and patience; and do you pray, my brother, as I know that you do, that I may have a heart more warm, and a zeal more ardent in this glorious cause. I marched back the same evening, with the troops. The surf on the shore was very high, but through mercy, we

* Missionaries of the United Brethren at Grœnekloof and Gnadenthal, and those belonging to the London Missionary Society at Bethelsdorp.

escaped that danger. But when we came to our ship's station, we found that she was gone ; having got under weigh some hours before. The sea ran high. Our men were almost spent, and I was very faint with hunger; but after a long struggle, we reached the Indiaman about midnight."

For the detail of the events which succeeded this most distressing day, and the incidents which occurred during his continuance at the Cape, we refer to the journal.

January 9th.—" Came on board early this morning. I was so sleepy and languid, I could do little or nothing, and at night was so oppressed with a sense of my un-profitableness, selfishness, and neglect of duty, that I felt shut out from God. I spread the matter before God, who knew the state of my case ; still I was wretched from the bondage of corruption, which seemed to chain me down to earth. Lying down in my bed, my wretchedness was brought to my mind, and would have overwhelmed me, but for the blood of Jesus Christ. There was very little firing to day. In the afternoon a flag of truce was observed."

January 10.—" I have been, through the mercy of God, in a more happy frame than for this week past. Meditation on Psalm ciii. 1—5, was much blest to me. Oh ! what happiness and benefit to my soul have I lost by neglecting to praise God. About five the commodore fired a gun, which was instantly answered by all the men-of-war. On looking out for the cause, we saw the British flag flying on the Dutch fort. Pleasing as the cessation of warfare was, I felt considerable pain at the enemy's being obliged to give up their fort and town, and every thing else, as a conquered people, to the will of their victor. I hate the cruel pride and arrogance that makes men boast over a conquered foe. And every observation of this sort which I hear cuts me to the very heart; whether from nature or from grace I do not know, but I had rather be trampled upon than be the trampler. I could find it more agreeable to my own feelings to go and weep with the relatives of the men whom the English have killed, than to rejoice at the laurels they have won. I had a happy season in prayer. No outward scene seemed to have power to distract my thoughts. I prayed that the capture of the Cape might be ordered to the advancement of Christ's kingdom ; and that England, whilst she sent the thunder of her arms to the distant regions of the globe, might not remain proud and ungodly at home ; but might show herself great indeed, by sending forth the ministers of her church to diffuse the gospel of peace."

January 12.—Sunday.—" Very unlike a Sabbath-day ; the whole morning, till dinner-time, was taken up in working the ship from her place to a station nearer the shore. There were so few hands on board, that I was obliged to take my place at the capstan. The wind now blows a hurricane over Table Mountain. I feel myself a guilty creature. Hide not thy face from me, O God."

January 13.—" Went on shore to Cape Town, and took lodgings. Walked about the Company's gardens and General Jansen's, whose family I saw. I felt much for the unfortunate females. Afterwards saw the menagerie. A lion and lioness, amongst the beasts, and the ostrich, led my thoughts very strongly to admire and glorify the power of the great Creator. 'Wilt thou hunt the prey for the lion?' I felt my insignificance,— but for a ransomed child, the strong hand of God can control all created power,—sweet and happy is it to have 'the everlasting arms underneath us.' From the first moment I arrived, I had been anxiously inquiring about Dr. Vanderkemp. I heard at last, to my no small delight, that he was now in Cape Town. But it was long before I could find him. At length I did. He was standing outside the house, silently looking up at the stars. A great number of black people were sitting around. On my introducing myself, he led me in, and called for Mr. Read. I was beyond measure delighted at the happiness of seeing him too. The circumstance of meeting with these beloved and highly honoured brethren, so filled me with joy and gratitude for the goodness of God's providence, that I hardly knew what to do."

January 14.—"Continued walking with Mr. Read till late. He gave me a variety of curious information respecting the mission. He told me of his marvellous success amongst the heathen,—how he had heard them amongst the bushes pouring out their hearts to God. At all this my 'soul did magnify the Lord, and my spirit rejoiced in God my Saviour.' Now that I am in a land where the Spirit of God appears, as in the ancient days, as in the generation of old, let a double portion of that Spirit rest upon this unworthy head, that I may go forth to my work 'rejoicing like a strong man to run his race.'"

January 15.—"Rose early, and obtained a serene and tender spirit from God."

January 16.—"Walked with brother Read, and was so charmed with his spiritual behaviour, that I fancied myself in company with David Brainerd. Sat at night in the open air, with Table Mountain before me, and endeavoured to meditate on Isaiah xi. 2."

January 17.—" Had some fervour in prayer for that blessed charity, described 1 Cor. xiii. Walked with Read, and continued to increase in love to him; we met in our walk Vanderlinger, who had been on a mission to the Briquas."

January 18.—" Having spoken in an unchristian spirit to a dear friend this morning, I retired in great grief to consider again 1 Cor. xiii. and Eph. iv. 5. I found my soul melted in prayer. Oh, when shall I learn humility! Cecil dined and walked with me;—not finding the missionaries at home, I returned and read Prideaux. After a short prayer, I found my soul blest with a most serene and tranquil sweetness; my thoughts seemed far from earth, and fixed on heavenly things."

January 19.—Sunday.—" The S.E. blew a hurricane all day, so I could not get to the Pitt, Botany Bay ship, as I had promised. I read prayers to most of the cadets and passengers in one of the parlours of the house, and expounded part of iv. and v. of Ephesians. Visited the hospital with brother Read, and then went to a church lately built for the instruction of slaves. There were about one hundred, sent from fifty different families. A black, who was employed in lighting the candles, was pointed out to me as one who was to go as a missionary to Madagascar."

January 20.—" Walking home I asked Dr. Vanderkemp if he had ever repented of his undertaking. 'No,' said the old man, smiling; 'and I would not exchange my work for a kingdom.' Read told me of some of his trials;—he has often been so reduced, for want of clothes, as to have scarcely any to cover him. The reasonings of his mind were;—I am here, Lord, in thy service;—why am I left in this state? It seemed to be suggested to him,—If thou wilt be my servant; be contented to fare in this way; if not, go and fare better. His mind was thus satisfied to remain God's missionary, with all its concomitant hardships. At night my sinful soul enjoyed a most reviving season in prayer; I rejoiced greatly in the Lord, and pleaded with fervour for the interests of his Church."

January 21.—"I sent to the Governor to offer my services on Sunday next at the church; he sent an immediate answer, that he could not avail himself of my offer, but assigned no reason. I was a little hurt, but my soul enjoyed sweet repose in God."

January 22.—"Went with Read to visit the hospital where the wounded English were."

January 23.—"Went on board, the S.E. blowing most violently; I did not think the boat could live it out, but through the mercy of God we shipped but one sea, and reached the ship in safety. Oh! may I love and serve Him with all my soul, till I

'reach that blissful shore,
Where storms and danger shall be known no more.'"

January 24.—"I came ashore, and walked with Lieutenant F——, and was much pleased with the sentiments he expressed; and with much affectionate regard for his welfare I suggested to him some advice. At night, the Lord helped me to plead long and earnestly for the ingathering of the heathen."

January 25.—"Employed in meditations on a sermon for to-morrow;—sat with Dr. Vanderkemp, conversing on metaphysics and divinity. Blessed with especial love of souls in prayer at night."

January 26.—Sunday.—"Had service in the house;

expounded 2 Cor. v. with such dulness, that I felt the
greatest shame before God. Walked near the sea, and
talked with some French prisoners;—went with Read to
the hospital, and left some Testaments. Dear Dr. Vanderkemp gave me a Syriac Testament as a remembrance
of him."

January 27.—" Preached at the hospital.—Many were
in tears."

January 28.—" I went this morning in a waggon drawn
by eight horses to Constantia, with a party of fellow-
passengers, and three officers of the 66th, but it was no
party of pleasure to me. I was disgusted at the conversation, which was trifling to the last degree. The farmer
was very civil, and gave me some of the celebrated wine.
The road was over a plain covered with beautiful shrubs ;
—there being no house there that was public, we went to
one two miles off :—here I walked on the heath alone,
seeking after God. Walked with brother Read in the
gardens, and continued to have much conversation on the
mission ; on our conversion ; and on the work of grace in
the heart. How profitable and heart-enlivening is conversation on experimental religion, when carried on without pride or display ! Preached at the hospital. In my
walk home by the sea-side, I sighed on thinking of L——,
with whom I had stood on the shore before coming away,
and of the long seas that were rolling between us : but
felt cheerful and strong in spirit to fulfil the word of
God."

January 30.—" Rose at five, and began to ascend Table
Mountain at six, with S—— and M——. I went on
chiefly alone. I thought of the Christian life,—what up-
hill work it is,—and yet there are streams flowing down
from the top, just as there was water coming down by the

Kloof, by which we ascended. Toward the top it was very steep, but the hope of being soon at the summit, encouraged me to ascend very lightly. As the Kloof opened, a beautiful flame-coloured flower appeared in a little green hollow, waving in the breeze. It seemed to be an emblem of the beauty and peacefulness of heaven, as it shall open upon the weary soul when its journey is finished, and the struggles of the death-bed are over. We walked up and down the whole length, which might be between two and three miles, and one might be said to look round the world from this promontory. I felt a solemn awe at the grand prospect,—from which there was neither noise nor smaller objects to draw off my attention. I reflected, especially when looking at the immense expanse of sea to the east, which was to carry me to India, on the certainty that the name of Christ should at some period resound from shore to shore. I felt commanded to wait in silence, and see how God would bring his promises to pass. We began to descend at half-past two. Whilst sitting to rest myself towards night, I began to reflect, with death-like despondency, on my friendless condition. Not that I wanted any of the comforts of life, but I wanted those kind friends who loved me, and in whose company I used to find such delight after my fatigues. And then, remembering that I should never see them more, I felt one of those keen pangs of misery that occasionally shoot across my breast. It seemed like a dream—that I had actually undergone banishment from them for life; or rather like a dream, that I had ever hoped to share the enjoyments of social life. But at this time I solemnly renewed my self-dedication to God; praying that I might receive grace to spend my days in his service, in continued suffering, and separation from all I held most dear in this life. Amen. How vain and transitory are those pleasures which the worldliness of my heart will ever be magnifying into real good! —The rest of the evening, I felt weaned from the world and all its concerns, with somewhat of a melancholy tranquillity."

January 31.—"From great fatigue of body, was in doubt about going to the hospital, and very unwilling to go. However, I went, and preached with more freedom than ever I had done there. Having some conversation with Colonel H——, I asked him 'whether, if the wound he had received in the late engagement had been mortal, his profaneness would have recurred with any pleasure to his mind on a death-bed.' He made some attempts at palliation, though in great confusion, but bore the admonition very patiently."

February 1.—"As yesterday evening, so to-day, I was happy with God."

February 2.—Sunday. "The purser of the William Pitt told me they were too busy to have service. Thus have these men contrived to prevent the word of God from being preached to the poor women, each Sunday as it came."

February 4.—"Read the Scriptures without a relish for them, and God's presence withdrawn. How dark and wretched this state of the soul!"

February 5.—"Rose early; walked out discouraged at the small progress I make in the eastern languages. My state of bodily and mental indolence were becoming so alarming, that I struggled hard against both, crying to God for strength. Notwithstanding the reluctance in my own heart, I went to the hospital, and preached on Matt. xi. 28; from this time I enjoyed peace and happiness. Dr. Vanderkemp called to take leave. I accompanied him and brother Smith out of the town, with their two waggons. The dear old man showed much affection, and gave me advice and a blessing at parting. While we were standing to take leave, Koster, a Dutch missionary, was just entering the town with his bundle, having been driven from his place of residence. Brother Read, also, appeared from another quarter, though we thought he had gone to sea. These, with Yons,* and myself, made six missionaries, who, in a few minutes, all parted again."

In the commencement of the voyage from the Cape, which took place not many days after this short, but most interesting meeting, Mr. Martyn's patience was exercised, as before, by the tediousness of the passage, by sickness, and by languor. But whether tossed on that stormy sea which roars round the Cape, or becalmed in the midst of the Indian ocean, or enfeebled by the recurrence of illness and extreme relaxation, he received all with the meekest resignation, as the special appointment of his God.

The violent and increasing opposition he experienced from many of the more intelligent part of the passengers, and the discouraging inattention he too often perceived amongst the other class of his hearers, caused him to "grieve on their account, and to humble himself before God." "I go down," he says, "and stand in the midst of a few, without their taking the slightest notice of me : Lord, it is for thy sake I suffer such slights,—let me persevere notwithstanding." But though he mourned on their account, "he was contented to be left without fruit, if such were the will of God." Conscious of having delivered his message faithfully, and trusting that, with respect to both descriptions of his auditors, he had commended

* Probably the Missionary destined for Madagascar.

himself to their consciences, if he had not reached their hearts, his own peace of mind was not affected : and he affirms, that he was "as happy as he could be without more grace ; enjoying peaceful thoughts, tender recollections, and happy prospects." How could he fail of pleasantness and peace, when this was the genuine expression of the sentiments of his soul,—"I am born for God only. Christ is nearer to me than father, or mother, or sister,— a nearer relation, a more affectionate friend ; and I rejoice to follow him, and to love him. Blessed Jesus ! thou art all I want—a forerunner to me in all I ever shall go through, as a Christian, a minister, or a missionary."

The sickness with which the ship's company had been affected before reaching the Cape, prevailed now more extensively than ever. Many fell a sacrifice to the disorder, and, amongst others, a devout soldier, with whom Mr. Martyn had often united in prayer and praise, and had often conversed on the things of eternity. It was a mournful satisfaction to him to attend his Christian brother in his last illness, and afterwards to commit his body to the deep, in certain expectation that the "sea should give up her dead," and he with him should enter into the joy of their Lord. "Thus," he says, "is my brother gone ;—he, with whom I have conversed on Divine things, and sung, and prayed, is entered into that glory of which we used to discourse. To his multiplied sorrows upon earth, he has bid an everlasting adieu. May I follow his faith and patience, till, with him, I inherit the promises."

Falling in with the trade-winds, the fleet now made rapid progress towards India ; and whilst the breezes wafted Mr. Martyn towards the destined scene of his labours, many a sigh did he continue to breathe, under a

sense of his own sinfulness and weakness, and many a
petition did he pour forth for the people to whom he was
sent. He felt it "good and suitable to walk through this
world, overwhelmed with contrition and love; receiving
with grateful contentment every painful dispensation,
because not worthy to enjoy the light of this world;"
praying that "God would glorify Himself by the gifts and
graces of all his creatures, and make him take his place
at the bottom of them all, unnoticed, unknown, and
forgotten." "Oh, when the Spirit is pleased," said he,
"to show his creature but a few scattered specimens of
his ungodly days,—yea, of his godly ones,—how universally
and desperately wicked doth he appear! Oh that I knew
how to be duly abased! What shall I think of myself, in
comparison of others? How ought I to kiss the very
dust beneath their feet, from a consciousness of my
inferiority; and in my thoughts of God, and his dealings
with me, how ought I to be wrapped up in constant
astonishment." Then, after setting apart a day for
fasting and humiliation, he began to pray for the setting
up of God's kingdom in the world, especially in India;
and had such energy and delight in prayer as he never
had before experienced. "My whole soul," he said,
"wrestled with God. I knew not how to leave off
crying to Him to fulfil his promises; chiefly pleading his
own glorious power. I do not know that anything would
be a heaven to me, but the service of Christ and the
enjoyment of his presence. O how sweet is life, when
spent in his service! I am going upon a work exactly
according to the mind of Christ; and my glorious Lord,
whose power is uncontrollable, can easily open a way for
his feeble follower, through the thickest of the ranks of

his enemies. And now, on let me go, smiling at my
foes ; how small are human obstacles, before this mighty
Lord ! How easy is it for God to effect his purposes in a
moment ! What are inveterate prejudices, when once the
Lord shall set to his hand ! In prayer I had a most
precious view of Christ, as a Friend that sticketh closer
than a brother. Oh, how sweet was it to pray to Him !
I hardly knew how to contemplate with praise enough
his adorable excellencies. Who can show forth all his
praise ! I can conceive it to be a theme long enough for
eternity. I want no other happiness—no other heaven."
With such holy, humble, and heavenly sentiments as
these did Mr. Martyn approach the shores of Hindostan ;
and, going as he was, into the vineyard of S. Bar-
tholomew and Pantenus, of Ziegenbalg and Schwartz,
it was in their spirit that he prepared to enter upon
his labours.

On the Good Friday shortly preceding his arrival in
India, which he passed in prayer and fasting, he represents
himself as enjoying throughout a most blessed and serene
view of Christ. The word of God was very sweet to
him, whilst reading the account of the sufferings and
death of Jesus. He was entirely withdrawn from all
other concerns, and felt his soul cleaving to Christ, his
Saviour, in tender seriousness ; thankful that such days
had been set apart by the Church. "In praying that
God would no longer delay exerting his power in the
conversion of the Eastern nations, I felt emboldened," he
observes, "to employ the most familiar petitions, by
Isa. lxii. 6, 7. Blessed be God for those words ! They
are like a cordial to my spirits ; because, even if the
Lord is not pleased, by me, or during my lifetime, to call

the Gentiles, yet He is not offended at my being urgent with Him, that the kingdom of God may come."

On the 19th of April, Ceylon was discovered, which Mr. Martyn describes as presenting a long range of hills, running north and south, broken in a picturesque manner, though not lofty, with low lands between the hills and sea, covered with trees; and whilst the breezes from the island regaled his senses by their soothing and refreshing fragrancy, his mind was filled with a train of delightful anticipations; he was thinking of the time when the name of Jesus should be as ointment poured forth, in temples raised by the Cingalese amidst their cinnamon-groves, and when supplications should there ascend, like clouds of incense, through the merits of the Redeemer.

The Sunday after this, presuming that it would be the last, Mr. Martyn addressed the ship's company in a farewell discourse. The occasion, it might have been conceived, was such as to preclude any disposition to ridicule, even in men pre-eminently disposed to scoffing and contempt. But those who had reviled him at first continued to revile him to the very last. "It pained me," he remarked, "that they should give a ridiculous turn to anything on so affecting an occasion as that of parting for ever in this life. But such is the unthankful office of a minister. Yet I desire to take the ridicule of men with all meekness and charity, looking forward to another world for approbation and reward."

And now, after a wearisome interval of above nine months, from the time of his leaving Portsmouth, the land which Mr. Martyn had so ardently longed to behold, appeared: on the 21st of April, 1806, "his eyes were gratified with the sight of India."

April 22.—"At sunrise we anchored," he says, "in Madras roads. Several doolbashees or interpreters came on board, dressed in white muslin. I went ashore in one of the country boats, made very high, in order to weather the surf, with the boards throughout sewed together very coarsely with straw, and the interstices filled with it. On shore I was surrounded by an immense crowd of coolies, I suppose two hundred, who caught up one box after another, and were going off in different directions, so that I was obliged to run instantly, and stop them ; and having, with some difficulty, got my things together, I went to the Custom-house, attended by four coolies, a doolbashee, an umbrella-carrier, and a boy, or waiting-man ; all of whom attached themselves to me, without at all consulting me on the occasion. Nothing as yet struck me as remarkable in the country, for the novelty of it had been anticipated in what I had seen at St. Salvador. The number of black people was immense, and the crowd of servants so great, that one would suppose they thought themselves made for the service of the English. The elegance of their manners I was much taken with ; but, in general, one thought naturally occurred,—the conversion of their poor souls. I felt a solemn sort of melancholy at the sight of such multitudes of idolaters. While the turbaned Asiatics waited upon us at dinner, about a dozen of them, I could not help feeling as if we had got into their places. But, now that I am actually treading on Indian ground, let me bless and adore my God, for doing so much for me ; and Oh, if I live, let me have come hither for some purpose ! "

April 26.—" Towards night, I walked out, with Samees, my servant, in a pensive mood; and went through his native village, Chindaput. Here all was Indian,—no vestige of anything European. It consisted of about two hundred houses,—those in the main street connected, and those on either side of the street separated from one another by little winding paths. Everything presented the appearance of wretchedness. I thought of my future labours among them with some despondency; yet I am willing, I trust, through grace, to pass my days among them, if, by any means, these poor people may be brought to God. The sight of men, women, and children, all idolaters, makes me shudder, as if in the dominions of the Prince of Darkness. I fancy the frown of God to be visible ; there is something peculiarly awful in the stillness that prevails. Whether it is the relaxing influence of the climate, or what, I do not know ; but there is everything here to depress the spirits : all nature droops."

April 27.—Sunday.—"Enjoyed some solemn moments this morning. This is my first Sabbath in India. May all the time I pass in it be a Sabbath of heavenly rest and blessedness to my soul ! Preached on Luke x. 41, 42. There was attention. After dinner I went to Black Town, to Mr. Loveless's chapel. I sat in the air at the door, enjoying the blessed sound of the Gospel on an Indian shore, and joining with much comfort in the song of Divine praise."

April 28.—"Had much conversation with Dr. Kerr. At night the Portuguese children sung—

" ' Before Jehovah's awful throne,'

very sweetly. It excited a train of affecting thoughts in my mind.

" 'Wide as the world is thy command,'

and therefore it is easy for thee to spread abroad thy

holy name. But oh, how gross the darkness here! The veil of the covering cast over all nations seems thicker here; the fiends of darkness seem to sit in sullen repose in this land."

April 30.—"Walked by moonlight, reflecting on the Mission. My soul was at first sore tried by desponding thoughts; but God wonderfully assisted me to trust him for the wisdom of his dispensations. Truly, therefore, will I say again, 'Who art thou, O great mountain? before Zerubbabel thou shalt become a plain.' How easy for God to do it; and it shall be done in good time: *and even if I never should see a native converted, God may design by my patience and continuance in the work to encourage future missionaries.* But what surprises me is the change of views I have here from what I had in England. There my heart expanded with hope and joy at the prospect of the speedy conversion of the heathen! but here the sight of the apparent impossibility requires a strong faith to support the spirits."

After being detained a short time at Madras the fleet sailed for the Hoogley; during which voyage Mr. Martyn again suffered, indescribably, from the relaxation of his frame. He rose in the morning with the deepest melancholy, and seemed, as he expressed it, *left without a motive.* "He looked forward to an idle, worthless life, spent in India to no purpose. Exertion seemed to him like death—indeed, absolutely impossible." But it pleased God at length to give him deliverance, by enabling him to exercise faith, and to remember that, as a sinner saved, he was bound to evince the most fervent gratitude to God.

The great Pagoda of Juggernaut, now becoming distinctly visible, was a sight sufficient to rouse Mr. Martyn from almost any depths of depression, either of body or mind. Contemplating that horrid altar of impurity and blood, his soul was excited to sentiments of the strongest commiseration for the children of wretched India, "who had erected such a monument of her shame on the coast, and whose heathenism stared the stranger in the face."

Leaving Juggernaut behind, a tremendous hurricane, such as is often experienced in those latitudes, descended on the fleet; and in an instant every sail of the Union was rent in pieces. All was uproar in the ship; nor was there any resource but to run before the gale, which, had they been further on their way, must have driven them upon some sandbanks at the mouth of the Hoogley. Incessant lightning rendered the scene still more dreadful. When nature began to shrink at the fear of dissolution, Mr. Martyn was much reconciled, he says, to it, by such thoughts as these :—"What have I here? Is it not better to go, and to be with Jesus, and to be free from this body of sin and death? But for the sake of the poor unconverted souls in the ship," he adds, "I prayed earnestly for her preservation."

To this danger, from which Mr. Martyn was mercifully delivered, another of a yet more formidable nature succeeded, when he had entered the mouth of the Hoogley, and was rejoicing in the happy termination of an eventful voyage.

On the 14th of May, the Union struck on a sand-bank near the diamond harbour; where her situation was awfully dangerous; for night came on, and the wind increased. The vessel was considered by the captain as lost, and all the passengers were in the utmost terror. Mr. Martyn "retired for prayer, and found his soul in

peace :" nor was the fervent prayer of this righteous man
ineffectual. After continuing in extreme peril for two
hours, the ship very unexpectedly floated into deep water.
Thus being yet more deeply convinced that in God and
in His hand were all his ways, and having his heart
humbled in thankfulness to Him as the Author of all his
mercies, Mr. Martyn arrived at Calcutta; from whence
he thus disclosed the sentiments of his heart to a beloved
Christian friend :—

"My long and wearisome voyage is concluded, and I
am at last arrived in the country in which I am to spend
my days in the work of the Lord. Scarcely can I
believe myself to be so happy as to be actually in
India ; yet this hath God wrought. Through changing
climates, and tempestuous seas, He has brought on his
feeble worm to the field of action ; and will, I trust,
speedily equip me for my work. I am now very far from
you all, and as often as I look around and view the Indian
scenery, I sigh to think of the distance that separates us.
Time, indeed, and reflection, have, under God, contributed
to make the separation less painful ; yet still my thoughts
recur with unceasing fondness to former friendships, and
make the duty of intercession for you a happy privilege.
Day and night I do not cease to pray for you, and I am
willing to hope that you also remember me daily at the
throne of grace. Let us not, by any means, forget one
another ; nor lose sight of the day of our next meeting.
We have little to do with the business of this world.
Place and time have not that importance in our views
that they have in those of others ; and therefore neither
changes of situation nor lapse of years should weaken our
Christian attachment. I see it to be my business to fulfil

as an hireling my day ; and then to leave the world.
Amen. We shall meet in happier regions. I believe
that those connexions, and comforts, and friendships,
which I have heretofore so desired, though they are the
sweetest earthly blessings, are earthly still."

CHAPTER V.

MR. MARTYN'S ARRIVAL AT CALCUTTA — RESIDENCE AT
ALDEEN—PREACHES AT CALCUTTA—IS APPOINTED TO
DINAPORE—LEAVES CALCUTTA—JOURNAL OF HIS VOYAGE
UP THE HOOGLEY AND GANGES.

DURING many years, supplications had incessantly ascended up to heaven from Christians in India, for the
spiritual prosperity of that benighted land; and, for a
considerable time, a stated weekly meeting had been held
at Calcutta, on the recommendation of Dr. Buchanan
and Mr. Brown, for the express purpose of beseeching the
Lord to send forth labourers into those fields which were
white unto the harvest. What a manifest answer to these
petitions was the appearance of Mr. Martyn amongst
those who had been thus offering up their prayers! One
of these, * a name dear to all who admire zeal, integrity,
liberality, and an entire consecration of the brightest
talents to the cause of Christian philanthropy, was now
about to commence his researches into the state of religion
amongst the Syrian Christians : and the ship which conveyed him on that interesting errand, left the mouth of
the Hoogley as the Union entered it. To him, doubtless,
the sight of Mr. Martyn would have seemed an answer to
prayer, demanding the warmest thanksgiving; the voice
of a Christian Missionary would have been sweeter in his
ears than even those sounds which he afterwards heard in

* Dr. Buchanan.

Travancore, from the bells amongst the hills, and which reminded him of another country.

At Aldeen, near Calcutta, the residence of the Rev. David Brown, Mr. Martyn was received and welcomed with all that cordiality of affection which characterizes the genuine servants of the Lord Jesus. Finding in him a spirit eminently congenial with his own, he gladly became one of his dear family, as he expresses it, and his days passed delightfully. In order that he might enjoy as much retirement as he deemed necessary, Mr. Brown prepared a pagoda for his habitation ; which was situate on the edge of the river, at no great distance from the house. There the vaulted roof was so changed from its original destination, as often to re echo the voice of prayer and the songs of praise ; and Mr. Martyn triumphed and rejoiced "that the place where once devils were worshipped, was now become a Christian oratory."

Soon after his being fixed at Aldeen, his affectionate friends there became seriously alarmed at an attack of fever which he experienced. His illness was of some continuance, and in it he was assaulted by a temptation more dangerous than uncommon,—a temptation to look to himself for some qualification with which to approach the Saviour,—for something to warrant his confidence in Him, and hope of acceptance from Him. Searching for evidences for the purpose of ascertaining *whether we are in Christ,* widely differs from searching for them to warrant a *boldness of access to Christ :* for the latter we require no evidence, but need only the passport of faith, and the plea of our own wretchedness : and as it is the design of our great adversary (such is his subtlety) to lead us to deny the evidences of faith altogether,— so it is a part of his plan to betray us into a legal and mistaken use of them. We find Mr. Martyn at this time expressing himself thus : "I could derive no comfort from reflecting on my past life. Indeed, exactly in proportion as I looked for evidences of grace, I lost that brokenness of spirit which I wished to retain, and could not lie with simplicity at the foot of the cross. I really thought that I was departing this life. I began to pray as on the verge of eternity ; and the Lord was pleased to break my hard heart. I lay, in tears, interceding for the unfortunate natives of this country ; thinking within myself that the most despicable soodar of India was of as much value in the sight of God as the king of Great Britain."

So pleasantly and sweetly, after his recovery, did the current of Mr. Martyn's days pass on at Aldeen and Calcutta, that he began to fear lest the agreeable society he met with there should induce a softness of mind, and an indisposition to solitude and bold exertion. Of this society he remarks, "I felt sometimes melancholy at the thought that I should soon be deprived of it. But alas ! why do I regret it ? Sweet is human friendship,—sweet is the communion of saints,—but sweeter far is fellowship with God on earth, and the enjoyment of the society of his saints in heaven."

The city of Calcutta was a place so evidently suited to that order of talent with which Mr. Martyn was endowed, that it is not to be wondered that the solicitations of his Christian friends there should pour in upon him at this time, with the view of persuading him to continue amongst them, in a sphere which they considered so well adapted for the exercise of his ministry. But it was truly said of him by one* now before the throne with him in the world of light,—that " he had a spirit to follow the

* Dr. Buchanan,—Christian Researches.

steps of Brainerd and Schwartz;" and "to be prevented
from going to the heathen," he himself remarked on this
occasion, "would almost have broken his heart."

In the vicinity of Aldeen, indeed, he witnessed, with
horror, the cruel rites and debasing idolatries of heathenism. The blaze of a funeral pile caused him one day to
hasten to endeavour, if possible, to rescue an unfortunate female, who was consumed, however, before he could
reach the spot. In a dark wood at no great distance from
Serampore, he heard the sound of the cymbals and drums,
summoning the poor natives to the worship of devils;—
sounds which pierced his heart. And before a black
image, placed in a pagoda, with lights burning around it,
he beheld his fellow-creatures prostrating themselves, with
their foreheads to the earth;—a sight which he contemplated with an overwhelming compassion, whilst "he
shivered," he says, "as if standing as it were in the
neighbourhood of hell."

Scenes so affecting as these might have pleaded with
him effectually in favour of the proposition of his friends,
had he not remembered that all these things happened at
no great distance from Aldeen, Serampore, and Calcutta,
—from whence many a holy man of God had already
come forth, and would again come forth, crying out to
the wretched idolaters, "Why do ye such things?"—
"Behold the Lamb of God, which taketh away the sin of
the world."

Detained as Mr. Martyn unavoidably was, at this time,
from what he considered his especial employment, he
applied himself more ardently than ever to the acquisition
of Hindoostanee, availing himself of the assistance of a
Cashmirian Brahmin, whom he wearied with his unceasing assiduity. He was also instant in preaching the

Gospel to his countrymen, both in the Mission Church,
and in the New Church, in Calcutta.

His first discourse in the New Church, on 1 Cor. i. 23,
24, occasioned a great sensation; of a kind very different,
indeed, from that which he heartily desired, but still one
which, from the treatment to which he had been accustomed on board the ship, he was not unprepared to
expect.

The plain exhibition of the doctrines of the Gospel
was exceedingly offensive to many of his hearers. Nor
did the ferment thus excited subside quickly, as it often
does, into pity or contempt. He had the pain, very
shortly after, of being personally attacked from the pulpit
by some of his brethren, whose zeal hurried them into
the violation not only of an express Canon of the Church,
but of the yet higher law of Christian charity; and led
them to make an intemperate attack upon him, and upon
many of the truths of the Gospel. Even when he was
himself present in church, Mr. —— spoke with sufficient
plainness of him and of his doctrines, calling them inconsistent, extravagant, and absurd; drawing a vast
variety of false inferences from them, and thence arguing
against them; declaring, for instance, that to affirm repentance to be the gift of God, and to teach that nature
is wholly corrupt, was to drive men to despair;—and that
to suppose the righteousness of Christ sufficient to justify,
is to make it unnecessary to have any of our own.
Though compelled to listen to such downright heresies;—
to hear himself described as knowing neither what he
said, nor whereof he affirmed,— and as aiming only to
gratify self sufficiency, pride, and uncharitableness,—" I
rejoiced," said this meek and holy man, " to receive the
Sacrament of the Lord's Supper afterwards,—as the

solemnities of that blessed ordinance sweetly tended to sooth my asperity of mind ; and I think that I administered the cup to —— and —— with sincere goodwill." When exposed to a similar invective from another preacher, who commenced a public opposition to him by denouncing his last sermon, in particular, as a rhapsody, —as unintelligible jargon,—as an enigma ;—declaring that the epistles of St. Paul were addressed to heathens alone, and that if the apostle could look down from heaven and see what use was made of his words to distress and agitate the minds of men, he would grieve at such perversions ; and who, in addition to this, pointedly addressed Mr. Martyn, and charged him with the guilt of distressing and destroying those for whom Christ died,— with taking away their only hope, and driving them to mopishness, melancholy, and despair,—and finally, with depriving them of the only consolation they could have on a death-bed ; he again observes, "We received the Sacrament of the Lord's Supper, and I was glad of the blessed ordinance, as it tended much to compose my mind, and to soften it in compassion and love towards all mankind."

But if Mr. Martyn had abundant reason to be grieved and pained at the conduct of some of his brethren at Calcutta, he had no small satisfaction in the wise and temperate line pursued by another chaplain in this season of doubtful and distressing disputation ; who, perceiving that the doctrines of the Church of England were becoming a matter of warm and general controversy, adopted the admirable plan of simply reading the Homilies to the congregation ;—thus leaving the Church to speak authoritatively for herself, and affording to all classes an opportunity of deciding which of the parties was most in accordance with her incomparable formularies, Mr. Martyn, or his opposers. "Mr. ——," he says, "to the great satisfaction of all serious people, after stating the diversity of opinion which had lately occurred in the pulpit, began to read a homily by way of sermon :" and again, "at the New Church, I read, and Mr. —— preached the second and third parts of the 'Homily on Salvation.' The clear exhibition of divine truth which was thus presented, was very rejoicing to our hearts."

Attached as Mr. Martyn was to the Church of England, he was far from either the apathy or the jealousy in which too many are apt to indulge, respecting the interests of other Christian communities. Very decidedly did he differ in some important points from the Baptists. But it was with the sincerest grief that he heard, during his abode at Aldeen, of an order issued by the government (though it afterwards proved that he was misinformed) to prevent their preaching and distributing tracts. So perplexed and excited was he by the intelligence, that it even deprived him of sleep ; and he spoke with so much vehemence against the measures of government, as, upon reflection, to afford him matter of self-condemnation. "I know not," he said, "what manner of spirit I am of ; I fancy it is all zeal for God ; but what a falsehood is this ! I am severe against a governor, not making allowances for what he knows. Oh ! does it become me to be judging others ? Did Jesus canvas the proceedings of government in the spirit of one of this world ? I pray to be preserved from ever falling into this snare again. May I, with poverty of spirit, go on my way, and never again trouble myself with what does not belong to me ! I trust I shall be able to distinguish between zeal and self-will. Let me never fancy I have zeal, till my heart overflows with love to every human being."

On the 13th of September, 1806, Mr. Martyn received his appointment to Dinapore; by which time, notwithstanding all his vigilance, the comforts of the life he had been leading had so far won upon him, that he suffered much at the thoughts of his removal. "It is an awful and an arduous thing," said he, "to root out every affection for earthly things, so as to live for another world. I was astonished at the attachment I felt for earthly things. The happiness of invisible and eternal things seemed something like a dream; the faint remains of what I had formerly known. In great melancholy, I determined before God to leave this wretched world once more; but my soul was greatly cast down. The affections were entwined around something or other here, so that it appeared like death to be torn from it."* So far, however, was he from yielding to selfishness or sloth, that, as the day of his departure drew near, he stirred himself up to the consideration of the greatness of his calling, and panted to begin his work.

At the beginning of October, Mr. Martyn prepared to leave that Christian family, in the bosom of which he had received such unremitted kindness; but not before he had welcomed the joyful arrival of two fellow-labourers from England; who, following his bright track, and imitating his self-denying example, had turned their backs on the beloved land of their nativity. This was an inexpressible joy to his heart. "I went down," he says in his journal, "to Calcutta, where we had the happiness of meeting our dear brethren. I rode out with them in the evening, and passed most of the time in conversing about European friends." And when, afterwards, he heard one of them (Mr. Corrie) preach, he thus expresses himself: "God be

* See Appendix, III., IV., V.

praised for another witness to his truth. Oh, may abundant grace and gifts rest on my beloved brother, that the works of God may show forth themselves in him." By these various circumstances, together with the letters which at the same time he received from those to whom he was so attached in England, his affections of love and joy were excited to such a degree, as to prove almost too much for his feeble frame.

A few days before he left Aldeen, several of Mr. Martyn's friends came together to his pagoda, in order that they might unite with him in imploring a blessing on his intended labours. Such a meeting could not fail of being highly interesting, and it was not the less so from a recollection of the place in which they were assembled :—a Christian congregation, in a building which once had been an idol's temple, seemed to supply a consolatory pledge, as well as a significant emblem, of what all earnestly prayed for, and confidently anticipated, for poor idolatrous India. "My soul," said Mr. Martyn, "never yet had such divine enjoyment. I felt a desire to break from the body, and join the high praises of the saints above. May I go, 'in the strength of this, many days.'—Amen. 'My soul doth magnify the Lord, and my spirit hath rejoiced in God my Saviour.' How sweet to walk with Jesus,—to love Him, and to die for Him. 'Surely goodness and mercy shall follow me all the days of my life : and I will dwell in the house of the Lord for ever.'" And again, the next day, he says, "The blessed God has again visited my soul in his power, and all that was within me blessed his holy name. I found my heaven begun on earth. No work so sweet as that of praying, and living wholly to the service of God."

On the 15th October, after taking leave of the Church at Calcutta in a farewell discourse, and of the family at Aldeen, in an exposition at morning worship, Mr. Martyn entered his budgerow,* which was to convey him to Dinapore, and sailed up the Ganges, accompanied by his brethren, Mr. Brown, Mr. Corrie, and Mr. Parsons. Mr. Marshman,† seeing them pass by the Mission House, could not resist joining the party, and, after going a little way, left them with prayer. At night, Mr. Martyn prayed with his brethren in the vessel, and the next day they devoted the whole morning to religious exercises. " How sweet is prayer," said he, " to my soul at this time. I seem as if I could never be tired, not only of spiritual joys, but of spiritual employments, since these are now the same."

The day after, the weather becoming tempestuous, his brethren sorrowfully and reluctantly left him to prosecute his voyage alone. Before they parted, however, they spent the whole morning (to use his own words) in a Divine ordinance, in which each of them read a portion of Scripture, and all them sang and prayed. " Mr. Brown's passage, chosen from the 1st of Joshua, was very suitable," said Mr. Martyn, " Have I not sent thee ?"—" Let this be an answer to my fears, O my Lord, and an assurance that I am in thy work ; and that therefore I shall not go forth at my own charges, or fight any enemies but thine. It was a very affecting

---

* A budgerow is "a travelling boat constructed like a pleasure barge. Some have cabins fourteen feet wide, and proportionably long, and draw from four to five feet of water. From seventeen to twenty miles a day is the greatest distance a large budgerow can be towed against the stream during the fair season."—RENNEL.

† One of the Baptist Missionaries.

season to me; but in prayer I was far from a state of seriousness and affection."

"I was left alone," he writes, October 17, in his journal, "for the first time with none but natives. The wind and rain became so violent,* that the men let the budgerow stay upon the shore the whole day; and, in consequence of beating on the ground, it leaked so much that the men were obliged to be in my cabin to bale her. Read with the Moonshee one of the tracts which he had himself translated from the Bengalee into verse. Perceiving him to be alarmed at the violence of the waves beating against the boat, I began to talk to him about religion. He began by saying, 'May God be our protector,'—this was a favourable beginning. The hurricane abated before midnight, through mercy."

Oct. 18.—"Reading hard all day;—wrote out a list of the errata in one of the tracts, and read Sanscrit grammar. In the evening, walked along the bank with my gun, and fired at some wild fowl, which the servants ate. At night read part of a Nagree tract with the Moonshee. Learnt some Arabic roots. Felt an occasional depression of spirits, but prayer instantly removed it; so that, in general, I was near to God and happy."

Oct. 19.—Sunday.—"The first solitary Sabbath spent amongst the heathen; but my soul not forsaken of God. The prayers of my dear friends were instant for me this day, I well perceive; and a great part of my prayer was occupied in delightful intercession for them. The account

* "The North-westers are the most formidable enemies that are to be met with in this inland navigation,—whole fleets of trading boats have been sunk by them almost instantaneously. But it is in the great rivers alone, when increased in width, that they are the most formidable."—RENNEL.

of the fall of man, in the third chapter of Genesis, and of his restoration by Christ, was unspeakably affecting to my soul. Indeed, everything I read seemed to be carried home to my soul with ineffable sweetness and power by the Spirit; and all that was within me blessed his holy name. In the afternoon, sent to the Moonshee, that he might hear the Gospel read, or read it himself. Began St. Mark; but our conversation turning from Christianity to Mohammedism, became deadening to my spirit. Our course to-day was along the eastern bank, which seems to have been lately the bed of the river, and is bare of trees for a considerable distance from the water. The western bank is covered with wood. In my evening walk saw three skeletons."

Oct. 20.—" Employed all the day in translating the first chapter of the Acts into Hindoostanee. I did it with some care, and wrote it all out in the Persian character; yet still I am surprised I do so little. In my morning walk shot a bird with a beautiful plumage, called a Culean; and, in the evening, a large bird called a Minca. Putting my gun into the boat, I walked into the village where the boat stopped for the night, and found the worshippers of Cali by the sound of their drums and cymbals. I did not think of speaking to them, on account of their being Bengalees. But being invited by the Brahmins to walk in, I entered within the railing, and asked a few questions about the idol. The Brahmin, who spoke bad Hindoostanee, disputed with great heat, and his tongue ran faster than I could follow; and the people, who were about one hundred, shouted applause. But I continued to ask my questions, without making any remarks upon the answers. I asked, among other things, whether what I had heard of Vishnu and Brahma was true; which he confessed. I forbore to press him with the consequences, which he seemed to feel; and then I told him what was my belief. The man grew quite mild, and said it was *chula bat* (good words); and asked me seriously, at last, what I thought, 'Was idol-worship true or false?' I felt it a matter of thankfulness that I could make known the truth of God, though but a stammerer; and that I had declared it in the presence of the devil. And this also I learnt, that the power of gentleness is irresistible. I never was more astonished than at the change in the deportment of this hot-headed Brahmin. Read the Sanscrit grammar till bedtime."

Oct. 21.—"Morning at Sanscrit, without gaining any ground. Afternoon, with my Moonshee, correcting Acts i.; and felt a little discouraged at finding I still wrote so incorrectly, though much pleased at this great apparent desire of having it perfectly accurate. Though not joyful in my spirit, as when my friends left me, I feel my God to be an all-satisfying portion, and find no want of friends. Read Genesis and Luke; at night in the Septuagint and Hindoostanee. Came-to at a desert place on the western bank."

Oct. 22.—"Shot a bird somewhat larger than a woodcock, but like it in taste, and a snipe. The Musalchee, who attended me, seeing an old man who had caught some fish, made a requisition of them. The old man understood the Musalchee's meaning better than I did; for he began to entreat me, saying, 'he was a poor man,' and was quite overjoyed to find that I had not given an order to plunder him, but meant to pay. I then recollected what Mr. Brown had told me of the custom the servants have of making requisitions from the natives in the name of their English masters. Alas! poor natives, how accustomed they are to injustice! They cannot believe their English masters to be better than their Mohammedan ones."

"A Brahmin of my own age was performing his devotions to Gunga early this morning, when I was going to prayer. My soul was struck with the sovereignty of God, who, out of pure grace, had made such a difference in all the external circumstances of our lives. O let not that man's earnestness rise up in judgment against me at the last day.—In the afternoon, they were performing the ceremony of throwing the effigies of Cali, collected from several villages, into the river. In addition to the usual music, there were trumpets. The objects of worship, which were figures in relief on the sector of a circle of about one hundred and twenty degrees, most gorgeously bedecked with tinsel, were kept under a little awning in their respective boats. As the budgerow passed through the boats, they turned so as to present the front of their goddess to me; and, at the same time, blew a blast with their trumpet, evidently intending to gratify me with a sight of what appeared to them so fine. Had their employment been less impious, I should have returned the compliment by looking, but I turned away. Yet I felt no tenderness of grief; nor in the morning did I feel any thing like due thankfulness for God's electing mercy, in making me thus to differ from the Brahmins. I have daily and hourly proofs of my corruption : for when does my heart come up to what my half-enlightened understanding approves? Yet I intend, through grace, to continue praying to the end for their poor precious souls, and that the kingdom of God may be set up here."

"Came-to on the eastern bank, below a village called

Ahgadeep. Wherever I walked, the women fled at the sight of me. Some men were sitting under the shed dedicated to their goddess ; and a lamp was burning in her place. A conversation soon began ; but there was no one who could speak Hindoostanee ; so all I could say was through the medium of my Mussulman Musalchee. They said that they only did as others did ; and that, if they were wrong, then all Bengal was wrong. I felt love for their souls, and longed for utterance to declare unto those poor simple people the holy gospel. I think that when my mouth is opened, I shall preach to them day and night. I feel that they are my brethren in the flesh ;— precisely on a level with myself."

"In the morning upon Sanscrit, though still quite in the dark. Afternoon with the Moonshee."

Oct. 23.—"The tow-rope broke, and we were hurried down the stream with great rapidity ; the stream running seven miles an hour. We ran foul of several large boats ; and I expected we should go to pieces. The people of the other boats would not afford the least help : so the Mangee and his assistant jumped overboard with a rope, and succeeded in getting ashore, but were unable to stop her till she ran foul of another, which was made fast. Came-to at night on the eastern bank. A delightful season to me, on account of the serenity of my mind, and of my happy and solemn reflections on the grace of my God towards his poor creature."

"I thought at night more than usual of my dear L——. But the more I exaggerate these ideal joys, the more do I treasure up subjects of woe. O what vanity has God written upon all things under the sun."—"As I returned late, I passed between the river and a party of jackals ; they kept at a little distance till we had passed."

Oct. 25.—"Passed the morning in writing out of the rules of Sundhi. Had a very solemn season of prayer, by the favour of God, over some of the chapters of Genesis ; but especially at the conclusion of the 119th Psalm. O that these holy resolutions and pious breathings were entirely my own ! Adored be the never-failing mercy of God ! He has made my happiness to depend, not on the uncertain connexions of this life, but upon his own most blessed self,—a portion that never faileth. Came-to on the eastern bank. The opposite side was very romantic ; —adorned with a stately range of very high forest-trees, whose deep dark shade seemed impenetrable to the light.—In my evening walk enjoyed great solemnity of feeling, in the view of the world as a mere wilderness, through which the children of God are passing to a better country. It was a comforting and a solemn thought, and was unspeakably interesting to me at the time,—that God knew whereabouts his people were in the wilderness, and was supplying them with just what they wanted."

"On my return towards the boat, I saw a wild boar, of a very large size, galloping parallel to the river. I had not a gun with me, or I might have killed him, as he was within reach of a fusee ball.—In my budgerow found great delight in Hart's Hymns at night."

October 26.—Sunday.—"Passed this Lord's day with great comfort, and much solemnity of soul. Glory to God for his grace ! Reading the Scriptures and prayer took up the first part of the day. Almost every chapter I read was blessed to my soul,—particularly the last chapter of Isaiah : 'It shall come, that I will gather all nations and tongues ; and they shall come, and see my glory,' &c. Rejoice, my soul, in the sure promises of Jehovah. How happy am I, when, in preparing for the work of declaring his glory among the Gentiles, I think, that many of the Lord's saints have been this day remembering their unworthy friend. I felt as if I could never be tired with prayer. In the afternoon, read one of Gibert's French Sermons,—Bates on Death,—and some of the Nagree Gospels. In the evening, we came-to on the eastern bank. I walked into a neighbouring village, with some tracts. The children ran away in great terror ; and though there were some men here and there, I found no opportunity or encouragement to try if there were any that could speak Hindostanee: however, I felt vexed with myself for not taking more pains to do them good. Alas ! while Satan is destroying their souls, does it become the servants of God to be lukewarm?—At night, read the third and fourth chapters of the Acts ; and lost much time and spirituality by indulging ideas of schemes about the Gospel, which had more of romance and pride in them than of wisdom and humiliation."

Oct. 27.—" Arrived at Berhampore. In the evening, walked out to see the cantonments at the hospital, in which there were one hundred and fifty European soldiers sick. I was talking to a man, said to be dying, when a surgeon entered. I went up, and made some apology for entering the hospital. It was my old schoolfellow and townsman, ———. The remainder of the evening he spent with me in my budgerow. He pressed me much to stay longer with him, which I refused ; but afterwards, on reflection, I thought it my duty to stay a little longer ; thinking I might have an opportunity of preaching to the soldiers."

Oct. 28.—" Rose very early, and was at the hospital at daylight. Waited there a long time, wandering up and down the wards, in hopes of inducing the men to get up and assemble ; but it was in vain. I left three books with them, and went away, amidst the sneers and titters of the common soldiers. Certainly it is one of the greatest crosses I am called to bear, to take pains to make people hear me. It is such a struggle between a sense of propriety and modesty, on the one hand; and a sense of duty, on the other ; that I find nothing equal to it. I could force my way anywhere, in order to introduce a brother minister ; but, for myself, I act with hesitation and pain. Mr. —— promised to ask the head surgeon's permission for me to preach, and appointed the hour at which I should come. I went there ; but, after waiting two hours, was told that the surgeon was gone without being spoken to; and many other excuses were made. So, as it was the heat of the day, I saw it was of no use to make any more attempts, and therefore I went on my way. At night, from mere thoughtlessness, went on shore without tracts, and lost a better opportunity than I have yet had of distributing them among the people. My soul was dreadfully wounded at the recollection of it ; and, O may the conviction of my wickedness rest upon my soul all my days ! How many souls will rise up in judgment against me at the last day, God only knows. The Lord forgive my guilty soul ; deliver me from blood guiltiness, and make me to remember for what purpose I came hither ! "

Oct. 29.—" Passed Cossim Buzar and Moorshedabad, in the middle of the day; and so my resolutions of repairing my past negligence were defeated, for we stopped at night where there was not a house. I talked with a party of boatmen, and begged them to take a tract ; but I could not prevail upon them. Though they were Rajemahl people, I could scarcely understand them, or they me, at all. I am grieved, and disappointed, and ashamed, at my extraordinary backwardness in the language; but I hope not to be discouraged. Employed the whole day in translating Acts, chap. ii., and correcting it with my Moonshee."

Oct. 30.—"Employed the whole day, as yesterday, about the same chapter. Read also the 'Ramayuna,' and Sale's 'Introduction to the Koran.' My views enlarge rapidly respecting the state of things among the Hindoos and Mohammedans. My soul was in a most awful state of impression. Satan was at work, and my soul found safety only in holding by God, as a child clings to the neck of its mother. Thánks be to God that I have the witness in myself. 'The anointing, which ye have received of him, abideth in you; and ye need not that any man teach you; but as the same anointing teacheth you of all things,' &c. O how refreshing and supporting to my soul was *the holiness of the word of God;* sweeter than the sweetest promise, at this time, was the constant and manifest tendency of the Word, to lead men to holiness and the deepest seriousness. What a contrast is it to the mock majesty of the Koran, and the trifling, indecent stuff of the Ramayuna. My whole soul seems at present engrossed in the work of being the messenger of truth; and, at every season of prayer, I found a peculiar tenderness in praying for those unenlightened people."

Oct. 31.—"Passed a very populous village, called Jungipore."

"Stopped at night again in a desert place. Employed as yesterday. My Moonshee said, 'How can you prove this book (putting his hand on the Gospel), to be the word of God?' I took him to walk with me on the shore, that we might discuss the matter; and the result of our conversation was, that I discovered that the Mussulmen allow the Gospel to be, in general, the command of God, though the words of it are not his, as the words of the Koran are; and contend that the actual words of God, given to Jesus, were burnt by the Jews; and that they also admit the New Testament to have been in force till the coming of Mahomet. When I quoted some passages which proved the Christian dispensation to be the final one, he allowed it to be inconsistent with the divinity of the Koran, but said, 'Then those words of the Gospel must be false.' The man argued and asked his questions seemingly in earnest, and another new impression was left upon my mind; namely, that these men are not fools; and that all ingenuity and clearness of reasoning are not confined to England and Europe. I seem to feel that these descendants of Ham are as dear to God as the haughty sons of Japheth; I feel, too, more at home with the Scriptures than ever. Everything I see gives light to, and receives it from, the Scriptures. I seem transported back to the ancient times of the Israelites and the apostles."

"My spirit felt composed, after the dispute, by simply looking to God as one who had engaged to support his own cause; and I saw it to be my part to pursue my way through the wilderness of this world, looking only to that redemption which daily draweth nigh. The same thoughts continued through the evening. I reflected, while looking at the stream gliding by, the smooth current of which showed its motion only by the moon shining upon it, that all are alike carried down the stream of time,—that in a few years there will be another generation of Hindoos, Mussulmen, and English in this country; and we are now but just speaking to each other as we are passing along. How should this consideration quell the tumult of anger and impatience, when I cannot convince men ! O how feeble an instrument must a creature so shortsighted be ! How necessary is it that God should be continually raising up new instruments ; and how easily can He do it. 'The government is on his shoulder ; ' Jesus is able to bear the weight of it ; therefore we need not be oppressed with care or fear ; but a missionary is apt to fancy himself an Atlas."

Nov. 1.—" Employed all day in translating the third chapter of the Acts. Came-to at a place where there was no house. For the first time since arriving in Bengal, saw some hills appearing in the N.W."

Nov. 2.—Sunday.—" My mind was greatly oppressed that I had done and was doing nothing in the way of distributing tracts. To free my conscience from the charge of unprofitableness and neglect, I wished to go ashore in the middle of the day, wherever I thought I might meet people ; but did not land till we came-to on the bank of the Ganges, which we entered just before sunset. Hills appeared from S.W. to N.W. Some of these were the Rajemahl hills. Walking on shore, I met with a very large party ; and, entering into conversation, I asked if any of them could read. One young man, who seemed superior in rank to the rest, said he could, and accordingly read some of the only Nagree tract that I had. I then addressed myself boldly to them, and told them of the Gospel. When speaking of the inefficacy of the religious practices of the Hindoos, I mentioned, as an example, the repetition of the name of Ram. The young man assented to this, and said, " Of what use is it ? " As he seemed to be of a pensive turn, and said this with marks of disgust, I gave him a Nagree Testament—the first I have given. May God's blessing go along with it, and cause the eyes of multitudes to be opened! The men said they should be glad to receive tracts; so I sent them back a considerable number by the young man. The idea of printing the Parables, in proper order, with a short explanation subjoined to each, for the purpose of distribution, and as school-books, suggested itself to me to-night, and delighted me prodigiously."

Nov. 3.—" Crossed the river in order to get to Chandry. But the wind growing very strong, we were obliged to come-to by a sand-bank. Began my work by writing a few remarks on one of the Parables. Finished "Sale's Preliminary Discourse to the Koran," and read the Ramayuna. Arrived at Chandry, and found —— and ——; walked with them over some of the ruins of Gour; a mosque, which was still standing entire, was indeed worth seeing. We observed several monkeys, and the print of a tiger's foot."

Nov. 4.—" After officiating at morning worship, I went up with my friends in a boat to Gomalty; stopping by the way to visit one of their schools at Mirdypore,* which much delighted me. The little boys, seated cross-legged on the ground all around the room, read some of the New Testament to us. While they displayed their powers of reading, their fathers and mothers crowded in great numbers round the doors."

Nov. 5.—" Received letters from Messrs. Brown, Corrie, and Parsons, which much revived me. At evening worship, discoursed from Isaiah lxiii. 1. My soul

* Here are thirteen or fourteen village schools, and, in consequence, a marked progress in civilization.

continued sweetly engaged with God; though the praises of the people of Calcutta were in some degree an interruption of that sweet peace, which is only to be found in being nothing before God."

Nov. 7.—" This morning, after speaking on Acts xx. 32, I took my leave; and, with Mr. ——, went in palanquins to Massamgung. Frequently cast down today. From want of diligent employment, my thoughts had time to wander in search of some earthly good; but I found that recollection of what I deserved at the hands of God restored me to greater peace."

Nov. 8.—" Early this morning reached Rajemahl, and walked to view the remains of its ancient splendour. Gave a tract or two to a Brahmin; but the Dak Moonshee, a Mussulman, when he received one of the Hindostanee tracts, and found what it was, was greatly alarmed : and, after many awkward apologies, returned it, saying, 'that a man who had his legs in two different boats was in danger of sinking between them.' Went on, much discouraged at the suspicion and rebuffs I met with,—or rather *pained ;* for I feel not the less determined to use every effort to give the people the Gospel. Oh ! that the Lord would pour out upon them a spirit of deep concern for their souls ! In a walk, at Rajemahl, met some of the hill people. Wrote down from their mouth some of the names of things. From their appearance, they seemed connected with the Hottentots and Chinese. Passed the day in correcting Acts, chap. iii., with the Moonshee. At night, walked with Mr. G—— into a village, where we met with some more of the hill people. With one of them, who was a Manghee, or chief of one of the hills, I had some conversation in Hindostanee ; and told him that wicked men, after death, go to a place of fire; and good men, above, to God. The former struck him exceedingly. He asked again, 'What! do they go to a place of great pain and fire?' These people, he said, sacrifice oxen, goats, pigeons, &c. I asked him if he knew what this was for, and then explained the design of sacrifices, and told him of the great sacrifice;—but he did not seem to understand me, and appeared pensive, after hearing that wicked men go to hell. He asked us, with great kindness, to have some of his wild honey : which was the only thing he had to offer. How surprising is the universal prevalence of sacrifices ! This circumstance will, perhaps, be made use of for the universal conversion of the nations. How desirable that some missionary should go among these people ! No prejudices ;—none of the detestable pride and self-righteousness of their neighbours in the plains."

Nov. 9.—"Passed the Sabbath rather uncomfortably. With Mr. —— I read several portions of the sacred Scriptures, and prayed in the afternoon. We reached Sicly gully, a point where the Rajemahl hills jut out into the Ganges. It was a romantic spot. We went ashore, and ascended an eminence to look at the ruins of a mosque. The grave of a Mussulman warrior, killed in battle, and a room over it, were in perfect preservation ; and lamps are still lighted there every night. We saw a few more of the hill people, one of whom had a bow and arrows; they were in a hurry to be gone, and went off, men, women, and children, into their native woods. As I was entering the boat, I happened to touch with my stick the brass pot of one of the Hindoos, in which rice was boiling. So defiled are we in their sight, that the pollution passed from my hand, through the stick and the brass, to the rice. He rose and threw it all away.

We read together at night an excellent sermon on 2 Cor. v. 1."

Nov. 10.—" Employed almost all the day in finishing the correction of the third of the Acts with my Moonshee, and in writing on some of the Parables. Went on the north side of the river, and set Mr. G—— ashore; walked with him to a nulla, expecting to find his boat, but it not being there, we were obliged to walk back by night. Happily we procured a torch in the village near. We were thus preserved from the wild buffaloes, whose recent footsteps in the path gave us no small alarm. I am *constantly* preserved through the good providence of the Lord. Employed in lessons of Persian, writing and reading Ramayuna."

Nov. 11.—" This morning, after prayer, Mr. G—— took his leave. I returned to my work without interruption, and with no small delight. The thought occurred to my mind very strongly,—How much have I to learn of Divine things,—if the Lord will be pleased to teach me. I want, above all, a meek, serious, resigned, Christ-like spirit. May I have grace to live above every human motive; simply with God, and to God, and not swayed, especially in the missionary work, by the opinions of people not acquainted with the state of things, whose judgment may be contrary to my own. But it is a matter of no small difficulty to keep one's eye from wandering to the church in Calcutta and in England."

Nov. 12.—" Employed all the day in translating, in which work the time passes away pleasantly and rapidly. The cold mornings and evenings begin to be very severe. Though the thermometer was only down to 61°, I should have been glad of a fire. It was 81° in the middle of the day. We passed this day out of Bengal into Bahar."

Nov. 13.—" This morning we passed Colgong. I went ashore and had a long conversation with two men. As I approached more and more to religion, they were the more astonished; and when I mentioned the day of judgment, they looked at each other in the utmost wonder, with a look that expressed, 'How should he know anything about that.' I felt some satisfaction in finding myself pretty well understood in what I said; but they could not read; and no people came near us, and so I had the grief of leaving this place without supplying it with one ray of light. I was much burdened with a consciousness of blood-guiltiness ; and though I cannot doubt of my pardon by the blood of Christ, how dreadful the reflection that any should perish who might have been saved by my exertions. Looking round this country, and reflecting upon its state, is enough to overwhelm the mind of a minister or missionary. When once my mouth is opened, how shall I ever dare to be silent ? Employed as yesterday. At night met some boatmen on the bank, and a Fakir with them : I talked a good deal, and some things they understood. The Fakir's words I could scarcely understand. As he said he could read, and promised to read a Testament, I gave him one and several tracts."

Nov. 14.—" Employed in writing out the Parables. Walked through a poor village in the evening, where there were none but women and children, who all ran away when they saw me, except one poor old woman who was ill, and begged. Though she spoke clearly enough, I could scarcely understand one of her words, so that I have quite a new language to learn. When she received half a rupee, she was mute with astonishment for a time, and at last said *Chula* (good). The name of the place was Nuckanpore."

Nov. 15.—" Morning spent on the Parables. After-wards with the Moonshee, correcting Acts iv. The boat stopping in the afternoon a short time, I went into a village, and finding a genteel-looking Hindoo smoking his hookah, I sat down with him, and a few people gathered round. But the old man, who had been a soldier, talked so incessantly about his campaigns, that I found no good would come if I did not interrupt him and introduce religion. From having been much with the English, he had more enlarged views than most of the Hindoos, and talked like a Mussulman,—that all were of one caste before God, that there would be a day of judgment, and that there was only one God. When I endeavoured to make him comprehend the nature of the death of Christ, he merely said, ' Ah! that is your shaster,'—so never was any effort more ineffectual. In the bazaar, I stood and asked if any one could read Nagree. There was only one who could, and he took a tract: about ten others were taken also. I suffered greatly from dejection most of the evening. But the Lord graciously came in the time of need and supported my sinking faith. 'The Lord reigneth,' and the people shall ' remember and turn to the Lord.'"

Nov. 16.—Sunday.—" Generally in a solemn tender spirit. Spent the first half of the day in reading the Scriptures and prayer. Many a word was brought home with abundance of consolation to my soul. 'Though I walk through the valley of the shadow of death, I will fear no evil, for thou art with me ; thy rod and thy staff they comfort me.' When do the sheep find the happiness of having a shepherd so much as when they are walking through a dark shadow? While Jesus lets me see his 'rod and staff,' I am comforted. In the afternoon read some French sermons. Walked in the evening to a poor village, where I only produced terror. One man, whom I at last met, told me that none could read in the village but a Brahmin, and he was gone to another town. I left two tracts for him, and told the man to be sure to give them to him when he came back. The man was in no small alarm at this, but asked only where I got them. Distressed at times: I fear that I am not acting faithfully in warning those around me. But the shortest way to peace is, to pray for a broken heart and submissive spirit: by these means my mind brightened up. At night was deeply affected about my two dear sisters, and felt the bowels of affection yearn over them; who knows what they have been suffering all this while! For my poor elder sister I interceded that she might be saved."

Nov. 17.—" Early this morning they set me ashore to see a hot spring. A great number of Brahmins and Fakirs were there. Not being able to understand them, I gave away tracts. Many followed me to the budgerow, where I gave away more tracts and some Testaments. Arrived at Monghir about noon. In the evening some came to me for books; and, among them, those who had travelled from the spring, having heard the report that I was giving away copies of the Ramayuna. They would not believe me when I told them that it was not the Ramayuna; I gave them six or eight more. In the morning tried to translate with the Moonshee one of the Nagree papers."

Nov. 18.—" A man followed the budgerow along the walls of the fort; and, finding an opportunity, got on board with another, begging for a book,—not believing but that it was the Ramayuna. As I hesitated, having given away as many as I could spare for one place, he prostrated himself to the earth, and placed his forehead in the dust ; at which I felt an indescribable horror. I gave them each a Testament. Employed in writing out the Parables, and translating. In the evening met with two villagers, and, finding they could read, I brought them to the boat, and gave them each a Testament and some tracts."

Nov. 19.—"Employed in translating the Parables all the day. Finished the first book of the Ramayuna. Came-to at a desert place on the north side, where, in my walk, I met with a man with whom I conversed; but we could understand each other but very little. To a boy with him, who could read, I gave some tracts. Felt extraordinarily wearied with my labou these two or three last days, and should have been glad of some refreshing conversation."

Nov. 20.—22.—"Employments,—the same, throughout these three days :—finished the sixth of Acts. Stopped each night at sand-banks."

Nov. 23.—"Sunday. Spent the day comfortably and solemnly, in reading and prayer ; but my conscience was grievously wounded in the evening, at the recollection of having omitted opportunities of leaving the word of God at a place. Yet will I adore the blessed Spirit, that He departs not, nor suffers my conscience to be benumbed. What a wretched life shall I lead, if I do not exert myself from morning till night in a place, where, through whole territories, I seem to be the only light."

Nov. 24.—"Employed in writing on a Parable all day. In my evening walk, finding an old Brahmin at work in the fields, I began to ask him 'How it came that he, a Brahmin, was obliged to work?' He concluded his answer by saying that we English had robbed them of their country. He was, for a considerable time, very violent; but another Brahmin, in some fright, coming up, set all right, as he thought, by speaking of 'the brave English,' &c. When I began to talk to them of the day of judgment, heaven, and hell, they seemed surprised and pleased, and gave great attention. But I have never had reason to believe, that the attention of the people to anything I have to say expresses anything more than mere respect for a 'Sahib.' They never ask a question about it, and probably do not understand one-half, even when my sentences are correct. The disaffection of the people gave rise, afterwards, to many reflections in my mind on what may be my future sufferings in this country: but, in proportion to the apparent causes of depression, did my faith and triumph in the Lord seem to rise. Come what will, —let me only be found in the path of duty, and nothing shall be wrong. Be my sufferings what they may, they cannot equal those of my Lord, nor, probably, even those of the apostles and early martyrs. They, 'through faith, subdued kingdoms, wrought righteousness, out of weakness were made strong,' &c., and why shall not I hope that I, too, who am indeed 'like one born out of due time,' shall receive strength according to my day."

Nov. 25.—"Reached Patna this afternoon;—walked about this scene of my future ministry, with a spirit almost overwhelmed at the sight of the immense multitudes. There was a Rajah sitting at the door of his tent, by the water-side. Came to the budgerow at night ill with a headache, and still more weak and feeble in faith. Pain in the head continued acute all night."

Nov. 26.—"The multitudes at the water-side prodigious. Arrived, in the afternoon, at Dinapore, but did not go on shore. Employed in translating and writing on the Parables. My spirit this evening was sweetly elevated beyond the people and the concerns of this world, while meditating on the words, 'I am the Almighty God : walk before me, and be thou perfect.'"

CHAPTER VI.

MR. MARTYN IS FIXED AT DINAPORE—COMMENCES HIS
MINISTRY—TRANSLATIONS—DISPUTES WITH HIS MOON-
SHEE AND PUNDIT — DIFFICULTIES RESPECTING THE
SCHOOLS—HIS HAPPINESS IN THE WORK OF TRANS-
LATION.

ON reaching Dinapore, which, for a considerable time,
was to be his permanent residence, Mr. Martyn's imme
diate objects were threefold: to establish native schools,
—to attain such readiness in speaking Hindostanee, as
might enable him to preach in that language the Gospel
of the grace of God,—and to prepare translations of the
Scriptures and religious tracts for dispersion. We have
already seen that the idea of translating the Parables,
accompanied by some remarks upon them, had occupied
his mind during his voyage up the Ganges. At Dinapore
he continued to engage in this employment with the same
earnestness. Of Hindostanee he already knew enough
to translate with grammatical accuracy; and his Moonshee was at hand to suggest the proper idiom, and, what
in that language is so difficult, the just and exact colloca-
tion of the words in the sentences. The obstacles which
he had to overcome in acquiring the languages of the
country, he represents as formidable. Passing out of
Bengal into Bahar, he found that he had to acquaint himself with the Baharree as well as the Hindostanee; and
the Baharree had its various dialects. "I am low-

spirited," he said, soon after reaching Dinapore, "about my work; I seem to be at a stand, not knowing what course to take." From the Pundit whom he employed he learned,—though the statement was probably exaggerated, —that every four *cos* (miles) the language changes; and by the specimens he gave of a sentence in the dialects across the water at Gyah, and some other places, they appeared to differ so much, that a book in the dialect of one district, would be unintelligible to the people of another. As the best mode of acquiring a knowledge of the various Oriental tongues, the study of Sanscrit was recommended to him by his Pundit, and with what spirit he laboured in this and other pursuits may be seen from his account of the work of a single day.

"Morning with the Pundit, occupied in Sanscrit. In the afternoon, hearing a Parable in the Bahar dialect. Continued till late at night writing on the Parables. My soul much impressed with the immeasurable importance of my work, and the wickedness and cruelty of wasting a moment, when so many nations are, as it were, waiting while I do my work. Felt eager for the morning to come again, that I might resume my work."

The difficulties of various kinds which presented themselves to Mr. Martyn, could not fail of being a source of pain to him, in proportion to his fervent anxiety to benefit all around him. But it was his privilege and consolation to remember that he was in His hands, in whom are "hid all the treasures of wisdom and knowledge," and "with whom all things are possible." Had he not sought and found refuge in the omnipotence of Christ, soon would he have sunk into despondency. To those who have not elevated their views above the feeble efforts of human agency, the conversion of the heathen cannot but appear to exceed the limits of possibility. Mr. Martyn, who in England had met with many such "disputers of this world," found that India was by no means destitute of them. A conversation into which he was led with one of these characters was painfully trying to him; "but in the multitude of my troubled thoughts," he said, "I still saw that there is 'strong consolation in the hope set before us.' Let me labour for fifty years, amidst scorn, and without seeing one soul converted,—still it shall not be worse for my soul in eternity, nor even worse for it in time. 'Though the heathen rage,' and the English people 'imagine a vain thing,' the Lord Jesus, who controls all events, is my friend,—my master,—my God —my all. On this rock of ages, on which I feel my foot to rest, 'my head is lifted up above all mine enemies round about me,' and I sing, 'yea, I will sing praises unto the Lord.'"

From much of the society Mr. Martyn found at Dinapore, he received more discomfort than disappointment;—some there were, indeed, who treated him from the first with the utmost kindness; who afterwards became his joy, and who one day will assuredly be his crown of rejoicing. But before that happy change in them was effected by the power of Divine grace, he found none to whom he could fully and freely unbosom himself. With what gladness and thankfulness, therefore, did he welcome the arrival of letters from his beloved Christian friends at Calcutta and in England. He speaks of being exceedingly comforted, on returning home after a melancholy walk, and finding letters from Mr. Brown and Mr. Corrie, and from two of his friends in England, who were as dear to him as he was to them. "How sweet," he said, after perusing these memorials of affection, "are the delights of Christian friendship; and what must heaven be, where there are none but humble, kind, and holy children of God! Such a society would of itself be a heaven to me; after what I feel at the ways of worldly people here." Nor was it only by the neglect, levity, and profaneness of many of his countrymen, where he was stationed, that Mr. Martyn was pained and grieved: his meek and tender spirit was hurt likewise at the manner in which he conceived himself to be regarded by the natives: by the anger and contempt with which multitudes of them eyed him in his palanquin at Patna, he was particularly affected; observing, "Here every native I meet is an enemy to me because I am an Englishman. England appears almost a heaven upon earth, because there one is not viewed as an unjust intruder. But oh! the heaven of my God,—the 'general assembly of the first-born, the spirits of just men made perfect,' and Jesus! Oh, let me, for a little moment, labour and suffer reproach."

The observations he was compelled to hear from his Moonshee and Pundit, often present a curious and affecting display of Pagan and Mohammedan ignorance.* "Upon showing," he writes, "the Moonshee the first part of John iii. he instantly caught at those words of our Lord, in which He describes Himself as having *come down* from heaven, and then calls Himself 'the Son of man which is *in* heaven.' He said that this was what the

---

* Many of these observations, as well as those made by the Persians with whom Mr. Martyn entered into religious discussion, cannot fail of giving pain to a Christian heart; but missionaries ought to be apprized of the nature of those weapons with which Christianity is assailed by Infidels. For their sakes much is inserted which otherwise had doubtless far better have been omitted.

philosophers call 'nickal,' or impossible,—even for God to make a thing to be in two different places at the same time. I explained to him, as soon as his heat was a little subsided, that the difficulty was not so much in conceiving how the Son of man could be, at the same time, in two different places, as in comprehending that union of the two natures in Him, which made this possible. I told him that I could not explain this union; but showed him the design and wisdom of God in effecting our redemption by this method. I was much at a loss for words, but I believe that he collected my meaning, and received some information which he did not possess before."

In another place he says : "On reading some parts of the epistles of St. John to my Moonshee, he seemed to view them with great contempt : so far above the wisdom of the world is their Divine simplicity ! The Moonshee told me, at night, that when the Pundit came to the part about the angels 'separating the evil from the good,' he said, with some surprise, 'that there was no such thing in his Shaster ; but that, at the end of the world, the sun would come so near, as first to burn all the men, then the mountains, then the debtas (inferior gods), then the waters : then God, reducing Himself to the size of a thumb-nail, would swim on the leaf of a peepul tree.'".

The commencement of Mr. Martyn's ministry amongst the Europeans of Dinapore, was not of such a kind as either to gratify or encourage him. At first he read prayers to the soldiers at the barracks from the drum-head, and as there were no seats provided, was desired to omit his sermon.

Arrangements being afterwards made for the perform-ance of Divine service with somewhat of that order and decency which becomes its celebration, the resident families at Dinapore assembled on the Sabbaths and attended Mr. Martyn's ministry. By many of these, offence was taken at his not reading to them a written sermon, and it was intimated to him, by letter, that it was their wish that he should desist from extempore preaching. At such an interference on the part of his flock, he confesses that he was at first roused into anger and displeasure ;—he could not but think that the people committed to his charge had forgotten the relation which subsisted between him and them, in dictating to him the mode in which they thought proper to be addressed. On mature reflection, however, he resolved upon compliance, for the sake of conciliation :—saying that " he would give them a folio sermon-book, if they would receive the word of God on that account."

Whilst the flock at Dinapore were thus overstepping the limits of respect and propriety, Mr. Martyn was informed that one of his brethren at Calcutta was about to transgress the rules of Christian charity very grievously, by publishing one of those pulpit invectives which had been fulminated against him on his arrival at Calcutta. Such an act in a brother chaplain would, in some minds, have excited vindictive feelings. In his, the chief excitement was a discomposure arising from an apprehension that he might be compelled to undertake a public refutation of this attack on his doctrines;—an undertaking which would consume much of that precious time which he wished wholly to devote to his missionary work.

Thus terminated the year 1806 ;—on the last day of which Mr. Martyn appears to have been much engaged in prayer and profitable meditation on the lapse of time : feeling communion with the saints of God in the world, whose minds were turned to the consideration of those awful things, which cannot but be suggested to a reflecting mind by a year irrecoverably past.

On the first day of the year 1807, Mr. Martyn was led to the following reflection, from whence we perceive that it is the work of the selfsame Spirit to convince the soul of sin ; to constrain it to unreserved obedience : and to fill it with unutterable consolation :—

"Seven years have passed away since I was first called of God. Before the conclusion of another seven years, how probable is it that these hands will have mouldered into dust ! But be it so : my soul through grace hath received the assurance of eternal life, and I see the days of my pilgrimage shortening, without a wish to add to their number. But oh, may I be stirred up to a faithful discharge of my high and awful work ; and, laying aside, as much as may be, all carnal cares and studies, may I give myself to this 'one thing.' The last has been a year to be remembered by me, because the Lord has brought me safely to India, and permitted me to begin, in one sense, my missionary work. My trials in it have been very few ; everything has turned out better than I expected ; lovingkindness and tender-mercies have attended me at every step : therefore here will I sing his praise. I have been an unprofitable servant, but the Lord hath not cut me off : I have been wayward and perverse, yet He has brought me further on the way to Zion : here, then, with sevenfold gratitude and affection, would I stop and devote myself to the blissful service of my adorable Lord. May He continue his patience, his grace, his direction, his spiritual influences, and I shall at last surely come off conqueror ! May He speedily open my mouth, to make known the mysteries of the Gospel, and in great mercy grant that the heathen may receive it and live ! "

The commencement of the New Year was devoted by Mr. Martyn to the work which was still before him, of translating and commenting on the Parables, as well as to the attainment of the Sanscrit. Sustained by the hope of future usefulness, he experienced much pleasure, not only in urging his toilsome way through the rudiments of that language, but even when he appeared, notwithstanding every exertion, to be making no sensible progress in it.

"Employed," he says, one day in the month of January, 1807, "morning and evening in Sanscrit grammar, and in the afternoon, in translating the Parables. Though I scarcely stirred in Sanscrit, yet, by keeping myself steady to the work, I had much comfort in my soul, and this day, like all others, fled swiftly away."

To these employments, he added another also—the translation into Hindostanee of those parts of the Book of Common Prayer which are most frequently used. This project, when it first occurred to him, so arrested his mind, that he instantly began to translate, and proceeded as far as the end of the "Te Deum." Fearing, however, as it was the Sabbath, that such an employment might not be in perfect harmony with the sacred solemnity of that day, inasmuch as it was not strictly of a devotional kind, he desisted from further progress,—so deep was his reverence for a Divine appointment—so jealous his fear of offending his God! After passing, therefore, the remainder of the day in reading the Holy Scriptures, and singing praises to the Lord, he closed it with these reflections :—" Oh, how shall I sufficiently praise my

God, that here in this solitude,—with people enough, indeed, but without a saint,—I yet feel fellowship with all those who, in every place, call on the name of our Lord Jesus Christ. I see myself travelling on with them, and I hope I shall worship with them in his courts above ! "

These peculiar studies, as well as the conversations which Mr. Martyn frequently had with the natives (for which purpose he went about without his palanquin), were regarded by many with a mixture of jealousy, fear, and contempt. Did he so much as speak to a native,—it was enough to excite wonder and alarm : nor is this a matter of surprise, when we consider, that all love for the soul and all fear of God are as certainly absent and inoperative in worldly characters, as the love of pleasure and the fear of man are present and predominant. And if, in ordinary circumstances, such a line of conduct as Mr. Martyn adopted in India was calculated to awaken the apprehensions of those who lived chiefly for this world, at this particular juncture it was still more likely to be attended with these effects. For, just at this time, the settlement was thrown into some consternation by hearing of the sudden arrival of twelve thousand Mahrattas in the neighbourhood ; of which event the alarmists at Dinapore might be ready to take advantage, and endeavour, in some way or other, to connect it with Mr. Martyn's plans for the conversion of the natives to Christianity. These troops, however, had other objects than those which the wakeful fear of some might have assigned them ; their destination being simply to attend one of their chiefs on a pilgrimage to Benares.

Religious discussions between Mr. Martyn, his Moonshee, and Pundit, were almost of daily occurrence; and, as they serve to throw light on his character, as well as on that of those with whom a missionary must be conversant in India, it may be useful again to refer to what his journals contain on this head :—

"Long disputes with the Moonshee on the enjoyments of heaven. I felt some mortification at not having a command of language. There are a variety of lesser arguments, the force of which consists in their being brought together in rapid succession in conversation, which nothing but a command of words can enable one to effect. However, I was enabled to tell the Moonshee one thing : that my chief enjoyment, even now on earth, was the enjoyment of God's presence, and a growing conformity to Him; and, therefore, I asked, what motives could the promise of houris, ghilmans, green meadows, and eating and drinking in paradise, afford me. My soul sweetly blessed the Lord in secret, that this testimony was true ; and oh, what a change must have been wrought in me !"

Jan. 16.—"Employed on the Sanscrit; in the afternoon, collecting idiomatic phrases for the Parables. Finished the First Epistle of St. John with the Moonshee. I asked him what he thought of those passages which so strongly express the doctrine of the Trinity and of the Divinity of Christ? He said he never would believe it; because the Koran declared it to be sinful to say that God had any Son. I told him that he ought to pray that God would teach him what the truth really is. He said he had no occasion to pray on this subject, as the word of God was express. I asked him whether some doubt ought not to arise in his mind whether the Koran is the word of God. He grew angry, and I felt hurt and vexed. I should have done better to have left the words of the chapter with him, without saying anything. I went also too far with the Pundit, in arguing against his superstition; for he also grew angry. If any qualification seems necessary to a missionary in India, it is wisdom,—operating in the regulation of the temper and the due improvement of opportunities."

"Dictating, to-day, the explanation of a parable to the Moonshee, I had occasion to give the proofs of the corruption of human nature, and drew the conclusion that, hence, till our hearts are changed, we are abominable in the sight of God, and our own works, however useful to men, are worthless in his sight. I think I never saw such a striking instance of the truth grappling with human nature. He seemed like a fish, when he first finds that the hook has hold of him. He was in a dreadful rage, and endeavoured to escape from the convictions these truths produced; but seemingly in vain. At last, recovering himself, he said he had a question to ask, which was, What would become of children, if the dispositions they were born with rendered them odious in the sight of God? I gave him the best answer I could; but he considered it nothing, because founded on Scripture; and said, with great contempt, that this was mere matter of faith,—the same sort of thing as when the Hindoos believed the nonsense of their shasters."

How delightful must it have been to Mr. Martyn to turn, as he did at this time, from controversies with these unbelievers, to the enjoyment of Christian converse and communion with his beloved friend and brother Mr. Corrie; who, towards the end of January, visited him, on his way to his station at Chunar. Many a happy hour did these servants of Jesus Christ then pass, in fellowship with each other; for truly their fellowship was with the Father, and with his Son Jesus Christ. With one accord they often fell at the feet of their Redeemer in supplication and thanksgiving; they read his Holy Word, they rejoiced together in its promises, they spake to one another of the glory of Christ's kingdom, and talked of his power; and they parted, sorrowfully indeed, yet earnestly desiring each to be employed in his proper work. "Our communion," said Mr. Martyn, respecting this interview, "has been refreshing, at least to me; and the Lord has sanctified our meeting by his presence and his gracious influences."

With respect to the Europeans, amongst whom Mr. Martyn ministered, he had much reason to be gratified with the reception he met with from those whom he attended in the hospital; but he had equal cause to be dissatisfied and grieved with the behaviour which he witnessed, too generally, in the houses of the wealthy. Can we be surprised, therefore, that he should prefer, as he did, the house of mourning, to that of feasting? In vain did he endeavour, amongst the upper ranks, to introduce religious topics in conversation. "I spoke," he said, after visiting some of these, "several times about religion to them; but the manner in which it was received, damped all further attempt. 'Who hath believed our report, and to whom is the arm of the Lord revealed?' How awful does the thought sometimes appear to me, that almost the whole world are united against God and his Christ. O thou injured Sovereign! O Lord, how long will it be ere thou plead thine own cause, and make bare thine arm in the sight of the nations? Let me in patience possess my soul; and, though iniquity abound, may I never wax cold, but be brought safely through all this darkness and danger to a happier world! To thousands my word will, perhaps, prove a 'savour of death unto death.' Let me, nevertheless, go on steadily in the path which the Lord hath marked out. Perhaps some poor soul may be converted by what he shall hear from me; or, if not, I shall have done my work." In such society, as might be expected, he found his desires and endeavours for the conversion of the heathen invariably discountenanced and opposed. Having, on one occasion, referred to the Company's charter, as not only permitting, but even enjoining, the communication of religious instruction to the natives, coldness and distance, on the part of those he was visiting, were the immediate consequences of his observations. But "his soul could rejoice in God, that if men were unkind, it was for Christ's sake; and he felt determined to go on with vigour, though the whole world of wretched men should oppose."

With respect to the conversion of the natives to the *nominal* profession of Christianity, in Mr. Martyn's opinion, the difficulty was by no means great. He was surprised at the laxity of principle among them, and could well perceive that the idea of embracing the religion of the English was very pleasant to the Pundit, and to other Hindoos. But he did not fail to explain to them "that it was no object of his to make them 'Feringees,' in the sense in which they understood it; and assured them that if all the Brahmins and Rajahs of the country would come to him for baptism, he would not baptize them, except he believed that they repented, and would renounce the world."

With the condition of the natives in a moral point of

view, Mr. Martyn had but too much reason to be shocked and affected ; and he was sometimes called upon to interfere, and that with some personal hazard, to prevent acts of the greatest turpitude and injustice among them. "My Surdar," he says, "was imprisoned by an unjust Cotwal. I sent word to him to give nothing for his release, and not to fear : the Cotwal was afraid, and let the man go, and ceased his claim upon his relations. This has been a long and iniquitous business. I felt quite thankful that the Lord had thus shown Himself the Father of the fatherless. I could hardly believe such barefaced oppression. How much has the Gospel done in producing sentiments of justice and equity in all ranks of people in Christendom !—The poor people *here* seem unable to comprehend it." "——," he adds, "developed a system of villany carried on in the country, through the supineness of ——, which astonished and grieved me beyond measure. I determined to go to —— myself, and tell him what I had heard, but thought it prudent to defer it till after my distant journey to Buxar ; in which the Cotwal, who is the head of a gang of robbers, with which the whole country is swarming, might easily procure my assassination, if, by getting him turned out, I should provoke him. I thought it, however, a duty I owed to God, to him, to the poor oppressed natives, and to my country, to exert myself in this business; and I felt authorized to risk my life."

The journey to Buxar, during which Mr. Martyn feared that, without prudence, he might possibly become a victim to the sudden revenge of one whose daily oppressions caused many to weep without a comforter,—was taken on the 16th of February : and it may surprise those who are not aware of the very slender proportion of chaplains then allotted to our empire in India, to be informed that he travelled *seventy miles* for the purpose of performing part of his pastoral duty in the celebration of a marriage. But, before we attend him on this journey, let us notice his abstraction from the world; his sacred peace; his holy aspirations; his deep contrition at this period.—" I felt more entirely withdrawn from the world than for a long time past: what a dark, atheistical state do I generally live in! Alas! that this creation should so engross my mind, and the Author of it be so slightly and coldly regarded. I found myself, at this time, truly a stranger and a pilgrim on the earth; and I did suppose that not a wish remained for anything here. The experience of my heart was delightful. I enjoyed a peace that passeth all understanding; no desire remained, but that this peace might be confirmed and increased. Oh, why should anything draw away my attention, whilst Thou art ever near and ever accessible through the Son of Thy love? Oh, why do I not always walk with God, forgetful of a vain and perishable world? Amazing patience! He bears with this faithless, foolish heart, and suffers me to come, laden with sins, to receive new pardon, new grace, every day. Why does not such love make me hate those sins which grieve Him, and hide Him from my sight? I sometimes make vain resolutions, in my own strength, that I will think of God. Reason, and Scripture, and experience, teach me that such a life is happiness and holiness; that by 'beholding his glory,' I should be changed 'into his image, from glory to glory,' and be freed from those anxieties which make me unhappy; and that, every motive to duty being strong, obedience would be easy."

Of his journey to Buxar, Mr. Martyn has left the following account. "February 16.—Rose very early, and accumulated work for my Moonshee in my absence. Made my will, and left it with ——. At half-past three set off in a palanquin, and in four hours reached the Soane. From thence travelled all night, and at nine next morning reached Buxar. Being unable to sleep, I arrived so sick and unwell, as to be convinced of the unprofitableness of travelling by night in this country. By reading some of the Epistle to the Ephesians before it grew dark, and meditating upon it afterwards, my time passed agreeably : and I thought with delight of the time when I should be able to adopt the apostle's words with respect to the heathen around me. After breakfast I lay down, and endeavoured in vain to get sleep. I was much assisted in conversation with the family after dinner, when we conversed much on religious subjects ; and I had as good an opportunity as I could have wished of explaining the nature of the Gospel, and offering considerations for embracing it. I retired to rest with my heart full of joy, at being thus assisted to pass the time profitably."

Feb. 18.—"My birthday,—twenty-six. With all the numerous occasions for deep humiliation, I have cause for praise in recollecting the promising openings and important changes which have occurred since my last birthday. The Lord, in love, make me wax stronger and stronger ! Walked after breakfast to a pagoda within the fort at Buxar, where a Brahmin read and expounded. It was a scene, I suppose, descriptive of the ancient times of Hindoo glory. The Brahmin sat under the shade of a large banyan near the pagoda ; his hair and beard were white, and his head most gracefully crowned with a garland of flowers. A servant of the Rajah sat on his right hand, at right angles ; and the venerable man then sung the Sanscrit verses of the Huribuns, and explained them to him without turning his head, but only his eyes, which had a very dignified effect. I waited for the first pause to ask some questions, which led to a long conversation; and this ended by my attempting to give them a history of redemption. The Rajah's servant was a very modest, pensive man, but did not seem to understand what I said so well as the old Brahmin, who expressed his surprise and pleasure, as well as the other, at finding a Sahib who cared anything about religion. I afterwards sent a copy of the Nagree Gospels to the servant, desiring that it might be given to the Rajah if he would accept it. In the evening I married and administered the sacrament to —— and —— at their own desire."

Feb. 19.—"Rose at four and left Buxar, and at nine in the evening reached Dinapore in safety, blessed be God! May my life, thus preserved by his unceasing providence, be his willing sacrifice."

The scene Mr. Martyn witnessed in the pagoda at Buxar was succeeded, soon after his return to Dinapore, by another, which he describes as still more interesting. "A poor Jew from Babylon came to me begging. He was tall, but stooping from weakness, and his countenance strongly marked with grief. When, at his first arrival, I asked him if he was a Mussulman, he said in a low and pensive tone of voice, No! an Israelee. Alas! poor people, still full of the fury of the Lord, the rebuke of thy God! I felt all the tenderness of a kinsman towards him, and found myself, as it were, at home with an Asiatic who acknowledged the God of Abraham. The passage in Isaiah ix. 5, 6, he rendered as meaning the Almighty God."

The state of the schools, five of which at his own expense solely, Mr. Martyn had instituted in and about Dinapore, now began to occasion him some anxiety. An alarm was spread that it was his intention to seize upon all the children, and, in some compulsory manner, make them Christians. The school at Patna, in consequence, suddenly sunk in number, from forty children to eight; and at Dinapore, a spot of ground which had been fixed upon for the erection of a schoolroom, could not be obtained from the Zemindar. In this perplexity Mr. Martyn lost no time in ascertaining what a soothing, and at the same time sincere, explanation of his sentiments might effect; and for this purpose he went to Patna. There, in addition to his present perplexities, he had the severe pain of beholding a servant of the Company, a man advanced in years, and occupying a situation of great respectability, living in a state of daring apostacy from the Christian faith, and openly professing his preference for Mohammedanism. He had even built a mosque of his own, which at this season, being the Mohurrun, was adorned with flags; and being illuminated at night, proclaimed the shame of the offender. It will readily be supposed that Mr. Martyn did not fail to sound a warning voice in the ears of this miserable apostate; he charged him to "remember whence he was fallen," and exhorted him to consider that "the Son of God had died for sinners."

At the school at Patna, neither children nor teacher were to be found; all, as if struck by a panic, had absented themselves. The people, however, quickly gathered in crowds, and to them Mr. Martyn declared that his intentions had been misunderstood; when, such was the effect of temperate reasonings and mild expostulations, that all apprehensions were removed almost as quickly as they had been excited, and in a few days the children came as usual to the schools of Patna and Dinapore.

By February 24, a work was completed by Mr. Martyn, which, had he effected nothing else, would have proved that he had not lived in vain,—the translation of the Book of Common Prayer into Hindostanee; and on Sunday, March 15, he commenced the performance of Divine worship in the vernacular language of India, concluding with an exhortation from the Scripture in the same tongue. The spectacle was as novel as it was gratifying, to behold two hundred women,—Portuguese, Roman Catholics, and Mohammedans,—crowding to attend the service of the Church of England, which had lost nothing, doubtless, of its beautiful simplicity and devout solemnity in being clothed with an Oriental dress.

Toward the latter end of the month of March another useful work was also brought to a conclusion, that of a Commentary on the Parables. "The little book of the Parables," Mr. Martyn wrote to Mr. Corrie at this time, "is finished, through the blessing of God: I cannot say that I am very well pleased on the reperusal of it ; but yet, containing, as it does, such large portions of the Word of God, I ought not to doubt its accomplishing that which He pleaseth."

"Talking to the Moonshee," he says in his journal, of the probable effects of that work, "he cut me to the very heart by his contemptuous reflections on the Gospel; saying that, after the present generation was passed away, a race of fools might perhaps arise, who would try to believe that God could be a man, and man God, and

who would say that this is the word of God. One
advantage I may derive from his bitterness and disrespect is, that I shall be surprised at no appearances
of the same temper in others in future. May my Lord
enable me to maintain an invincible spirit of love ! How
sweet that glorious day when Jesus Christ shall reign !
Death at several times of this day appeared infinitely
sweet in this view of it,—that I shall then go to behold
the glory of Christ."

Mr. Martyn's duties on the Sabbath had now increased ;
—consisting of one service at seven in the morning to the
Europeans, another at two in the afternoon to the
Hindoos, and an attendance at the hospital : after
which, in the evening, he ministered privately at his
own rooms to those soldiers who were most seriously
impressed with a sense of divine things. From the following statement we may see and appreciate his exertions :—
" The English service, at seven in the morning. I
preached on Luke xxii. 22. As is always the case
when I preach about Christ, a spiritual influence was
diffused over my soul. The rest of the morning, till
dinner time, I spent not unprofitably in reading Scripture
and David Brainerd, and in prayer. That dear saint of
God, David Brainerd, is truly a man after my own heart.
Although I cannot go halfway with him in spirituality
and devotion, I cordially unite with him in such of his
holy breathings as I have attained unto. How sweet and
wise, like him and the saints of old, to pass through this
world as a serious and considerate stranger ! I have had
more of this temper to-day than of late, and every duty
has been in harmony with my spirit. The service in
Hindostanee was at two o'clock. The number of women
not above one hundred. I expounded chap. iii. of St.

Matthew. Notwithstanding the general apathy with
which they seemed to receive everything, there were two
or three who, I was sure, understood and felt something.
But, beside them, not a single creature, European or
native, was present. Yet true spirituality, with all its
want of attraction for the carnal heart, did prevail over
the splendid shows of Greece and Rome, and shall again
here. A man at the hospital much refreshed me, by
observing, that if I made an acquisition of but one convert
in my whole life, it would be a rich reward ; and that I
was taking the only possible way to this end. This man's
remark was much more sensible than ——'s yesterday,
who, it seems, had full information of my schools, &c., and
said that I should make no proselytes. 'Thy judgments
are far above out of their sight.' How positively they
speak, as if there were no God who could influence the
heart. At night B——, and S——, came, and we had
the usual service."

With those soldiers who attended Mr. Martyn always
on the evening of the Sabbath, and often on some other
evenings of the week, he enjoyed true spiritual communion. Their number was at first very small, amounting at the most to five ; sometimes, indeed, only one
could attend, but with him he would gladly unite in
prayer and praise, and in reading the Scriptures ; and
the presence of the Redeemer's gracious presence was
verified, to their abundant consolation.

Over some few of the officers stationed at Dinapore he
now began to rejoice, with that joy which those faithful
ministers alone can estimate, who, after much earnest
preaching and admonition, and after many prayers and
tears, at length perceive a fruitful result of their anxious
endeavours to win souls, and glorify their Lord. One of

these, "who from the first," to use Mr. Martyn's own
words, "had treated him with the kindness of a father,"
at this time excited expectations, which soon ripened into
a delightful certainty, that he had turned with full
purpose of heart to his Redeemer. But if Mr. Martyn's
happiness was great, in witnessing this effect of the Divine
blessing on his ministry ; so also was his anxiety, lest this
new convert should relapse, and walk again according to
the course of this world ; and he began, for the first time,
he said, in reference to him, to enter into the spirit of the
Apostle's words,—"Now we live, if ye stand fast in the
Lord."

To those ministerial duties in which he was now
engaged, Mr. Martyn considered that in prudence he
ought, for the present, to confine himself ;—had he
given way at once to the strong and full-flowing tide of his
zeal and love, it would immediately have carried him,
with the Bible in his hand, into the streets of Patna ;
though to have commenced his ministry in that idolatrous
city would, as he confesses to Mr. Corrie, have cost him
much. He wrote to Mr. C. in these ardent and energetic
terms :—"Oh that the time were come that I should be
able to carry the war into the enemy's territory. It will
be a severe trial to the flesh, my dear brother, for us
both,—but it is sufficient for the disciple to be as his
master, and the servant as his Lord. We shall be
'accounted as the filth of the world, and the off-scour-
ing of all things.' But glory be to God, if we shall
be accounted worthy to suffer shame for the name of
the Lord Jesus. The cause we undertake is, if possible,
more odious and contemptible in the eyes of the people of
this country than it was in the primitive times : and that
because of the misconduct of the Roman Catholic mission-

aries, in administering baptism to people without repentance. It is no more than natural, that 'Christian' should be a name of execration, to those who know no more of Christianity than what they have hitherto observed in this country."

To that unrestrained intercourse by letter, which Mr. Martyn held weekly with Mr. Corrie, he was indebted for much of the purest felicity of his life. Such a friend, stationed near him in such a country, he ranked amongst the richest blessings showered down upon him from on high. For—if we except his other brethren in India, with whom he statedly corresponded every quarter, and often also at other times, and never but with great delight—he had no one like-minded who could naturally care for the souls of the heathen ; but Mr. Corrie was of one heart with himself.

An interruption of this correspondence which now took place, painful as it was in itself to Mr. Martyn, was more so with respect to its cause. The military station at Chunar is considered more adverse to the constitution of an European than almost any other in India; and the heat, which in the month of March raised the thermometer at Dinapore to 92° in the shade, at Chunar was still more oppressively intense. Mr. Corrie's health began in consequence to be seriously affected, and many apprehensions for his most valuable life forced themselves upon the mind of Mr. Martyn.

The following extract of a letter written upon this occasion, shows Mr. Martyn's anxiety for his friend, and evinces also how fully he was alive to the necessity of subjecting the impetuosity of zeal to the discriminating correction of wisdom. "If there is nothing on the rock of Chunar which occasions your frequent illness, I am sure

I am not one to advise you to leave the flock. But if there is,—as I have much reason to believe,—then the mere loss of your services to the few people there is, I think, not sufficient reason for hazarding your life, in which the interests of millions of others are immediately involved. Consider, you bring a fixed habit of body with you, and must humour it as much as possible, at first. When, after the experience of a year or two, you know what you can bear, go, if you please, to the extent of your powers. It is not agreeable to the pride and self-righteous parts of our nature, to be conferring with flesh and blood : nature, under a religious form, would rather squander away life and strength, as David Brainerd did. You know that I regard him as one 'the latchet of whose shoes I am not worthy to unloose;' and yet, considering the palpable impropriety of his attempting to do what he did, when he ought to have been in medical hands,—and not being able to ascribe it to folly, in such a sensible man,—I feel disposed, perhaps from motives of censoriousness, to ascribe it to the desire of gaining his own good opinion." Then proceeding to the subject which lay so near both their hearts—the conversion of the heathen—he thus concludes, "I long to hear of a Christian school established at Benares : it will be like the ark of God brought into the house of Dagon. But do not be in a hurry : let your character become known, and you may do anything. If nothing else comes of our schools, one thing I feel assured of—that the children will grow up ashamed of the idolatry and other customs of their country. But surely the general conversion of the natives is not far off; the poverty of the Brahmins makes them less anxious for the continuance of the present system, from which they gain but little. But the translation of the Scriptures is the grand point. I trust we shall have the heavenly pleasure of dispersing the Scriptures together through the interior. Oh, the happiness and honour of being the children of God, the ministers of Christ!"

Mr. Martyn's own health, as well as that of his friend, was reduced at this time to a weak and languid state. To the debilitating effects of the heated atmosphere, this was, in part, perhaps, to be attributed; but it was certainly increased, if not induced, by his too severe abstinence. Most strictly did he observe the holy seasons set apart by the Church for fasting and prayer; but the illness under which he now laboured was so evidently aggravated, if not occasioned by abstinence, that he became convinced that the exercise of fasting was so injurious to his health as to be improper, in the degree and frequency in which he had been accustomed to use it.

In this sickness, however, though an extreme languor accompanied it, he was not only *patient*, but *active*. On the Sabbath he would by no means desist from his work. "I was assisted," he says, "to go through the usual ministrations without pain. In the morning I preached on Psalm xvi. 8, 10, and administered the Lord's Supper with rather more solemnity and feeling than I usually have. The rest of the morning I could do little but lie down. In the afternoon I found, I suppose, two hundred women, and expounded again at considerable length. Read the 'Pilgrim's Progress' at the hospital. In exposition with the soldiers I found great enlargement."

In proof of that wretchedness and ignorance in the natives which so excited Mr. Martyn's compassion for them, we may adduce two instances with which he himself has furnished us, in the cases of a Brahmin and a Ranee or native princess; though, perhaps, the Brahmin may be considered as only avowing sentiments too common amongst many who are yet called Christians, and have the Book of God in their hands. "A Brahmin," he says, "visiting my Pundit, copied out the parable in which the Ten Commandments were written, with a determination to put them all accurately into practice, in order to be united with God. He had, however, an observation to make, and a question to ask. 'There was nothing,' he said, 'commanded to be *done*, only things to be *abstained from ;* and if he should be taken ill in the bazaar, or while laughing, and die ; and, through fear of transgressing the third commandment, should not mention the name of God, should he go to heaven ?' The Ranee of Daoud-nagur, to whom I had sent a copy of the Gospels by the Pundit, returned her compliments, and desired to know what must be done for obtaining benefit from the Book ; whether prayer, or making a salaam (a bow) to it ? I sent her word that she must seek Divine instruction by secret prayer, and I also added some other advice."

Little as there appeared of a promising nature in either of these characters, there was yet more of what might be thought hopeful in them, than in Mr. Martyn's Moonshee and Pundit, whom he still continued to labour incessantly, though unsuccessfully, to convince of their awful errors.

"My faith," he complains again, "is tried by many things ; especially by disputes with the Moonshee and the Pundit. The Moonshee shows remarkable contempt for the doctrine of the Trinity. 'It shows God to be weak,' he says, 'if He is obliged to have a fellow. God was not obliged to become man, for if we had all perished, He would have suffered no loss. And as to pardon, and the difficulty of it, I pardon my servant very easily, and there is an end. As to the Jewish Scriptures, how do I know but that they were altered by themselves? They were wicked enough to do it, just as they made a calf.' In all these things, I answered so fully that he had nothing to reply."—"In the afternoon I had a long argument again with the Pundit. He, too, wanted to degrade the Person of Jesus, and said that neither Brahma, Vishnu, nor Siva were so low as to be born of a woman; and that every sect wished to exalt its teacher, and so the Christians did Jesus."

March 14.—"The quotations which I collected from Scripture this day, in treating on the Parable of the Inconsiderate King, in order to illustrate the idea of the sufferings to which Christians are exposed, seemed to offend both the Moonshee and the Pundit very much. In considering the text,—' The time cometh when he that killeth you shall think he doeth God service,' he defended the practice of putting Infidels to death, and the certainty of salvation to Moslems dying in battle with the Infidels; and said that it was no more strange than for a magistrate to have power to put an offender to death. He took occasion also to say, that both the New Testament, as we gave it, and the Church Service also, were stuffed with blasphemies. With the benighted Pundit I had a long conversation, as he seemed to be more in earnest than I had yet seen him. He asked whether, by receiving the Gospel, he should see God in a visible shape; because, he said, he had seen Sargoon the deity made visible : this he affirmed with great gravity and earnestness. At night I lost time and temper in disputing with the Moonshee, respecting the lawfulness of putting men to death for blasphemy. He began by cavilling at the Lord's Prayer, and ridiculing it, particularly the expression, 'Hallowed be thy name,' as if the name of the Deity was not already holy. He said that 'prayer was not a duty amongst the Mohammedans ; that reading the Numaz was merely the praise of God ; and that, as when a servant, after doing his master's duty well, thought it a favourable opportunity for asking a favour, so the Moslem, after doing his duty, might ask of God riches, or a son, or, if he pleased, patience in affliction.' This, then, is Mohammedanism,— to murder, as Infidels, the children of God, and to live without prayer."

"The conversation with the Pundit was more serious than it has yet been ; and I find that seriousness in the declaration of the truths of the Gospel is likely to have more power, than the clearest argument conveyed in a trifling spirit. I told him, that now he had heard the Word of Christ, he would not be tried at the Last Day by the same law as the other Brahmins and Hindoos, who had never heard it, but in the same manner as myself and other Christians ; and that I feared, therefore, that he was in great danger. He said, as usual, that there were many ways to God ; but I replied that there was no other Saviour than Christ, because no other had bought men with his blood, and suffered their punishment for them. This effectually silenced him on that head. He then said, that 'he had a house and children, and that to preserve them he must retain the favour of the world ; that he and his friends despised idol-worship, but that the world would call him wicked if he forsook the service of the gods.'"

"My Pundit grieved me, by showing that he knew no more of the way of salvation than before. Alas ! how poor and contemptible are all my efforts for God, if efforts they can be called. He observed, that 'there was nothing express in the Book about the way of salvation, or as to *what one must do* to be saved,'—the legalist's question in every land."

"My Pundit observed, that I had said that forgiveness would not be given for repentance only; whereas, in the third Parable, in chap. xv. of St. Luke, the repentant sinner was received at once. How could this be? For his part, he would rest his hope on the Parables, in preference to the other statements. How strange is the reluctance which men have to depend on the righteousness of another! He affirmed, that he was keeping all the commandments of God. But when I charged him with worshipping the sun at his morning devotions, he confessed it, and said that it was not forbidden in the Ten Commandments. I then read him the passages relating to the worship of the host of heaven, but he could see no harm in this species of worship more than in making his salam to any other superior. With respect to the Sabbath, he said, that he had always kept that day by fasting, and that all Hindoos did the same; but that no reason was given in the Shaster why it was holy."

"Talking with the Moonshee on the old subjects,—the divinity of Christ, Mahomet's challenge, &c.,—he did not know of the system of the Mohammedan Doctors, that one passage abrogates another, but said, that if I could produce two commandments undeniably opposite, he would throw away the book, and seek a new religion. Respecting the promise of Mahomet, that they who died fighting for Islam should certainly go to heaven, I said, that my objection was, that the person thus dying might be full of envy, &c.; and could such a person go to God? In answer to this, he denied that the sins of the heart were sins at all, and I could say nothing to convince him that they were. To refute what he had said at some former times, about Mussulmen not remaining in hell for ever, I applied our Saviour's parable of the servant beaten with many stripes, and asked him, 'If I had two servants, one of whom knew my will, and the other did not, and both committed the same fault,—which was the more culpable?' He answered, 'I suppose, he who knew his master's will.' I replied, 'Yet, according to you, the enlightened Mussulmen are to come out of hell, while Jews and Christians, for the same sin, are to remain there for ever.' He had not a word to reply, but said he could give no answer, 'uglee,' but only 'nuglee,'—contradicting it on the authority of the Koran. He spoke of the ineffectual endeavours of men to root out Islamism, as a proof of its being from God; and objected to Christianity, because there were no difficulties in it,—devotion only once a-week,—prayer or no prayer, just when or where we pleased,—eating with or without washing; and that, in general, it was a life of carelessness with us."

Toward the middle of the month of April, another summons, similar to that which had carried Mr. Martyn to Buxar, called him from his studies and labours at Dinapore, to Monghir. Not long before he undertook this expedition, we find him thus expressing himself, after an examination into the state of his heart before God :—

"My mind much as usual, not tried by any violent assault of sin or Satan ; but the daily cause of grief and shame, and indeed the root of all sin, is forgetfulness of God. I perceive not in what state I have been till I come to pray."—"Enjoyed a greater stability of faith in the Divine Redeemer. May He make his servant steady,

brave, and vigilant in his service!"—"Satan assaults me
in various ways. Some of his temptations, respecting
the person of my Lord, were dreadfully severe; but he
triumphed not a moment. I am taught by these things
to see what would become of me if God should withdraw
his mighty hand. Is there any depth into which Satan
would not plunge me?"

"My soul is sometimes tried with the abounding of
iniquity, and wounded by infidel thoughts. But my
Redeemer has risen triumphant, and will not suffer his
feeble servant to be tempted above what he is able
to bear."—"If there is one thing that refreshes my soul
above all others, it is that I shall behold the Redeemer
gloriously triumphant, at the winding-up of all things. O
Thou injured Sovereign, how long dost Thou bear this
ingratitude from wicked mankind!"

"Still permitted to find sweet refuge, in the presence
of my Lord, from infidelity, and from the proud world,
and the vanities of time."

"In prayer had an affecting sense of my shameful ingratitude. Had I behaved thus to an earthly benefactor,
showing so little regard for his company and his approbation,—how should I abhor myself and be abhorred by
all! Oh, what a God is our God! How astonishingly
rich in grace, bearing all with unceasing patience, and
doing nothing but crowning his sinful creature with loving-kindness and tender mercies."

"This is the day on which I left Cambridge. My
thoughts frequently recurred, with many tender recollections, to that seat of my beloved brethren; and I again
wandered in spirit amongst the trees on the banks of the
Cam."

"Employed in writing a sermon, and translating; but

heavenly things become less familiar to my mind whilst I am so employed without intermission. Yet the whole desire of my heart is towards spiritual enjoyment. Oh, when shall body, soul, and spirit, be all duly employed for God!"

"Dull and poor as my miserable soul is, and thinking very little about heaven, yet, for aught else that is in this world, existence is scarcely worth having. The world seems as empty as air."

On the 18th of April, Mr. Martyn commenced his voyage of nearly a hundred miles to Monghir. The following is an extract from his journal during the eight days that were consumed in thus leaving his station to marry a couple, and in returning afterwards to Dinapore.

"After finishing the correction of the Parables, I left Dinapore to go to Monghir. Spent the evening at Patna with Mr. G——, in talking on literary subjects; but my soul was overwhelmed with a sense of my guilt in not striving to lead the conversation to something that might be for his spiritual good. My general backwardness to speak on spiritual subjects before the unconverted, made me groan in spirit at such unfeelingness and unbelief. May the remembrance of what I am made to suffer for these neglects be one reason for greater zeal and love in the time to come."

April 19.—"A melancholy Lord's-day! In the morning, at the appointed hour, I found some solemnity and tenderness; the whole desire of my soul seemed to be, that all the ministers in India might be eminently holy, and that there might be no remains of that levity or indolence in any of us which I found in myself. The rest of the day passed heavily, for a hurricane of hot wind fastened us on a sand-bank for twelve hours; whilst the dust was suffocating, and the heat increased the sickness which was produced by the tossing of the boat, and I frequently fell asleep over my work. However, the more I felt tempted to impatience and unhappiness, the more the Lord helped me to strive against it, and to look to the fulness of Jesus Christ. Several hymns, particularly

" 'There is a fountain filled with blood,'

were very sweet to me. After all the acquisitions of human science, what is there to be compared with the knowledge of Christ, and him crucified ?—Read much of the Scripture history of Saul, and the predictions in the latter end of the Revelation. Read also Marshall on Sanctification, Gibert's Sermons, and Thomas à Kempis."

April 20.—" A day very little better. I could scarcely keep myself alive, and was much tried by evil temper. Employed in writing to ——, and Mr. —— ; but all I did was without energy: the long-wished-for night came at last, and my feeble body found rest and restoration in sleep."

April 21.—" Again the love and mercy of the Lord restored me to health and spirits. Began to write a sermon on walking in Christ, and found my soul benefited by meditation on the subject. In the afternoon went on with translations. Arrived at sun-set at Monghir."

April 22.—" Spent the day at ——'s. Found two or three opportunities to speak to him about his soul. —— threw out some infidel sentiments, which gave me an opportunity of speaking. But to none of the rest was I able to say anything. Alas ! in what a state are mankind everywhere; living without God in the world. Married —— to ——."

April 23.—"After baptizing a child of ——'s, I left Monghir, and got on twenty-three miles toward Dinapore: very sorrowful in mind, both from the recollection of having done nothing for the perishing souls I have been amongst, and from finding myself so unqualified to write on a spiritual subject which I had undertaken. Alas! the ignorance and carnality of my miserable soul! how contemptible must it be in the sight of God!"

April 24.—"Still cast down at my utter inability to write anything profitable on this subject, and at my execrable pride and ease of heart. O that I could weep in the dust, with shame and sorrow, for my wickedness and folly! Yet, thanks are due to the Lord for showing me, in this way, how much my heart has been neglected of late. I see by this, how great are the temptations of a missionary to neglect his own soul. Apparently outwardly employed for God, my heart has been growing more hard and proud. Let me be taught that the first great business on earth is to obtain the sanctification of my own soul; so shall I be rendered more capable also of performing the duties of the ministry, whether amongst the European or heathen, in a holy and solemn manner. Oh, how I detest that levity to which I am so subject! How cruel and unfeeling is it! God is my witness that I would rather, from this day forward, weep day and night, for the danger of immortal souls. But my wickedness seems to take such hold of me, that I cannot escape; and my only refuge is to commit my soul, with all its corruption, into the hands of Christ, to be sanctified and saved by His Almighty grace. For what can I do with myself? my heart is so thoroughly corrupt, that I cannot keep myself one moment from sin.—Finished the Koran to-day, and considered within myself, why I rejected it as an imposition, and the reasons appeared clear and convincing."

" The budgerow struck with such violence against a sand-bank, that a poor Mohammedan boy, falling with all the rest, broke his arm. We did all that we could, but the cries of the poor boy went through my heart. At night a tremendous north-wester came on, but the Lord kept us in safety."

April 25.—" The morning employed, with little success, on the same subject. I still find it too spiritual for my carnal heart. My mind distressed with doubts whether I shall make the people observe the Sabbath by causing them to lie by ; but on considering that they would not think it a favour, but, on the contrary, a vexation,—that they could not sanctify it, and that I had not given the mangee notice before setting out, I resolved to go on, though I felt by no means easy. Before setting out again, I hope to make up my mind satisfactorily on this subject."

April 26.—" In prayer at the appointed hour. I felt solemnity of mind, and an earnest desire that the Lord would pour out a double portion of his Spirit upon us his ministers in India, that every one of us may be eminent in holiness and ministerial gifts. If I were to judge for myself, I should fear that God had forsaken his Church, for I am most awfully deficient in the knowledge and experience requisite for a minister; but my dear brother Corrie, thanks be to God, is a man of a better spirit,— may he grow more and more in grace, and continue to be an example to us all. Passed the day in reading and prayer, such as my prayers are. My soul struggled with corruption, yet I found the merit and grace of Jesus all-sufficient and all-supporting. Though my guilt seemed like mountains, I considered it as no reason for departing from Christ, but rather for clinging to Him more closely. Thus I got through the day, cast down but not destroyed. The account of David's fall affected me more tenderly than ever it did, and I could not help weeping over the fall of that man of God. Began Scott's Essays, and was surprised indeed at the originality and vigour of the sentiments and language. At eight arrived at Patna."

April 27.—" Left Patna and arrived at Dinapore. The concourse of people in that great city was a solemn admonition to me to be diligent in study and prayer. Thousands of intelligent people together;—no Sabbath, no word of God, no one to give them advice : how inscrutable the ways of God!"

Mr. Martyn had no sooner returned to Dinapore than he heard, to his sorrow and surprise, that the Ranee, to whom he had sent a Testament, together with some advice upon the subject of religion, was about to despatch a messenger to him to request a letter of recommendation to one of the judges, before whom she had a cause pending in which her dominions were at stake. "I felt hurt," he says, "at considering how low a sovereign princess must have fallen to make such a request, but lost no time in apprising her that our laws were perfectly distinct from the Divine laws; and that, therefore, this was no affair of mine, as she seemed to suppose it to be."

In Mr. Martyn's schools so much progress had now been made, that it became necessary to determine what books should be placed in the hands of the children who could read. To give them at first the book of the Parables which he had prepared for their use, would, it was feared, awaken suspicion in the breasts of their parents, who had already shown much jealousy respecting his designs. He therefore deemed it the wisest measure to permit them to use one of the Hindoo books, after having had it previously read to him. It was a book which, if it did no good, could, he thought, do no harm, as it was an old Hinduwee poem, on an Avater of Vishnu, which it was impossible for the children to understand.

His judgment on this question,—one of some difficulty and embarrassment,—is thus given in a letter to Mr. Corrie:—" Your schools flourish; blessed be God ! The Dinapore school is resorted to from all quarters, even from the other side of the river. The Bankipore school is also going on well. I do not institute more till I see the Christian books introduced. The more schools the more noise, and the more inquiry, and the greater suspicion of its being of a political nature. Besides, if all the schools were to come to a demur together, I fear their deciding against us; but if one or two schools, with much thought about it, comply with our wishes, it will be a precedent and example to others. I think you should not dictate which of their books should be given, but only reserve the power of rejecting, amongst those which they propose. I bless God that you are brought to act with me on a broad and cautious plan; but I trust our motto will be, 'constant, though cautious,'—never ceasing to keep our attention steadily fixed on the state of things, and being swift to embrace every opportunity."

Amidst many causes of discouragement,—from the inattention of the women who attended his expositions on the Sabbath,—the general profanation of that holy day by Europeans, notwithstanding his solemn and repeated remonstrances,—and the vacillating conduct of some of his flock, whom he had hoped to have seen stronger and bolder in their Master's cause,—a letter from a young officer, desiring at this time an acquaintance with Mr. Martyn on a religious account, was to him a source of the most cheering delight. And yet, even before the receipt of it, he could bless God that he "felt impregnable to any discouragement." "It was not," said he, "that I was indifferent, or that I saw some encouraging circumstances, but I was made to reflect that I was the servant of God in these things, and that He would surely bring his purposes to pass in some way or other."

In addition to Mr. Martyn's studies in Sanscrit, Persian, and Hindostanee, we find him now sedulously employed in reading Leland against the deistical writers ; and thence drawing out arguments against the Koran. But being fearful lest, in the midst of these pursuits, his spirit should decline as to more important points, he thus speaks :—"May my soul, in prayer, never rest satisfied without the enjoyment of God ! May all my thoughts be fixed on Him ! May I sit so loose to every employment here, that I may be able, at a moment's warning, to take my departure for another world ! May I be taught to remember that all other studies are merely subservient to the great work of ministering holy things to immortal souls ! May the most holy works of the ministry, and those which require most devotedness of soul, be the most dear to my heart ! "

Mr. Martyn, whilst thus occupied, was called to the decision of a practical question of greater moment and difficulty than that respecting the introduction of books into the schools ;—application having been made to him for baptism by one of the native women. This request, as the candidate manifested no signs of penitence or faith, and could by no means be made to comprehend that anything further was necessary to constitute a Christian, than to say the Lord's Prayer,—he found himself compelled to refuse. "The party," he writes, "went away in great distress, and I felt much for them ; but the Lord, I trust, will not suffer me to listen to my own feelings, and profane his holy ordinances." That this point had been a matter of anxious consideration with him, we learn from a letter to Mr. Corrie. "Your account of a native woman whom you baptized, came in season for me ; I have been subjected to similar perplexities ; but I think no one could refuse baptism in the case you mention. The woman who is now making the same petition here promises to marry, and comes frequently for instruction, but her heart is not touched with any tender sense of sin, or of her need of mercy. Yet if there be no scandal in her life, and she profess her belief on those points on which candidates are interrogated in the baptismal service, may I lawfully refuse ? I cannot tell what to do ; but I seem almost resolved not to administer the ordinance till convinced in my own mind of the true repentance of the person. The eventual benefit will be great, if we both steadily adhere to this purpose ; they will see that our Christians and those of the Papists are different ; and will be led to investigate what it is, which, in our opinion, is wanted." The determination to reject those candidates for admission into the Church of England, who were manifestly ignorant of the spirit of Christianity, though convinced of the truth of it, was fully adopted by Mr. Martyn, after mature consideration ; and the decision was doubtless agreeable to the word of God, and to the practice of the primitive times.

Much time, as we have already seen, had been devoted

by Mr. Martyn to the translation of the Scriptures into Hindostanee ; both before and after he quitted Calcutta. To these exertions for the honour and glory of God, a new stimulus was added, in the month of June in this year, by a proposal from the Rev. David Brown, that he would engage more directly in that important work, in which he had already proceeded to the end of the Acts of the Apostles ; and, also, that he would superintend the translation of the Scriptures into Persian. This proposal he eagerly, yet diffidently, accepted ;—and, animated by the expectation of beholding his labours brought to a successful termination, he prosecuted them with a delight commensurate with his ardent diligence.

"The time fled imperceptibly," he observes, "while so delightfully engaged in the translations ; the days seemed to have passed like a moment. Blessed be God for some improvement in the languages ! May everything be for edification in the Church ! What do I not owe to the Lord, for permitting me to take part in a translation of his word : never did I see such wonder and wisdom and love in that blessed book, as since I have been obliged to study every expression ; and it is a delightful reflection, that death cannot deprive us of the pleasure of studying its mysteries."

"All day on the translations :—employed a good while at night in considering a difficult passage ; and being much enlightened respecting it, I went to bed full of astonishment at the wonders of God's word : never before did I see anything of the beauty of the language, and the importance of the thoughts, as I do now. I felt happy that I should never be finally separated from the contemplation of them, or of the things concerning which they are written. Knowledge shall vanish away, but it shall be because perfection shall come. Then shall I see as I am seen, and know as I am known."

"What a source of perpetual delight have I in the precious book of God! O that my heart were more spiritual, to keep pace with my understanding; and that I could feel as I know! May my root and foundation be deep in love, and may I be able to ' comprehend, with all saints, what is the breadth, and length, and depth, and height, and to know the love of Christ which passeth knowledge!' And may I be filled with all the fulness of God!" He adds, in his accustomed spirit of incessant watchfulness,—" May the Lord, in mercy to my soul, save me from setting up an idol of any sort in his place; as I do by preferring even a work professedly done for Him, to communion with Him. How obstinate is the reluctance of the natural heart to love God! But, O my soul, be not deceived; thy chief work upon earth is to obtain sanctification, and to walk with God. ' To obey is better than sacrifice, and to hearken than the fat of rams.' Let me learn from this, that to follow the direct injunctions of God, as to my own soul, is more my duty than to be engaged in other works, under pretence of doing Him service."

CHAPTER VII.

SCARCELY had Mr. Martyn girded up his loins with the great and heavenly design of completing a version of the scriptures in Hindostanee, and of superintending one in the Persian tongue,—when the sovereign, wise, and infinite love of his God summoned him to endure an affliction, more grievous than any which had befallen him since those first bitter tears which he shed at the death of his father. Apprehensions of the loss of his eldest sister had been excited in his mind, by some expressions she herself had dropped, in a letter which reached him a few weeks before he received the fatal intelligence that she was no more. A period of torturing suspense terminated in one of inexpressible sorrow. But "blessed is the man whom thou chastenest, O Lord." Gleams of this blessedness shone forth from the clouds of that dark dispensation with which Mr. Martyn was now visited. "O my heart, my heart," he exclaimed, "is it, can it be true, that she has been lying so many months in the cold grave ! Would that I could always remember it, or always forget it ;—but to think for a moment of other things, and then to feel the remembrance of it coming, as if for the first time, rends my heart asunder. When I look round upon the creation, and think that her eyes see it not, but have closed upon it for ever,—that I lie down in my bed, but that she has lain down in her grave,—Oh ! is it possible ! I wonder to find myself still in life ;—that the same tie which united us in life, has not brought death at the same moment to both. O great and gracious God ! what should I do without Thee ! But now thou art manifesting thyself as the God of all consolation to my soul ;—never was I so near Thee :—I stand on the brink, and long to take my flight. There is not a thing in the world for which I could wish to live, except the hope that it may please God to appoint me some work. And how shall my soul ever be thankful enough to Thee, O thou most incomprehensibly glorious Saviour Jesus ! O what hast thou done to alleviate the sorrows of life ! and how great has been the mercy of God towards my family, in saving us all ! How dreadful would be the separation of relations in death, were it not for Jesus ! "

Mr. Martyn's mind, under this painful deprivation, was exceedingly comforted by a sure and certain hope, as it respected her for whom he mourned. That delightful expectation of meeting her in glory, which she has now realized, was one powerful support to his heart, then overwhelmed within him : for the letter which contained the account of his loss, happily left him no room to doubt of his sister's eternal gain ; and that, through the grave and gate of death, she had passed into the consummation of bliss, in the eternal and everlasting kingdom of Christ.

"The European letter," he wrote to Mr. Brown, " contained the intelligence of the death of my eldest sister. A few lines received from herself about three weeks ago, gave me some melancholy forebodings of her danger. But though the Lord thus compassionately prepared me for this affliction, I hardly knew how to bear it. We were more united in affection to each other, than to any of our relations : and now she is gone, I am left to fulfil as a hireling my day, and then I shall follow her. She had been many years under some conviction of her sins, but not till her last illness had she sought in earnest for salvation. Some weeks before her death she felt the burden of sin, and cried earnestly for pardon and deliverance ; and continued in the diligent use of the appointed means of grace. Two days before her death,—when no immediate danger was apprehended,—my youngest sister visited her ; and was surprised and delighted at the change which had taken place. Her convictions of sin were deep, and her views clear ; her only fear was on account of her own unworthiness. She asked, with many tears, whether there was mercy for one who had been so great a sinner ;— though in the eyes of the world she had been an exemplary wife and mother ; and said that she believed the Lord would have mercy upon her, because she knew he had wrought on her mind by His Spirit. Two days after this conversation, she suddenly and unexpectedly left this world of woe, while her sister was visiting a dying friend at a distance. This, you will tell me, is precious consolation ; indeed I am constrained to acknowledge that I could hardly ask for greater ; for I had already parted with her for ever in this life ; and, in parting, all I wished for, was, to hear of her being converted to God ; and, if it was His will, taken away in due time, from the evil to come ; and brought to glory before me. Yet human nature bleeds ;—her departure has left this world a frightful blank to me ; and I feel not the smallest wish to live, except there be some work assigned for me to do in the church of God."

Acutely as Mr. Martyn suffered, such importance did he attach to those studies which had in view the manifestation of the gospel to regions " sitting in darkness and the shadow of death," that he omitted the prosecution of them, at this period, only for a single day. It was a duty, he thought, incumbent on him, to return to his work as soon as possible, however heavily his mind might be burdened; but his expressions many days afterwards declare into what depths of grief he was sunk. " My heart," said he, " is still oppressed, but it is not ' a sorrow that worketh death.' Though nature weeps at being deprived of all hopes of ever seeing this dear companion on earth ; faith is thereby brought the more into exercise. How sweet to feel dead to all below ; to live only for eternity ; to forget the short interval that lies between us and the spiritual world ; and to live always *seriously*.— The *seriousness* which this sorrow produces, is indescribably precious ; O that I could always retain it, when these impressions shall be worn away ! My studies have been the Arabic grammar, and Persian ;—writing Luke for the women, and dictating 1 Peter i. to my Moonshee. Finished the Gulistan of Sadi, and began it again in order to mark all the phrases which may be of use in the translation of the scriptures."

One fruit of Mr. Martyn's prayers, and result of his prudence, was, the successful introduction into his schools, shortly after this, of the Sermon on the Mount ; and on the 21st of September he had the exquisite joy of hearing the poor heathen boys reading the words of the Lord Jesus. " A wise man's heart," saith Solomon, " discerneth

both time and judgment." It was in this spirit of patient
and dependent wisdom that Mr. Martyn had acted respecting the schools ; and it was the same rare temper of mind
which prevailed on him still to abstain from preaching
publicly to the natives ; again and again did he burn to
begin his ministry in Patna ; but again and again did he
feel deeply the importance of not being precipitate. It
was not, however, without much difficulty that he checked
the ardour of his zeal. He was determined to see what
the institution of schools, and the quiet distribution of the
Scriptures would effect, and was convinced that public
preaching *at first* was incompatible with his plan of procedure ; whereas it was clear that a way would thus be
opened for preaching, of which object he never lost sight.
It was this which made him resist the solicitations of those
friends who would have detained him at Calcutta ; and
this it was which now occasioned him to decline a very
pressing invitation from Mr. Brown, urging him to take
the Mission Church at the Presidency. Dinapore was in
the midst of the heathen ; and Dinapore, further, was a
scene of tranquil retirement. These two considerations
caused Mr. Martyn to refuse to comply with the very
earnest desire of one whom he entirely esteemed and
loved. "If ever I am fixed at Calcutta," he wrote in
reply, "I have done with the natives ; for, whatever
might be my previous determination, the churches and
people at Calcutta are enough to employ twenty ministers.
This is one reason for my apparently unconquerable
aversion to being fixed there. The happiness of being
near and with you and your dear family would not be a
compensation for this disappointment ; and having said
this, I know of no stronger method of expressing my

dislike to the measure. If God commands it, I trust I shall have grace to obey; but let me beseech you all to take no step towards it, for I shall resist it as long as I can with a safe conscience."

"I am happier here in this remote land," he wrote in his journal, "where I hear so seldom of what happens in the world, than in England, where there are so many calls to look at 'the things that are seen.' How sweet the retirement in which I here live! The precious Word is now my only study, in the work of translation. Though, in a manner, buried to the world,—neither seeing nor seen by Europeans,—the time flows on here with great rapidity: it seems as if life would be gone before anything is done, or even before anything is begun. I sometimes rejoice that I am not twenty-seven years of age; and that, unless God should order it otherwise, I may double the number in constant and successful labour. If not, God has many, many more instruments at command; and I shall not cease from my happiness, and scarcely from my work, by departing into another world. Oh, what shall separate us from the love of Christ! Neither death nor life, I am persuaded. Oh, let me feel my security, that I may be, as it were, already in heaven; that I may do all my work as the angels do theirs; and oh, let me be ready for every work!—be ready to leave this delightful solitude, or remain in it,—to go out, or go in,—to stay, or depart, just as the Lord shall appoint. Lord, let me have no will of my own; nor consider my true happiness as depending in the smallest degree on anything that can befal my outward man; but as consisting altogether in conformity to God's will. May I have Christ here with me in this world; not substituting imagination in the place of faith; but seeing outward things as they really are, and thus obtaining a radical conviction of their vanity."

Mr. Martyn's spirits being much depressed by his recent affliction, an invitation, or rather entreaty, so strongly pressed upon him by one who had a great share in his affection and esteem,—but which called, as he conceived, for a direct and firm rejection,—could not but be a matter of some disquiet to him.   He had not, however, the additional pain of witnessing the slightest variation in his friend's attachment : a circumstance which does not always occur on similar occasions : for the fondness even of Christian friendship will sometimes suffer an interruption, from a disagreement respecting favourite projects and designs.

To this perturbation of mind, comparatively light, a very severe disappointment from another quarter succeeded ; a disappointment intended, doubtless, like his other troubles, for the augmentation of his faith.   Such strong representations had been made by those whose judgment he highly valued, respecting the dreariness of a distant station in India, and the evils of solitude, that he had deemed it agreeable to the will of God to make an overture of marriage to her, for whom time had increased rather than diminished his affection.   This overture, for reasons which afterwards commended themselves to Mr. Martyn's own judgment, was now declined ; on which occasion, suffering sharply as a man, but most meekly as a Christian, he said, "The Lord sanctify this ; and, since this last desire of my heart is also withheld, may I turn away for ever from the world, and henceforth live, forgetful of all but God.   With Thee, O my God, is no disappointment.   I shall never have to regret that I have loved Thee too well.   Thou hast said, 'Delight thyself in the Lord, and he shall give thee the desires of thy heart.' " *

"At first I was more grieved," he wrote some time afterwards, "at the loss of my gourd, than for all the perishing Ninevehs around me; but now my earthly woes and earthly attachments seem to be absorbing in the vast concern of communicating the Gospel to these nations. After this last lesson from God, on the vanity of the creature, I feel desirous to be nothing, to have nothing, to ask for nothing, but what He gives."

Providentially for Mr. Martyn's comfort, his thoughts were much occupied, just after the receipt of this letter, by the arrival of his coadjutors in the work of translation ; one of them, Mirza, of Benares, well known in India, as an eminent Hindostanee scholar ; the other, Sabat, the Arabian, since but too well known, both in India and England, by his rejection of that faith, which he then appeared to profess in sincerity and truth. In the latter of these, Mr. Martyn confidently trusted that he had found a Christian brother. Nor were these hopes respecting Sabat's religious character more sanguine than both in reason and charity he might fairly have entertained. Of his abilities a most favourable report had been made by Dr. Kerr, of Madras, who represented him as a man of good family in Arabia,—as having been employed as an expounder of Mohammedan law, at Masulipatam,—and as being well skilled in the literature of his country. With respect to the reality of his belief in Christianity, although Mr. Martyn immediately discovered in him an unsubdued Arab spirit, and witnessed, with pain, many deflections from that temper and conduct which he himself so eminently exemplified, yet he could

* See Appendix VI.

not but 'believe all things, and hope all things,' even while he continued to suffer much from him, and, for a length of time, with unparalleled forbearance and kindness. How could he allow himself to cherish any doubt, when he beheld the tears he shed in prayer, and listened to the confessions he made of his sinfulness, and to the professions he uttered of his willingness to correct whatever was reprehensible in his behaviour. No sooner had he arrived at Dinapore, than he opened to Mr. Martyn the state of his mind; declaring, with seeming contrition, that the constant sin he found in his heart filled him with fear. "If the spirit of Christ is given to believers, why," said he, "am I thus, after three years' believing? I determine, every day, to keep Christ crucified in sight; but soon I forget to think of Him. I can rejoice, when I think of God's love in Christ; but then I am like a sheep that feeds happily, whilst he looks only at the pasturage before him, but when he looks behind and sees the lion, he cannot eat." "His life," he avowed, "was of no value to him; the experience he had had of the instability of the world had weaned him from it; his heart was like a looking-glass, fit for nothing except to be given to the glass-maker to be moulded anew." Can we wonder, concerning one who uttered, with apparent sincerity and much earnestness, sentiments such as these,—that Mr. Martyn should observe to Mr. Brown, who had sent him from Calcutta to Dinapore, that "not to esteem him a monument of grace, and to love him, is impossible." And truly, notwithstanding all that time has since developed, who will not hesitate in attributing to Sabat the guilt of a systematic and well-concerted tissue of hypocrisy; and prefer to conclude that his judgment was at that time enlightened, and his heart in some measure impressed with a sense of what he believed? Very soon, indeed, was Mr. Martyn called to rejoice over this Mohammedan convert with great fear and trembling; for scarcely had he reached Dinapore, when the violence of his temper began to manifest itself. The first Sunday after his arrival, on coming to church, conceiving that all due respect was not shown him, he would not wait till service began, but abruptly left the church and returned home; yet, on Mr. Martyn's expostulations on his turning his back upon the house of God, on account of an insult which was unintended, he instantly confessed, with seeming humiliation, that he had two dispositions; the one, his old one, which was a soldier's, and the other a Christian's.

Many other signs of an unhumbled spirit in Sabat gave rise to differences which were singularly distressing to a man of such meekness as Mr. Martyn. Even before the conclusion of that year, which when Sabat entered under Mr. Martyn's roof was drawing to a close, he was so grieved at his spirit, that he could find relief only in prayer for him. Yet, however disquieted he might and could not but be, at what he was called hourly to witness, in one brought into such near contact with him, and bearing the name of a Christian brother, his own mind, nevertheless, enjoyed a large measure of "that perfect peace" in which those are kept whose minds are stayed on God. He was continually "rejoicing in the solid ground of Jesus' imputed righteousness,"—the greatness, the magnificence, the wisdom of which filled his mind; and he was continually thinking, "Oh! how is every hour lost that is not spent in the love and contemplation of God, my God. Oh, send out Thy light and Thy truth, that I may live always sincerely, always affectionately towards Thee!" "To live without sin, I cannot expect in this world; but to desire to live without it may be the experience of every moment." And he closed the year like him who, at the end of a psalm of holy and joyful aspirations, exclaims, "I have gone astray like a lost sheep," in the following strain of brokenness of spirit and abasement of soul: "I seem to myself permitted to exist only through the inconceivable compassion of God. When I think of my shameful incapacity for the ministry, arising from my own neglect, I see reason to tremble, though I cannot weep. I feel willing to be a neglected outcast, unfit to be made useful to others, provided my dear brethren are prosperous in their ministry."

In the midst of various weighty employments, and of much tribulation, Mr. Martyn passed into the year 1808; on the first day of which he thus reverted to his past life :— "Few or no changes have occurred in the course of the last year. I have been more settled than for many years past. The events which have taken place, most nearly interesting to myself, are my sister's death, and my disappointment about L——; on both these afflictions I have seen love inscribed, and that is enough. What I think I want it is better still to want; but I am often wearied with this world of woe. I set my affections on the creature, and am then torn from it; and from various other causes, particularly the prevalence of sin in my heart, I am often so full of melancholy, that I hardly know what to do for relief. Sometimes I say, 'Oh, that I had wings like a dove, then would I flee away and be at rest;' at other times, in my sorrow about the creature, I have no wish left for my heavenly rest. It is the grace and favour of God that have saved me hitherto; my ignorance, waywardness, and wickedness would long since have plunged me into misery; but there seems to be a mighty exertion of mercy and grace upon my sinful nature, every day, to keep me from perishing at last. My attainments in the Divine life, in this last year, seem to be none at all; I appear, on the contrary, to be more self-willed and perverse, and more like many of my countrymen, in arrogance and a domineering spirit over the natives. The Lord save me from my wickedness! Henceforth let my soul, humbly depending upon the grace of Christ, perfect holiness in the fear of God, and show towards all, whether Europeans or natives, the mind that was in Christ Jesus."

In the beginning of this year Mr. Martyn's situation at Dinapore was rendered far less agreeable than heretofore,—much as he loved retirement,—by the removal of the only family with whom he lived upon terms of Christian intimacy,—a family for whom he had no common affection; to whom he had been the means of first imparting serious impressions; whom he had exhorted, watched over, and prayed for, and whom he unceasingly followed with his intercessions when he could no longer reach them with his exhortations. "The departure of ——," he writes, "seemed to leave me without human comfort; my regard for them has increased very much of late; I have seen marks of grace more evidently. It is painful to be deprived of them just at this time, yet the Lord knoweth them that are his, and will keep them, through faith, unto eternal salvation."

The following is an extract of a letter to Mrs. —— on this occasion :—

"*Dinapore, January* 8, 1808.

"Your departure has left the Arab and me in such gloom, that I cannot yet find in his society a supply for yours. I still continue, therefore, one of your camp-followers; often every day accompanying you in my thoughts as you travel along, and I now despatch some china paper, to overtake you and assure you once more of my good wishes and prayers. After leaving you on Monday, I crossed the river and solemnized the nuptials of ——, without the intervention of anything untoward. Next morning, at Patna, I walked out in hopes of having one more sight of the battalion and my friends in it. But some of the slow-moving baggage hackeries only, in the rear, showed where you had passed. The nearness of your second day's camp was a strong temptation to add myself again to your number; and it might have been easily accomplished, but the pain of repeated farewells deterred me from going. So I set my face towards Dina-pore again, and now as often as I traverse, in my evening walk, the spot where the pale grass marks your former abode, and as often as I bring out the Koran from the book room, without taking up the Hebrew for you, I join with Sabat in regretting that 'the faithful is gone.' But only continue to deserve the name, my dear friends, and we shall sorrow the less at your departure. Cleave to Him,—in duty, in affection, in bearing his reproach, and we are never separated. If I am so happy as to hear good tidings of you, and that you grow in faith and love, I shall be contented. Friendship must not selfishly repine at a separation appointed by God. Yesterday a letter came from P——, who says that trials are awaiting you; that your gay friends will oppose, &c.,—but enter Berhampore armed with strong resolutions, and depending on the grace that is in Christ Jesus, and you will stand firm."

This separation affected him the more sensibly because it was not in every family at that station that he met with a kind, much less a cordial, reception. "I called," says he, "on the 15th of January, on one of the Dinapore families, and felt my pride rise at the uncivil manner in which I was received. I was disposed at first to determine never to visit the house again, but I remembered the words, 'Overcome evil with good.'"

So much as Mr. Martyn was concerned for the salvation of the heathen, it will readily be surmised that the state of the native Christians,—sunk as they were into a condition of equal ignorance and wickedness with the heathen,—would excite his peculiar sympathy and anxiety. Their lamentable case was never forgotten by him. At the commencement of the present year, especially, it lay so near his heart, that he resolved to ascertain what might be affected at Patna in behalf of those wretched people, who "had a name to live, but were dead.' Without loss of time, therefore, he made an offer to the Roman Catholics there of preaching to them on Sundays, but the proposal was rejected. Had it been accepted, he purposed to have made it the groundwork of a more extensive publication of the Gospel to the inhabitants at large. "Millions perishing," he said, much affected at the reflection, "in the neighbourhood of one who can preach the Gospel to them! how wonderful! I trust the Lord will soon open a great and effectual door. Oh! for faith, zeal, courage, love!"

In consequence of the state of the weather at this season of the year, the public celebration of Divine service on the Sabbath was suspended for a considerable time at Dinapore; a circumstance as painful to Mr.

Martyn, as it was pleasing to the careless and worldly part of his congregation. Upon the serious inconvenience, and yet more serious detriment to the spiritual interest of his flock, arising from the want of a church, he had already presented a memorial to the Governor-General; and orders to provide a proper place for public worship had been issued. Nothing effectual, however, was yet done; and Mr. Martyn's love for the souls entrusted to him, not allowing him to bear the thought of their being scattered for a length of time, as sheep without a shepherd, he came to the resolution of opening his own house, as a place in which the people might assemble, in this emergency. About the middle of February, he writes :—

" As many of the European regiment as were effective were accommodated under my roof, and, praised be God, we had the public ordinances once more. My text was from Isaiah iv. 5,—'The Lord will create upon every dwelling-place of Mount Zion, and upon her assemblies, a cloud and smoke by day, and the shining of a flaming fire by night; for upon all the glory shall be a defence.' In the afternoon, I waited for the women, but not one came; perhaps, by some mistake, notice had not been given them. At the hospital, and with the men at night, I was engaged, as usual, in prayer. My soul panted after the living God, but it remained tied and bound with corruption. I felt as if I could have given the world to be brought to be alone with God; and the promise that 'This is the will of God, even our sanctification,' was the right hand that upheld me, while I followed after Him. When low in spirits, through an unwillingness to take up the cross, I found myself more resigned in endeavouring to realize the thought which had often composed me in my trials on board the ship,—namely, that I was born to suffer,—that suffering is my appointed daily portion;— let this reconcile me to everything! To have a will of my own, not agreeable to God's, is a most tremendous wickedness. I own it is so, for a few moments; but, Lord, write it on my heart! In perfect meekness and resignation, let me take whatever befals me in the path of duty, and never dare to think of being dissatisfied."

As far as it respected Mr. Martyn's health, a temporary interruption of his ministerial duty would have proved a favourable occurrence. He was beginning again to suffer from some severe pains in the chest, which first attacked him in the autumn of the preceding year. Desiring to be as "a flame of fire in the service of his God, and panting for the full enjoyment of every day," the early morning, as well as the closing evening, found him engaged in his delightful labours; but he perceived that the body could not keep pace with the soul, in this career of unceasing activity. "The earthly tabernacle weighed down the spirit, whilst musing upon many things," and compelled him, for awhile, at least, to moderate the vehemence of these exertions. By the month of March, however, the great work, for which myriads in the ages yet to come will gratefully remember and revere the name of Martyn,—*the Version of the New Testament in Hindostanee*,—was brought to a completion; nor,—if we consider how much time he had spent upon it, ever since he arrived at Calcutta, and how laboriously he prosecuted it, after Mr. Brown had summoned him to direct all his efforts to that end,—can it be affirmed that it was hurried to a conclusion with a heedless and blameable precipitancy.

> " 'Twas not the hasty product of a day;
> But the well-ripen'd fruit of wise delay."

"It is a real refreshment to my spirit," Mr. Martyn remarks to Mr. Corrie, just at the moment of sending off the first page of the Testament to Calcutta, in the beginning of April, "to take up my pen to write to you. Such a week of labour I believe I never passed, not excepting even the last week before going into the Senate-House. I have read and corrected the manuscript copies of my Hindostanee Testament so often that my eyes ache. The heat is terrible, often at 98°; the nights insupportable." Such was his energy, in a climate tending to beguile him into ease and indolence; so entirely, "whatsoever he had to do," did he "do it with all his might."

Throughout the remainder of the year 1808, till his removal to Cawnpore, Mr. Martyn's life flowed on in the same tranquil course of usefulness and uniformity. He was occupied in revising the sheets of the Hindostanee version of the New Testament, which he had completed; he superintended the Persian translation, confided to Sabat; he gave himself to the study of Arabic, that he might be qualified to take part with Sabat in another version of the New Testament into that tongue; he continued also to minister to the Europeans and the natives at the hospital; and he daily received the more religious part of his flock at his own house, whilst his health permitted. A serious attack, similar to that which he experienced on his journey to Portsmouth, occurred towards the end of the summer, and was productive of the following effusion, bearing a pre-eminent impress of the Spirit of God. No one, surely, ever touched a string more in unison with the harps of angels and saints in light, than he who wrote thus on the evening of a day expected to be his last:—

"I little thought to have had my faith brought to a trial so soon. This morning, while getting up, I found a pain in the centre of my body, which increased to such a degree, that fever and vertigo came on, and I fainted. The dreadful sensation was like what I once felt in England, but by no means so violent or long-continued; as then, also, I was alone. After recovering my senses, and lying in pain which made me almost breathless, I turned my thoughts to God; and oh, praise to his grace and love, I felt no fear; but I prayed earnestly that I might have a little relief, to set my house in order, and make my will. I also thought with pain of leaving the Persian Gospels unfinished. By means of some ether, the Lord gave me ease, and I made my will. The day was spent in great weakness, but my heart was often filled with the sweetest peace and gratitude for the precious things God hath done for me."

"I found delight at night in considering, from the beginning, all that God had done in creation, providence, and grace, for my soul. O God of love, how shall I praise Thee! Happiness, bliss for ever, lies before me! Thou hast brought me upon this stage of life, to see what sin and misery are; myself, alas! most deeply partaking in both. But the days and the works of my former state, fraught with danger and with death, are no more; and the God of benevolence and love hath opened to me brighter prospects. Thine I am; 'My Beloved is mine, and I am his;' and now I want none but Thee. I am alone with Thee in this world, and when I put off this mortal tabernacle, I shall still be with Thee, whatever that unknown change may be; and I shall be before

Thee, not to receive honour, but to ascribe praise. Yes, I shall then have power to express my feelings. I shall, then, without intermission, see and love; and no cloud of sorrow overcast my mind. I shall then sing, in worthy, everlasting strains, the praises of that Divine Redeemer, whose works of love now reach beyond my conception."

From the even tenor of his life at this period, it cannot be expected that incidents of a very striking nature should arise; yet the description which he himself has given of it in the following extracts, drawn chiefly from a free and frequent correspondence with his endeared friends and brethren, the Rev. David Brown and the Rev. Daniel Corrie, will not be wholly devoid of interest to those who have hitherto watched him, with love and admiration, on his way to heaven.

April 16, 1808.

"This day I have received yours of the 8th; like the rest of your letters, it set my thoughts on full gallop, from which I can hardly recover my breath. Sabat's letter I hesitate to give him, lest it should make him unhappy again. He is at this moment more quiet and Christian in his deportment than I have yet seen him. Arabic now employs my few moments of leisure. In consequence of reading the Koran with Sabat, audibly, and drinking no wine, the slander has gone forth amongst the Christians at Patna,—that the Dinapore Padre has turned Mussulman."

" *To the Rev. D. Brown.*"

" *April* 26, 1808.

"This day I sent off a chapter of Hindostanee, of St.

Matthew. The name I design for my work is,—Benoni, the son of my affliction : for through great tribulation will it come out. Sabat has kept me much upon the fret this week : when he had reached the ninth chapter, the idea seized him, that Mirza might receive some honour from his inspecting the work. He stopped immediately ; and, say what I will, he determines not to give me the smallest help in correcting the Hindostanee."

"*To the Rev. D. Brown.*"

"*May* 9, 1808.

"Sabat having one of his headaches, leaves me at liberty to take a complete sheet. This week has passed, as usual, in comparing the Persian and Greek ; yet we are advanced no further than the end of the 15th of Matthew. Notwithstanding the vexation and disappointment Sabat has occasioned me, I have enjoyed a more peaceable week than ever since his arrival. I do not know how you find the heat, but here it is dreadful ; in one person's quarters yesterday it was at 102° ; perhaps it was on that account that scarcely any women came. Another reason I assign is, that I rebuked one of them last Sunday, yet very gently, for talking and laughing in the church before I came ; so yesterday they showed their displeasure by not coming at all. I spoke to them on the Parable of the Great Supper : the old woman, who is always so exemplary in her attention, shed many tears ; I have sometimes endeavoured to speak to her, but she declines conversation. I feel interested about her, there is so much sorrow and meekness depicted in her countenance ; but she always crosses herself after the service is over. Yesterday, for the first time, I baptized a child in Hindostanee. My Europeans, this week, have not attended very well;—fifteen only, instead of twenty-five; some of them, indeed, are in the hospital; and the hospital is a town of itself;—how shall I ever be faithful to them all."

"*To the Rev. D. Corrie.*"

"*May* 31, 1808.

"Yours of the 24th instant arrived to-day, and relieved me from much anxiety respecting your own health. Still you do not say whether the Hindostanee sheets have arrived. I do not wonder at your inquiring about the Persian. To-day we finish comparing St. Matthew with the Greek, if it may be called a comparison; for, partly owing to the errors of the scribe, rendering whole verses unintelligible,—and partly on account of Sabat's anxiety to preserve the rhythm, which often requires the change of a whole sentence for a single word,—it is a new translation. We have laboured hard at it to-day; from six in the morning till four in the afternoon."

"*To the Rev. D. Brown.*"

June 6, 1808.

"To-day we have completed the Persian of St. Matthew, and to-morrow it is to be sent off to be printed. Sabat desired me to kneel down to bless God for the happy event, and we joined in praise of 'the Father of Lights.' It is a superb performance in every respect. Sabat is prodigiously proud of it: I wish some mistakes may not be found in it, to put him to shame. Among the events of the last week is the earthquake; we were just reading the passage of the 24th of Matthew, on "earthquakes in divers places," when I felt my chair shake under me; then some pieces of the plaister fell; on which I sprang up and ran out :—the doors had still a tremulous motion.

The edition of the Gospel must be announced as 'printed at the expense of the British and Foreign Bible Society.'"

" *To the Rev. D. Corrie.*"

"*June* 7, 1808.

"This day we have sent the Persian of St. Matthew. Sabat is not a little proud of it. Your design of announcing the translation, as printed at the expense of the British and Foreign Bible Society, I highly approve; I wish to see honour put upon so godlike an Institution. Mirza returned yesterday, and again there are symptoms of disquiet in Sabat. Pray for us."

" *To the Rev. D. Brown.*"

"*Bankipore, June* 23, 1808.

" I groan at the wickedness and infidelity of men, and seem to stretch my neck every way to espy a righteous man. All at Dinapore treat the gospel with contempt; here there is nothing but infidelity. I am but just arrived, and am grieved to find in my old friend —— less proofs of real acquaintance with the gospel than I used to hope. On my way here I called on Col. ——, and advised him to marry or separate;—the alternative I am ever insisting on. As soon as I arrived, Mr. —— informed me that the reason why no one came to hear me, was, 'that I preached faith without works, and that little sins are as bad as great ones,' and that thus I tempted them to become great sinners. A young civilian, who some time ago came to me desiring satisfaction on the evidences of Christianity, and to whom I spoke very freely, and with some regard, as I could not doubt his sincerity, now holds me up to ridicule. Thus, through evil report, we go on. Oh! my brother! how happy I feel, that all have not forsaken Christ; that I am not left alone even in India. 'Cast thy burden on the Lord, and he shall sustain thee,' is the text I carry about with me, and I can recommend it to anybody as an infallible pre servative from the fever of anxiety."

"*To the Rev. D. Corrie.*"

"*June* 26, 1808.

"The day after I wrote to you from Bankipore, I called on the Nawaub, Babir Ali Khan, celebrated for his sense and liberality. I stayed two hours with him, conversing in Persian, but badly. He began the theological discussion by requesting me to explain necessity and free-will; I instantly pleaded ignorance. He gave me his own opinion; on which I asked him for his proofs of the religion of Mahomet. His first argument was the eloquence of the Koran, but he at last acknowledged that this was insufficient. I then brought forward a passage or two in the Koran, containing sentiments manifestly false and foolish; he flourished a good deal, but concluded by saying, that I must wait till I could speak Persian better, and had read their logic. His whole manner, look, authority, and copiousness, reminded me constantly of Dr. ——. This was the first visit, and I returned highly delighted with his sense, candour, and politeness. Two days after I went to breakfast with him, and conversed with him in Hindostanee. He inquired what were the principles of the Christian religion; I began with the Atonement, the divinity of Christ, the corruption of human nature, the necessity of regeneration, and a holy life. He seems to wish to acquire information, but discovers no spiritual desire after the truth. So much for this Mussulman lord: now for Antichrist in another shape—the Popish padre, Julius Cæsar. I asked him whether the doctrine I had heard from the Franciscan brethren was his :—*Extra Ecclesiam Romanam salus non esse potest ?* He said that it was a question on which disputations were constantly held at Rome. By some means we got upon the additions made to the Commandments by the Church of Rome ; he said that Christianity without Councils was a city without walls ; and that Luther, Calvin, &c., had made additions : all which I denied, and showed him the last verses in the Revelation. Upon the whole, our conversation seemed without benefit."

" *To the Rev. D. Corrie.*"

" *July* 2, 1808.

" My work is very delightful in itself, but it is doubly so by securing me so much of your correspondence. My eyes seized your beloved handwriting with more eagerness than even if the letter had been from Europe. I rejoice with you, and praise God for one Gospel in Persian. With elegance enough to attract the careless and please the fastidious, it contains enough of Eternal Life to save the reader's soul ; therefore, if we do no more, we are happy that something is done. We are safe with the Hindostanee ; it wants but little correction, and, in case of my death, could be easily prepared by any one. I am anxious to hear of the new plans you are about to propose to me : let them not be in the way of *recreation ;* my only exertion, and that, through indolence, is small, is to keep my heart rightly disposed to minister to my congregation at night. I shrink from the idea of Sanscrit : the two or three months I spent in striving to penetrate its unwieldy grammar were more painful to me than any since the sorrowful days when I first began to learn Greek."

"*To the Rev. D. Brown.*"

"*July* 4, 1808.

"I have received no letter from you this week. When Sunday came and no letter arrived from you, I began to entertain the romantic notion that perhaps my brother himself would come and preach for me at night. I am now on my way to Patna by water. The Italian Padre came to Dinapore again on Saturday, but did not call upon me : the men sent him a letter, to which he replied in French, that he lamented he could not speak their language, but should remember them in his prayers, and spoke of them as brethren in Christ. When he came into the barracks, the Catholics crowded round him by hundreds, and in a tone of triumph pointed out his dress - that of a Franciscan friar—to the Protestants ; contrasting it with that of a clergyman of the Church of England, booted and spurred, and ready for a hunt. The Catholics in this regiment amount to a full thousand,— the Protestants are scarcely discernible. Who would think that we should have to combat Antichrist again at this day? I feel my spirit roused to preach against Popery with all the zeal of Luther. How small and unimportant are the hair splitting disputes of the blessed people at home, compared with the formidable agents of the devil with whom we have to combat here ! There are four castes of people in India : the first, heathen ; the second, Mohammedans ; the third, Papists ; the fourth, infidels. Now I trust that you and I are sent to fight this four-faced devil, and, by the help of the Lord Jesus, whom we serve, we will. I was rather apprehensive yesterday that my female hearers would have forsaken me ; but they came as usual, and the words, 'Search the Scriptures,' occurring in the chapter of the day, I took occasion to point out to them the wickedness of the Church of Rome, in forbidding the use of the Scriptures."

" *To the Rev. D. Corrie.*"

" *July* 11, 1808.

" A loquacious Brahmin having interrupted us in our work, I leave him to Sabat, and turn my thoughts with more pleasure Chunar-ward. My last letter left me at Patna. The Catholic Padre, Julius Cæsar, had gone to Dinapore that very day to say mass ; but at Babir Ali's I met with a very agreeable Armenian Padre, named Martin, who kept my tongue employed nearly the whole of the day. I tried him once or twice in spiritual things, but on these he had nothing to say. His dress was a little black cassock, exactly such as we wear, or ought to wear : the top of his head was shaved like the Franciscans. I am almost ashamed of my secular appearance before these very venerable and appropriate figures. The Catholics in the regiment are a thousand strong, and are disposed to be malicious ; they respect me, however, and cannot help thinking that I have been taught by Roman Catholics, or have been in some way connected with them : at the hospital, the greater number keep themselves aloof. My society, this week, has occasioned me great trouble ; one man was the occasion of it : still his professions, and earnestness not to be excluded, make it difficult to know how to deal with him. Certainly there is infinitely better discipline in the Romish Church than in ours, and if ever I were to be the pastor of native Christians, I should endeavour to govern with equal strictness. My female hearers do not give me half such encouragement as yours ; probably because I do not take such pains with them ; yet there is no trouble I would spare if I knew how to reach their minds. There were only fourteen yesterday. I spoke to them on the text, 'Lord, to whom shall we go ? Thou hast the words of eternal life.' To whom shall we go ?—To the Padre,—to the Virgin Mary,—to the Saints, —to the world,—to works,—to repentance ? No : to Christ."

" *To the Rev. D. Corrie.*"

" *July* 18, 1808.

"I mentioned to you that I had spoken very plainly to the women last Sunday, on the delusions of the papists : yesterday only seven came. I ascribed it to what I had said; but to-day Sabat tells me that they pour contempt upon it all. Sabat, instead of comforting and encouraging me in my disappointments and trials, aggravates my pain by contemptuous expressions of the perfect inutility of continuing to teach them. He may spare his sarcastic remarks, as I suppose that after another Sunday none at all will come. I find no relief but in prayer : to God I can tell all my griefs, and find comfort. Last Tuesday the Padre, Julius Cæsar, came and staid with me four hours. We argued with great vehemence : when I found that he had nothing to say in defence of the adoration of the Virgin Mary and the saints, I solemnly charged him and his church with the sin of idolatry :—he started, and said that if I had uttered such a sentiment in Italy, I should have been burned. He certainly seems sincere ; and at one time he lifted up his eyes and prayed that I might not convert him, and that God would never suffer the Protestant religion to enter Italy. His main argument against me was, the disorder and impiety prevalent among the Protestants, whom he had had an opportunity of observing in Geneva and Leghorn. This disputation has brought us to be quite familiar in our acquaintance ; he looked over all my books, and found a French one, called ' the Crimes of the Popes; ' which he desired to have ; but recollected afterwards that his coadjutor might see it. I feel a regard for him : he is a serious and unassuming young man."

" *To the Rev. D. Corrie.*"

"*August* 1, 1808.

"One day this week, on getting up in the morning, I was attacked with a very serious illness. I thought I was leaving this world of sorrow ; and, praised be the God of grace, I felt no fear. The rest of the day I was filled with sweet peace of mind, and had near access to God in prayer. What a debt of love and praise do we owe ! Yesterday I attempted to examine the women who attended (in number about thirty) in Christian knowledge : they were very shy, and said that they could say no prayers but in Portuguese. It appears that they were highly incensed, and went away, saying to Joseph, 'We know a great deal more than your Padre himself. ' The services much weakened me after my late attack."

" *To the Rev. D. Corrie.*"

"*August* 8, 1808.

"I called on the Commander-in chief here on Saturday morning, and was received very graciously. I told him that it was a duty we owed to God, as a nation, to erect churches ; and asked whether Lord Minto was disposed to go on with it ; to which he replied in the affirmative. I enlarged on the shame I felt in my disputes with the Popish Padres, as often as they threw out reflections on the utter disregard of the Protestants to religion. Julius, the Padre, has been here twice this week, but staid only a very short time. He began to assert, with very great vehemence, the necessity of an infallible judge, in order to settle all disputes on religion ; and mentioned how much he had been agitated by his last dispute with me : he could do nothing but walk about that night ;—yet looked up to God, and became tranquil. The men are fast dying in the hospital, yet they would rather be sent to Patna for some holy oil, than hear the word of eternal life. Two or three of my evening hearers are in the hospital ; one is prepared to die : blessed sight ! The Persian of St. Mark is to be sent to-morrow, and five chapters of St. Luke, corrected. There is no news from down the stream ; but always glad tidings for us from the world above."

"*To the Rev. D. Corrie.*"

"*Aug.* 15, 1808.

"Glad am I that we are likely to meet so soon ; may it be 'in the fulness of the blessing of the gospel of peace.' Last week Mahomed Babir, the Mahomedan lord, and Padre Martino, spent three days here. Little, I am sorry to say, has been done. Sabat did not appear to advantage : instead of speaking about the gospel to Babir, he was reciting poetry, particularly his own ; and seemed more anxious to gain admirers than converts. We did, however, at last converse about religion ; but Mahomed confessed himself an infidel, and required proof of the truth of any religion. Sabat was not prepared for this, so I attempted to speak to Babir upon the nature of probable evidence, but he did not understand me : so this came to nothing. One day we sat down to dinner before Sabat came ; and, to our great astonishment, he rebuked us, with much wrath and pride. With all Babir's gentleness, he rebuked him in his turn, and told him that the Persians and English knew how to behave, but the Arabs did not. Babir was so lavish in his compliments to us all, that it was difficult to get at his real sentiments ; but he praised Sabat's Persian translation to the stars ; which I was glad to hear. As for the poor Padre, with an exterior so imposing that you would think St. Peter himself was present, he knows nothing at all. I tried him on spiritual things again and again ; but he could say nothing. Alas ! how fallen from what their fathers were ! When shall the churches of Asia recover their ancient glory ? You will see both the Nabob and the Padre soon, I hope. Last Tuesday we sent off the Persian of St. Mark."

" *To the Rev. D. Corrie.*"

" *September* 9, 1808.

" Corrie is here, and likely to remain, to my joy. You will have some happy hours together, I doubt not : with all your cares and trials, you claim all the consolation we can give ; and you shall have more than that, if we can obtain anything for you by our prayers. Corrie will bring you but a poor account of my congregation : I am much neglected on all sides, and without the work of translation, I should fear that my presence in India were useless."

" *To the Rev. D. Brown.*"

" *October,* 1808.

" I deserve your reproof for not having written to you

oftener; and I am pained at the anxiety I have thought-lessly occasioned you. I console myself, however, by reflecting that a letter must have reached you a few weeks after you sent your last. I am sorry that I have not good accounts to give of my health; yet no danger is to be apprehended. My services on the Lord's-day always leave me a pain in the chest, and such a great degree of general relaxation, that I seldom recover it till Tuesday. A few days ago I was attacked with a fever, which, by the mercy of God, lasted but two days. I am now well, but must be more careful for the future. In this debili-tating climate, the mortal tabernacle is frail indeed: my mind seems as vigorous as ever, but my delicate frame soon calls for relaxation; and I must give it, though un-willingly; for such glorious fields for exertion open all around, that I could with pleasure be employed from morning to night. It seems a providential circumstance, that the work at present assigned me is that of transla-tion; for had I gone through the villages, preaching, as my intention led me to do, I fear that, by this time, I should have been in a deep decline. In my last, I gave you a general idea of my employments. The society still meet every night at my quarters, and, though we have lost many by death, others are raised up in their room; one officer, a lieutenant, is also given to me; and he is not only a brother beloved, but a constant companion and nurse; so you need feel no apprehension that I should be left alone in sickness; neither on any other account should you be uneasy. You know that we must meet no more in this life; therefore, since we are, as I trust, both children of God by faith in Jesus Christ, it becomes a matter of less consequence when we leave this earth. Of the spread of the Gospel in India I can say little, because

I hear nothing. Adieu, my dearest sister : let us live in constant prayer, for ourselves, and for the Church."

To his Sister.

"*October* 19, 1808.

"I have just come from my chapel, where, with my little flock, I have once more resumed my duties. The infrequency of my appearance among them of late has thinned them considerably; and this effect, which I foresaw, is one of the most painful and lamentable consequences of my withdrawing from them ; but it is unavoidable if I wish to prolong my life. My danger is from the lungs, though none of you seem to apprehend it. One complete service at church does more to consume my strength and spirits, than six days of the hardest study or bodily labour. Pray for me, my dear brother, that I may be neither rash nor indolent.

"*To the Rev. D. Corrie.*"

"*October* 24, 1808.

"You mention a letter enclosed, but none came. The intelligence, however, intended to be conveyed by it, met my delighted eyes. Thomason is coming. This is good. Praise be to the Lord of the harvest, for sending out labourers ! Behold how the prayers of the society at Calcutta have been heard. I hope they will continue their supplication ; for we want more yet, and it may please God yet further to bless us. You cannot leave Calcutta by the middle of November, and must therefore apply for one month's extension of leave. But you are unwilling to leave your flock ; and I do not wonder, as I have seen my sheep grievously dispersed during my absence. Uncertain when I may come amongst them, they seldom come at all, except the ten or twelve who meet one another. My morning congregation increases as the cold weather advances, and yesterday there seemed to be a considerable impression. I spoke in a low tone of voice, and therefore did not feel much fatigue;—after the Hindostanee service I was very weak, but, at night, tolerably strong again. On the whole, my expectations of life return. May the days thus prolonged be entirely His who continues them! and may my work not only move on delightfully, but with a more devout and serious spirit! You are too many for me to mention each; suffice it to say that my heart is with you, and daily prays for blessings upon you all!

"*To the Rev. D. Corrie.*"

The early part of the year 1809 produced no variation in the life of Mr. Martyn, until the month of April, when he was removed from his station at Dinapore to Cawnpore. The following extracts are selected from the continuation of his correspondence with Mr. Corrie, in the interval which passed between the end of the year 1808, and the termination of his ministry at Dinapore.

"*January* 10, 1809.

"Your letter from Buxar found me in much the same spiritual state as you describe yourself to be in; though your description, no doubt, belongs more properly to me. I no longer hesitate to ascribe my stupor and formality to its right cause,—unwatchfulness in worldly company. I thought that any temptation arising from the society of the people of the world, at least of such as we have had, was not worthy of notice; but I find myself mistaken. The frequent occasions of being among them of late, have proved a snare to my corrupt heart. Instead of returning with a more elastic spring to severe duties, as I expected, my heart wants more idleness, more dissipation. David Brainerd in the wilderness,—what a contrast to Henry Martyn! But, God be thanked, that a start now and then interrupts the slumber. I hope to be up, and about my Master's business ; to cast off the works of darkness, and to be spiritually-minded, which alone is life and peace. But what a dangerous country it is that we are in ; hot weather or cold, all is softness and luxury ; all a conspiracy to lull us to sleep in the lap of pleasure. While we pass over this enchanted ground, call, brother, ever and anon, and ask, ' Is all well ?' We are as shepherds keeping watch over our flocks by night ; if *we* fall asleep, what is to become of them ! "

"*January* 30, 1809.

" I have been seized with a sudden desire for reading Hebrew, chiefly from a wish to see language in its simplest and purest state. It is my belief that language is from God ; and that therefore, as in his other works, so in this, the principles must be extremely simple. My present labour is to find a reason for there being but two tenses in Hebrew. I have read, or rather devoured, the first four chapters in the Hebrew Bible, in order to account for the apparently strange use of these two tenses, and am making hypotheses every moment,—when I walk, and when I awake in the night. One thing I have found, which is, that there are but two tenses in English and in Persian. *I will go :*—in that sentence the principal verb is *I will*, which is the present tense. *I would have gone :*—the principal verb is, *I would*, or *I willed. Should*, also, is a preterite, namely, *shalled*, from *to shall*. Another thing I observe is, that both in Persian and in English the preterite is formed in the same way, viz., by the addition of *ed ; porsum, porsedum,—ask, asked*. I should not wonder if, in the Saxon, or some other ancient northern language, from which the English comes, it is *askedum*. Thus you have a letter of philology. If I make any other *great* discoveries, and have nothing better to write about, I shall take the liberty of communicating them. *Scire tuum nihil est, nisi te scire hoc sciat alter :—* but this, I trust, is not my maxim. ' *Whatsoever ye do, do all to the glory of God*,' is much better."

"*February* 13, 1809.

"Last Friday we had the happiness and honour of finishing the four Gospels in Persian. The same evening, I made some discovery respecting the Hebrew verb; but was, unfortunately, so much delighted, that I could not sleep ; in consequence of which, I have had a headache ever since. Thus, even intellectual joys are followed by sorrow ; not so spiritual ones. I pray continually that *order* may be preserved in my heart ; that I may esteem and delight most in that work which is really most estimable and delightful,—the work of Christ and his apostles. When this is in any measure the case, it is surprising how clear and orderly the thoughts are on other subjects. I am still a good deal in the dark respecting the objects of my pursuit ; but have so far an insight, that I read both Hebrew and Arabic with increasing pleasure and satisfaction."

"*February* 29, 1809.

"Your attack proves the necessity of diminishing your Sabbath services. I scarcely know how this week has passed; nor can I call to mind the circumstances of one single day; so absorbed have I been in my new pursuit. I remember, however, that during one night I did not sleep a wink. Knowing what would be the consequence the next day, I struggled hard, and turned every way, that my mind might be diverted from what was before it; but all in vain. One discovery succeeded another, in Hebrew, Arabic, and Greek, so rapidly, that I was sometimes almost in ecstacy; but, after all, I have moved but a step; you may scold me, if you please, but I am helpless. I do not turn to this study of myself, but it turns to me, and draws me away almost irresistibly. Still I perceive it to be a mark of a fallen nature to be so carried away by a pleasure merely intellectual; and, therefore, while I pray for the gifts of his Spirit, I feel the necessity of being still more earnest for his grace. 'Whether there be tongues, they shall cease; whether there be knowledge, it shall vanish away;' but 'Charity never faileth.' Yesterday my mind was mercifully kept free the whole day, and I ministered without distraction, and, moreover, without fatigue. I do not know when I have found myself so strong. The state of the air affects me more than anything else. On Saturday, I completed my twenty-eighth year. Shall I live to see another birthday? It will be better to suppose not. I have not read 'Faber' yet; but it seems evident to me that the eleventh of Daniel, almost the whole of it, refers to future times. But, as the time of accomplishing the Scriptures draws on, knowledge shall increase. In solemn expectation we must wait, to see how our God will come. How interesting are his doings! We feel already some of that rapture wherewith they sing above,

'Great and wonderful are thy works, Lord God Almighty! Just and true are thy ways, thou King of saints!'"

"*March* 3, 1809.

"I did not write to you last week, because I was employed night and day, on Monday and Tuesday, with Sabat, in correcting some sheets for the press. I begin my letter, now, immediately on receiving yours of last week. The account of your complaint, as you may suppose, grieves me exceedingly; not because I think that I shall outlive you, but because your useful labours must be reduced to one quarter of their present amount; and that you may, perhaps, be obliged to take a voyage to Europe, which involves loss of time and money. But, O brother beloved, what is life or death? Nothing, to the believer in Jesus. 'He that believeth, though he were dead, yet shall he live: and he that liveth, and believeth in me, shall never die.' The first and most natural effect of sickness, as I have often found, is to cloud and terrify the mind. The attention of the soul is arrested by the idea of soon appearing in a new world; and a sense of guilt is felt, before faith is exercised in a Redeemer: and for a time this will predominate; for the same faith that would overcome fear in health, must be considerably strengthened, to have the same ascendancy in sickness. I trust you will long live to do the work of your Lord. My discoveries are all at an end. I am just where I was,—in perfect darkness, and tired of the pursuit. It is, however, likely that I shall be constantly speculating on the subject. My thirst after knowledge is very strong; but I pray continually that the Spirit of

God may hold the reins,—that I may mind the work of God above all things, and consider all things else as merely occasional."

" How delightful it is to me, at this moment, to commune with a dear brother, who 'is not of the world, as the Lord was not of the world.' I am just come from the mess of the ———. This morning the Regiment was reviewed, and I, among the staff,* was invited to a public *déjeûné* and dinner. As I had no pretence for not going, I went. Yesterday our new place of worship was opened. It is a room eighty-one feet long, with a very large verandah. It will be a noble church, but, I fear, will diminish somewhat of my strength. My text was, ' In all places where I record my name, I will come unto thee and bless thee.' Oh may the promise be fulfilled to us ! "

At Cawnpore, the hand of friendship and hospitality was stretched out to welcome Mr. Martyn, and to afford him those attentions which, after a wearisome and perilous journey, were not only most gratifying to his feelings, but almost indispensable to the preservation of his life. From the pen of the lady† of that friend who then received him,—a pen which has been often and happily employed in the sacred cause for which Mr. Martyn lived and laboured,—we have the following account of his arrival at the new station to which he was appointed :—

"The month of April, in the Upper Provinces of

---

* Mr. Martyn was Military Chaplain.   † Mrs. Sherwood.

Hindostan, is one of the most dreadful months for travelling throughout the year : indeed, no European, at that time, can remove from place to place, but at the hazard of his life. But Mr. Martyn had that anxiety to be in the work which his heavenly Father had given him to do, that, notwithstanding the violent heat, he travelled from Chunar to Cawnpore, the space of about four hundred miles. At that time, as I well remember, the air was hot and dry as that which I have sometimes felt near the mouth of a large oven ;—no friendly cloud or verdant carpet of grass to relieve the eye from the strong glare of the rays of the sun, pouring on the sandy plains of the Ganges. Thus, Mr. Martyn travelled, journeying night and day, and arrived at Cawnpore in such a state, that he fainted away as soon as he entered the house. When we charged him with the rashness of hazarding his life in this manner, he always pleaded his anxiety to get to the great work. He remained with us ten days, suffering considerably, at times, from fever and pain in the chest."

Mr. Martyn's own account of this dreadful and most distressing journey, is thus briefly detailed to Mr. Corrie :—

"*Cawnpore, May* 1, 1809.

"The entrance to this place is through plains of immeasurable extent, covered with burning sand. The place itself I have not yet been able to see, nor shall, I suppose, till the rains : at present it is involved in a thick cloud of dust. So much for exordium. Let me take up my narrative from Mirzapoor, from whence I wrote you a note. I reached Tarra about noon. Next day, at noon, reached Allahabad, and was hospitably

CAWNPORE.

Page 260.

CAWNPORE.

[Page 286.

received by Mr. G——; at night dined with him at the Judge's, and met twenty-six people. From Allahabad to Cawnpore, how shall I describe what I suffered! Two days and two nights was I travelling without intermission. Expecting to arrive early on Saturday morning, I took no provision for that day. Thus I lay in my palanquin, faint, with a headache, neither awake nor asleep, between dead and alive; the wind blowing flames. The bearers were so unable to bear up, that we were six hours coming the last six *kos* (twelve miles). However, with all these frightful circumstances, I was brought, in mercy, through. It was too late on Saturday to think of giving notice of my arrival, that we might have service; indeed, I was myself too weak. Even now the motion of the palanquin is not out of my brain, nor the heat out of my blood."

Mr. Martyn's removal from Dinapore to Cawnpore was to him, in many respects, a very unpleasant arrangement. He was several hundred miles farther distant from Calcutta, and was far more widely separated than before from his friend Mr. Corrie: he had new acquaintances to form at his new abode; and, after having with much difficulty procured the erection of a church at Dinapore, he was transported to a spot where none of the conveniences, much less the decencies and solemnities of public worship, were visible. We find him, soon after he arrived there, preaching to a thousand soldiers, drawn up in a hollow square, when the heat was so great, although the sun had not risen, that many actually dropped down unable to support it. What must such services as these have been to a minister too faithful and zealous to seek refuge in indolent formality, and already weakened in health by former ministrations. He complained—if, indeed, he might ever be said to complain—of an attack of fever soon after the commencement of these services; and there can be little doubt that they contributed very materially to undermine his constitution. No time, indeed, was lost by him on this occasion, as before, in remonstrating upon this subject; and his remonstrances procured a promise that a church should be built. This expectation, however, was not fulfilled until his health was too much shaken to profit by its accomplishment.

At Cawnpore Mr. Martyn's ministerial duties varied little from those which had occupied him at Dinapore. Prayers and a sermon with the regiment at the dawn of the morning; the same service at the house of the General of the station at eleven o'clock; attendance at the hospital; and in the evening, that part of his work which was the most grateful and refreshing to his spirit, though performed under the pressure of much bodily fatigue,—an exposition to the more devout part of his flock, with prayer and thanksgiving,—made up the ordinary portion of his labours.

The love of philology—in which science he fondly hoped to effect discoveries conducive to the elucidation of difficulties in the Scriptures—followed him from Dinapore to his new residence; and so haunted his mind, that, whether at home or abroad, whether by day or by night, he could not divest himself of it. For many successive days did he intensely pursue this study, and for many sleepless nights did this study pursue him. At length he thought that he had ascertained the meaning of almost all the Hebrew letters: by degrees, however, he became less ardent in these inquiries; either from questioning the truth of those axioms which he had laid down, or from finding their inutility after he had established them.

These abstruse speculations, together with duties of a more important character, one of the chief of which was the superintendence of the Arabic translation of the New Testament, now begun and carried on conjointly with a new Persian version, were soon interrupted, and for a time suspended, by a summons he received to Lucknow, for the purpose of celebrating a marriage, and by a similar call to Pretabjush. Concerning the latter, he thus writes to Mr. Simeon, lamenting the inconvenience to which he was exposed by such distant demands upon his services. " Just after the last ship from Europe arrived, and I was hourly expecting my letters, I was summoned to a distant station to marry a couple, and did not return till three weeks after. It was a great disappointment to be thus suddenly sent to roam amongst jungles and jackals, when I was feasting my fancy with delightful letters from my friends at home, though Europe is no longer my home. However, my mind was soon reconciled to it, and I was often able to recite, with some sense of their sweetness, Mr. Newton's beautiful lines,—

> " ' In desert tracts, with Thee, my God,
> How happy could I be!'

'The place to which I was called is Pretabjush, in the territory of Oude, which is still under the government of the Nabob. Oppression and insecurity of property seemed to have stripped the country of its inhabitants. From Manicpore, where I left the river, to Pretabjush, a distance of fifty miles, I saw but two or three miserable villages, and no agriculture. The road was nothing more than a winding footpath, through a continued wood, and that in consequence of the rains was often lost. Indeed, all the lowlands were under water, which, added to the circumstance of travelling by night, made the journey by no means a pleasant one. Being detained one Lord's-day at the place, I assembled all the officers and company at the commanding officer's bungalow, and preached the Gospel to them. There were five and-thirty officers, besides ladies and other Europeans. You will have an idea of the Nabob's country when you are informed that last September a young officer, going from his station to Lucknow, was stopped by robbers, and literally cut to pieces in his palanquin. Since that time, the Nabob has requested that every English gentleman wishing to visit his capital, may give notice of his intention to the Resident, in order that a guard may be sent. Accordingly, a few months ago, when I had occasion to go to Lucknow, I had a guard of four troopers, armed with matchlocks and spears. I thought of Nehemiah, but was far too inferior to him in courage and faith, not to contemplate the fierce countenances of my satellites with great satisfaction."

Not long after Mr. Martyn's return from this expedition, letters from Europe reached Cawnpore, bringing intelligence of a similar nature with that which had overwhelmed him in the preceding year. They contained intimations of the dangerous illness of that sister who had been so instrumental to his conversion to the Lord; and they were but too quickly followed by an account of her death. "Oh, my dearest S——," he began to write, with a faint hope at first of the possibility of her receiving his letter, "that disease which preyed upon our mother and dear sister, and has often shown itself in me, has, I fear, attacked you. Although

I parted from you in the expectation of never seeing you in this life; and though I know that you are, and have long been, prepared to go, yet to lose my last near relation, my only sister, in nature and grace, is a dreadful stroke."—"Dearest brother," he continued to her husband, from whom he had, in the meantime, received a more alarming account, "I can write no more to my sister. Even now something tells me that I have been addressing one in the world of spirits. But yet it is possible that I may be mistaken. No! I dare not hope. Your loss is greater than mine, and therefore it would become me to offer consolation; but I cannot. I must wait till your next; and in the meantime I will continue to pray for you, that the God of all consolation may comfort you, and make us both, from this time, live more as pilgrims and strangers upon the earth. In the first three years after leaving my native land, I have lost the three persons whom I most loved in it. What is there now that I should wish to live for? Oh, what a barren desert, what a howling wilderness, does this world appear! But for the service of God in his Church, and the preparation of my own soul, I do not know that I would wish to live another day."

With a grateful tenderness, also, in the midst of this affliction, he thus addressed Mr. Simeon : —" My ever dear friend and brother,—I address you by your true title, for you are a friend and brother, and more than a brother to me. Your letter, though it contains much afflictive intelligence, contains also much that demands my gratitude. In the midst of judgment He remembers mercy. He has been pleased to take away my last remaining sister (for I have no hopes of my poor S——'s recovery) ; He has reduced the rest of my family, but He has raised up a friend for me and mine. Tears of gratitude mingle with those of sorrow, whilst I think of the mercy of God, and the goodness of you, his instrument."

The close of the year 1809 was distinguished by the commencement of Mr. Martyn's first public ministration among the heathen. A crowd of mendicants, whom, to prevent perpetual interruptions, he had appointed to meet on a stated day, for the distribution of alms, frequently assembled before his house in immense numbers, presenting an affecting spectacle of extreme wretchedness. To this congregation he determined to preach the Word of the Saviour of all men, who is no respecter of persons. Of his first attempt at this new species of ministration, he thus speaks :—"I told them, after requesting their attention, that I gave with pleasure the alms I could afford, but wished to give them something better ; namely, eternal riches, or the knowledge of God, which was to be had from God's Word ; and then producing a Hindostanee translation of Genesis, read the first verse, and explained it word by word. In the beginning, when there was nothing, no heaven, no earth, but only God, he created all these, without help, for his own pleasure. But who is God ? One so great, so good, so wise, so mighty, that none can know him as he ought to know : but yet we must know that He knows us. When we rise up, or sit down, or go out, He is always with us. He created heaven and earth ; therefore everything in heaven,—sun, moon, and stars. Therefore how should the sun be God; or the moon be God ? He created everything on earth, therefore Ganges also ; therefore, how should Ganges be God ? Neither are they like God. If a shoemaker make a pair of shoes, are the shoes like him ? If a man make an image, the image is not like man his maker. Infer secondly : if God made the heaven and earth for you, and made the meat also for you, will he not also feed you? Know also, that He that made heaven and earth, can destroy them, and will do it : therefore fear God, who is so great; and love God, who is so good." Such was the substance of his first discourse, the whole of which was preached, sentence by sentence, for at the end of each clause there followed applause and explanatory remarks from the wiser among them. "I bless my God," said Mr. Martyn, "for helping me beyond my expectations. Yet still my corrupt heart looks forward to the next attempt with some dread."

The following Sunday he preached again to the beggars, in number about five hundred, on the work of the first and second day, when all he said was received with great applause. And on the last day of the year he again addressed them, their numbers amounting to about five hundred and fifty; taking for his subject the works of the third and fourth day. "I did not," he remarks, "succeed so well as before ; I suppose because I had more confidence in myself, and less in the Lord. I fear they did not understand me well ; but the few sentences that were clear they applauded. Speaking to them of the sea and rivers, I spoke to them again of the Ganges, that it was no more than other rivers. God loved the Hindoos,—but He loved other people too ; and whatever river, or water, or other good thing He gave Hindoos, He gave other people also : for all are alike before God. Ganges therefore is not to be worshipped ; because, so far from being a God, it is not better than other rivers. In speaking of the earth and moon, 'as a candle in the house, so is the sun,' I said, 'in the heavens.' But would I worship a candle in my

hand? These were nice points : I felt as if treading on
tender ground, and was almost disposed to blame myself
for imprudence. I thought that, amidst the silence these
remarks produced, I heard hisses and groans ; but a few
Mohammedans applauded."

With these new labours of love the year 1809 terminated. "Ten years have elapsed," observed Mr.
Martyn on the last day of it, "since I was first called of
God into the fellowship of the Gospel; and ten times
greater than ever ought to be my gratitude to the tender
mercy of my God, for all that He has done for me. The
ways of wisdom appear more sweet and reasonable than
ever, and the world more insipid and vexatious. The
chief thing I have to mourn over is my want of more
power and fervour in secret prayer, especially when
attempting to plead for the heathen. Warmth does not
increase with me in proportion to my light."

To the temporal and spiritual necessities of those
wretched beings who statedly assembled before his house,
Mr. Martyn continued to minister assiduously in the early
part of the year 1810 ; nor did he cease to do so, whilst
his health permitted, during the remainder of his residence at Cawnpore. The satisfaction of seeing their
numbers increase, sometimes amounting to as many as
eight hundred persons, was exceeded by the more solid
gratification of witnessing in them a growing attention to
the instructions he delivered. By degrees, tumultuous
applauses were succeeded by pertinent remarks, or were
lost in a serious and pensive silence. On one occasion
particularly, the apparent effect produced by his discourse
was highly encouraging. An extraordinary impression was
made on his Mohammedan and pagan auditory, whom he
had been addressing on the awful subject of the destruction

of Sodom and Gomorrah, with equal simplicity and solemnity. "After finishing," he observes, "the narrative of the fall of Sodom, I said, without further preparation, 'Do you, too, repent of your sins, and turn to God?' It was this simple sentence that seemed to come with great power, and prevented my proceeding for a time. 'For though you are not like the men of Sodom,—God forbid! —you are nevertheless sinners. Are there no thieves, fornicators, railers, extortioners among you? Be you sure that God is angry. I say not that He will burn your town; but that He will burn you. Haste, therefore, out of Sodom. Sodom is the world, which is full of sinners and of sin. Come out, therefore, from amongst them : forsake not your worldly business, but your sinful companions. Do not be like the world, lest you perish with the world. Do not, like Lot, linger; say not, 'To-morrow we will repent,' lest you never see to-morrow ;— repent to-day. Then, as Lot, seated on the hill, beheld the flames in safety, you also, sitting on the hills of heaven, shall behold the ruins of the world without fear."

In the midst of these exertions, an attack of pain in the chest, of a severer kind than he had before experienced, forced upon Mr. Martyn's mind the unwelcome conviction of the necessity of some quiet and relaxation.

Upon the subject of his health,—a subject which was becoming but too interesting and alarming to his friends in general,—he thus wrote to Mr. Simeon, who, long before, had warmly urged him to the most watchful care and prudence. "I read your letter of the 6th July, 1809, cautioning me against over-exertion, with the confidence of one who had nothing to fear. This was only three weeks ago. Since the last Lord's-day, your kind advice was brought home to my mind, accompanied with painful regret that I had not paid more attention to it. My work last Sunday was not more than usual, but far too much for me, I can perceive. First, service to his Majesty's 53rd Regiment, in the open air; then at headquarters; in the afternoon, preached to eight hundred natives; at night, to my little flock of Europeans. Which of these can I forego? The ministration of the natives might be in the week; but I wish to attach the idea of holiness to the Sunday. My evening congregation, on Sunday, is attended by twice as many as that on the week-day; so how can I let this go?"

With what extreme reluctance Mr. Martyn "spared himself," we see from the above letter. The progress of his complaint, however, compelled him to overcome this reluctance; and to the Indian congregation, when they next assembled, he was obliged to declare that his ill-health prevented him from addressing them; upon which, hundreds of voices were heard invoking for him long life and health; and when he dispensed his alms among them, their thankfulness seemed to know no bounds. Shortly after, however, he ventured to finish with these mendicants the history of Joseph, upon which he had entered; and to resume also the whole of his duty on the Sabbath, with the exception of one service. And, notwithstanding his extreme caution on that point, he administered the rite of baptism to an old Hindoo woman, "who, though she knew but little, was," he said, "lowliness itself."

Whilst Mr. Martyn was thus labouring in the very fire, sometimes yielding to the pressure of his complaint, and affording himself a little ease and relaxation; at others, renewing it, either by private conversation or public services,—providentially for the preservation of the remnant of his health, in the beginning of June his friend and brother, Mr. Corrie, arrived at Cawnpore, on his journey to his new station at Agra. This proved a most seasonable refreshment and relief to Mr. Martyn, both in body and mind; for his friend, though himself in a weak state of health, undertook, by the permission of the Commander-in-Chief,—who showed a kind consideration for Mr. Martyn, in his drooping condition,—part of the duty, leaving to Mr. Martyn only the services of preaching to the natives at noon, and to the soldiers in the evening, in the performance of which he persuaded himself that he ought to persevere.

How greatly his friends became alarmed at this juncture, will appear from the following animated and anxious letter from Mr. Brown:—" You will know, from our inestimable brother Corrie, my solicitude about your health. If it could make you live longer, I would give up any child I have, and myself into the bargain. May it please the adorable and unsearchable Being with whom we have to do, to lengthen your span! Amidst the dead and the dying, nothing can be more apparently prosperous to the Church of God, than the overwhelmings now taking place in the earth. Christ will find his way to the hearts of men, and there will be a great company to praise Him. I know not why we should wish to be saved, but for this purpose; or why, but for this purpose, we should desire the conversion of Heathens, Turks, and Infidels. To find them at the feet of Jesus will be a lovely sight. Our feeble voices cannot praise him much. We shall be glad to see them clapping their hands and casting their crowns before Him; for all in heaven and earth cannot sufficiently praise Him. I see no cause to wish for anything but the advancement of that knowledge by which there is some accession of praise to his holy and blessed name. We grasp, and would wish to gather all to Christ; but without Him we can do nothing : He will gather to Himself those that are his."

From this time till the month of September, Mr. Martyn persisted in his ministration to the natives, taking for the subject of several successive discourses, the Ten Commandments. On one of these occasions, he describes himself as speaking with great ease in his body and joy in his heart. "Blessed be God," he says, "my strength is returning. Oh may I live to proclaim salvation through a Saviour's blood!" But this sunshine was soon overclouded ; for he shortly after again relapsed.

Such was the sinking state of his health, notwithstanding the seasonable and important assistance derived from the presence of Mr. Corrie, that a removal from Cawnpore, either to make trial of the effect of a sea-voyage, or to return for a short time to England, became now a matter of urgent necessity. The adoption of the latter expedient he had once determined upon, conceiving that his complaint might arise from relaxation, and that a bracing air would in that case be beneficial. Nor was this resolution formed without a reluctant struggle in his mind : India held out to him the most powerful attractions; however strongly his affections were drawn towards his native country. That he had not forgotten one peculiarly dear to him, is shown by the following record, breathing equally a spirit of touching tenderness, and of meek resignation.

Sept. 22.—"Was walking with L——; both much affected, and speaking on the things dearest to us both. I awoke, and behold, it was a dream! My mind remained very solemn and pensive; I shed tears. The clock struck three, and the moon was riding near her highest noon; all was silence and solemnity; and I thought with pain of the sixteen thousand miles between us. But good is the will of the Lord, even if I see her no more." *

The precise period of his departure from Cawnpore, as well as the place of his ultimate destination, was fixed by information received from Calcutta, concerning the Persian Version of the New Testament.

The version which had first been made in that language, two Gospels of which had been printed, had been considered, on further inspection and more mature consideration, to require too many amendments to admit of its immediate publication. It was accordingly returned to the translator, who, under the superintendence of Mr. Martyn, bestowed so much pains and attention upon it, as to render it a new, and, it was hoped, a sound and accurate work. By those, however, who were considered competent judges at Calcutta, it was still deemed unfit for general circulation, inasmuch as it was thought to abound with Arabic idioms, and to be written in a style, pleasing indeed to the learned, but not sufficiently level to the capacities of the mass of modern readers.

At this decision, Mr. Martyn was as keenly disappointed, as he was delighted at the complete success of the Hindostanee version, which, on the minutest and most rigorous revision, was pronounced to be idiomatic and plain. But, meeting the disappointment with that spirit and elasticity of mind which is the result of lively

* See Appendix VII., VIII., IX., X.

faith, he instantly resolved—after committing his way to God in prayer, and consulting his friends, Mr. Corrie and Mr. Brown, on the subject—to go into Arabia and Persia, for the purpose of collecting the opinions of learned natives, with respect to the Persian translation which had been rejected, as well as of the Arabic version, which was yet incomplete, though nearly finished.

Mr. Brown's reply, on this purpose being communicated to him, is too characteristic, both of himself and of Mr. Martyn, to be omitted. " But can I then," said he, " bring myself to cut the string, and let you go ? I confess I could not, if your bodily frame were strong, and promised to last for half a century. But, as you burn with the intenseness and rapid blaze of heated phosphorus, why should we not make the most of you ? Your flame may last as long, and perhaps longer, in Arabia, than in India. Where should the phœnix build her odoriferous nest, but in the land prophetically called 'the blessed ?' and where shall we ever expect, but from that country, the True Comforter to come to the nations of the East ? I contemplate your New Testament, springing up, as it were, from dust and ashes, but beautiful 'as the wings of a dove covered with silver, and her feathers like yellow gold.' "

Towards the end of September, therefore, Mr. Martyn put himself in readiness to leave Cawnpore; and, on his preaching for the last time to the natives, and giving them an account of the life, the miracles, the death, and the resurrection of Jesus, as well as a summary of His heavenly doctrine,—exhorting them to believe in Him, and taking them to record that he had declared to them the glad tidings of the Gospel,—it was but too apparent that they would never again hear those sounds of wisdom and mercy from his lips. On the opening of the new church, also, where he preached to his own countrymen, amidst the happiness and thankfulness which abounded at seeing "a temple of God erected, and a door opened for the service of the Almighty, in a place, where from the foundation of the world, the tabernacle of the true God had never stood,"—a mournful foreboding could not be suppressed, that he who had been the cause of its erection, and who now ministered in it for the first time, in the beauty of holiness, would minister there no more. They beheld him as standing on the verge of the eternal world, and ready to take a splendid flight. "My father, my father, the chariot of Israel and the horsemen thereof," were the sentiments with which many gazed on him. One of his auditors, on this solemn occasion,* describes, in the following words, the feelings of many others, while depicting her own :—

"He began in a weak and faint voice, being, at that time, in a very bad state of health ; but, gathering strength as he proceeded, he seemed as one inspired from on high. Never was an audience more affected. The next day this holy and heavenly man left Cawnpore, and the society of many who sincerely loved and admired him. He left us, with little hope of seeing him again, until, by the mercy of our Saviour, we meet with him in our Father's house."

On the first day of October, the day following the delivery of this affecting discourse, after fervently uniting in prayer with his beloved friend and brother, Mr. Corrie, with whom he was not again to meet and worship, until separation shall cease for ever and prayer be changed into endless hallelujahs, Mr. Martyn

* Mrs. Sherwood.

departed from Cawnpore for Mr. Brown's residence at Aldeen, which he safely reached on the evening of the last day of the month. In his voyage down the Ganges, nothing of particular moment occurred, except that he visited the remains of his flock of the 67th at Gazeepore, "where," said he, "sad was the sight. Many of the most hopeful were ashamed to look me in the face, and sorrow appeared in the faces of those who had remained faithful. About nine of these came to me in my boat, where we sang the hymn which begins,

"'Come ye that love the Lord;'

after which I spoke to, and prayed with them, earnestly and affectionately, if ever I did in my life." This painful interview was succeeded by another, not uninteresting, with Antonio, a monk, at Boglipore. "We sat in the evening," Mr. Martyn writes, "under a shed on the banks of the river, and began to dispute in Latin, about the church. He grew a little angry, and I do not know what might have been the end of it, but the church-bells rang for vespers, and terminated the controversy. The church is in his garden; a very neat building, hung round with some mean little engravings. A light was burning in the chancel, and an image of the Virgin, behind a curtain, as usual, was over the table. Antonio did not fail to bow to the image; but he did it in a way which showed that he was ashamed of himself; at least, so I thought. He read some passages from the Hindostanee Gospels, which I was surprised to find so well done. I begged him to go on with the Epistles. He had translated also the Missal, equally well done. He showed me the Four Gospels in Persian, very poorly done. I rejoiced unfeignedly at seeing so much done, though he followeth not with us. The Lord bless his labours; and while he watereth others, may he be watered himself!"

Restored, after an absence of four years, to an intercourse with his friends, who, on beholding his pallid countenance and enfeebled frame, knew not whether most to mourn or to rejoice, Mr. Martyn partook largely of that pure and refined happiness, which is peculiar to one of his vivid feelings and heavenly affections, in that society where they that "fear the Lord speak often one to another, and the Lord hearkens and hears, and a book of remembrance is written before Him for them that fear the Lord, and think upon his name."

The following letter to Mr. Simeon expresses the heartfelt sentiments of one of those friends,* to whom India in general, and Calcutta in particular, stand so greatly indebted, after an interview chequered alternately by the varying lights and shades of joy and distress :—

"This bright and lovely jewel first gratified our eyes on Saturday last. He is on his way to Arabia, where he is going in pursuit of health and knowledge. You know his genius, and what gigantic strides he takes in everything. He has some great plan in his mind, of which I am no competent judge; but, as far as I do understand it, the object is far too grand for one short life, and much beyond his feeble and exhausted frame. Feeble it is, indeed! how fallen and changed! His complaint lies in his lungs, and appears to be an incipient consumption. But let us hope that the sea-air may revive him; and that change of place and pursuit may do him essential service, and continue his life many years. In all other respects, he is exactly the same as he was. He shines in all the dignity of love, and seems to carry about him such

* The Rev. Mr. Thomason.

a heavenly majesty, as impresses the mind beyond description. But if he talks much, though in a low voice, he sinks, and you are reminded of his being 'dust and ashes.'

So infirm was the state of Mr. Martyn's health, that the indulgence of conversation with his friends soon produced a recurrence of those symptoms which had occasioned alarm at Cawnpore; and yet, notwithstanding this, he preached every Sabbath at Calcutta, with one exception only, until he finally left it. Animated with the zeal of that apostle who at Troas continued his discourse until midnight, he could not refrain from lifting up his voice, weak as it was, in divine warnings and invitations, in a place where something seemed to intimate that he should never again declare God's judgments against the impenitent, nor invite the weary and heavy-laden to Jesus Christ for rest.

"I now pass," said Mr. Martyn on the first day of the year 1811, "from India to Arabia, not knowing the things that shall befal me there, but assured that an ever-faithful God and Saviour will be with me in all places whithersoever I go. May He guide and protect me, and, after prospering me in the thing whereunto I go, bring me back again to my delightful work in India! I am perhaps leaving it to see it no more;—but the will of God be done; my times are in his hand, and He will cut them as short as shall be most for my good: and with this assurance, I feel that nothing need interrupt my work or my peace."

On the 7th day of January, after having preached a sermon on the anniversary of the Calcutta Bible Society, which was afterwards printed, and entitled, "Christian India; or, an Appeal on behalf of Nine hundred thousand

Christians in India who want the Bible ;" and after having for the last time addressed the inhabitants of Calcutta, from the text of Scripture, "But one thing is needful,"—Mr. Martyn departed for ever from those shores, on which he had fondly and fully purposed to spend all his days.

CHAPTER VIII.

MR. MARTYN LEAVES BENGAL FOR SHIRAZ—OCCURRENCES
DURING HIS JOURNEY—ARRIVES AT SHIRAZ — COM-
MENCES A NEW TRANSLATION—DISCUSSIONS WITH THE
PERSIAN MOOLLAHS.

IN the former periods of Mr. Martyn's life, we have seen
in him, the successful candidate for academical distinctions,—the faithful and laborious Pastor,—the self-denying and devoted Missionary,—the indefatigable Translator
of the Scriptures,—the Preacher of the Gospel to the
heathen. In this, the last and shortest portion of the
contracted term of his earthly existence, we are called to
contemplate his character in a new and yet more striking
light, and shall have occasion to admire in him the erect
and courageous spirit of the Christian confessor.

The occurrences which transpired between his departure from the mouth of the Hoogley and his arrival at
Shiraz, occupy a period of five months. They are partly
recorded in the following extracts from his private journal,
and partly related in a letter to Mr. Corrie, from Shiraz.

"Bay of Bengal, January, 1811.

"I took a passage in the ship Ahmoody, Captain
Kinsay, bound to Bombay. One of my fellow-passengers
was the Honourable Mr. Elphinstone, who was proceeding
to take the Residency of Poonah. His agreeable manners
and classical acquirements made me think myself fortunate

indeed in having such a companion, and I found his company the most agreeable circumstance in my voyage."

"Our captain was a pupil of Swartz, of whom he communicated many interesting particulars.—Swartz, with Kolhoff and Jœnicke, kept a school for half-caste children, about a mile and a-half from Tanjore ; but went every night to the Tanjore church, to meet about sixty or seventy of the king's regiment, who assembled for devotional purposes ; after which he officiated to their wives and children in Portuguese. At the school Swartz used to read, in the morning, out of the German "Meditation for every day in the year ;" at night, he had family prayer. Jœnicke taught geography ; Kolhoff, writing and arithmetic.—They had also masters in Persian and Malabar.

"At a time when the present Rajah was in danger of his life from the usurper of his uncle's throne, Swartz used to sleep in the same room with him. This was sufficient protection, "for (said the Captain) Swartz was considered by the natives as something more than mortal." The old Rajah, at his death, committed his nephew to Swartz."

"All down the Bay of Bengal I could do nothing but sit listless on the poop, viewing the wide waste of water ; a sight that would have been beautiful, had I been well."

"On the 18th, we came in sight of the Island of Ceylon."

"In my Hebrew researches I scarcely ever felt so discouraged. All the knowledge I thought I had acquired became uncertain, and consequently I was unhappy. It was in vain that I reflected that thousands live and die happy, without such knowledge as I am in search of."

Jan. 20.—Sunday.—"Had divine service in the cabin

in the morning, but waited in vain for what seemed a proper opportunity of introducing family prayer. When shall I have done with this pernicious delicacy, which would rather yield up souls than suffer a wound itself?"

Jan. 22.—"Came to an anchor off Columbo. In the afternoon, went on shore with Mr. Elphinstone, and walked to a cinnamon-garden. The road all along was beautiful; tall groves of cocoa-nut trees on each side, with the tents of the natives among them, opened here and there, and gave a view of the sea. The Cingalese who accompanied us, told the natives who saw us, that we were Protestant Christians. On our way back, we saw a party of Cingalese Christians returning home from a church-yard, where they had been burying a corpse. I crossed over to them, and found their Catechist, who, however, spoke too little English to give me any information."

Jan. 23.—"Sailed from Ceylon across the Gulf of Manaar, where there is generally a swell, but which we found smooth. Having passed Cape Comorin, and come into smooth water, I proposed having family prayer every night in the cabin, and no objection was made. Spoke a ship to-day, which was conveying pilgrims from Manilla to Jidda. The first object discernible under the high mountains of Cape Comorin was a church. As we passed along the shore, churches appeared every two or three miles, with a row of huts on each side. These churches are like the meeting-houses in England, with a porch at the west end. Perhaps many of these poor people, with all the incumbrances of Popery, are moving towards the kingdom of heaven."

Jan. 26.—"Anchored off Allepie. Learned that there were here about two hundred Christians, Portuguese, besides the fisherman caste. The church was a temporary erection, but a stone edifice is to be raised on the spot. The Portuguese Padre resides at another church about three miles off."

Jan. 27 to 31.—"Generally unwell. In prayer, my views of my Saviour have been inexpressibly consolatory. How glorious the privilege that we exist but in Him; without Him I lose the principle of life, and am left to the power of native corruption,—a rotten branch, a dead thing, that none can make use of. This mass of corruption, when it meets the Lord, changes its nature and lives throughout, and is regarded by God as a member of Christ's body. This is my bliss, that Christ is all. Upheld by Him, I smile at death. It is no longer a question about my own worthiness. I glory in God, through our Lord Jesus Christ." *

Feb. 7.—"Arrived at Goa. Spent the evening at Mr. ——'s, to whom I had letters of recommendation. The next day I went up with Mr. Elphinstone and others to Old Goa, where we were shown the convents and churches. At the convent of the nuns, observing one reading, I asked to see the book. It was handed through the grate, and as it was a Latin prayer-book, I wrote in it something about having the world in the heart, though flying from it to a convent. I tried to converse with two or three half-native monks, but they knew so little Latin that I could not gain much from them, and the Portuguese Padres seemed to know still less. After visiting the tomb of Francis Xavier, we went to the Inquisition, but we were not admitted beyond the antechamber. The priest we found there (a secular) conversed a little on the subject, and said that it was the ancient practice, that if

* See Appendix XI.

any spoke against religion, they were conducted thither and chastised ; and that there were some prisoners there under examination at that time. No one dares resist the officers of the Inquisition; the moment they touch a man he surrenders himself. Colonel ——, who is writing an account of the Portuguese in this settlement, told me that the population of the Portuguese territory was two hundred and sixty thousand ; of whom two hundred thousand, he did not doubt, were Christians."

Feb. 17.—Sunday.—"A tempestuous sea throwing us all into disorder, we had no service."

Feb. 18.—"Anchored at Bombay. This day I finished the thirtieth year of my unprofitable life ; the age at which David Brainerd finished his course. I am now at the age at which the Saviour of men began his ministry, and at which John the Baptist called a nation to repentance. Let me now think for myself, and act with energy. Hitherto I have made my youth and insignificance an excuse for sloth and imbecility : now let me have a character, and act boldly for God."

Feb. 19.—"Went on shore. Waited on the Governor, and was kindly accommodated with a room at the Government-house."

Feb. 21.—"Talked to the Governor about what we had been doing at Bengal, and begged that he would interest himself, and procure us all the information he could about the native Christians : this he promised to do. At Bombay there are twenty thousand Christians ; at Salsette twenty-one thousand ; and at this place there are forty-one thousand, using the Mahratta language."

Feb. 22.—"At the 'Courier' press I saw the Malayalim New Testament in print, as far as the eleventh of John."

Feb. 24.—"Preached at the Bombay church."

March 5.—"Feeroz, a Parsee, who is considered the most learned man here, called to converse about religion. He spoke Persian, and seemed familiar with Arabic. He began with saying that no one religion had more evidences of its truth than another, for that all the miracles of the respective founders depended upon tradition. This I denied. He acknowledged that the writer of the Zendavesta was not contemporary with Zoroaster. After disputing and raising objections, he was left without an answer, but continued to cavil. 'Why,' said he, 'did the Magi see the star in the East, and none else? From what part of the East did they come? and how was it possible that their king should come to Jerusalem in seven days?' The last piece of information he had from the Armenians. I asked him, 'Whether he had any thoughts of changing his religion.' He replied with a contemptuous smile, 'No; every man is safe in his own religion.' I asked him, 'What sinners must do to obtain pardon?' 'Repent,' said he. I asked, 'Would repentance satisfy a creditor or judge?' 'Why, is it not said in the Gospel,' rejoined he, 'that we must repent?' I replied, 'It cannot be proved from the Gospel, that repentance alone is sufficient, or good works, or both.' 'Where, then, is the glory of salvation?' he said. I replied, 'In the atonement of Christ.' 'All this,' said he, 'I know; but so the Mohammedans say, that Hosyn was an atonement for the sins of men.' He then began to criticise the translations which he saw on the table, and wondered why they were not made in such Persian as was now in use. He looked at the beginning of the eighth of Romans, in the Christian Knowledge Society's Arabic Testament, but could gather no meaning at all from it."

March 6.—"Feeroz called again, and gave me some

account of his own people. He said that they considered the terms Magi and Guebr as terms of reproach, and that their proper name was Musdyasni; that no books were written in their most ancient language, namely, the Pahlavee, but Zoroaster's twenty-one; of these twenty-one, only two remain. He showed me a part of a poem which he is writing; the subject is the conquest of India by the English; the title, Georgiad. He is certainly an ingenious man, and possesses one of the most agreeable qualities a disputant can possess, which is, patience : he never interrupted me; and, if I rudely interrupted him, he was silent in a moment."

March 7.—" Mahomed Jan, a very young man, son of Mehdee Ali Kahn, Lord Wellesley's Envoy to Persia, called. I should not have thought him worth arguing with, he seemed such a boy; but his fluency in Persian pleased me so much, that I was glad to hear him speak; he was, besides, familiar with all the arguments the Mouluwees usually bring forward; moreover, I thought that perhaps his youthful mind might be more open to conviction than that of the hoary Moollahs."

March 9.—" Visited the Elephanta Island."

March 10.—Sunday.—" This morning Feeroz called before church. He said that their order of priesthood consisted in the descendants of Zoroaster, and were called Mobid : that four times a month they assembled, viz., the 6th, 13th, 20th, and 27th : strangers were not allowed to see the sacred fire, ' though,' said the old man, significantly, ' I think there is nothing unlawful in it, but the common people do.' He began to profess himself a Deist. ' In our religion,' said he, ' they believe as Zoroaster taught ; that the heavens and earth were made; but I believe no such thing.' "

March 16.—" Walked at night with a respectable Jew

of Bussorah, whose name was Ezra; he knew next to nothing."

March 25.—"Embarked on board the Benares, Captain Sealy; who, in company with the Prince of Wales, Captain Hepburn, was ordered to cruise in the Persian Gulf against the Arab pirates. We got under weigh immediately, and were outside the land before night."

March 31.—"The European part of the ship's crew, consisting of forty-five sailors and twelve artillerymen, were assembled on the quarter deck to hear divine service. I wondered to see so many of the seamen inattentive; but I afterwards found that most of them were foreigners, French, Spanish, Portuguese, &c. We had prayers in the cabin every night. In the afternoon I used to read to a sick man below, and two or three others would come to hear."

April 14.—Easter Sunday.—"Came in sight of the Persian coast, near Tiz, in Meehran."

April 21.—"Anchored at Muscat, in Arabia."*

April 23.—"Went on shore with the Captain to the Indian broker's, at whose house we met the Vizier, by appointment. There was an unimportant conference, at which I assisted as interpreter. The Sultan was a few miles off, fighting with the Wechabites."

April 24.—"Went with our English party, two Armenians, and an Arab soldier, to see a garden: there was nothing very wonderful in the garden, but a little green in this frightful wilderness was, no doubt, to the Arab, a great curiosity. His African slave argued with me for Mahomet, and did not know how to let me go, he was so interested in the business."

April 25.—"The Arab soldier and his slave came on

* See Appendix XII.

board to take leave. They asked to see the Gospel. The instant I gave them a copy in Arabic, the poor boy began to read, and carried it off as a great prize, which I hope he will find it to be. This night we warped out of the Cove, and got under weigh. I had not had a night's rest from the day we entered it."

April 26.—" Came in sight of the Persian shore again."

April 28.—Sunday.—" At anchor in Jasques Bay, which the artillery officer surveyed. Captain Hepburn brought his crew to church. Went on board his ship to see two Armenian young men, who informed me of the conversion of Mirza Ishmael, son of Shehool Islam, of Isfahan, who was gone to Bombay for baptism."

May 7.—" Finished a work on which I have been engaged for a fortnight;—a new arrangement of all the Hebrew roots, classing them according to the last letter, the last but one, &c."

May 20.—" After a troublesome north-wester, we have now a fair wind, carrying us gently to Bushire."

May 22.—" Landed at Bushire."

In his journey from Bushire to Shiraz, it was not merely the ordinary inconveniences of travelling in Persia which Mr. Martyn had to combat. So intense was the heat of the sun in the month of June, as to endanger his life; a peril of which he had no previous apprehension: though, with so great an object before him, he would have been warranted in knowingly incurring great danger towards the attainment of his purpose.

Seventeen days elapsed, after landing at Bushire, before he reached Shiraz; of these, eight were consumed in preparation for travelling, and the remainder in accomplishing his journey. The whole period is embraced, and

TO SHIRAZ. 289

the very interesting events of it are recorded, in the following letter to Mr. Corrie.

"A few days after my letter to you from Muscat, we sailed for the Gulf, and continued cruising a month, generally in sight of Persia or Arabia, sometimes of both. On the 22d of May, we landed at Bushire, and took up our lodging with Mr. ———. We are now in a new situation. Mrs. ——— and her sister, both Armenians, spoke nothing but Persian at table ; the servants and children the same. One day a party of Armenian ladies came to kiss my hand,—the usual mark of respect shown to their own priests ; I was engaged at the time, but they begged to have it explained that they had not been deficient in their duty. The Armenian priest was as dull as they usually are. He sent for me, one Sunday evening, to come to church ; though he was ministering when I entered, he came out, and brought me within the rails of the altar ; and at the time of incense, censed me four times, while the others were honoured with only one fling of the censer: this the old man begged me afterwards to notice. But, though his civility was well meant, I could hardly prevail upon myself to thank him for it. It was due, he said, to a *Padre ;* thus we provide for the honour of our own order, not contented with that degree of respect which really belongs to us. Walking afterwards with him by the sea-shore, I tried to engage him in a conversation respecting the awful importance of our office ; but nothing could be more vapid and inane than his remarks.

"One day we called on the Governor, a Persian Khan ; he was very particular in his attentions, seated me in his own seat, and then sat by my side. After the usual salutations and inquiries, the calean (or hookah) was introduced; then coffee, in china cups placed within silver ones; then calean; then some rose-water syrup; then calean. As there were long intervals, often, in which naught was heard but the gurgling of the calean, I looked round with some anxiety for something to discourse upon, and observing the windows to be of stained glass, I began to question him about the art of colouring glass; observing that the modern Europeans were inferior to the ancient in the manufacture of that article. He expressed his surprise that Europeans, who were so skilful in making watches, should fail in any handicraft-work. I could not help recollecting the Emperor of China's sarcastic remark on the Europeans and their arts, and therefore dropped the subject. On his calean,—I called it hookah at first, but he did not understand me,—I noticed several little paintings of the Virgin and Child, and asked him whether such things were not unlawful among the Mohammedans? He answered very coolly, 'Yes;' as much as to say, 'What then?' I lamented that the Eastern Christians should use such things in their churches. He repeated the words of a good man, who was found fault with for having an image before him while at prayer: 'God is nearer to me than that image, so that I do not see it.' We then talked of the ancient Caliphs of Bagdad; their magnificence, regard for learning, &c. This man, I afterwards found, is, like most of the other grandees of the East, a murderer. He was appointed to the Government of Bushire, in the place of an Arab Shekh, in whose family it had been for many years. The Persian, dreading the resentment of the other Arab families, invited the heads of them to a feast. After they had regaled themselves a little, he proposed to them to take off their swords, as they were all friends together: they did so, a signal was given, and a band of ruffians murdered them all immediately. The Governor rode off with a body of troops to their villages, and murdered or secured their wives and children. This was about two years and a-half ago.

"Abdalla Aga, a Turk, who expects to be Pasha of Bagdad, called to examine us in Arabic; he is a great Arabic scholar himself, and came to see how much we knew; or rather, if the truth were known, to show how much he himself knew. There was lately a conspiracy at Bagdad to murder the Pasha. He was desired to add his name, which he did by compulsion, but secured himself from putting his seal to it, pretending he had lost it: this saved him. All the conspirators were discovered and put to death; he escaped with his life, but was obliged to fly to Bushire.

"On the 30th of May, our Persian dresses were ready, and we set out for Shiraz. The Persian dress consists of, first, stockings and shoes in one; next, a pair of large blue trousers, or else a pair of huge red boots; then the shirt; then the tunic; and above it the coat, both of chintz, and a great-coat. I have here described my own dress, most of which I have on at this moment. On the head is worn an enormous cone, made of the skin of the black Tartar sheep, with the wool on. If to this description of my dress I add that my beard and moustaches have been suffered to vegetate undisturbed ever since I left India,— that I am sitting on a Persian carpet, in a room without tables or chairs,—and that I bury my hand in the pillau, without waiting for spoon or plate, you will give me credit for being already an accomplished Oriental.

"At ten o'clock on the 30th, our cafila began to move.

It consisted chiefly of mules, with a few horses. I wished to have a mule, but the muleteer favoured me with his own pony; this animal had a bell fastened to its neck. To add solemnity to the scene, a Bombay trumpeter, who was going up to join the embassy, was directed to blow a blast as we moved off the ground; but whether it was that the trumpeter was not an adept in the science, or that his instrument was out of order, the crazy sounds that saluted our ears had a ludicrous effect. At last, after some jostling, mutual recriminations, and recalcitrating of the steeds, we all found our places, and moved out of the gate of the city in good order. The Resident accompanied us a little way, and then left us to pursue our journey over the plain. It was a fine moonlight night, the scene new, and perfectly Oriental, and nothing prevented me from indulging my own reflections. I felt a little melancholy, but commended myself anew to God, and felt assured of His blessing, presence, and protection. As the night advanced, the cafila grew quiet; on a sudden one of the muleteers began to sing, and sang in a voice so plaintive, that it was impossible not to have one's attention arrested. Every voice was hushed. As you are a Persian scholar, I write down the whole, with a translation:—

        "'Think not that e'er my heart could dwell
           Contented far from thee:
        How can the fresh-caught nightingale
           Enjoy tranquillity?

        "'O then forsake thy friend for naught
           That slanderous tongues can say;
        The heart that fixeth where it ought,
           No power can rend away.'

"Thus far my journey was agreeable: now for miseries.

At sunrise we came to our ground at Ahmedee, six para-sangs, and pitched our little tent under a tree : it was the only shelter we could get. At first the heat was not greater than we had felt in India ; but it soon became so intense as to be quite alarming. When the thermometer was above 112°, fever-heat, I began to lose my strength fast ; at last it became quite intolerable. I wrapped my-self up in a blanket and all the warm covering I could get, to defend myself from the external air ; by which means the moisture was kept a little longer upon the body, and not so speedily evaporated as when the skin was exposed : one of my companions followed my example, and found the benefit of it. But, the thermometer still rising, and the moisture of the body being quite ex-hausted, I grew restless, and thought I should have lost my senses. The thermometer at last stood at 126° ; in this state I composed myself, and concluded that, though I might hold out a day or two, death was inevitable. Captain ——, who sat it out, continued to tell the hour, and height of the thermometer ; and with what pleasure did we hear of its sinking to 120°, 118°, &c. At last the fierce sun retired, and I crept out, more dead than alive. It was then a difficulty how I could proceed on my jour-ney ; for, besides the immediate effects of the heat, I had no opportunity of making up for the last night's want of sleep, and had eaten nothing. However, while they were loading the mules, I got an hour's sleep, and set out, the muleteer leading my horse, and Zachariah, my servant, an Armenian, of Isfahan, doing all in his power to encourage me. The cool air of the night restored me wonderfully, so that I arrived at our next munzil with no other de-rangement than that occasioned by want of sleep. Expect-ing another such day as the former, we began to make preparation the instant we arrived on the ground. I got a tattie made of the branches of the date-tree, and a Persian peasant to water it; by this means the thermometer did not rise higher than 114°. But what completely secured me from the heat was a large wet towel, which I wrapped round my head and body, muffling up the lower part in clothes. How could I but be grateful to a gracious Providence, for giving me so simple a defence against what, I am persuaded, would have destroyed my life that day. We took care not to go without nourishment, as we had done; the neighbouring village supplied us with curds and milk. At sunset, rising up to go out, a scorpion fell upon my clothes; not seeing where it fell, I did not know what it was; but Captain —— pointing it out, gave the alarm, and I struck it off, and he killed it. The night before we found a black scorpion in our tent; this made us rather uneasy; so that, though the cafila did not start till midnight, we got no sleep, fearing we might be visited by another scorpion.

"The next morning we arrived at the foot of the mountains, at a place where we seemed to have discovered one of Nature's ulcers. A strong suffocating smell of naphtha announced something more than ordinarily foul in the neighbourhood. We saw a river;—what flowed in it, it seemed difficult to say, whether it were water or green oil; it scarcely moved, and the stones which it laved, it left of a greyish colour, as if its foul touch had given them the leprosy. Our place of encampment this day was a grove of date-trees, where the atmosphere, at sunrise, was ten times hotter than the ambient air. I threw myself down on the burning ground, and slept: when the tent came up, I awoke, as usual, in a burning fever. All this day I had recourse to the wet towel, which kept me alive, but would allow of no sleep. It was a sorrowful Sabbath ; but Captain —— read a few hymns, in which I found great consolation. At nine in the evening we decamped. The ground and air were so insufferably hot, that I could not travel without a wet towel round my face and neck. This night, for the first time, we began to ascend the mountains. The road often passed so close to the edge of tremendous precipices, that one false step of the horse would have plunged his rider into inevitable destruction. In such circumstances, I found it useless to attempt guiding the animal, and therefore gave him the rein. These poor animals are so used to journeys of this sort, that they generally step sure. There was nothing to mark the road, but the rocks being a little more worn in one place than in another. Sometimes my horse, which led the way, as being the muleteer's, stopped, as if to consider about the way : for myself, I could not guess, at such times, where the road lay, but he always found it. The sublime scenery would have impressed me much in other circumstances ; but my sleepiness and fatigue rendered me insensible to everything around me. At last we emerged *superas ad auras*, not on the top of a mountain, to go down again,—but on a plain or upper world. At the pass, where a cleft in the mountain admitted us into the plain, was a station of Rahdars. While they were examining the muleteer's passports, &c., time was given for the rest of the cafila to come up, and I got a little sleep for a few minutes. We rode briskly over the plain, breathing a purer air, and soon came in sight of a fair edifice, built by the king of the country for the refreshment of pilgrims. In this caravansera we took up our abode for the day. It was more calculated for Eastern than European travellers, having no means of keeping

out the air and light. We found the thermometer at 110°.
At the passes we met a man travelling down to Bushire
with a load of ice, which he willingly disposed of to us.
The next night we ascended another range of mountains,
and passed over a plain, where the cold was so piercing,
that, with all the clothes we could muster, we were shi-
vering. At the end of this plain, we entered a dark
valley, formed by two ranges of hills converging to one
another. The muleteer gave notice that he saw robbers.
It proved to be a false alarm; but the place was fitted to
be a retreat for robbers, there being, on each side, caves
and fastnesses from which they might have killed every
man of us. After ascending another mountain, we descended by a very long and circuitous route into an extensive valley, where we were exposed to the sun till eight
o'clock. Whether from the sun, or from continued want
of sleep, I could not, on my arrival at Carzeroon, compose
myself to sleep; there seemed to be a fire within my
head, my skin like a cinder, and the pulse violent. Through
the day it was again too hot to sleep; though the place
we occupied was a sort of summer house, in a garden of
cypress-trees, exceedingly well fitted up with mats and
coloured glass. Had the cafila gone on that night, I
could not have accompanied it; but it halted here a day;
by which means I got a sort of night's rest, though I
awoke twenty times to dip my burning hand in water.
Though Carzeroon is the second greatest town in Fars,
we could get nothing but bread, milk, and eggs, and those
with difficulty. The governor, who is under great obli-
gations to the English, heard of our arrival, but sent no
message."

June 5.—"At ten we left Carzeroon, and ascended a
mountain: we then descended from it, on the other side,

into a beautiful valley, where the opening dawn discovered to us ripe fields of wheat and barley, with the green oak, here and there in the midst of it. We were reminded of an autumnal morning in England. Thermometer, 62°.

June 6.—"Half way up the Peergan mountain we found a caravansera. There being no village in the neighbourhood, we had brought supplies from Carzeroon. My servant Zachary got a fall from his mule this morning, which much bruised him; he looked very sorrowful, and had lost much of his garrulity. Zachary had become remarkable throughout the cafila for making speeches; he had something to say to all people, and on all occasions."

June 7.—" Left the caravansera at one this morning; and continued to ascend. The hours we were permitted to rest, the mosquitoes had effectually prevented me from using; so that I never felt more miserable and disordered; the cold was very severe; for fear of falling off, from sleep and numbness, I walked a good part of the way.—We pitched our tent in the vale of.Dustarjan, near a crystal stream, on the banks of which we observed the clover and golden cup : the whole valley was one green field, in which large herds of cattle were browsing. The temperature was about that of spring in England. Here a few hours' sleep recovered me, in some degree, from the stupidity in which I had been for some days. I awoke with a light heart, and said, 'He knoweth our frame, and remembereth that we are dust. He redeemeth our life from destruction, and crowneth us with loving-kindness and tender mercies. He maketh us to lie down on the green pastures, and leadeth us beside the still waters.' And when we have left this vale of tears, there is 'no more sorrow, nor sighing, nor any more pain.' 'The sun shall not light upon thee, nor any heat : but the Lamb shall lead thee to living fountains of waters.'"

June 8.—"Went on to a caravansera, three parasangs, where we passed the day. At night set out upon our last march for Shiraz. Sleepiness, my old companion and enemy, again overtook me. I was in perpetual danger of falling off my horse, till at last I pushed on to a considerable distance beyond the cafila, planted my back against a wall, and slept I know not how long ; till the good muleteer came up and gently waked me.

"On the morning of the 9th we found ourselves in the plain of Shiraz. We put up at first in a garden, but are now at Jaffier Ali Khan's."

Arrived at the celebrated seat of Persian literature, Mr. Martyn having ascertained the general correctness of the opinion delivered at Calcutta, respecting the translation of the New Testament by Sabat, immediately commenced another version in the Persian language. An able and willing assistant, in this arduous and important work, presented himself in the person of Mirza Seid Ali Khan, the brother-in-law of his host, Jaffier Ali Khan. His coadjutor, he soon discovered, was one of a numerous and increasing religious community, whose tenets—if that term be not inapplicable to anything of so fluctuating and indefinite a nature as their sentiments—appear to consist in a refined mysticism of the most latitudinarian complexion ; a quality, be it remembered, entirely opposite to the exclusive character and inflexible spirit of Christianity ; and which, pervading, as it does so completely, the system of Soofeism, sufficiently accounts for its toleration under a Mohammedan despotism, of a purer

WHIMPER.

SHIRAZ.

Page 298.

SHIRAZ.

and more absolute kind than exists even in the Turkish dominions.

In Jaffier Ali Khan, a Mohammedan of rank and consequence, to whom Mr. Martyn had letters of recommendation, he found a singular urbanity of manners, united to a temper of more solid and substantial excellence,—a kindness of disposition, ever fertile in expedients conducive to the comforts and convenience of his guest. There was in him also, as well as in his brother-in-law, what was still more gratifying, an entire absence of bigotry and prejudice ; and on all occasions he was ready to invite, rather than decline, the freest interchange of opinion on religious topics.

The work for which Mr. Martyn had come to Shiraz, was commenced on the 17th of June, little more than a week after his reaching that city. It was preceded by a very pleasing interview with two priests of the Mohammedan faith, of which we have this account :—" In the evening Seid Ali came with two Moollahs, disciples of his uncle Mirza Ibraheem, and with them I had a very long and temperate discussion. One of them read the beginning of St. John, in the Arabic, and inquired very particularly into our opinions respecting the person of Christ; and when he was informed that we did not consider his human nature eternal, nor his mother divine, seemed quite satisfied, and remarked to the others, 'How much misapprehension is removed when people come to an explanation.'"

As Mr. Martyn was himself an object of attention and curiosity in Shiraz, and the New Testament itself was wholly new to his coadjutor, he was not suffered to proceed with his work without many interruptions. "Seid Ali," he writes, June 17, "began translating the Gospel of John with me. We were interrupted by the entrance of two very majestic personages, one of whom was the great-grandson of Nadir Shah. The uncle of the present king used to wait behind his father's table. He is now a prisoner here, subsisting on a pension."

June 18.—"At the request of our host, who is always planning something for our amusement, we passed the day at a house built half way up one of the hills which surround the town. A little rivulet, issuing from the rock, fertilizes a few yards of ground, which bear, in consequence, a cypress or two, sweet-brier, jessamine, and pinks. Here, instead of a quiet retreat, we found a number of noisy, idle fellows, who were gambling all day, and as loquacious as the men who occupy an alehouse bench. The Persians have certainly a most passionate regard for water : I suppose because they have so little of it. There was nothing at all in this place worth climbing so high for, except the little rivulet."

June 22.—"The prince's secretary, who is considered to be the best prose-writer in Shiraz, called upon us. One of his friends wanted to talk about Soofeism. They believe they know not what. It is mere vanity that makes them profess this mysticism. He thought to excite my wonder by telling me, that I, and every created thing, was God. I asked him how this was consistent with his religion ? He then mentioned the words from the Koran, 'God can be with another thing only by pervading it.' Either from curiosity, or to amuse themselves at an Indian's expense, they called in an Indian Moonshee, who had come with us from Bengal, and requested him to recite some of his poetry. Thus I had an opportunity of witnessing this exhibition of Eastern folly. After a few modest apologies, the Indian grew bold, and struck off a few stanzas. The Persians affected to admire them, though it was easy to see that they were laughing at his pronunciation and foreign idiom. However, they condescended to recite, in their turn, a line or two of their own composition; and, before they went away, wrote down a stanza or two of the Indian's, to signify that they were worth preserving."

June 26.—"Two young men from the college, full of zeal and logic, came this morning to try me with hard questions, such as, Whether being be one or two? What is the state and form of disembodied spirits? and other foolish and unlearned questions, ministering strife, on all which I declined wasting my breath. At last one of them, who was about twenty years of age, discovered the true cause of his coming, by asking me bluntly to bring a proof for the religion of Christ. 'You allow the Divine mission of Christ,' said I, 'why need I prove it?' Not being able to draw me into an argument, they said what they wished to say, namely, 'that I had no other proof for the miracles of Christ than they had for those of Mahomet; which is tradition.' 'Softly,' said I; 'you will be pleased to observe a difference between your books and ours. When, by tradition, we have reached our several books, our narrators were eye-witnesses; yours are not, nor nearly so.' In consequence of the interruption these lads gave me, for they talked a long time with great intemperance, I did little to-day.

"In the evening, Seid Ali asked me 'the cause of evil?' I said, 'I knew nothing about it.' He thought he could tell me, so I let him reason on, till he soon found he knew as little about the matter as myself. He wanted to prove that there was no real difference between good and evil,— that it was only apparent. I observed that this difference, if only apparent, was the cause of a great deal of real misery.

"While correcting the fifth of John, he was not a little surprised at finding such an account as that of an angel coming down and troubling the waters. When he found that I had no way of explaining it, but was obliged to understand it literally, he laughed, as if saying, 'there are other fools in the world besides Mohammedans.' I tried to lessen his contempt and incredulity by saying, that 'the first inquiry was,—Is the book from God ?' 'Oh, to be sure !' said he, 'it is written in the Bible ; we must believe it.' I asked him 'whether there was anything contrary to reason in the narrative ? whether it was not even possible that the salubrious powers of other springs were owing to the descent of an angel ?' Lastly, I observed, 'that all natural agents might be called the angels of God.' 'This,' said he, 'was consonant to their opinions ; and that when they spoke of the angels of the winds, the angel of death, &c., nothing more was meant than the cause of the winds,' &c."

June 27.—"Before I had taken my breakfast, the younger of the youths came in, and forced me into a conversation. As soon as he heard the word 'Father,' in the translation, used for 'God,' he laughed, and went away. Soon after, two men came in, and spoke violently for hours. Seid Ali, and a respectable Moulwee, whom he brought to introduce to me, took up the cudgels against them, and said that 'the *onus probandi* rested with them, not with me.' Zachariah told me this morning that I was the town talk ; that it was asserted that I was come to Shiraz to be a Mussulman, and should then bring five thousand men to Shiraz, under pretence of making them Mussulmans, but in reality to take the city."

June 28.—"The poor boy, while writing how one of the servants of the high-priest struck the Lord on the face, stopped, and said, 'Sir, did not his hand dry up?'"

June 30.—Sunday.—"Preached to the Ambassador's suite on the 'Faithful Saying.' In the evening baptized his child."

July 1.—"A party of Armenians came, and said among other things, that the Mohammedans would be glad to be under our English Government. Formerly they despised and hated the Feringees, but now they begin to say, 'What harm do they do? They take no man's wife,—no man's property.'

"Abdoolghunee, the Jew Mohammedan, came to prove that he had found Mahomet in the Pentateuch. Among other strange things, he said that the Edomites meant the Europeans, and that Mount Sion was in Europe. Afterwards Seid Ali asked me to tell him in confidence, why I believed that no prophet could come after Christ. I chose to begin with the Atonement, and wished to show that it was of such a nature that salvation by another was impossible. 'You talk,' said he, 'of the Atonement, but I do not see it anywhere in the Gospels.' After citing two passages from the Gospels, I read the third chapter of Romans, and the fifty-third of Isaiah. With the latter he was much struck. He asked many more questions, the scope of which was, that though Islam might not be true, he might still remain in it, and be saved by the Gospel. I said, 'You deny the divinity of Christ.'—'I see no difficulty in that,' said he. 'You do not observe the institutions of Christ,—Baptism and the Lord's Supper.'—'These,' said he, 'are mere emblems, and if a man have the reality, what need of emblems?' 'Christ,' said I, 'foresaw that the reality would not be so constantly

perceived without them, and therefore enjoined them.'
He said that 'in his childhood he used to cry while
hearing about the sufferings of Christ,' and he wept while
mentioning it."

The 3d of July was distinguished by a conversation
kept up between Mr. Martyn and two Moollahs, one of
whom displayed a very different spirit from that which
had actuated those ministers of the Mohammedan religion
who first visited him. "The Jewish Moollah Abdoolghunee, with Moollah Abulhasan," he writes, "came
prepared for a stiff disputation, and accordingly the altercation was most violent. Jaffier Ali Khan and Mirza
Seid Ali were present, with many others. The Jew
began by asking whether we believed that Jesus suffered.
I referred him to the 9th of Daniel, 'Messiah shall be cut
off, but not for himself.' I begged him to show who was
the Messiah, of whom Daniel spoke, if it was not Jesus.

"At Abulhasan's request, he began to give his reasons
for believing that Mahomet was foretold in the Old
Testament. The Jew wanted to show that when it is
said, 'Moses went out, and the twelve princes with him,'
the meaning is, that Moses had twelve religious Khaleefs,
just like Mahomet. I explained to the Mussulman that
they were not for religious affairs, but worldly,—for
deciding causes, &c.; and that religious services were
confined to one tribe.

"He proceeded to Deut. xviii. 18, 'The Lord will
raise from among their brethren.' 'Brethren,' he said,
'must mean some other than Jews. That Moses and
Jesus were not alike. Moses gave a law before he went;
Jesus did not; his disciples made one for Him; whereas
Mahomet left a book himself. That Moses was a warrior;

that Christ was not; but that Mahomet was.' I replied,—
"that the words of God, 'from among their *brethren*,'
Moses explained by those, 'from among *thee*;' and that
this excludes the possibility of Mahomet being meant."
After they were gone, I found Lev. xxvi. 46, which
supplies a complete answer. In reply to the objection
that Moses and Christ were not alike, I said, 'that in
respect of the *prophetic office*, there was such a likeness as
did not exist between any other two prophets;—in that
each *brought a new law*, and each was a *Mediator*.'

"The Jews next read the sixty-first of Isaiah, and
commented. I then read the same chapter, and observed
that Christ had cited one of the passages for Himself.
'The spirit of the Lord is upon me,' &c. This they
attended to, *because Christ had said so;* but as for
Peter's appropriating the passage in Deuteronomy to
Christ (Acts iii.), they made no account of it. So
ignorant are they of the nature of revelation.

"When we were separating, the Moollah Abulhasan
gravely asked me whether, if I saw proof of Mahomet's
miracles, I would believe and act as one who sought
the truth?' I told him, 'I wished for nothing but the
truth.' He then said, 'We must have an umpire.' 'But
where,' said I, 'shall we find an impartial one.' 'He
must be a Jew,' said one. 'Well, then,' added another,
'let Abdoolghunee be the man.' The apostate Jew
swore, by the four sacred books, that he would give
'just judgment.' I could not conceal my indignation
at such a ridiculous proposal, and said to the Jew, 'You
impartial! As a Mohammedan, you ought to speak well
of Christ; but it is easy to see that, like your brethren,
you hate Jesus as bitterly as ever.' He was quite alarmed
at this charge before the Mohammedans, by whom he has

long been considered as no true Mohammedan; and, in the most gentle manner possible, he assured me that 'none could have a greater respect for Jesus than he had; and that, *possibly*, in the text in Deuteronomy Jesus might be meant as well as Mahomet.'

"At the end of this vehement controversy, when they were most of them gone, I told Seid Ali 'that I had thought, that whatever others did, he would not have denied me common justice.' He took me aside, and said to me very earnestly, 'You did not understand me. Abulhasan is my enemy: nothing does he want so much as to bring me into danger; I must therefore show some little regard for the religion.' He told me that Mirza Ibrahim, the preceptor of all the Moollahs, was now writing a book in defence of Mohammedanism, and that it was to this that Abulhasan alluded, as that which was to silence me for ever.

July 4.—"Seid Ali having informed the Jew that I had found an answer to his argument from Genesis xiv., he came to know what it was, and stayed the whole morning asking an infinity of questions. He showed himself extremely well read in the Hebrew Bible and Koran, quoting both with the utmost readiness. He argued a little for the Koran, but very coldly. He concluded by saying, 'he must come to me every day; and either make me a Mussulman, or become himself a Christian.'"

The progress of the translation gave rise to the following affecting discourse between Seid Ali and Mr. Martyn. "Seid Ali, while perusing the twelfth of John, observed,— 'How he loved these twelve persons!' 'Yes,' said I; 'and all those who believe on Him through their word.' After our work was done, he began to say, 'From my childhood I have been in search of a religion, and am still undecided. Till now, I never had an opportunity of conversing with those of another religion: the English I have met in Persia have generally been soldiers, or men occupied with the world.' To some remarks I offered on the necessity of having the mind made up upon such a subject, considering the shortness of our stay here, he seemed cordially to assent, and shed tears. I recommended prayer and the consideration of that text, 'If any man will do his will, he shall know of the doctrine;' and spoke as having found it verified in my own experience; that when I could once say before God, 'What wilt thou have me to do!'—I found peace. I then went through all the different states of my mind at the time I was called to the knowledge of the Gospel. He listened with great interest and said, 'You must not regard the loss of so much time as you give me, because it does me good.' "

The situation of those whose forefathers crucified the Lord of glory, is ever pitiable to a Christian mind: but how much more are the Jews entitled to compassion, when groaning under the iron rod of oppression on the one hand, and tempted on the other to exchange their own religion for a base imposture, upon the basest considerations. Who can read the following account of their condition at Shiraz, without sighing over the depth of their temporal and spiritual degradation!

July 5.—"The Jew came again with another Jew; both Mussulmen. The prince gives every Jew, on conversion, an honorary dress; so they are turning Mohammedans every day. A young man, son of the old Jew, asked, 'How it could be supposed that God would leave so many nations so long in darkness, if Islam be in error?' The father sat with great complacency to see how I could get over this. I asked, 'Why God, for four thousand years, made himself known to their nation only, and left all the rest of the world in darkness?' They were silent.

"The old man, forgetting he was a Mussulman, asked again,—'If Jesus was the Messiah, why did not the fiery wrath of God break out against them, as it did formerly for every small offence?' 'But first,' said he, 'what do you think of God's severity to the Jews at other times?' I said, 'If my son do anything wrong, I punish him; but with the thieves and murderers out of doors, I have nothing to do.' This affected the old man; and his son recollected many passages in the Bible appropriate to this sentiment, and said,—'Yes, they were indeed a chosen generation.' I proceeded—'But did not the wrath of God break out against you at the death of Christ, in a more dreadful manner than ever it did?' They mentioned the captivity. 'But what,' said I, 'was the captivity? it lasted but seventy years. But now seventeen hundred years have passed away; and have you a king? or a temple? Are you not mean and despised everywhere?' They seemed to feel this, and nodded assent.

"During this conversation, I said,—'God has raised up a great prophet from the midst of you, and now you have gone after a stranger, of a nation who were always your enemies. You acknowledge Jesus, indeed; but it is only for fear of the sword of the Ishmaelite.' They wondered why the Christians should love them more than they do the Mohammedans, as I told them we did; and pretended to argue against it, as unreasonable; evidently from a wish to hear me repeat a truth which was so agreeable to them."

On the morning of the 6th, Mr. Martyn, ever anxious to pay all due reverence to 'the powers that be,' presented himself, with the Ambassador and suite, before Prince Abbas Mirza : He thus describes the ceremony : —"Early this morning I went with the Ambassador and his suite to court, wearing, agreeably to costume, a pair of red cloth stockings, with green high-heeled shoes. When we entered the great court of the palace, a hundred fountains began to play. The prince appeared at the opposite side, in his talar, or hall of audience, seated on the ground. Here our first bow was made. When we came in sight of him, we bowed a second time, and entered the room. He did not rise, nor take notice of any but the Ambassador, with whom he conversed at the distance of the breadth of the room. Two of his ministers stood in front of the hall, outside ; the Ambassador's Mihmander, and the Master of the Ceremonies, within, at the door. We sat down in order, in a line with the Ambassador, with our hats on. I never saw a more sweet and engaging countenance than the Prince's ; there was such an appearance of good nature and humility in all his demeanour, that I could scarcely bring myself to believe that he would be guilty of anything cruel or tyrannical."

The Jewish Moollah, who, a few days before, had attempted to support a heresy which he himself did not believe, revisited Mr. Martyn, accompanied by one of his brethren who had apostatized. These were followed, on the same day, by two other visitors, one of whom was a man of great consequence, and of equal courtesy.—"The Jew came again," he says, "with one of his apostate brethren from Bagdad. As he was boasting to Seid Ali, that he had gained one hundred Jews to Islam, I could not help saying, 'I will tell you how Jews are made Mohammedans. First, the Prince gives them a dress; secondly,'—here the old man coloured, and, interrupting me, began to urge, that it was not with the hope of any worldly advantage.

"His object to-day was, to prove that the passages in the Old Testament, which we applied to Jesus, did not belong to him. I referred him to the 16th Psalm. He said, 'that none of the prophets saw corruption.' He did not recollect the miracle wrought by the bones of Elisha; neither did I at the time.

"Mohammed Shareef Khan, one of the most renowned of the Persian generals, having served the present royal family for four generations, called to see me, out of respect for General Malcolm. An Armenian priest also, on his way from Bussorah to Isfahan : he was as ignorant as the rest of his brethren. To my surprise I found that he was of the Latin Church, and read the service in Latin ; though he confessed he knew nothing about the language."

Mr. Martyn, unwilling to lose any opportunity (if it were the will of God) of benefiting the inhabitants of Shiraz, was never inaccessible to them. Strict as he was in the observance of the Sabbath, he admitted them even on that day to speak with him, for he had learnt the import of those words, "I will have mercy and not sacrifice." In consequence, however, of his removal, in the middle of the month of July, to a garden in the suburbs of the city, where his kind host had pitched a tent for him, to relieve the tedium of confinement within the walls of Shiraz,—he prosecuted the work before him uninterruptedly. "Living amidst clusters of grapes, by the side of a clear stream," as he describes it, and frequently sitting under the shade of an orange-tree, which

Jaffier Ali Khan delighted to point out to visitors, he passed many a tranquil hour, and enjoyed many a Sabbath of holy rest and divine refreshment. Of one of these Sabbaths, he thus writes, July 14.—"The first Sabbath morning I have had to myself this long time, and I spent it with comfort and profit. Read Isaiah, chiefly ; and hymns, which, as usual, brought to my remembrance the children of God in all parts of the earth : remembered, especially, dear ——, as he desired me, on this his birthday."

CHAPTER IX.

FIRST PUBLIC DISCUSSION AT SHIRAZ—MR. MARTYN RE-
PLIES TO A DEFENCE OF MOHAMMEDANISM—INTERVIEW
WITH THE HEAD OF THE SOOFIES—VISITS PERSEPOLIS
—TRANSLATIONS—DISCUSSIONS.

THE day following this happy, though solitary Sabbath,
formed a contrast to its peaceful and sacred serenity ;
being the day of Mr. Martyn's first public controversy
with the Mohammedans.

After some hesitation and demur, the Moojtuhid, or
Professor of Mohammedan Law, consented to a discussion
upon religious topics. He was a man of great consequence
in Shiraz, being the last authority in the decision of all
matters connected with his profession ; so that a contest
with him, as it respected rank, prejudice, popularity, and
reputation for learning, was manifestly an unequal one.
Mr. Martyn, however, fearlessly engaged in it, knowing
in whom he had believed.

The subjoined is the account he has left of this disputation,—if such, indeed, it can be called ;—for the Professor, it seems, could not so far forget his official dignity,
as to dispute fairly and temperately ;—he preferred the
easier task of dogmatising magisterially.

"He first ascertained from Seid Ali," says Mr. Martyn,
" that I did not want demonstration, but admitted that
the prophets had been sent. So, being a little easy at

this assurance, he invited us to dinner. About eight o'clock at night we went, and after passing along many an avenue, we entered a fine court, where was a pond, and by the side of it a platform, eight feet high, covered with carpets. Here sat the Moojtuhid in state, with a considerable number of his learned friends,—among the rest I perceived the Jew. One was at his prayers. I was never more disgusted at the mockery of this kind of prayer. He went through the evolutions with great exactness, and pretended to be unmoved at the noise and chit-chat of persons on each side of him. The Professor seated Seid Ali on his right hand, and me on his left. Everything around bore the appearance of opulence and ease; and the swarthy obesity of the little personage himself, led me to suppose that he had paid more attention to cooking than to science. But when he began to speak, I saw reason enough for his being so much admired. The substance of his speech was flimsy enough; but he spoke with uncommon fluency and clearness, and with a manner confident and imposing. He talked for a full hour about the soul; its being distinct from the body; superior to the brutes, &c. ; about God; his unity, invisibility, and other obvious and acknowledged truths. After this followed another discourse. At length, after clearing his way for miles around, he said, ' that philosophers had proved, that a single being could produce but a single being ;—that the first thing God had created was *Wisdom*,—a being perfectly one with Him; after that, the souls of men, and the seventh heaven; and so on, till he produced matter, which is merely passive.' He illustrated the theory, by comparing all being to a circle ; at one extremity of the diameter is God, at the opposite extremity of the diameter is matter, than which nothing in the world is meaner. Rising from thence, the highest stage of matter is connected with the lowest stage of vegetation; the highest of the vegetable world, with the lowest of the animal; and so on, till we approach the point from which all proceeded. 'But,' said he, 'you will observe, that next to God, something ought to be, which is equal to God; for since it is equally near, it possesses equal dignity. What this is, philosophers are not agreed. You,' said he, 'say it is Christ; but we, that it is the Spirit of the Prophets. All this is what the philosophers have proved, independently of any particular religion.' I rather imagined that it was the invention of some ancient Oriental Christian, to make the doctrine of the Trinity appear more reasonable. There were a hundred things in the Professor's harangue that might have been excepted against, as mere dreams supported by no evidence; but I had no inclination to call in question dogmas, on the truth or falsehood of which nothing in religion depended.

" He was speaking, at one time, about the angels; and asserted that man was superior to them, and that no being greater than man could be created. Here the Jew reminded me of a passage in the Bible, quoting something in Hebrew. I was a little surprised, and was just about to ask where he found anything in the Bible to support such a doctrine; when the Moojtuhid, not thinking it worth while to pay any attention to what the Jew said, continued his discourse. At last the Jew grew impatient, and, finding an opportunity of speaking, said to me, 'Why do not you speak?—Why do not you bring forward your objections?' The Professor, at the close of one of his long speeches, said to me, 'You see how much there is to be said on these subjects; several visits will be necessary; we must come to the point by degrees.' Perceiving how much he dreaded a close discussion, I did not mean to hurry him, but let him talk on, not expecting we should have anything about Mohammedanism the first night. But at the instigation of the Jew I said, 'Sir, you see that Abdoolghunee is anxious that you should say something about Islam.' He was much displeased at being brought so prematurely to the weak point, but could not decline accepting so direct a challenge. 'Well,' said he to me, 'I must ask you a few questions. Why do you believe in Christ?' I replied, 'That is not the question. I am at liberty to say, that I do not believe in any religion; that I am a plain man, seeking the way of salvation; that it was, moreover, quite unnecessary to prove the truth of Christ to Mohammedans, because they allowed it.' 'No such thing,' said he. 'The Jesus we acknowledge is he who was a prophet, a mere servant of God, and one who bore testimony to Mahomet; not your Jesus, whom you call God,' said he, with a contemptuous smile. He then enumerated the persons who had spoken of the miracles of Mahomet, and told a long story about Salmon, the Persian, who had come to Mahomet. I asked 'whether this Salmon had written an account of the miracles he had seen?' He confessed that he had not. 'Nor,' said I, 'have you a single witness to the miracles of Mahomet.' He then tried to show, that though they had not, there was still sufficient evidence. 'For,' said he, 'suppose five hundred persons should say that they heard some particular thing of a hundred persons who were with Mahomet, would that be sufficient evidence or not?' 'Whether it be or not,' said I, 'you have no such evidence as that, nor anything like it; but if you have, as they are something like witnesses, we must proceed to examine them, and see whether their testimony deserves credit.'

"After this, the Koran was mentioned; but as the company began to thin, and the great man had not a sufficient audience before whom to display his eloquence, the dispute was not so brisk. He did not, indeed, seem to think it worth while to notice my objections. He mentioned a well-known sentence in the Koran, as being inimitable. I produced another sentence, and begged to know why it was inferior to the Koranic one. He declined saying why, under pretence that it required such a knowledge of rhetoric in order to understand his proofs, as I probably did not possess. A scholar afterwards came to Seid Ali, with twenty reasons for preferring Mahomet's sentence to mine.

"It was midnight when dinner, or rather supper, was brought in: it was a sullen meal. The great man was silent, and I was sleepy. Seid Ali, however, had not had enough. While burying his hand in the dish of the Professor, he softly mentioned some more of my objections. He was so vexed, that he scarcely answered anything; but, after supper, told a very long story, all reflecting upon me. He described a grand assembly of Christians, Jews, Guebres, and Sabians (for they generally do us the honour of stringing us with the other three), before Iman Ruza. The Christians were of course defeated and silenced. It was a remark of the Iman's, in which the Professor acquiesced, 'that it is quite useless for Mohammedans and Christians to argue together, as they had different languages and different histories.' To the last I said nothing; but to the former replied by relating the fable of the lion and the man, which amused Seid Ali so much, that he laughed out before the great man, and all the way home."

So universal a spirit of inquiry had been excited in the city of Shiraz, by Mr. Martyn's frequent disputations, as well as by the notoriety of his being engaged in a translation of the New Testament into Persian, that the *Preceptor of all the Moollahs* began greatly to 'fear whereunto this would grow.' On the 26th of July, therefore, an Arabic defence of Mohammedanism made its appearance from his pen. A considerable time had been spent in its preparation; and on seeing the light, it obtained the credit of surpassing all former treatises upon Islam.

This work, as far as a judgment of it can be formed from a translation discovered amongst Mr. Martyn's papers, is written with much temper and moderation, and with as much candour as is consistent with that degree of subtilty which is indispensable in an apology for so glaring an imposture as Mohammedanism.

The chief Moollah begins by declaring his desire to avoid all altercation and wrangling; and expresses his hope that God would guide into the right way those whom He chose. He then endeavours, in the body of the work, to show the superiority of the single perpetual miracle of the Koran, addressed to the understanding, above the variety of miracles wrought by Moses and by Christ, which were originally addressed only to the senses; and that these, from lapse of time, become every day less and less powerful in their influence. And he concludes with the following address to Mr. Martyn :—

"Thus behold, then, O thou that art wise, and consider with the eye of justice, since thou hast no excuse to offer to God. Thou hast wished to see the truth of miracles. We desire you to look at the great Koran: that is an everlasting miracle.

"This was finished by Ibraheem ben al Hosyn, after

the evening of the second day of the week, the 23rd of the month Iemadi, the second in the year 1223 of the Hegira of the Prophet. On him who fled be a thousand salutations!"

This work Mr. Martyn immediately set himself to refute, in dependance on his Saviour to "give him a wisdom which his adversaries should not be able to gainsay." His answer was divided into two parts: the first was principally devoted to an attack upon Mohammedanism; the second was intended to display the evidences and establish the authority of the Christian faith. It was written in Persian; and, from a translation of the first part, which has been found, we perceive that Mr. Martyn, "having such hope, used great plainness of speech;" whilst at the same time he treated his opponent with meekness and courtesy.

After replying to the various arguments of Mirza Ibraheem, Mr. Martyn shows why men are bound to reject Mohammedanism;—that Mahomet was foretold by no prophet;—that he worked no miracles;—that he spread his religion by means merely human, and framed his precepts and promises to gratify men's sensuality, both here and hereafter;—that he was most ambitious, both for himself and his family;—that his Koran is full of gross absurdities and palpable contradictions;—that it contains a method of salvation wholly inefficacious; which Mr. Martyn contrasted with the glorious and efficacious way of salvation held out in the Gospel, through the divine atonement of Jesus Christ. He concludes by addressing Mirza Ibraheem in these words:—

"I beg you to view these things with the eye of impartiality. If the evidence be indeed convincing, mind not the contempt of the ignorant, nor even death itself;—for the vain world is passing away like the wind of the desert.

"If you do not see the evidence to be sufficient, my prayer is, that God may guide you; so that you, who have been a guide to men in the way you thought right, may now both see the truth, and call men to God through Jesus Christ, 'who hath loved us, and washed us from our sins in his blood.' His glory and dominion be ever-lasting!"

Reverting to the Journal, we meet with the following statements illustrative of the Persian character, and descriptive of the genius of Soofeism. From these also, we discover that, notwithstanding individuals were to be found in Shiraz, who professed Mohammedanism without having imbibed the spirit of cruelty and extermination which belongs to it, Mr. Martyn was nevertheless exposed to personal danger there, and subject to much contempt and many insults.

July 29.—"Mirza Ibraheem declared publicly, before all his disciples, 'that if I really confuted his arguments, he should be bound in conscience to become a Christian.' Alas! from such a declaration I have little hope. His general good character, for uprightness and unbounded kindness to the poor, would be a much stronger reason with me for believing that he may perhaps be a Cornelius"

Aug. 2.—"Much against his will, Mirza Ibraheem was obliged to go to his brother, who is Governor of some town, thirty-eight parasangs off. To the last moment, he continued talking with his nephew on the subject of his book, and begged that, in case of his detention, my reply might be sent to him."

Aug. 7.—"My friends talked, as usual, much about

what they call Divine Love; but I do not very well comprehend what they mean. They love not the holy God, but the God of their own imagination;—a God who will let them do as they please.

"I often remind Seid Ali of one defect in his system, which is, that there is no one to stand between his sins and God. Knowing what I allude to, he says, 'Well, if the death of Christ intervene, no harm; Soofeism can admit this too.'"

Aug. 14.—"Returned to the city in a fever, which continued all the next day, until the evening."

Aug. 15.—"Jani Khan, in rank corresponding to one of our Scotch dukes, as he is the head of all the military tribes of Persia, and chief of his own tribe, which consists of twenty thousand families, called on Jaffier Ali Khan, with a message from the king. He asked me a great number of questions, and disputed a little. 'I suppose,' said he, 'you consider us all as infidels?' 'Yes,' replied I, 'the whole of you.' He was mightily pleased with my frankness, and mentioned it when he was going away."

Aug. 22.—"The copyist having shown my answer to a Moodurris, called Moollah Acber, he wrote on the margin with great acrimony, but little sense. Seid Ali having shown his remarks in some companies, they begged him not to show them to me, for fear I should disgrace them all through the folly of one man."

Aug. 23.—"Ruza Cooli Mirza, the great grandson of Nadir Shah, and Aga Mahomet Hasan, called. The prince's nephew, hearing of my attack on Mahomet, observed that 'the proper answer to it was the sword;' but the prince confessed that he began to have his doubts. On his inquiring what were the laws of Christianity,— meaning the number of times of prayer, the different washings, &c.,—I said that we had two commandments, 'Thou shalt love the Lord thy God with all thy heart, and all thy soul, and all thy strength; and thy neighbour as thyself.' He asked, 'What could be better?' and continued praising them.

"The Moollah Aga Mahommed Hasan, himself a Moodurris, and a very sensible, candid man, asked a good deal about the European philosophy; particularly what we did in metaphysics;—for instance, 'How, or in what sense, the body of Christ ascended into heaven?' He talked of free-will and fate, and reasoned high, and at last reconciled them according to the doctrines of the Soofies, by saying, that 'as all being is an emanation of the Deity, the will of every being is only the will of the Deity; so that, therefore, in fact, free-will and fate are the same.' He has nothing to find fault with in Christianity, except the Divinity of Christ. It is this doctrine that exposes me to the contempt of the learned Mohammedans, in whom it is difficult to say whether pride or ignorance predominates. Their sneers are more difficult to bear than the brickbats which the boys sometimes throw at me: both, however, are an honour of which I am not worthy. How many times in the day have I occasion to repeat the words,

> "'If on my face, for Thy dear name,
> Shame and reproaches be;
> All hail, reproach, and welcome, shame,
> If Thou remember me.'

"The more they wish me to give up this one point,—the Divinity of Christ, the more I seem to feel the necessity of it, and rejoice and glory in it. Indeed, I trust I would sooner give up my life than surrender it."

The following account of an interview to which Mr.
Martyn was admitted, with the head of the sect of the
Soofies, will interest those whose thoughts are turned
towards the state of religion in the East : a large proportion of the people of Shiraz, it is computed, are either
the secret or avowed disciples of Mirza Abulcasim.
Whenever "a great and effectual door" is opened for
Christianity, "there are many adversaries." It is otherwise with a delusion congenial to the "desires of the flesh
and of the mind" in fallen man. Such a system the god
of this world is concerned to uphold rather than oppose.

"In the evening we went to pay a long-promised visit
to Mirza Abulcasim, one of the most renowned Soofies in
all Persia. We found several persons sitting in an open
court, in which a few greens and flowers were placed ; the
master was in a corner. He was a very fresh-looking old
man, with a silver beard. I was surprised to observe the
downcast and sorrowful looks of the assembly, and still
more at the silence which reigned. After sitting some
time in expectation, and being not at all disposed to waste
my time in sitting there, I said softly to Seid Ali, 'What
is this?' He said, 'It is the custom here, to think much
and speak little.' 'May I ask the master a question?'
said I. With some hesitation he consented to let me : so
I begged Jaffier Ali to inquire, 'Which is the way to be
happy?'

"This he did in his own manner : he began by observing,
that 'there was a great deal of misery in the world, and
that the learned shared as largely in it as the rest ;
that I wished, therefore, to know what we must do to
escape it.' The master replied, that, 'for his part, he did
not know, but that it was usually said that the subjugation of the passions was the shortest way to happiness.'

" After a considerable pause, I ventured to ask 'what were his feelings in the prospect of death,—hope, or fear, or neither?' 'Neither,' said he, and that 'pleasure and pain were both alike.' I then perceived that the Stoics were Greek Soofies. I asked, 'whether he had attained this apathy?' He said, 'No.' 'Why do you think it attainable?' He could not tell. 'Why do you think that pleasure and pain are not the same?' said Seid Ali, taking his master's part. 'Because,' said I, 'I have the evidence of my senses for it. And you also act as if there was a difference. Why do you eat, but that you fear pain?' These silent sages sat unmoved.

" One of the disciples is the son of the Moojtuhid, who, greatly to the vexation of his father, is entirely devoted to the Soofie doctor. He attended his calean with the utmost humility. On observing the pensive countenance of the young man, and knowing something of his history from Seid Ali, how he had left all to find happiness in the contemplation of God, I longed to make known the glad tidings of a Saviour, and thanked God, on coming away, that I was not left ignorant of the Gospel. I could not help being a little pleasant on Seid Ali, afterwards, for his admiration of this silent instructor. 'There you sit,' said I, 'immersed in thought, full of anxiety and care, and will not take the trouble to ask whether God has said anything or not. No: that is too easy and direct a way of coming at the truth. I compare you to spiders, who weave their house of defence out of their own bowels; or to a set of people who are groping for a light at noon-day.' "

Mr. Martyn's mathematical acquirements were to him invaluable, inasmuch as they gave him that habit of patient and persevering study, which was sanctified in the application of his powers to the highest ends and purposes. There were also occasions in which this and other sciences were of service to the cause he had at heart, by procuring for him that attention and respect, which learning ever secures in countries where the light of civilization shines, even though but faintly and imperfectly. Of this we have an instance in the following account :—

August 26.—" Waited this morning on Mohammed Nubee Khan, late ambassador at Calcutta, and now Prime Minister of Fars. There were a vast number of clients in his court, with whom he transacted business while chatting with us. Amongst the others who came and sat with us was my tetric adversary, Aga Acbar, who came for the very purpose of presenting the minister with a little book he had written in answer to mine. After presenting it in due form, he sat down, and told me he meant to bring me a copy that day—a promise which he did not perform, through Seid Ali's persuasion, who told him it was a performance that would do him no credit. Aga Acbar gave me a hint respecting its contents, namely, that there were four answers to my objections to Mohammedans using the sword.

" He then, without any ceremony, began to question me, before the company (there were more than fifty in the hall, and crowds in front, all listening), about the European philosophy; and brought objections against the world's motion with as much spleen as if he had an estate which he was afraid would run away from him. As it was a visit of mere ceremony, I was not a little surprised, and looked at the minister, to know if it would not be a breach of good manners to dispute at such a time; but it seemed there was nothing contrary to custom, as he rather expected my answer. I explained our system to Aga Acbar; but there were many things not to be understood without diagrams; so a scribe in waiting was ordered to produce his implements, and I was obliged to show him, first, the sections of the cone, and how a body revolves in an ellipse round the sun in one focus, &c. He knew nothing of mathematics, as I suspected, so it was soon found useless to proceed; he comprehended nothing.

" On my return, Jaffier Ali Khan and Mirza Seid Ali requested me to explain to them my proofs. I did my best; but there were so many things they were obliged to take for granted, that all my endeavours were to little purpose. So much Mirza Seid Ali comprehended, that the hypothesis of a force varying inversely as the square of the distance, was sufficient to account for every phenomenon; and that therefore, according to the rules of philosophy, a more complex hypothesis was not to be admitted. This he had sense enough to see."

There is something so estimable in the character of Mr. Martyn's opponent, Mirza Ibraheem, that it will not fail to secure the attention of the reader, in perusing the subjoined relation of the effect produced on his mind by Mr. Martyn's defence of Christianity and attack upon Mohammedanism:—

Aug. 29.—"Mirza Ibraheem begins to inquire about the Gospel. The objections he made were such as these:—How sins could be atoned for before they were committed? Whether, as Jesus died for all men, all would necessarily be saved? If faith be the condition of salvation, would wicked Christians be saved, provided they believe? I was pleased to see, from the nature of the objections, that he was considering the subject. To this last objection I remarked, that to those who felt themselves sinners, and came to God for mercy, through Christ, God would give his Holy Spirit, which would progressively sanctify them in heart and life."

August 30.—"Mirza Ibraheem praises my answer, especially the first part."

Mr. Martyn's mind, we have had frequent occasion to notice, closed as it was against trifling vanities, was ever open and alive to many of those subjects which arrest the attention, and interest the curiosity of men of science and research, and which form one great source of intellectual gratification. Whilst the moral depravity of Shiraz chiefly occupied his thoughts and excited his commiseration, he could also find a mournful pleasure in musing over the fallen grandeur of Persepolis.

He has left the following observations and reflections, on visiting these celebrated remains of antiquity:—

"I procured two horsemen, as guards, from the minister, and set off about two hours before sunset. At a station of Rahdars we fed the horses, and then continued our course, through a most dismal country, till midnight, when we entered a vast plain, and two or three hours before day crossed the Araxes, by a bridge of three arches, and coming in sight of the ruins, waited for the day. I laid down upon the bare ground, but it was too cold to sleep.

"When the sun rose, we entered. My guards and servant had not the smallest curiosity to see ruins, and therefore the moment they mounted the terrace they laid down and fell asleep. These people cannot imagine why the Europeans come to see these ruins. One of them said to me, 'A nice place, Sahib; good air and a fine garden; you may carry brandy, and drink there at leisure.' Thus he united, as he thought, the two ingredients of human happiness,—the European enjoyment of drinking, and the Persian one of straight walks, cypress-trees, and muddy water in a square cistern. One of my guards was continually reminding me, on my way thither, that it was uninhabited. Finding me still persist, he imagined that my object must be to do something in secret; and accordingly, after I had satisfied my curiosity and was coming away, he plainly asked me whether I had been drinking;—observing, perhaps my eyes, which were red with cold and want of sleep. When I gravely told them that drunkenness was as great a sin with us as with them, they altered their tone, and said that wine was not only unlawful, but odious and filthy.

"After traversing these celebrated ruins, I must say, that I felt a little disappointed: they did not at all answer my expectation. The architecture of the ancient Persians seems to be much more akin to that of their clumsy neighbours the Indians, than to that of the Greeks. I saw no appearance of grand design anywhere. The chapiters of the columns were almost as long as the shafts,—though they are not so represented in Niebuhr's plate,—and the mean little passages into the square court, or room, or whatever it was, make it very evident that the taste of the Orientals was the same three thousand years ago as it is now.

"But it was impossible not to recollect that here Alexander and his Greeks passed and repassed;—here they sat, and sang, and revelled: now all is silence;—generation on generation lie mingled with the dust of their mouldering edifices:—

> " ' Alike the busy and the gay,
> But flutter in life's passing day,
> In fortune's varying colours drest.'

"From the ruins I rode off to a neighbouring village, the head man of which, at the minister's order, paid me every attention. At sunset, we set out on our return, and lost our way. As I particularly remarked where we entered the plains, I pointed out the track, which afterwards proved to be right ; but my opinion was overruled, and we galloped further and further away. Meeting, at last, with some villagers, who were passing the night at their threshing-floor in the field, we were set right. They then conceived so high an idea of my geographical skill, that, as soon as we re-crossed the Araxes, they begged me to point out the Keblah to them, as they wanted to pray. After setting their faces towards Mecca, as nearly as I could, I went and sat down on the margin near the bridge, where the water, falling over some fragments of the bridge under the arches, produced a roar, which, contrasted with the stillness all around, had a grand effect. Here I thought again of the multitudes who had once pursued their labours and pleasures on its banks. Twenty-one centuries have passed away since they lived : how short, in comparison, must be the remainder of my days ! What a momentary duration is the life of man ! *Labitur et labetur in omne volubilis œvum*, may be affirmed of the river ; but men pass away as soon as they begin to exist. Well, let the moments pass—

> " ' They'll waft us sooner o'er
> This life's tempestuous sea,
> And land us on the peaceful shore
> Of blest Eternity.'

"The Mohammedans having finished their prayers, I

mounted my horse, and pursued my way over the plain.
We arrived at the station of the Rahdars so early, that
we should have been at Shiraz before the gates were
opened, so we halted. I put my head into a poor corner
of the caravansera, and slept soundly upon the hard
stone, till the rising sun bid us continue our course.

"One of my guards was a pensive, romantic sort of a
man, as far as Eastern men can be romantic; that is, he
is constantly reciting love-verses. He often broke a long
silence by a sudden question of this sort: 'Sir, what is
the chief good of life?' I replied, 'The love of God.'
'What next?' 'The love of man.' 'That is,' said he,
'to have men love us, or to love them?' 'To love them.'
He did not seem to agree with me. Another time he
asked, 'Who were the worst people in the world?' I
said, 'Those who know their duty, and do not practise it.'
At the house where I was entertained, they asked me the
question which the Lord once asked, 'What think ye of
Christ?' I generally tell them at first what they expect
to hear, 'The Son of God;' but this time I said, 'The
same as you say,—the Word of God.' 'Was He a
Prophet?' 'Yes, in some sense, He was a Prophet; but,
what it chiefly concerns us to know,—He was an Atonement for the sins of men.' Not understanding this, they
made no reply. They next asked, 'What did I think of
the soul? was it out of the body or in the body?' I
supposed the latter. 'No,' they said, 'it was neither the
one nor the other; but next to it, and the mover of the
body.'"

The details Mr. Martyn gives of the fast of Ramazan,
which he witnessed on his return to Shiraz, whilst they

show that he was far from being an unobservant spectator of what was passing around him, afford a striking view of the interior of Mohammedanism. We plainly discover from them that a love for particular popular preachers—a fiery zeal in religion—a vehement excitation of the animal feelings, as well as rigid austerities,—are false criterions of genuine piety; for we see all these in their full perfection amongst the real followers of the Crescent, as well as amongst the pretended disciples of the Cross.

Sept. 20.—"First day of the fast of Ramazan.—All the family had been up in the night, to take an unseasonable meal, in order to fortify themselves for the abstinence of the day. It was curious to observe the effects of the fast in the house. The master was scolding and beating his servants;—they equally peevish and insolent; and the beggars more than ordinarily importunate and clamorous. At noon, all the city went to the Grand Mosque. My host came back with an account of new vexations there. He was chatting with a friend, near the door, when a great preacher, Hagi Mirza, arrived, with hundreds of followers. 'Why do you not say your prayers?' said the new-comers to the two friends. 'We have finished,' said they. 'Well,' said the other, 'if you cannot pray a second time with us, you had better move out of the way.' Rather than join such turbulent zealots, they retired. The reason of this unceremonious address was, that these loving disciples had a desire to pray all in a row with their master, which, it seems, is the custom. There is no public service in the Mosque; every man there prays for himself.

"Coming out of the Mosque, some servants of the prince, for their amusement, pushed a person against a poor man's stall, on which were some things for sale, a few European and Indian articles, also some valuable Warsaw plates, which were thrown down and broken. The servants went off without making compensation. No cazi will hear a complaint against the prince's servants.

"Hagi Mohammed Hasan preaches every day during the Ramazan. He takes a verse from the Koran, or more frequently tells stories about the Imans. If the ritual of the Christian churches, their good forms, and everything they have, is a mere shadow, unless a Divine influence attend on them, what must all this Mohammedan stuff be? and yet how impossible is it to convince the people of the world, whether Christian or Mohammedan, that what they call religion, is merely a thing of their own, having no connection with God and his kingdom. This subject has been much on my mind of late. How senseless the zeal of churchmen against dissenters, and of dissenters against the Church! The kingdom of God is neither meat nor drink, nor anything perishable; but righteousness, and peace, and joy in the Holy Ghost.

"Mirza Ibraheem never goes to the Mosque; but he is so much respected, that nothing is said: they conclude that he is employed in devotion at home. Some of his disciples said to Seid Ali, before him, 'Now the Ramazan is come, you should read the Koran and leave the Gospel.' 'No,' said his uncle, 'he is employed in a good work; let him go on with it.' The old man continues to inquire with interest about the Gospel, and is impatient for his nephew to explain the evidences of Christianity, which I have drawn up."

Sept. 22.—Sunday.—"My friends returned from the Mosque, full of indignation at what they had witnessed there. The former governor of Bushire complained to the vizier, in the Mosque, that some of his servants had treated him brutally. The vizier, instead of attending to his complaint, ordered them to do their work a second time; which they did, kicking and beating him with their slippers, in the most ignominious way, before all the Mosque. This unhappy people groan under the tyranny of their governors; yet nothing subdues or tames them. Happy Europe! how has God favoured the sons of Japheth, by causing them to embrace the Gospel. How dignified are all the nations of Europe compared with this nation! Yet the people are clever and intelligent, and more calculated to become great and powerful than any of the nations of the East, had they a good government and the Christian religion."

Sept. 29.—"The Soofie, son of the Moojtuhid, with some others, came to see me. For fifteen years he was a devout Mohammedan; visited the sacred places, and said many prayers. Finding no benefit from austerities, he threw up Mohammedanism altogether, and attached himself to the Soofie master.

"I asked him, what his object was, all that time? He said, 'he did not know, but he was unhappy.' I began to explain to him the Gospel; but he cavilled at it as much as any bigoted Mohammedan could do, and would not hear of there being any distinction between Creator and creature. In the midst of our conversation, the sun went down, and the company vanished, for the purpose of taking an immediate repast.

"Aga Baba was also for many years a zealous Mohammedan, often passing whole nights in prayer. His father, who at first had encouraged his religious propensities, found them at last so troublesome, that he was obliged to leave the house, not being able to get sleep for the noise his son made in prayer. Finding, after many years, that he was growing more and more proud and contemptuous, he could ascribe it to nothing but his prayers, and therefore, from really conscientious motives, left them off.

"Jaffier Ali Khan was also once a great sayer of prayers, and regularly passed every afternoon, for fourteen years, in cursing the worshippers of Omar, according to the prescribed form; but perceiving that these zealous maledictions brought no blessing on himself, he left them off, and now just prays for form's sake. His wife says her prayers regularly five times a-day, and is always up before sun-rise for the first prayer.

"Mirza Seid Ali seems sometimes coming round to Christianity, against Soofeism. The Soofies believe in no prophet, and do not consider Moses to be equal to Mirza Abulcasim. 'Could they be brought,' Seid Ali says, 'to believe that there has been a prophet, they would embrace Christianity.' And what would be gained by such converts? 'Thy people shall be willing in the day of thy power.' It will be 'an afflicted and poor people,' that shall call upon the name of the Lord, and such the Soofies are not: professing themselves to be wise, they have become fools."

October 1.—"Thousands every day assemble at the Mosque; it is quite a lounge with them. Each, as soon as he has said his prayers, sits down and talks to his friend. The multitude press to hear Hagi Mohammed Hasan. One day they thronged him so much that he made some error in his prostrations. This put him into such a passion, that he wished that Omar's curse might come upon him, if he preached to them again. However, a day or two after, he thought better of it. This preacher is famous for letting out his money for interest; and therefore, in spite of his eloquence, he is not very popular. About two years ago, Shekh Jaffier came here and preached,—'The Persians are all murderers! adulterers!' 'What does the Shekh mean?' said his followers. 'Why,' said he, 'the Persians take usury; and he that does that, is worse than a murderer or adulterer.'"

Oct. 7.—"I was surprised by a visit from the great Soofie doctor, who, while most of the people were asleep, came to me for some wine. I plied him with questions innumerable; but he returned nothing but incoherent answers, and sometimes no answer at all. Having laid aside his turban, he put on his night-cap, and soon fell asleep upon the carpet. Whilst he lay there, his disciples came, but would not believe, when I told them who was there, till they came and saw the sage asleep. When he awoke, they came in, and seated themselves at the greatest possible distance, and were all as still as if in a church.

"The real state of this man seems to be despair, and it will be well if it do not end in madness. I preached to him the kingdom of God: mentioning particularly how I had found peace from the Son of God and the Spirit of God: through the first, forgiveness; through the second, sanctification. He said it was good, but said it with the same unconcern with which he admits all manner of things, however contradictory. Poor soul! he is sadly bewildered.

"At a garden called Shah Chiragh, in which is the tomb of the brother of one of the Imans, who was killed on the spot, a miracle is wrought every Ramazan. The Mootuwulli, or proprietor of the garden, in whose family it has been for ages, finds its supposed sanctity abundantly profitable, as he is said to make 2,000*l*. a-year of it. To keep alive the zeal of the people, who make their offerings there every day, he procures a villager, who is at first sick and crying to Ali for help; and then, on the appointed day, recovers. This year a man was recovered of the palsy, and our servants came in quite full of it. Though this farce is played off every year, the simpletons are never undeceived. Presents of sheep, fowls, sweetmeats, money, flowed in upon the Mootuwulli, who skilfully turned all to the best advantage. Those who wished to see the man's face, were to pay so much; those who were anxious to touch him, were to pay so much more; and so on.

"On two days in the Ramazan, tragedies were acted at our house in the women's court. Two or three men, dressed in the Khan's court-robes, spouted and sang for an hour, before an immense concourse of women, all veiled. The subject on the first day was the death of Mahomet; on the second, that of Iman Hosyn."

Oct. 18.—"The Ramazan ended, or ought to have ended, but the moon disappointed them. The Moollahs not having seen the new moon, would not allow the fast to be over, and the people were, in consequence, all in confusion; for not having eaten in the night, they were not at all disposed to go through the day fasting. At last some witnesses appeared, who vowed that they had seen the silver bow. These were from the prince; but the Moollahs refused to admit them till seventy-two of the same kind bore the same testimony. This was no great number for a prince to produce; so the seventy-two appeared, and the feast was proclaimed."

Towards the end of November, great progress having been made in the Persian translation of the New Testament, Mr. Martyn ordered two splendid copies of it to be prepared, designing to present the one to the king of Persia, and the other to the prince Abbas Mirza, his son. It being now also his fixed intention to pass the winter at Shiraz, he resolved to commence another eminently useful and, to him, most delightful, work,—a translation of the Psalms of David into Persian, from the original Hebrew. The divine Songs of Sion became thus the subject of his critical examination, close meditation, and frequent prayer; and whilst engaged in this sacred employment, often did he find his soul elevated, and his spirit refreshed in a "strange land."

The events of the last month of the year stand thus recorded in his Journal:—

Dec. 3.—"Attended the lecture of Aga Mahommed Hasan. He read and commented on three books of metaphysics, and at intervals conversed with me. Amongst other things we discussed the cause of the ascent of a light body in a fluid. Our argument came at last to this,—that if one particle of fluid were on another, it would, from its gravity, move ever horizontally off, in order to be nearer the centre. 'If,' said he, 'a body can move towards the centre only directly, how do you account for its falling down an inclined plane?' I began to explain the composition and resolution of forces; but some disciples coming, he could not stay to hear what I had to say, but went on with his lecture. At one time he asked me some questions about genera and species."

Dec. 6.—"Aga Boozong, and his disciple, Aga Ali, a Mede, came and sat many hours. The former, from love to the Gospel, as he said, had desired a friend at Isfahan to send him Luke's Gospel, translated from the Arabic.

He asked me about the Trinity, and said that, 'for himself, he had no objection to the doctrine.' So say all the Soofies, but they will only concede to Jesus a nature which they conceive to belong to all the prophets, and all the illuminated. He stated his sentiments; I asked for reasons, but asked in vain. 'Proofs,' he said, 'were cobwebs,—a breath destroyed them: nothing but a Divine teacher could make known the mystery.' Aga Ali, in order to prove to me that proofs were nothing, adduced the instance of Matthew the publican, who rose at the call of Christ, without seeing a miracle. They are fond of producing what they know of the Gospel, in confirmation of their mystic fancies. The Atonement they would not hear of, because the Mohammedans pretended, in the same way, that Hosyn was sacrificed for the sins of men. Thus Satan has contrived Mohammedanism with more craft than at first appears; for the impostor of Mecca, by making common cause with the prophets of God, has taken care, that if any forsake him, they shall at the same time forsake the messengers of God; of whom they know nothing but just what he tells them,—which is far enough from the truth."

Dec. 8.—"The Soofies breakfasted with me. Aga Boozong talked dogmatically about the unity of all being, and quoted large portions from the Munari of Mouluwee Room. Another part of the conversation was about India. The Soofies consider all the Brahmins as philosophers of the same school with themselves. One of them asked me gravely, 'whether I had met with any in whom was the Holy Ghost?' This, he supposed, was the only way of expressing what they mean by being enlightened."

Dec. 12.—"Letters, at last, from India. Mirza Seid

Ali was curious to know in what way we corresponded, and made me read Mr. Brown's letter to me, and mine to Corrie. He took care to let his friends know that we wrote nothing about our own affairs: it was all about translations, and the cause of Christ: with this he was delighted."

Dec. 16.—"In translating 2 Cor. i. 22, 'Who hath given the earnest of the Spirit in our hearts,' he was much struck when it was explained to him. 'O that I had it!' said he; 'have you received it?' I told him that, as I had no doubt of my acceptance through Christ, I concluded that I had. Once before, on the words, 'Who are saved,' he expressed his surprise at the confidence with which Christians spoke of salvation. On 1 Cor. xi. he observed, that the doctrine of the resurrection of the body was unreasonable; but that as the Mohammedans understood it, it was impossible; on which account the Soofies rejected it.'"

Christmas-day.—"I made a great feast for the Russians and Armenians; and, at Jaffier Ali Khan's request, invited the Soofie master with his disciples. I hoped there would be some conversation on the occasion of our meeting, and, indeed, Mirza Seid Ali did make some attempts, and explained to the old man the meaning of the Lord's Supper; but the sage maintaining his usual silence, the subject was dropped.

"I expressed my satisfaction at seeing them assembled on such an occasion, and my hope that they would remember the day in succeeding years, and that, though they would never see me again in those succeeding years, they would not forget that I had brought them the Gospel. The old man coldly replied, that 'God would guide those whom He chose.' Most of the time they continued was before dinner; the moment that was despatched, they rose and went away. The custom is, to sit five or six hours before dinner; and at great men's houses, singers attend."

Dec. 27.—"Carapet invited me this evening to his wedding; but just before the guests were to have assembled, the Darogha's servants seized his father-in-law, and carried him away to be bastinadoed, or else to pay five hundred piastres. It seems he had given a bond to that amount, never to sell wine to Mohammedans; and yesterday he was detected in the act. Jaffier Ali Khan wrote, in my name, to the Vizier, to request his release. The Vizier replied, that Carapet, for my sake, should not be molested; but that the other man had forfeited his money, and, in evidence, sent his bond. Finding that it was not a piece of villany on the part of the Government, as I had apprehended, I declined having anything to do in the business; the law might take its course. But Jaffier Ali Khan begged, as a favour, of the servant of the Vizier, who had formerly been a servant of his, to represent the matter in such a light to his master as to excite his compassion. After he was gone away, the Armenians came in great numbers, and begged I would procure the pardon of the poor man; and obtained a promise from me to that effect; when the servant came back with the poor Greek, and said that the Vizier had released him and forgiven him the forfeit for my sake. The Armenians were in ecstasies of joy, and did not know how enough to express their gratitude to me, though it was rather due to Jaffier Ali Khan. I was unable to attend the wedding, from a cough, which made it unsafe to be out at night. They sat up all night, according to the Armenian custom, eating and drinking,

and about two hours before day went to church, where
the marriage was solemnized: the feasting continues two
days longer.

"On the strength of the narrow escape the Greek had
experienced, some of the Vizier's servants came, the day
after, to feast themselves at his expense. They first called
for a calean, which was brought them; then for the wine
he had promised them, though he had promised none.
This unfortunate people have been visited almost like the
Jews. When will the Lord pity them! An Armenian,
if he gets a new coat, makes the sleeves of patches, as he
will be sure to have it taken from him if it looks new.
Carapet was insulted, for being a little better dressed
than they thought a Christian ought to be."

Dec. 31.—"The accounts of the desolations of war
during the last year, which I have been reading in some
Indian newspapers, make the world appear more gloomy
than ever. How many souls hurried into eternity unprepared! How many thousands of widows and orphans
left to mourn! But admire, my soul, the matchless power
of God, that out of this ruin He has prepared for himself
an inheritance. At last the scene shall change, and I
shall find myself in a world where all is love."

The early part of the year 1812, that year in which
Mr. Martyn "rested from his labours," and "found
himself in a world where all was love," was ushered in
by him in the following strain of singular pathos and
piety:—

"The last has been, in some respects, a memorable
year. I have been led, by what I have reason to consider as the particular providence of God, to this place;
and have undertaken an important work, which has gone

on without material interruption, and is now nearly finished. I like to find myself employed usefully, in a way I did not expect or foresee, especially if my own will is in any degree crossed by the work unexpectedly assigned me, as there is then reason to believe that God is acting. The present year will probably be a perilous one; but my life is of little consequence, whether I live to finish the Persian New Testament, or do not. I look back with pity and shame upon my former self, and on the importance I then attached to my life and labours. The more I see of my own works, the more I am ashamed of them. Coarseness and clumsiness mar all the works of man. I am sick when I look at man and his wisdom and his doings; and am relieved only by reflecting that we have a city, whose builder and maker is God. The least of *his* works it is refreshing to look at. A dried leaf or a straw makes me feel myself in good company: complacency and admiration take place of disgust.

"I compared, with pain, our Persian translation with the original; to say nothing of the precision and elegance of the sacred text, its perspicuity is that which sets at defiance all attempts to equal it."

In the succeeding portion of Mr. Martyn's journal we are presented with a statement, from which it is scarcely possible not to infer that the civil government of Persia is in a condition of extreme weakness and wretchedness.

Jan. 15.—"I went with Jaffier Ali Khan to see the College. It is almost in ruins, not having been repaired these two hundred years. It contains sixty or seventy sets of rooms, in many of which we observed teachers and scholars giving and hearing lectures. It was formerly richly endowed; but the rapacity of the kings has stripped it of everything; only a small stipend is now allowed to the principal teachers. Near it is an octagonal caravansera, where goods were formerly exposed to sale, and a tax levied, which was appropriated to the College; but this is nearly gone. The best way of laying out money at this time is to build a caravansera for merchants to lodge their goods in, and expose them to sale. In this way they make about fifteen per cent.; but these warehouses are heavily taxed by Government.

"We called on several people; among the rest, on Mirza Abulcasim Kalantar, a man of large landed property, who was very courteous. Conversation, as usual, about the happiness of India and England.

"We called on Aga Boozong, an old man of ninety, whose house, or rather college, is a kind of asylum; for he is so venerated, that even the Vizier dare not drag an offender thence. A poor ragged fellow came while we were there, and said that the Vizier had sent him. 'Go and tell the Vizier,' said he, 'to knock his head against the pavement, and not send such messengers to me.'

"A poor blind man whom we met begging, the Khan pointed out to me, as one who formerly was a general, and one of Kureen Khan's family; but, by a change of dynasty, had lost his eyes. Nobody took any notice of him."

Who can read some of the ensuing remarks without discovering how abundantly those words of our Saviour were verified in Mr. Martyn,—"Neither pray I for these alone, but for them also which shall believe on me through their word: that they all may be one, as thou, Father, art in me, and I in thee, that they also may be one in us;

that the world may believe that thou hast sent me."
(John xvii. 20, 21.)

Jan. 16.—"Mirza Seid Ali told me accidentally, to-day,
of a distich made by his friend Mirza Koochut, at Teheran,
in honour of a victory obtained by Prince Abbas Mirza
over the Russians. The sentiment was, that he had
killed so many of the Christians, that Christ, from the
fourth heaven, took hold of Mahomet's skirt to entreat
him to desist. I was cut to the soul at this blasphemy.
In prayer I could think of nothing else but that great
day when the Son of God shall come in the clouds of
heaven, taking vengeance on them that know not God,
and convincing men of all their hard speeches which they
have spoken against Him.

"Mirza Seid Ali perceived that I was considerably disordered, and was sorry for having repeated the verse; but
asked what it was that was so offensive. I told him that
'I could not endure existence if Jesus was not glorified;
—it would be hell to me, if he were to be always thus
dishonoured.' He was astonished, and again asked, why?
'If any one pluck out your eyes,' I replied, 'there is no
saying *why* you feel pain;—it is feeling. It is because I
am one with Christ that I am thus dreadfully wounded.'
On his again apologizing, I told him that 'I rejoiced at
what had happened, inasmuch as it made me feel nearer
the Lord than ever. It is when the head or heart is
struck, that every member feels its membership.' This
conversation took place while we were translating. In
the evening, he mentioned the circumstance of a young
man's being murdered,—a fine athletic youth, whom I
had often seen in the garden. Some acquaintance of his,
in a slight quarrel, had plunged a dagger in his breast.
Observing me look sorrowful, he asked why. 'Because,'

said I, 'he was cut off in his sins, and had no time to repent.' 'It is just in that way,' said he, 'that I should like to die; not dragging out a miserable existence on a sick bed, but transported at once into another state.' I observed that 'it was not desirable to be hurried into the immediate presence of God.' 'Do you think,' said he, 'that there is any difference between the presence of God here or there?' 'Indeed I do,' said I. 'Here we see through a glass, darkly; but there face to face.' He then entered into some metaphysical Soofie disputation about the identity of sin and holiness, heaven and hell; to all which I made no reply."

The subjoined conversation, into which Mr. Martyn was led, exhibits the ignorance of the natural man, and the knowledge of the spiritual man, in striking contrast.

Jan. 18.—"Aga Ali, of Media, came; and with him and Mirza Ali, I had a long and warm discussion about the essentials of Christianity. The Mede seeing us at work upon the Epistles, said, 'he should be glad to read them; as for the Gospels, they were nothing but tales, which were of no use to him;—for instance,' said he, 'if Christ raised four hundred dead to life, what is that to me?' I said, 'It certainly was of importance, for his works furnished a reason for our depending upon his words.' 'What did he say,' asked he, 'that was not known before? the love of God, humility,—who does not know these things?' 'Were these things,' said I, 'known before Christ, either among Greeks or Romans, with all their philosophy?' They averred that the Hindoo book Juh contained precepts of this kind. I questioned its antiquity; 'but however that may be,' I added, 'Christ came not to *teach* so much as to *die;* the truths I spoke of, as confirmed by his miracles, were those relating to his person, such as, 'Come unto me, all ye that labour and are heavy-laden, and I will give you rest.' Here Mirza Seid Ali told him, that I had professed to have no doubt of my salvation. He asked what I meant. I told him 'that though sin still remained, I was assured that it should not regain dominion; and that I should never come into condemnation, but was accepted in the Beloved.' Not a little surprised, he asked Mirza Seid Ali whether he comprehended this? 'No,' said he, 'nor Mirza Ibraheem, to whom I mentioned it.' The Mede again turning to me, added, 'How do you know this? How do you know you have experienced the second birth?' 'Because,' said I, 'we have the Spirit of the Father; what He wishes, we wish; what He hates, we hate.' Here he began to be a little more calm and less contentious, and mildly asked how I had obtained this peace of mind. 'Was it merely those books?' said he, taking up some of our sheets. I told him 'These books, with prayer.' 'What was the beginning of it?'—said he,—'the society of some friends?' I related to him my religious history, the substance of which was, that I took my Bible before God, in prayer, and prayed for forgiveness through Christ; assurance of it through his Spirit, and grace to obey his commandments. They then both asked whether the same benefit would be conferred on them. 'Yes,' said I, 'for so the Apostles preached, that all who were baptized in his name, should receive the gift of the Holy Ghost.' 'Can you assure me,' said Mirza Seid Ali, 'that the Spirit will be given to me?—if so, I will be baptized immediately.' 'Who am I, that I should be surety?'—I replied;—'I bring you this message from God, that he who, despairing of himself, rests for righteousness on the Son of God, shall receive the gift of the Holy Ghost; and to this I can add my testimony, if that be worth anything, that I have found the promise fulfilled in myself. But if, after baptism, you should not find it so in you, accuse not the Gospel of falsehood; it is possible that your faith might not be sincere; indeed, so fully am I persuaded that you do not believe on the Son of God, that if you were to entreat ever so earnestly for baptism, I should not dare to administer it at this time, when you have shown so many signs of an unhumbled heart.' 'What! would you have me believe,' said he, 'as a child?' 'Yes,' said I. 'True,' said he, 'I think that is the only way.' Aga Ali said no more, except, 'Certainly he is a good man!'"

Shortly after this discussion, Mr. Martyn states himself to have attended a public exhibition of a religious kind. The reason why he did not repeat his attendance, whether well-grounded or not, is at least a proof that patriotic feelings in his mind were not extinguished by Christianity.

Jan. 23.—" Put on my English dress, and went to the Vizier's, to see part of the tragedy of Hosyn's death, which they contrive to spin out so as to make it last the first ten days of the Mohurrin. All the apparatus consisted of a few boards for a stage, two tables, and a pulpit, under an immense awning, in the court where the company were assembled. The *dramatis personæ* were two ; the daughter of Hosyn, whose part was performed by a boy, and a messenger ; they both read their parts. Every now and then loud sobs were heard all over the court. After this, several feats of activity were exhibited before the altar, where the Vizier sat with the Moollahs. I was appointed to a seat, where, indeed, I saw as much as I wanted, but which, I afterwards perceived, was not the place of honour. As I trust I am far enough from desiring the chief seats in the synagogues, there was nothing in this that could offend me ; but I do not think it right to let him have another opportunity of showing a slight to my country in my person."

Those who know not what it is to pass a dreary season of long seclusion from Christian society, surrounded by those who are immersed in all wickedness, can form but an inadequate idea of the sacrifices to which Mr. Martyn submitted, in continuing so great a length of time at Shiraz : yet we may, in some measure, see what he endured, from the expression of sentiments such as these :—

Feb. 2.—" From what I suffer in this city, I can understand the feelings of Lot. The face of the poor Russian appears to me like the face of an angel, because he does not tell lies. Heaven will be heaven, because there will not be one liar there. The word of God is more precious to me at this time that I ever remember it to have been ; and of all the promises in it, none is more sweet to me than this,—' He shall reign till He hath put all enemies under his feet.' "

Feb. 3.— " A packet arrived from India, without a single letter for me. It was some disappointment to me ; but let me be satisfied with my God ; and if I cannot have the comfort of hearing from my friends, let me return with thankfulness to his word, which is a treasure of which none envy me the possession, and where I can find what will more than compensate for the loss of earthly enjoyments. Resignation to the will of God is a lesson which I must learn, and which I trust He is teaching me."

What an influence a departure from the *precepts* of the Gospel has upon the determination of the judgment with respect to its *doctrines*, appears from the representation Mr. Martyn gives of the conduct of Mirza Seid Ali at this period.

Feb. 4.—"Mirza Seid Ali, who has been enjoying himself in dissipation and idleness these two days, returned full of evil and opposition to the Gospel.

"Alluding to some remarks he had made, 'I suppose,' said he, 'you think it is sinful to sport with the characters of holy men.' 'I have no objection,' I replied, 'to hear your sentiments; but I cannot bear to hear anything spoken disrespectfully of the Lord Jesus; and yet there is not one of your Soofies but has said something against Him.' 'You never heard me speak lightly of Jesus,' he replied. 'No, there is something so awfully pure about Him, that nothing can be said.'"

Recovering somewhat of a more serious spirit, Seid Ali joined with Aga Boozong, whom Mr. Martyn describes as one of the most magisterial of the Soofies, in a conversation in which a real desire for religious information seems to have been indicated. The day on which it took place was almost entirely consumed in discussions with a variety of visitors respecting the Scriptures; it concluded with a very pleasing confession on the part of Seid Ali.

Feb. 9.—"Aga Boozong came. After much conversation, he said, 'Prove to me, from the beginning, that Christianity is the way: how will you proceed? what do you say must be done?' 'If you would not believe a person who wrought a miracle before you,' said I, 'I have nothing to say; I cannot proceed a step.' 'I will grant you,' said Seid Ali, 'that Christ was the Son of God, and more than that.' 'That you despair of yourself, and are willing to trust in Him alone for salvation?' 'Yes.'

'And are ready to confess Christ before men, and act conformably to his word?' 'Yes: what else must I do?' 'Be baptized in the name of Christ.' 'And what shall I gain?' 'The gift of the Holy Ghost. The end of faith is salvation in the world to come; but even here you shall have the Spirit to purify your heart, and to give you the assurance of everlasting happiness.' Thus Aga Boozong had an opportunity of hearing those strange things from my own mouth, of which he had been told by his disciple the Mede. 'You can say, too,' said he, 'that you have received the Spirit?' I told them I believed I had; 'for, notwithstanding all my sins, the bent of my heart was to God, in a way it never was before; and that according to my present feelings, I could not be happy if God was not glorified, and if I had not the enjoyment of His presence, for which I felt that I was now educating.' Aga Boozong shed tears.

"A Russian officer coming in at the time, the subject of religion was dropped, except that while speaking of the convicts of Calcutta, whom I had seen at the gaol, Mirza Seid Ali asked me how I addressed them? I told him that I cautioned them against despair, assured them that they might come at the eleventh hour, that it was never too late for mercy, if they came to God through Christ.

"After this came Aga Ali, the Mede, to hear, as he said, some of the sentences of Paul. Mirza Seid Ali had told them, 'that if they had read nothing but the Gospels, they knew nothing of the religion of Christ.' The sheet I happened to have by me was the one containing the fourth, fifth, and sixth chapters of the second epistle to the Corinthians, which Aga Ali read out.

"At this time the company had increased considerably.

I desired Aga Ali to notice particularly the latter part
of the fifth chapter, 'God was in Christ, reconciling the
world unto himself.' He then read it a second time, but
they saw not its glory ; however, they spoke in high terms
of the pith and solidity of Paul's sentences.

"They were evidently on the watch for anything that
tallied with their own sentiments. Upon the passage—
'Always bearing about in the body the dying of the Lord
Jesus,' the Mede observed, 'Do you not see that Jesus
was in Paul, and that Paul was only another name for
Jesus ?' And the text, 'Whether we be beside ourselves,
it is to God ; or whether we be sober, it is for your
sakes,' they interpreted thus :—'We are absorbed in the
contemplation of God, and when we recover, it is to
instruct you.'

"Walking afterwards with Mirza Seid Ali, he told me,
how much one of my remarks had affected him, namely,
that he had no humility. He had been talking about
simplicity and humility as characteristic of the Soofies.
'Humility !' I said to him, 'if you were humble, you
would not dispute in this manner ; you would be like a
child.' He did not open his mouth afterwards, but to
say, 'True ; I have no humility.' In evident distress, he
observed, ' The truth is, we are in a state of compound
ignorance ;—ignorant, yet ignorant of our ignorance.' "

On the last birthday Mr. Martyn lived to com-
memorate, we find him speaking in affecting terms
with respect to his privations as a missionary ; yet expressing himself with ardent and humble gratitude, as a
believer in the Lord Jesus Christ.

Feb. 8.—" While walking in the garden, in some disorder from vexation, two Mussulmen Jews came up, and

asked me what would become of them in another world ?
the Mohammedans were right in their way, they supposed, and we in ours ?—but what must they expect ?
After rectifying their mistake as to the Mohammedans, I
mentioned two or three reasons for believing that we are
right : such as their dispersion, and the cessation of
sacrifices, immediately on the appearance of Jesus.
'True, true,' they said, with great feeling and seriousness ; indeed, they seemed disposed to yield assent to anything I said. They confessed they had become Mohammedans only on compulsion : and that Abdoolghunee
wished to go to Bagdad, thinking he might throw off
the mask there with safety ;—but they asked, what I
thought ? I said that the governor was a Mohammedan. 'Did I think Syria safer ?' 'The safest place in
the east,' I said, 'was India.' Feelings of pity for God's
ancient people, and having the awful importance of
eternal things impressed on my mind by the seriousness of their inquiries as to what would become of them,
relieved me from the pressure of my comparatively insig-
nificant distresses. I, a poor Gentile, blest, honoured,
and loved ; secured for ever by the everlasting covenant,
whilst the children of the kingdom are still lying in outward darkness ! Well does it become me to be thankful.

" This is my birth-day, on which I complete my thirty-
first year. The Persian New Testament has been begun,
and, I may say, finished in it, as only the last eight
chapters of the Revelation remain. Such a painful
year I never passed ; owing to the privations I have
been called to, on the one hand, and the spectacle before
me of human depravity, on the other. But I hope that
I have not come to this seat of Satan in vain. The word
of God has found its way into Persia, and it is not in

Satan's power to oppose its progress, if the Lord hath sent it."

The effect upon the natural conscience, of a plain and solemn declaration of the awful truths of Scripture, may be seen in the case of one of Mr. Martyn's visitors, who to great libertinism of practice added extreme latitudinarianism of principle.

Feb. 23.—" Aga Neeser came, and talked most captiously and irrelevantly against all revealed religion. Three years ago, he had thrown off the shackles of Mohammed, and advised me to do the same with my yoke. I told him, that I preferred my yoke to his freedom. He was for sending me naked into a wilderness; but I would rather be a child under the restraints of a parent, who would provide me with food and clothing, and be my protector and guide. To everything I said, he had but one answer. ' God is the sole agent;—sin and holiness, happiness and misery, cause and effect, are all perfectly one.' Finding him determined to amuse himself in this way, I said, ' These things will do very well for the present, while reclining in gardens and smoking caleans; but not for a dying hour. How many years of life remain? You are about thirty, perhaps thirty more remain. How swiftly have the last thirty passed : how soon will the next thirty be gone ; and then we shall see. If you are right, I lose nothing : if I am right, you lose your soul. Leaving out the consideration of all religion, it is probable that the next world may be akin to this, and our relation to both not dissimilar. But here we see that childhood is a preparation for manhood, and that neglect of the proper employments of childhood entails miseries in riper years.' The thought of death, and of separation from his pleasures.

made him serious; or perhaps he thought it useless to press me with any more of his dogmas."

On the 24th of February, 1812, the last sheet of the Persian New Testament was completed. "I have many mercies," said the author of this great work, on bringing it to a termination, "for which to thank the Lord, and this is not the least. Now may that Spirit who gave the word, and called me, I trust, to be an interpreter of it, graciously and powerfully apply it to the hearts of sinners, even to the gathering an elect people from amongst the long-estranged Persians!"

The version of the Psalms in Persian, "a sweet employment," as Mr. Martyn terms it, and which, to use his own language, "caused six weary moons, that waxed and waned since its commencement, to pass unnoticed," was finished by the middle of the month of March.

Mr. Martyn had now been resident for the space of ten months at Shiraz, during the whole of which time he had been almost incessantly engaged, as we have seen, in endeavouring to reclaim the wretched race of infidels around him from the error of their ways. So far was he from shrinking from any fair opportunity of confessing Christ before men, that he gladly embraced, and boldly sought out, every occasion of avowing "whose he was, and whom he served." Nor was this conduct in him the fruit of a contentious spirit: it was the genuine offspring of that heavenly charity, which, "rejoicing in the truth," is ever ready to "contend earnestly for the faith once delivered to the saints." No one could have a more deep-rooted antipathy to controversy, at all times, and with all persons, than Mr. Martyn: a paramount regard to what was indispensably due to the cause of his Redeemer could alone induce him to engage in it.

One public argument he had already held with the chief professor of Mohammedan law; a second disputation, of a similar, but far more decided character, he was led to enter into, at this time, with Mirza Ibraheem. The scene of this discussion was a court in the palace of one of the Persian princes, where a numerous body of Moollahs were collected, with Mirza Ibraheem at their head. In this assembly Mr. Martyn stood up, as the single advocate of the Christian faith. Fearing God, like Micaiah the son of Imlah, he feared not man. In the midst, therefore, of a Mohammedan conclave, he proclaimed and maintained that prime and fundamental article of true religion, the Divinity of the Son of God.

"On the 23rd," Mr. Martyn writes, "I called on the Vizier, and afterwards on the secretary of the Kermanshah prince. In the court where he received me, Mirza Ibraheem was lecturing. Finding myself so near my old and respectable antagonist, I expressed a wish to see him; on which Jaffier Ali Khan went up to ascertain if my visit would be agreeable. The master consented, but some of the disciples demurred. At last, one of them observing that 'by the blessing of God on the master's conversation, I might possibly be converted,' it was agreed that I should be invited to ascend. Then it became a question, where I ought to sit. Below all, would not be respectful to a stranger; but above all the Moollahs, could not be tolerated. I entered, and was surprised at the numbers. The room was lined with Moollahs on both sides, and at the top. I was about to sit down at the door, but I was beckoned to an empty place near the top, opposite to the master, who, after the usual compliments, without further ceremony, asked me, 'what we meant by calling Christ, God?' War being thus unequivocally declared, I had nothing to do but to stand upon the defensive. Mirza Ibraheem argued temperately enough, but of the rest, some were very violent and clamorous. The former asked, 'if Christ had ever called himself God;— was he *the Creator or a creature?*' I replied, 'The CREATOR.' The Moollahs looked at one another. Such a confession had never before been heard among these Mohammedan doctors.

"One Moollah wanted to controvert some of my illustrations, by interrogating me about the personality of Christ. To all his questions I replied by requesting the same information respecting his own person.

"To another, who was rather contemptuous and violent, I said, 'If you do not approve of our doctrine, will you be so good as to say what God is, according to you; that I may worship a proper object?' One said, 'The author of the universe.' 'I can form no idea from these words,' said I, 'but of a workman at work upon a vast number of materials. Is that a correct notion?' Another said, 'One who came of himself into being.' 'So, then, he came,' I replied,—'he came out of one place into another; and before he came he was not. Is this an abstract and refined notion?' After this no one asked me any more questions; and, for fear the dispute should be renewed, Jaffier Ali Khan carried me away."

After making this intrepid and memorable confession of the divinity of our Lord and Saviour Jesus Christ, in which he might be described as

" Faithful found
Among the faithless ; faithful only he :
Unshaken, unseduced, unterrified,
His loyalty he kept, his zeal, his love ; "

Mr. Martyn continued only a short time at Shiraz. From his own hand we have this brief account of that interesting period which immediately preceded his departure.

" Mirza Seid Ali never now argues against the truth, nor makes any remarks but of a serious kind. He speaks of his dislike to some of the Soofies, on account of their falsehood and drunken habits. This approach to the love of morality is the best sign of a change for the better which I have yet seen in him. As often as he produces the New Testament, which he always does when any of his friends come, his brother and cousin ridicule him ; but he tells them that, supposing no other benefit to have been derived, it is certainly something better to have gained all this information about the religion of Christians, than to have loitered away the year in the garden."

April 27.—"Four Moollahs, of Mirza Ibraheem's school, came to dispute against European philosophy and European religion.

" Mirza Seid Ali requested, at Mirza Ibraheem's desire, to know where we got our notions concerning the Holy Spirit ? He, for his part, did not remember any passage in the New Testament which bore upon the subject. I referred them to the second chapter of the first epistle to the Corinthians."

May 10.—" Passed some days at Jaffier Ali Khan's garden, with Mirza Seid Ali, Aga Baba, and Shekh Abulhasan, reading, at their request, the Old Testament histories. Their attention to the word, and their love and attention to me, seemed to increase as the time of my departure approached.

"Aga Baba, who had been reading St. Matthew, related very circumstantially to the company, the particulars of the death of Christ. The bed of roses on which we sat, and the notes of the nightingales warbling around us, were not so sweet to me as this discourse from the Persian.

"Telling Mirza Seid Ali, one day, that I wished to return to the city in the evening, to be alone, and at leisure for prayer,—he said, with seriousness, 'Though a man had no other religious society, I suppose he might, with the aid of the Bible, live alone with God?' This solitude will, in one respect, be his own state soon;—may he find it the medium of God's gracious communications to his soul! He asked in what way God ought to be addressed: I told him, as a Father, with respectful love; and added some other exhortations on the subject of prayer."

May 11.—"Aga Baba came to bid me farewell, which he did in the best and most solemn way, by asking, as a final question, 'Whether, independently of external evidences, I had any internal proofs of the doctrine of Christ?' I answered, 'Yes, undoubtedly: the change from what I once was is a sufficient evidence to me.' At last he took his leave, in great sorrow, and, what is better, apparently in great solicitude about his soul.

"The rest of the day I continued with Mirza Seid Ali, giving him instructions what to do with the New Testament in case of my decease, and exhorting him, as far as his confession allowed me, to stand fast. He had made many a good resolution respecting his besetting sins. I hope, as well as pray, that some lasting effects may be seen at Shiraz, from the word of God left among them."

CHAPTER X.

MR. MARTYN LEAVES SHIRAZ, IN ORDER TO LAY BEFORE
THE KING HIS TRANSLATION OF THE NEW TESTAMENT.——
ARRIVES AT THE CAMP.——IS NOT ADMITTED TO AN AUDI-
ENCE.——PROCEEDS TO TEBRIZ.——SEVERE ILLNESS.

ON the evening of the 24th of May, one year after
entering Persia, Mr. Martyn left Shiraz, in company
with an English clergyman, with the intention of laying
before the King his translation of the New Testament;
but finding that, without a letter of introduction from
the British Ambassador, he could not, consistently with
established usage, be admitted into the Royal presence,
he determined to proceed to Tebriz, where, at that time,
Sir Gore Ouseley, his Britannic Majesty's Minister, resided.

His journey from Shiraz to Tebriz was not accomplished
in less than eight weeks, including one week spent at
Isfahan, and a few days at the King's camp; and the
latter part of it was a time of great and unforeseen
suffering to him. Had he known to what peril his life
would be subjected, he, doubtless, would have deemed his
object of too insufficient a magnitude to justify his
exposing himself to so much danger.

"A little before sunset," Mr. Martyn writes, "I left
the city, and at ten o'clock at night the cafila started.
Thus ended my stay at Shiraz. No year of my life was

ever spent more usefully, though such a long separation from my friends was often a severe trial. Our journey to Persepolis was performed in ten hours. I had a fall from my horse, owing to the saddle coming off, but a gracious providence preserved me from harm."

May 12.—"Stayed at Futihabad, a village about a parasang from the ruins."

May 13.—"At three in the morning, we pursued our way, and at eight reached a village at the north-eastern extremity of the plain of Persepolis. Remained all day at the caravansera, correcting the Prince's copy."

May 14. — "Continued our journey through two ridges of mountains to Imanzadu : no cultivation to be seen anywhere, nor scarcely any natural vegetable production, except the broom and hawthorn. The weather was rather tempestuous, with cold gusts of wind and rain.

"The inhabitants of the village, this being the Imanzadu's tomb, do no work, and pay no tax ; but are maintained by the surrounding villages, and the casual offerings of visitors to the tomb. The caravansera being in ruins, we stayed all this rainy day at a private house, where we were visited by people who came to be cured of their distempers."

May 15.—"From the top of a mountain, just behind Imanzadu, we descended into a vast plain, entirely uninhabited, except where the skirts of it were spotted with the black tents of the wandering tribes. Crossing the plain obliquely, we passed over a mountain into another plain, where was the same scene of desolation. After a journey of ten parasangs, arrived at two in the afternoon at the caravansera Khooshee Zar, which, being in ruins, let in the wind upon us at night in all directions. '

"On rising on the morning of the 16th, we found

a hoar frost, and ice in the pools. The excessive cold at this place is accounted for, by its being the highest land between the Persian Gulf and the Caspian Sea. The baggage not having come up, we were obliged to pass another day in this uncomfortable neighbourhood, where nothing was to be procured for ourselves or our horses; the scarcity of rain this year having left the ground destitute of verdure, and the poor people of the village near us having nothing to sell."

May 17.—"Our way to-day lay along the same plain; on the left was a ridge of hills covered with snow. Entering another plain, into which the former led, we reached a caravansera, near a small walled village, called Dih Serdoo."

May 18.—"After a journey of much the same length, over uneven ground, where the view was much obstructed, we arrived at a caravansera, in a great cleft, which divides Fars from Irak."

May 19.—"Moved forward six parasangs, to a private house at Mujrood. The plain, as usual, uninhabited; but we passed one village."

May 20.—"Continued our march, over the same plain, to Comesha, four parasangs."

May 21.—"To Mygar, five parasangs.—Finished the revision of the Prince's copy. At eleven at night we started for Isfahan, where we arrived soon after sunrise on the 22d, and were accommodated in one of the King's palaces. Found my old Shiraz scribe here, and corrected with him the Prince's copy."

May 23.—"Called on the Armenian Bishops at Julfa, and met Matteus. He is certainly vastly superior to any Armenian I have yet seen. We went next to the Italian missionary, Joseph Carabiciate, a native of Aleppo, but educated at Rome. He spoke Latin; was very sprightly, considering his age, which was sixty-six, but discovered no sort of inclination to talk about religion. Until lately, he had been supported by the Propaganda; but weary, at last, of exercising his functions without remuneration, and even without the necessary provision, he talked of returning to Aleppo."

May 24.—Sunday.—"Went early this morning to the Armenian Church attached to the Episcopal residence. Within the rails were two out of the four Bishops, and other ecclesiastics; but in the body of the church, only three people. Most of the Armenians at Julfa, which is now reduced to 500 houses, attended at their respective parish churches, of which there are twelve, served by twenty priests. After their pageantry was over, and we were satisfied with processions, ringing of bells, waving of colours, and other ceremonies, which were so numerous as entirely to remove all semblance of spiritual worship, we were condemned to witness a repetition of the same mockery at the Italian's church, at his request. I could not stand it out; but those who did, observed, that the priest ate and drank all the consecrated elements himself, and gave none to the few poor women who composed his congregation, and who, the Armenians said, had been hired for the occasion.

"In our way back, we called at the convent of Armenian nuns, a company of ignorant old women, who screamed out something in the church, which they called a welcome anthem. I tried to converse with the abbess, through Matteus, and was not much surprised to find her utterly without information, when the bishops have so little. I wished to learn Matteus's sentiments on the subject of monachism. Though his defence of it showed that he was not strong in his belief of its utility, I was grieved to see that he did not perceive how far the Christian way of sanctification differed from these human devices to attain that object. I talked to him a good deal about the office of the Holy Spirit, but he did not, while assenting, seem to feel its importance. Before returning to Isfahan, we sat a short time in the garden, with the bishops. They, poor things! had nothing to say, and could scarcely speak Persian; so that all the conversation was between me and Matteus. At my request he brought what he had of the Holy Scriptures, in Persian and Arabic. They were Wheloi's 'Persian Gospels,' and an Arabic version of the Gospels, printed at Rome. I tried in vain to bring him to any profitable discussion : with more sense than his brethren, he is not more advanced in spiritual knowledge. Returned much disappointed. Julfa had formerly twenty bishops, and about one hundred clergy, with twenty-four churches. All the Armenians can read, and have the New Testament ; but family prayer is not known. They may go every day to church prayers. Matteus preaches every Sunday, he says, and this day expounded the first of John, which was the Gospel for the day."

May 26.—"The Armenian bishops and three priests came to return our visit. Matteus brought with him a copy of the Gospels, Armenian and Persian, done by Joannes, the late Bishop here, who, he says, was a good scholar, and wrote on the divinity of Christ."

At the end of the month of May, Mr. Martyn departed from Isfahan, and thus describes a route in which the extremes of lovely fertility and sterile desolation seem to have been united.

June 1.—" Continued winding through the mountains to Caroo, situated in a deep dell. Here were trees, green corn-fields, and running streams; it was the first place I have seen in Asia which exhibited anything of the scenery of England."

June 2.—" Soon after midnight we mounted our horses. It was a mild moonlight night, and a nightingale filled the whole valley with his notes. Our way was along lanes, over which the wood on each side formed a canopy, and a murmuring rivulet accompanied us, till it was lost in a lake. At daylight we emerged into the Plain of Cashan, which seems to be a part of the Great Salt Desert. On our arrival at the King's garden, where we intended to put up, we were at first refused admittance, but an application to the Governor was soon attended to. We saw here huge snowy mountains on the north-east beyond Tehran."

June 5.—" Reached Kom. The country uniformly desolate.

"The chief Moojtuhid in all Persia being a resident of this city, I sent to know if a visit would be agreeable to him. His reply was, that if I had any business with him, I might come; but if otherwise, his age and infirmities must be his excuse. Intending to travel a double stage, started soon after sunset; and on

June 6.—"Crossed the desert, which we had been skirting from the day we came in sight of Cashan. After travelling ten parasangs, reached the caravansera of Hour Sultania. Here first we seemed to be approaching the Tartar regions."

June 7.—"Arrived at a caravansera, with villages in the neighbourhood, seven parasangs. A large party gathered about me in the evening, and, from asking questions about Europe, proceeded, as usual, to interrogate me concerning Christ. They continued about me till I mounted my horse, and rode from amongst them, to prosecute my journey."

June 8.—" Arrived, two hours before daybreak, at the walls of Tehran. I spread my bed upon the high road, and slept till the gates were open; then entered the city, and took up my abode at the ambassador's house."

As no muleteers could be procured at Tehran to proceed to Tebriz, it was considered advisable that Mr. Martyn should travel alone to the king's camp, for the purpose of seeing Mirza Shufi, the Premier, or Ameenoddoula, and soliciting his assistance in obtaining for him an introduction to the king; for he was "anxious to lose no time in presenting his book." So "leaving the city," he says, "just before the gates were shut, and giving the cattle their feed outside the walls, I went on, and travelled all night, till sunrise, when I arrived at the caravansera, close to the king's camp at Carach. I lost no time in forwarding Jaffier Ali Khan's letter to the Premier, who sent to desire that I would come to him. I found him lying ill in the verandah of the king's tent of audience. Near him were sitting two persons, who I was afterwards informed were Mirza Khanter and Mirza Abdoolwahab; the latter being a Secretary of State, and a great admirer of the Soofie sage. They took very little notice, not rising when I sat down, as is their custom to all who sit with them; nor offering me calean. The two secretaries, on learning my object in coming, began a conversation with me on religion and metaphysics, which lasted two hours. As they were both well-educated, gentlemanly men, the discussion was temperate, and, I hope, useful. What I remember of it was as follows :—' Do you consider the

New Testament as the word spoken by God?' 'The sense from God, but the expression from the different writers of it.' Here the Premier asked how many languages I understood; whether I spoke French; where I was educated; whether I understood astronomy and geography; and then observed to the others, that I spoke good Persian; to which they assented. They resumed,—'We want to know what your learned men think about the state of the soul after death, till the resurrection?' I mentioned the different opinions. 'But how, think you, does the spirit exist without a body?' 'Tell me,' said I, 'how the angels exist, and I will tell you.' 'In what sense do you believe the resurrection of the body; that every particle buried shall rise?' I mentioned the Scripture metaphor of the wheat dying and rising, with which the Soofie secretary appeared much pleased. 'What are the principles of your religion?' 'They are all centred in Jesus; not in his precepts, but in himself.' 'What are your opinions concerning Christ? was He a prophet created?' 'His manhood was created; his Godhead, of course, was not.' 'Now we much wish to hear what are your notions on that extraordinary subject, the Trinity?' I explained them, and began with observing, that the doctrine was by no means so extraordinary as at first sight it appeared to be; and then brought forward the illustration from the words, 'the Image of the invisible God.' 'Have you read the Koran?' 'Yes.' 'Is it not a miracle?' 'Prove it to be so.' The Soofie said, as if from me, 'The Arabs say it is inimitably elegant: how do I, who am a Persian, know it to be so?' 'What do you say to the division of the moon?' 'That there is no sufficient evidence for it.' 'What superior evidence have you for the miracles of Christ?' I was

about to answer, when the Soofie, not thinking it would
be satisfactory, said, rather dogmatically, that no religion
could be proved demonstratively. I said that ' If such a
degree of probable evidence was adduced as we acted upon
in common life, we should be inexcusable in rejecting it.'

"On the top of the caravansera, at sunset, I had a
conversation of a different kind on these subjects. A
man, seated on his rug, asked me what I walked up
and down for, and told me to come and sit with him on
his carpet. I did so, and found him to be a plain Mohammedan, that is, a compound of bigotry and ignorance.
Everything I said went for nothing. I knew nothing
at all about the Gospel. He had talked with Armenian
preachers, and therefore knew more about the matter
than myself. They had told him that the story of Jesus
and Mary in the Koran was exactly true ; this he took to
be an acknowledgment that the book was from God.
Thinking it worth while to see the state of the middling
rank of Mohammedans, I let him talk away. He supposed that the Mohammedans had formerly taken all
Europe, and that we still paid tribute for being permitted
to live. That the mother of Mehdi was the daughter of
Simon Peter or Plato ; he could not tell which, but rather
thought it was Constantine, Emperor of Rome. He could
not understand how Europe should be on one side of
Persia, and India on the other. Such geographical
difficulties are not to be wondered at in such a poor
fellow, though he had travelled as a merchant a good
deal,—when the Moollahs, and probably even the
Ministers of State, do not know the relative situation
of the provinces of their own kingdom.

"This man was very angry at my presuming to ask
why he was a Mohammedan. Finding me at last more

disposed to hear than to speak, he began to think that his discourse had made some impression upon me; and with eyes sparkling with hopes of a conquest, told me, with great affection, what I should do to get a knowledge of the truth. 'Drink,' said he, 'no wine for three days: pray, according to your own form, for Divine direction,—and depend upon it you will find it.' 'But supposing,' said I, 'that I have no such doubts in my mind, as to feel my need of Divine direction in this particular! what then?' 'Why, then,' said he, looking grimly, 'I have nothing more to say to you; and so, good night.'"

The third day after the above conversations, Mr. Martyn was called to a severer trial of his faith and patience than any to which he had yet been exposed. Several of the most intemperate Moollahs set themselves in array against him, and contended with him in behalf of Mohammedanism, in the presence of the prime minister of the kingdom. There it was demanded of him that he should deny that Saviour who had bought him with his blood; but he "witnessed a good confession," and fearlessly acknowledged Jesus as his Lord.

June 12.—"I attended the Vizier's levee, where there was a most intemperate and clamorous controversy kept up for an hour or two; eight or ten on one side, and I on the other. Amongst them were two Moollahs, the most ignorant of any I have yet met with in either Persia or India. It would be impossible to enumerate all the absurd things they said. Their vulgarity, in interrupting me in the middle of a speech; their utter ignorance of the nature of an argument; their impudent assertions about the law and the Gospel, neither of which they had ever seen in their lives, moved my indignation a little. I wished, and I said it would have been well, if Mirza

Abdoolwahad had been there; I should then have had a man of sense to argue with. The Vizier, who set us going at first, joined in it latterly, and said, 'You had better say, God is God, and Mahomet is the prophet of God.' I said, 'God is God,' but added, instead of 'Mahomet is the prophet of God,' 'and Jesus is the Son of God.' They had no sooner heard this, which I had avoided bringing forward till then, than they all exclaimed in contempt and anger, 'He is neither born nor begets,' and rose up, as if they would have torn me in pieces. One of them said, 'What will you say when your tongue is burnt out for this blasphemy?'

"One of them felt for me a little, and tried to soften the severity of this speech. My book which I had brought, expecting to present it to the king, lay before Mirza Shufi. As they all rose up, after him, to go, some to the king, and some away, I was afraid they would trample on the book; so I went in among them to take it up, and wrapped it in a towel before them; while they looked at it and me with supreme contempt.

"Thus I walked away alone to my tent, to pass the rest of the day in heat and dirt. What have I done, thought I, to merit all this scorn? Nothing, I trust, but bearing testimony to Jesus. I thought over these things in prayer, and my troubled heart found that peace which Christ hath promised to his disciples :—

'If on my face, for thy dear name,' &c.

"To complete the trials of the day, a message came from the Vizier in the evening, to say, that it was not the custom of the king to see any Englishman, unless presented by the ambassador or accredited by a letter from him; and that I must therefore wait till the king reached Sultania, where the ambassador would be."

After this "day of rebuke and blasphemy,"—when that divine promise was eminently fulfilled towards Mr. Martyn, "Thou shalt hide them in the secret of thy presence from the pride of man ; thou shalt keep them secretly in thy pavilion from the strife of tongues ; "—when having heard the "slander of many," and being made "a reproach amongst all his enemies," he could nevertheless exclaim with the Psalmist, "O how great is thy goodness, which thou hast laid up for them that fear thee, which thou hast wrought for them that trust in thee before the sons of men,"—he turned his back upon the king's camp, having been joined by his companion from Tehran, and prosecuted his journey towards Tebriz.

June 13.—"Disappointed," he writes, "of my object in coming to the camp, I lost no time in leaving it, and proceeded in company with Mr. C——, who had just joined me from Tehran, towards Casbin ; intending there to wait the result of an application to the ambassador. Started at eleven, and travelled till eleven next morning, having gone ten parasangs, or forty miles, to Quishlag. The country all along was well watered and cultivated. The mules being too much tired to proceed, we passed the day at the village ; indeed, we all wanted rest. As I sat down in the dust, on the shady side of a walled village by which we passed, and surveyed the plains over which our road lay, I sighed at the thoughts of my dear friends in India and England ; of the vast regions I must traverse before I can get to either, and of the various and unexpected hindrances which present themselves to my going forward ! I comfort myself with the hope that my God has something for me to do, by thus delaying my exit."

June 16.—"Continued at the village, in consequence of an illness with which Mr. C—— was attacked; but at night we moved forward, and after travelling seven parasangs over the same fine plain, reached Casbin."

June 17.—"In the caravansera there, they were collecting straw, &c., for the king, whom they expected in ten days. On this plea, they refused to allow us to unload there."

June 18.—"Endeavoured to get a muleteer to go to the ambassador, but could agree with none, so I determined to stay at Casbin. I had at first intended to go on to Sultania, there to wait for the King."

June 20.—"Left this place, not a little disgusted at the reception we had met with there. One parasang off, we stopped at a village to get something for breakfast. One of the people there asked a good many questions about our religion. It was such an unusual thing to be travelling coolly, in the middle of the day, in the East, that it produced a new train of ideas: indeed I thought of nothing but of my dear friends in England, and of the days when, in weather like this, I walked with them 'taking sweet counsel.' While passing over the plain, mostly on foot, I had them all in my mind, and bore them upon my heart in prayer. The north wind from the Caspian, I suppose, blowing through some clouds which rested on the mountains on our right, made the air excessively cold.

"Arrived, between twelve and one o'clock, at Scah Dulir, where a villager gave us his house; and though the room we were in was so constructed as scarcely to admit the light, we had need of all our skins to keep us warm."

June 21.—"On account of the coldness of the weather,

we did not think it necessary to start till seven o'clock, after breakfast. Arrived at the village of Aber at four in the afternoon, having taken the shortest route. Till we reached the high and frequented road, all was barrenness; but from thence we found a good deal of cultivation, as also all the way from Casbin: near which city the vineyards were all open to the road; there was not so much as a fence."

June 22.—"Left Sangla at a quarter past five in the morning, and at a quarter past ten reached Sultania. The weather was perfectly cool and agreeable, and all around were the pastures of the wilderness. We met with the usual insulting treatment at the caravansera, where the king's servants had got possession of a good room, built for the reception of the better order of guests; —they seemed to delight in the opportunity of humbling an European. Sultania is still but a village; yet the Zengan prince has quartered himself and all his attendants, with their horses, on this poor little village. All along the road where the king is expected, the people are patiently waiting, as for some dreadful disaster:—plague, pestilence, or famine, are nothing to the misery of being subject to the violence and extortion of this rabble soldiery. One of our servants, who himself had formerly been a soldier in the king's camp, said that the troops were raised from the wandering tribes, and from the cities. Those from the tribes are paid by the king, the others by the cities. Sons of the chiefs of the tribes, and, indeed, of all unimportant Governments, are detained at court as hostages."

June 24.—"Left Sultania at half-past three. Saw some water-tortoises on the edge of the little stream which watered the vale. Continued our course to Zengan, a walled city, distant from Sultania six parasangs. Here we found, in the caravansera, large bales of cotton brought by merchants from Tehran, intended for Turkey. There were also two Tartar merchants, natives of Astracan, who had brought iron and tea for sale. They wished to know whether we wanted tea of Cathay. I was curious to know something about the countries they had visited; but they spoke nothing but Turkish, without which language a person may travel to very little purpose in these parts: Persian is quite a foreign language."

June 25.—"After a restless night, rose so ill with a fever that I could not go on. My companion, Mr. C——, was nearly in the same state. We touched nothing all day."

June 26.—"After such another night, I had determined to go on, but Mr. C—— declared himself unable to stir; so here we dragged through another miserable day. What added to our distress was, that we were in danger, if detained here another day or two, of being absolutely in want of the necessaries of life before reaching Tebriz. We made repeated applications to the moneyed people, but none would advance a piastre. Where are the people who flew forth to meet General Malcolm with their purses and their lives? Another generation is risen up, 'who know not Joseph.' Providentially a poor muleteer arriving from Tebriz became security for us, and thus we obtained five tomans. This was a heavensend; and we lay down quietly, free from apprehensions of being obliged to go a fatiguing journey of eight or ten hours, without a house or village in the way, in our present weak and reduced state. We had now eaten nothing for two days. My mind was much disordered from headache and giddiness, from which I was seldom free; but my heart, I trust, was with Christ and his saints. To live much longer in this world of sickness and pain, seemed no way desirable; the most favourite prospects of my heart seemed very poor and childish; and cheerfully would I have exchanged them all for the unfading inheritance."

June 27.—"My Armenian servant was attacked in the same way. The rest did not get me the things that I wanted, so that I passed the third day in the same exhausted state; my head, too, was tortured with shocking pains, such as, together with the horror I felt at being exposed to the sun, showed me plainly to what to ascribe my sickness. Towards evening, two more of our servants were attacked in the same way, and lay groaning from pains in the head."

June 28.—"All were much recovered, but in the afternoon I again relapsed. During a high fever, Mr. C—— read to me, in bed, the Epistle to the Ephesians, and I never felt the consolations of that Divine revelation of mysteries more sensibly and solemnly. Rain in the night prevented our setting off."

June 29.—"My ague and fever returned, with such a headache, that I was almost frantic. Again and again I said to myself, 'Let patience have her perfect work;' and kept pleading the promises, 'When thou passest through the waters, I will be with thee,' &c.; and the Lord did not withhold his presence. I endeavoured to repel all the disordered thoughts that the fever occasioned, and to keep in mind that all was friendly; a friendly Lord presiding; and nothing exercising me but what would show itself at last friendly. A violent perspiration at last relieved the acute pain in my head, and my heart rejoiced; but as soon as that was over, the exhaustion it occasioned, added to the fatigue from the pain, left me in as low a state of depression as ever I was in. I seemed about to sink into a long fainting fit, and I almost wished it; but at this moment, a little after midnight, I was summoned to mount my horse, and set out, rather dead than alive. We moved on six parasangs. We had a thunderstorm with hail."

July 1.—"A long and tiresome march to Sarehund. In seven parasangs there was no village. They had nothing to sell but buttermilk and bread; but a servant of Abbas Mirza, happening to be at the same caravansera, sent us some flesh of a mountain cow which he had shot the day before. All day I had scarcely the right recollection of myself, from the violence of the ague. We have now reached the end of the level ground, which we have had all the way from Tehran, and are approaching the boundaries of Parthia and Media; a most natural boundary it is, as the two ridges of mountains we have had on the left and right, come round and form a barrier."

July 2.—"At two in the morning we set out. I hardly know when I have been so disordered. I had little or no recollection of things, and what I did remember, at times, of happy scenes in India or England, served only to embitter my present situation. Soon after removing into the air, I was seized with a violent ague, and in this state I went on till sunrise. At three parasangs and a-half we found a fine caravansera, apparently very little used, as the grass was growing in the court. There was nothing all round but the barren rocks, which generally roughen the country before the mountain rears its height. Such an edifice, in such a situation, was cheering. Soon after, we came to a river, over which was a high bridge; I sat down in the shade under it, with two camel-drivers. The cafila, as it happened, forded the river, and passed on without my perceiving it. Mr. C——, seeing no signs of me, returned, and, after looking about for some time, espied my horse grazing; he concluded immediately that the horse had flung me from the bridge into the river, and was almost ready to give me up for lost. My speedy appearance from under the bridge relieved his terror and anxiety. The pass was a mere nothing to those at Bushire; in fact, it was no part of the mountain we climbed, but only a few hills. In a natural opening in the mountains, on the other side, was a river, with most of its bed dry, and over it a bridge of many arches; which led us to an unwalled village, surrounded by cornfields, which we reached at ten o'clock. Half the people still continue ill. For myself, I am, through God's infinite mercy, recovering."

July 3.—"Started at three, full three hours after we ought; and, as was to be expected, we all got ill again, from being exposed to the sun six hours; for we did not get to our ground, Turcoman, till eleven o'clock. It was a poor village among the hills, over which our whole way from Mianu lay. Ascending one, and descending another, was the whole of the variety, so that I do not know when we have had a more tiresome day."

July 4.—"I so far prevailed as to get the cafila into motion at midnight. Lost our way in the night, but, arriving at a village, were set right again. At eight came to Kilk caravansera, but not stopping there, went on to a village, where we arrived at half-past nine. The baggage not coming up till long after, we got no breakfast till one o'clock. In consequence of all these things,—want of sleep, want of refreshment, and exposure to the sun,—

I was presently in a high fever, which raged so furiously all the day, that I was nearly delirious, and it was some time before I could get the right recollection of myself. I almost despaired, and do now, of getting alive through this unfortunate journey. Last night I felt remarkably well, calm, and composed, and sat reflecting on my heavenly rest, with more sweetness of soul, abstraction from the world, and solemn views of God, than I have had for a long time. Oh for such sacred hours! This short and painful life would scarcely be felt, could I live thus at heaven's gate. It being impossible to continue my journey in my present state, and one of the servants also being so ill that he could not move with safety, we determined to halt one day at the village, and sent on a messenger to Sir Gore, at Tebriz, informing him of our approach."

July 5.—"Slept all day, and at sunset prepared to proceed all the way to Tebriz, or at least to Seid Abad; but we did not set out till one in the morning. I was again dreadfully disordered with headache and fever. We got into a wretched hovel, where the raging fever almost deprived me of reason. In the cool of the evening we set out to go to Seid Abad, distant about three parasangs. When the cafila arrived near Seid Abad, it was a dark night, about eleven o'clock, and not one of the party knew where it was, nor could we discover it by the barking of the dogs, the usual sign. Once we heard the bark, and made sure of having attained our object, but found only some shepherds keeping watch over their flocks by night. These boors showed us which road to take, which we soon found end in nothing; so, returning, we tried to induce one of them to serve as a guide, with the promise of any sum of money he required; but all in vain. The only thing that remained to be done was to lie down on the spot, and wait patiently for the day, which I did, and caught such a cold as, with all our other exposures, consummated my disorders. As soon as it was day, we found our way to the village, where Dr. —— was waiting for us. Not being able to stay for us, he went on to Tebriz, and we as far as Wasmuch, where he promised to procure for us a fine upper room furnished ; but when we arrived, they denied that there was any such place: at last, after an hour's threatening, we got admittance to it. An hour before break of day, I left it, in hopes of reaching Tebriz before sunrise. Some of the people seemed to feel compassion for me, and asked me if I was not very ill. At last I reached the gate, and feebly asked for a man to show me the way to the Ambassador's."

By a fever of nearly two months' continuance, which, during the greater portion of that period, raged with unremitting severity, Mr. Martyn was defeated in his intention of presenting in person his translation of the New Testament to the King of Persia and to the Prince his son.* His disappointment, however, on this occasion was greatly diminished by the kindness of Sir Gore Ouseley, who, together with his lady, was tenderly and assiduously attentive to Mr. Martyn throughout the whole of his illness; and who, in order that nothing might be wanting conducive to the favourable acceptance of the New Testament by the King, promised himself to present it at Court.†

* See Appendix XVI.

† Sir Gore Ouseley, according to his promise, laid the New Testament before the King, who publicly expressed his approbation of the work. He also carried the MS. to St. Petersburg, where, under his superintendence, it was printed and put into circulation.

The idea of returning to England, which first occurred to Mr. Martyn at Cawnpore, was, as we have seen, instantly abandoned by him, on its appearing to be the Divine will that he should visit Persia. After accomplishing his great object in that country, the general state of his health seeming to him to render the measure requisite, he reverted to his original intention, in the prosecution of which he was confirmed by his long illness at Tebriz, which had been induced by exposure to a heated atmosphere.

Happy would it have been, speaking after the manner of men, had he been less precipitate in putting his design in execution; but, on the tenth day after his recovery, he commenced his journey. What he felt when deprived of health, and what were his sensations when in a considerable degree restored to it, may be seen in extracts from two letters,—the one addressed to Mr. Simeon, from the bed of suffering; the other sent to a friend exceedingly beloved by him, in Cornwall:—*

"I would not pain your heart," he said, in the first; "but we who are in Jesus have the privilege of viewing life and death as nearly the same, since both are ours; and I thank a gracious Lord that sickness never came at a time when I was more free from apparent reasons for living. Nothing, seemingly, remains for me to do, but to follow the rest of my family to the tomb."

"It has pleased God," he wrote in the second, "to restore me to life and health again; not that I have yet recovered my former strength, but I consider myself sufficiently restored to prosecute my journey. My daily prayer is, that my late chastisement may have its intended effect, and make me, all the rest of my days, more

* See Appendix XVII.

humble and less self-confident. Self-confidence has often let me down fearful lengths, and would, without God's gracious interference, prove my endless perdition. I seem to be made to feel this evil of my heart, more than any other, at this time. In prayer, or when I write or converse on the subject, Christ appears to me my life and strength; but, at other times, I am thoughtless and bold, as if I had all life and strength in myself. Such neglects on our part are a diminution of our joys; but the Covenant! the Covenant stands fast with Him for his people evermore. I mentioned my conversing sometimes on Divine subjects. In these I am sometimes led on by the Soofie Persians, and tell them all I know of the very recesses of the sanctuary. But to give an account of all my discussions with these mystic philosophers must be reserved to the time of our meeting. Do I dream, that I venture to think and write of such an event as that? Is it possible that we shall ever meet again below? Though it is possible, I dare not indulge such a pleasing hope.

" In three days I intend setting my horse's head towards Constantinople, distant about 1,300 miles. Nothing, I think, will occasion any further detention here, if I can procure servants who know both Persian and Turkish. Ignorant as I am of Turkish, should I be taken ill on the road, my case would be pitiable indeed. The Ambassador and his suite are still here; his and Lady Ouseley's attentions to me during my illness, have been unremitted. The Prince Abbas Mirza, the wisest of the King's sons, and heir to the throne, was here some time after my arrival. I much wished to present a copy of the Persian New Testament to him; but I could not rise from my bed. The book, however, will be given him

by the Ambassador. Public curiosity about the Gospel,
now, for the first time in the memory of the modern
Persians, introduced into the country, is a good deal
excited here and at Shiraz, and in other places; so that,
upon the whole, I am thankful for having been led
hither, and detained; though my residence in this
country has been attended with many unpleasant circumstances. The way of the Kings of the East is
preparing : thus much may be said with safety, but
little more. The Persians will also probably take the
lead in the march to Sion."

CHAPTER XI.

WITH such feeble hopes of reaching England, Mr. Martyn
commenced a journey which was the most painful, and
at the same time the most joyful one, he ever undertook.
The miseries he endured in it were intense; but it ended
in heaven.

Sept. 2.—"All things being ready," he says, "I· set
out on my long journey of 1,300 miles, carrying letters
from Sir G. Ouseley, for the Governors of Erivan, Cars,
and Erzerum, and the Ambassador at Constantinople.
My party consisted of two Armenian servants,—Antoine
the groom, and Sergius, who was to accompany me all the
way to Constantinople; he professing to speak Persian
and Turkish, and to be qualified to act as my interpreter;
but his knowledge of the former I soon found to be
rather scanty. These were mounted, and two other horses
carried my luggage. My Mihmander had also Chappar*
horses, and I rode my own. There was also a man on

* Mr. Martyn, through the friendly interference of the Ambassador,
travelled with what are termed *Chappar Horses*, for an account of
which see Burder's " Oriental Customs," p. 260.

foot, to bring back the cattle. As we passed through the
bazaars of Tebriz, I saw quantities of the finest fruit
displayed on every stand. At sunset we left the western
gate of Tebriz behind us. The horses proved to be sorry
animals. One sunk so often under his load, that we were
six hours going what the Mihmander called two parasangs, but which was undoubtedly three or four. It was
midnight before we arrived at Sangla, a village in the
middle of the plain of Tebriz. There they procured me a
place in the Zabit's house. I slept till after sunrise of
the 3d, and did not choose to proceed at such an hour;
so I passed most of the day in my room. At three in the
afternoon proceeded towards Sofian. My health being
again restored, through infinite and unbounded mercy, I
was able to look round the creation with calm delight.
The plain of Tebriz, towards the west and south-west,
stretches away to an immense distance, and is bounded in
these directions by mountains so remote, as to appear,
from their soft blue, to blend with the skies. The baggage having been sent on before, I ambled on with my
Mihmander, looking all around me, and especially towards
the distant hills, with gratitude and joy. Oh! it is necessary to have been confined to a bed of sickness, to know
the delight of moving freely through the works of God,
with the senses at liberty to enjoy their proper objects.
My attendant not being very conversant with Persian, we
rode silently along. For my part, I could not have
enjoyed any companion so much as I did my own feelings.
At sunset we reached Sofian, a village with gardens, at
the north-west end of the plain, which is usually the first
stage from Tebriz. The Zabit was in his corn-field, under
a little tent, inspecting his labourers, who were cutting the
straw fine, so as to be fit to be eaten by cattle. This was

done by drawing over it a cylinder armed with blades of a triangular form, placed in different planes, so that their vertices should coincide in the cylinder.

"The Zabit paid me no attention, but sent a man to show me a place to sleep in, who took me to one with only three walls. I demanded another with four, and was accordingly conducted to a weaver's, where, notwithstanding the mosquitoes and other vermin, I passed the night comfortably enough. On my offering money, the Mihmander interfered, and said that if it were known that I had given money, he should be ruined; and added,—'they, indeed, dare not take it;' but this I did not find to be the case."

Sept. 4.—"At sunrise mounted my horse, and proceeded north-west, through a pass in the mountains, towards Murun. By the way, I sat down by the brook, and there ate my bread and raisins, and drank of the crystal stream; but either the coldness of this unusual breakfast, or the riding after it, did not at all agree with me. The heat oppressed me much, and the road seemed intolerably tedious; at last we got out from among the mountains, and saw the village of Murun, in a fine valley on the right. It was about eleven o'clock when we reached it. As the Mihmander could not immediately find a place to put me in, we had a complete view of this village. They stared at my European dress, but no disrespect was shown. I was deposited, at last with —— Khan, who was seated in a place with three walls. Not at all disposed to pass the day in company, as well as exposed, I asked for another room: on which I was shown to the stable, where there was a little place partitioned off, but so as to admit a view of the horses. The smell of the stable, though not in general disagreeable to me, was so strong, that I was quite unwell, and strangely dispirited and melancholy. Immediately after dinner, I fell fast asleep, and slept four hours; after which I rose and ordered them to prepare for the next journey. The horses being changed here, it was some time before they were brought, but by exerting myself, we moved off by midnight. It was a most mild and delightful night, and the pure air, after the smell of the stable, was quite reviving. For once, also, I travelled all the way without being sleepy ; and beguiled the hours of the night by thinking of the 14th Psalm,—especially the connection of the last three verses with the preceding."

Sept. 5.—" In five hours we were just on the hills which face the pass out of the valley of Murun, and in four hours and a-half more, emerged from between the two ridges of mountains, into the valley of Gurjur. Gurjur is eight parasangs from Murun, and our course to it was nearly due north. This long march was far from being a fatiguing one. The air, the road, and my spirits were good. Here I was well accommodated, but had to mourn over my impatient temper towards my servants ; there is nothing that disturbs my peace so much. How much more noble and godlike to bear with calmness, and observe with pity, rather than anger, the failings and offences of others. O that I may, through grace, be enabled to recollect myself in the time of temptation ! O that the Spirit of God may check my folly, and at such times, bring the lowly Saviour to my view."

Sept. 6.—" Soon after twelve we started with fresh horses, and came to the Arar, or Araxes, distant two parasangs, and about as broad as the Isis, with a current as strong as that of the Ganges. The ferry-boat

being on the other side, I lay down to sleep till it came,
but observing my servants do the same, I was obliged to
get up and exert myself. It dawned, however, before we
got over. The boat was a huge fabric in the form of a
rhombus. The ferryman had only a stick to push with ;
an oar, I dare say, he had never seen or heard of, and
many of my train had probably never floated before ;—
so alien is a Persian from everything that belongs to
shipping. We landed safely on the other side in about
two minutes. We were four hours in reaching Nackshan,
and for half an hour more I was led from street to street,
till at last I was lodged in a wash-house belonging to a
great man, a corner of which was cleaned out for me. It
was near noon, and my baggage was not arrived ; so that
I was obliged to go without my breakfast ; which was
hard after a ride for four hours in the sun. The baggage
was delayed so long, that I began to fear ; at last, however, it arrived. All the afternoon I slept, and at sunset
arose, and continued wakeful till midnight, when I roused
my people, and with fresh horses set out again. We
travelled till sunrise. I scarcely perceived that we had
been moving,—a Hebrew word in the 16th Psalm, having
led me gradually into speculations on the eighth conjuga-
tion of the Arabic verb. I am glad that my philological
curiosity is revived, as my mind will be less liable to idleness."

Sept. 7.—" Arrived at Khoock, a poor village distant
five and a-half parasangs from Nackshan, nearly west. I
should have mentioned, that on descending into the plain
of Nackshan, my attention was arrested by the appearance of a hoary mountain, opposite to us at the other end,
rising so high above the rest that they sunk into insignificance. It was truly sublime, and the interest it excited

was not lessened, when, on inquiring its name, I was told it was Agri, or Ararat. Thus I saw two remarkable objects in one day,—the Araxes, and Ararat. At four in the afternoon we set out for Shurror. The evening was pleasant; the ground over which we passed was full of rich cultivation and verdure, watered by many a stream, and containing forty villages, most of them with the usual appendage of gardens. To add to the scene, the great Ararat was on our left. On the peak of that hill the whole church was once contained; it has now spread far and wide, even to the ends of the earth, but the ancient vicinity of it knows it no more. I fancied many a spot where Noah perhaps offered his sacrifices; and the promise of God, 'that seed-time and harvest should not cease,' appeared to me to be more exactly fulfilled in the agreeable plain in which it was spoken than elsewhere; as I had not seen such fertility in any part of the Shah's dominions. Here the blessed saint landed in a new world; so may I, safe in Christ, outride the storm of life, and land at last on one of the everlasting hills!

"Night coming on, we lost our way, and got intercepted by some deep ravines, into one of which the horse that carried my trunks sunk so deep, that the water got into one of them, wetted the linen, and spoiled some books. Finding it in vain to attempt gaining our munzil, we went to another village, where, after a long delay, two aged men with silver beards opened their house to us. Though it was near midnight, I had a fire lighted to dry my books, took some coffee, and sunk into deep sleep; from which awaking at the earliest dawn of

Sept. 8.—"I roused the people, and had a delightful ride of one parasang to Shurror, distant four parasangs from Khoock. Here I was accommodated by the great man with a stable, or winter room; for they build it in such a strange vicinity, in order to have it warm in winter. At present, while the weather is still hot, the smell is at times overpowering. At eleven at night we moved off, with fresh horses, for Duwala; but though we had guides in abundance, we were not able to extricate ourselves from the ravines with which this village is surrounded. Procuring another man from a village we happened to wander into, we at last made our way, through grass and mire, to the pass, which led us to a country as dry as the one we had left was wet. Ararat was now quite near : at the foot of it is Duwala, six parasangs from Nackshan, where we arrived at seven in the morning of

Sept. 9.—"As I had been thinking all night of a Hebrew letter, I perceived little of the tediousness of the way. I tried also some difficulties in the 16th Psalm, without being able to master them. All day on the 15th and 16th Psalms, and gained some light into the difficulties. The villagers not bringing the horses in time, we were not able to go on at night; but I was not much concerned, as I thereby gained some rest."

Sept. 10.—"All day at the village, writing down notes on the 15th and 16th Psalms. Moved at midnight, and arrived early in the morning at Erivan."

Sept. 11.—"I alighted at Hosyn Khan, the governor's palace, as it may be called, for he seems to live in a style equal to that of a prince. Indeed, commanding a fortress on the frontier, within six hours of the Russians, he is entrusted with a considerable force, and is nearly independent of the Shah. After sleeping two hours, I was summoned to his presence. He at first took no notice of me, but continued reading his Koran, it being the Mo-

hurrun. After a compliment or two he resumed his
devotions. The next ceremony was to exchange a rich
shawl dress for a still richer pelisse, on pretence of its
being cold. The next display was to call for his physician,
who, after respectfully feeling his pulse, stood on one side :
this was to show that he had a domestic physician. His
servants were most richly clad. My letter from the ambassador, which till now had lain neglected on the ground,
was opened and read by a Moonshee. He heard with
great interest what Sir Gore had written about the translation of the Gospels. After this he was very kind and
attentive, and sent for Lieutenant M——— of the engineers,
who was stationed, with two sergeants, at this fort. In
the afternoon, the governor sent for me again in private.
A fountain, in a basin of white marble, was playing before
him, and in it water-grapes and melons were cooling; two
time-pieces were before him, to show the approach of the
time of lawful repast; below the window, at a great depth,
ran a broad and rapid stream, over rocks and stones, under
a bridge of two arches, producing an agreeable murmur :
on the side of the river were gardens, and a rich plain ;
and directly in front, Ararat. He was now entirely free
from ceremony, but too much fatigued to converse. I
tried to begin a religious discussion, by observing that
' he was in one paradise now, and was in quest of another
hereafter,' but the remark produced no effect. He ordered
for me a Mihmander, a guard and four horses, with which
a Turk had just come from Cars. Lieutenant M———
dined and passed the rest of the evening with us."

Sept. 12.—" The horses not being ready for me according to my order, I rode alone, and found my way to Ech-
Miazin (or Three Churches), two and a half parasangs
distant. Directing my course to the largest church, I

found it enclosed by some other buildings and a wall. Within the entrance, I found a large court, with monks, cowled and gowned, moving about. On seeing my Armenian letters, they brought me to the patriarch's lodge, where I found two bishops, one of whom was Nestus, at breakfast on pilaws, kubebs, wine, arrack, &c., and Serafino with them. As he spoke English, French, and Italian, I had no difficulty in communicating with my hosts. After breakfast, Serafino showed me the room appointed for me, and sat down and told me his story. His proper name, in Armenian, is Serope; he was born at Erzerum, of Armenian Roman Catholic parents. His father dying when he was young, his mother intrusted him to the care of the missionaries, to be carried to Rome to be educated. There he studied eight years, and became perfectly Europeanized. At eighteen or twenty he left Rome, and repaired to Mount Libanus, where he was ordained; and there his eyes were opened to the falsehood of the Pope's pretensions. After this he served the Armenian church at Erzerum, and then at Cars, after which he went to Bagdad. Receiving at this time an invitation from the patriarch at Ech-Miazin to join their body, he consented, on condition that he should not be considered as a common monk; and accordingly he is regarded with that deference which his talents and superior information demand. He is exerting himself to extend his influence in the monastery, for the purpose of executing some plans he has formed for the improvement of the Armenians. The monastery, and consequently the whole of the Armenians, are under the direction of Nestus, one of the bishops; for the patriarch Ephraim is a mere cypher, and passes most of his time in bed. About three years ago, Nestus succeeded in forming a synod for the management of the business of the church, consisting of eight bishops, in which, of course, he is all-powerful. The patriarch is elected by twelve bishops. One member alone of the synod is a man of any ability, and he sometimes ventures to differ from Nestus. The object which Serope has at heart is a college, to teach the Armenian youth logic, rhetoric, and the other sciences. The expediency of this is acknowledged, but they cannot agree about the place where the college should be. Serope, considering the danger to which the cathedral seat is exposed, from its situation between Russia, Persia, and Turkey, is for building it at Teflis. Nestus, on the contrary, considering that Ech-Miazin is the spot appointed by heaven, according to a vision of Gregory, for the cathedral seat, and so sanctified, is for having it there. The errors and superstitions of his people were the subject of Serope's conversation the whole morning, and seemed to be the occasion of real grief to him. He intended, he said, after a few more months' trial of what he could do here, to retire to India, and there write and print some works in Armenian, tending to enlighten the people with regard to religion, in order to introduce a reform. I said all I could to encourage him in such a blessed work: promising him every aid from the English, and proving to him, from the example of Luther, and the other European reformers, that, however arduous the work might seem, God would surely be with him to help him. I mentioned the awful neglect of the Armenian clergy, in never preaching; as thereby the glad tidings of a Saviour were never proclaimed. He made no reply to this, but that 'it was to be lamented, as the people were never called away from vice.' When the bells rang for vespers, we went together to the great church. The ecclesiastics, consisting of ten bishops and other monks, with the choristers, were drawn up in a semicircle fronting the altar, for a view of which the church-door was left open. Serope fell into his place and went through a few of the ceremonies; he then took me into the church, never ceasing to remark upon the ignorance and superstition of the people. Some of his Catholic prejudices against Luther seemed to remain. The monks dined together in the hall at eleven; at night each sups in his own room. Serope, Nestus, and two or three others, form a party of themselves, and seldom dine in the hall; where coarseness, both of meals and manners, too much prevails."

Sept. 13.—"I asked Serope about the 16th Psalm in the Armenian version; he translated it into correct Latin. In the afternoon I waited on the patriarch; it was a visit of great ceremony. He was reclining on a sort of throne, placed in the middle of the room. All stood, except the two senior bishops; a chair was set for me on the other side, close to the patriarch; at my right hand stood Serope, to interpret. The patriarch had a dignified, rather than a venerable appearance. His conversation consisted in protestations of sincere attachment, in expressions of his hopes of deliverance from the Mohammedan yoke, and inquiries about my translations of the Scriptures; and he begged me to consider myself as at home in the monastery. Indeed, their attention and kindness are unbounded: Nestus and Serope anticipate my every wish. I told the patriarch, that I was so happy in being here, that, did duty permit, I could almost be willing to become a monk with them. He smiled, and fearing, perhaps, that I was in earnest, said that they had quite enough. Their number is a hundred, I think. The church was immensely rich till about ten years ago; when, by quarrels between two contending patriarchs, one of whom is still in the monastery in disgrace, most of their money was expended in referring their disputes to the Mohammedans as arbitrators. There is no difficulty, however, in replenishing their coffers; their merchants in India are entirely at their command."

Sept. 15.—"Spent the day in preparing, with Serope, for the mode of travelling in Turkey. All my heavy and expensive preparations at Tebriz prove to be incumbrances which must be left behind: my trunks were exchanged for bags; and my portable table and chair, several books, large supplies of sugar, &c., were condemned to be left behind. My humble equipments were considered as too mean for an English gentleman; so Serope gave me an English bridle and saddle. The roads in Turkey being much more infested with robbers than those of Persia, a sword was brought for me. My Armenian servant, Sergius, was also to be armed with a gun and sword, but it was determined that he was unfit for the journey; so a brave and trusty man of the monastery, named Melcom, was appointed in his stead, and he had arms of his own; —he speaks nothing but Turkish."

Sept. 16.—"I conversed again with Serope on his projected reformation. As he was invited to Ech-Miazin for the purpose of educating the Armenian youth for the ministry, he has a right to dictate in all that concerns that matter. His objection to Ech-Miazin is, that from midnight to sunrise all the members of the monastery must attend prayers; this requires all to be in bed immediately after sunset. The monks are chiefly from the neighbourhood of Erivan, and were originally singing-boys; into such hands is this rich and powerful foundation fallen. They have no vows upon them but those of celibacy."

The hospitable and benevolent conduct of the interesting society at Ech-Miazin,* made a deep impression upon the feeling mind of their guest:—received by them as a brother, he left them with sentiments of fraternal regard, and no doubt his heart swelled with grateful recollections of peculiar strength, when the kindness he had experienced in the bosom of an Armenian monastery was brought into contrast with that Mohammedan inhospitality and cruelty to which in a short time he was subjected.

"At six in the morning of September 17," Mr. Martyn writes, "accompanied by Serope, one bishop, the secretary, and several servants of the monastery, I left Ech-Miazin. My party now consisted of two men from the Governor of Erivan, a Mihmander, and a guard; my servant Sergius, for whom the monks interceded, as he had some business at Constantinople; one trusty servant from the monastery, Melcom, who carried my money; and two baggage-horses with their owners. The monks soon returned, and we pursued our way over the plain of Ararat. At twelve o'clock reached Quila Gazki, about six parasangs from Ech-Miazin. The Mihmander rode on, and got a good place for me."

Sept. 18.—"Rose with the dawn, in hopes of going this stage before breakfast, but the horses were not ready. I set off at eight, fearing no sun, though I found it at times very oppressive when there was no wind. At the

* For the interest the Armenians excite in a missionary point of view, see Dr. Buchanan's "Christian Researches."

end of three hours we left the plain of Ararat, the last of
the plains of modern Persia in this quarter. Meeting
here with the Araxes again, I undressed and plunged
into the stream. While hastening forward with the
trusty Melcom, to rejoin my party, we were overtaken
by a spearman, with a lance of formidable length: I did
not think it likely that one man would venture to attack
two, both armed; but the spot was a noted one for
robbers, and very well calculated, by its solitariness, for
deeds of privacy: however, he was friendly enough.
He had, however, nearly done me a mischief. On the
bank of the river we sprung a covey of partridges:
instantly he laid his lance under him across the horse's
back, and fired a horse-pistol at them. His horse,
starting at the report, came upon mine, with the point of
the spear directly towards me, so that I thought a wound
for myself or horse was inevitable; but the spear passed
under my horse. We were to have gone to Hagi-
Buhirem, but finding the head man of it at a village a
few furlongs nearer, we stopped there. We found him
in a shed outside the walls, reading his Koran, with his
sword, gun, and pistol by his side. He was a good-
natured farmer-looking man, and spoke in Persian. He
chanted the Arabic with great readiness, and asked me
whether I knew what that book was? 'Nothing less
than the great Koran!'"

Sept. 19.—"Left the village at seven in the morning,
and as the stage was reputed to be very dangerous,
owing to the vicinity of the famous Cara Beg, my Mihmander took three armed men from the village in addition to the one we brought from Erivan. We continued
going along, through the pass, two or three parasangs,
and crossed the Araxes three times. We then ascended

the mountains on the north, by a road, if not so steep, yet
as long and difficult as any of the cotuls of Bushire. On
the top we found table-land, along which we moved many
a tedious mile, expecting every minute that we should
have a view of a fine champaign country below; but dale
followed dale, apparently in endless succession, and though
at such a height, there was very little air to relieve the
heat, and nothing to be seen but barren rocks. One part,
however, must be excepted, where the prospect opened to
the north, and we had a view of the Russian territory;
so that we saw at once, Persia, Russia, and Turkey. At
length we came to an Armenian village, situated in a
hollow of these mountains, on a declivity. The village
presented a singular appearance, being filled with conical
piles of peat, for they have no firewood. Around there
was a great deal of cultivation, chiefly corn. Most of the
low land from Tebriz to this place is planted with cotton,
palma Christi, and rice. This is the first village in
Turkey; not a Persian cap was to be seen; the respectable
people wore a red Turkish cap. The great man of the
village paid me a visit; he was a young Mussulman, and
took care of all my Mussulmen attendants; but he left me
and my Armenians where he found us, at the house of an
Armenian, without offering his services. I was rather
uncomfortably lodged, my room being a thoroughfare for
horses, cows, buffaloes, and sheep. Almost all the village
came to look at me. The name of this village is Fiwick,
it is distant six parasangs from the last; but we were eight
hours accomplishing it, and a cafila would have been twelve.
We arrived at three o'clock, both horses and men much
fatigued."

Sept. 20.—"From daybreak to sunrise I walked, then
breakfasted, and set out. Our course lay north, over a

mountain; and here danger was apprehended; it was, indeed, dismally solitary all around. The appearance of an old castle on the top of a crag was the first occasion on which our guard got their pieces ready, and one rode forward to reconnoitre; but all there was as silent as the grave. At last, after travelling five hours, we saw some men: our guard again took their places in front. Our fears were soon removed by seeing carts and oxen. Not so the opposite party; for my baggage was so small as not to be easily perceived. They halted, therefore, at the bottom, towards which we were both descending, and those of them who had guns advanced in front and hailed us. We answered peaceably; but they, still distrusting us, as we advanced nearer, cocked their pieces: soon, however, we came to a parley. They were Armenians, bringing wood from Cars to their village in the mountain: they were hardy, fine young men, and some old men who were with them were particularly venerable. The dangerous spots being passed through, my party began to sport with their horses;—galloping across the path, brandishing their spears or sticks; they darted them just at the moment of wheeling round their horses, as if that motion gave them an advantage. It struck me that this, probably, was the mode of fighting of the ancient Parthians, which made them so terrible in flight. Presently after these gambols, the appearance of some poor countrymen with their carts put into their heads another kind of sport; for knowing, from the ill fame of the spot, that we should easily be taken for robbers, four of them galloped forward, and by the time we reached them, one of the carters was opening a bag to give them something. I was, of course, very much displeased, and made signs to him not to do it. I then told them all, as we quietly pursued our course, that such kind of sport was not allowed in England: they said it was the Persian custom. We arrived at length at Ghanikew, having ridden six hours and a half without intermission. The Mihmander was for changing his route continually, either from real or pretended fear. One of Cara Beg's men saw me at the village last night, and as he would probably get intelligence of my intended route, it was desirable to elude him. But after all, we went the shortest way, through the midst of danger, if there was any, and a gracious Providence kept all mischief at a distance. Ghanikew is only two parasangs from Cars, but I stopped there, as I saw it was more agreeable to the people; besides which, I wished to have a ride before breakfast. I was lodged in a stable-room, but very much at my ease, as none of the people of the village could come at me without passing through the house."

Sept. 21.—"Rode into Cars. Its appearance is quite European, not only at a distance, but within. The houses all of stone; streets with carts passing; some of the houses open to the street; the fort on an uncommonly high rock; such a burying-ground I never saw;— there must be thousands of gravestones. The Mihmander carried me directly to the Governor, who, having just finished his breakfast, was, of course, asleep, and could not be disturbed; but his head man carried me to an Armenian's house, with orders to live at free quarter there. The room at the Armenian's was an excellent one, upstairs, facing the street, fort, and river, with a bow containing five windows, under which were cushions. As soon as the Pasha was visible, the chief Armenian of Cars, to whom I had a letter from Bishop Nestus, his relation, waited upon him on my business. On looking over my letters of recommendation from Sir Gore Ouseley, I found there was none for Abdallah, the Pasha of Cars; however, the letter to the Governor of Erivan secured all I wanted. He sent to say I was welcome; that if I liked to stay a few days, he should be happy; but that if I was determined to go on to-morrow, the necessary horses, and ten men for a guard, were all ready. As no wish was expressed of seeing me, I was of course silent upon that subject."

Sept. 22.—"Promises were made that everything should be ready at sunrise, but it was half-past nine before we started, and no guard present but the Tartar. He presently began to show his nature, by flogging the baggage-horse with his long whip, as one who was not disposed to allow loitering; but one of the poor beasts presently fell with his load, at full length, over a piece of timber lying in the road. While this was setting to rights, the people gathered about me, and seemed more engaged with my Russian boots than with any other part of my dress. We moved south-west, and after five hours and a-half reached Joula. The Tartar rode forward, and got the coffee-room at the post-house ready. The coffee-room has one side raised and covered with cushions, and on the opposite side cushions on the ground; the rest of the room was left with bare stones and timbers. As the wind blew very cold yesterday, and I had caught cold, the Tartar ordered a great fire to be made. In this room I should have been very much to my satisfaction, had not the Tartar taken part of the same bench; and many other people made use of it as a public room. They were continually consulting my watch, to know how near the hour of eating approached. It was evident that the Tartar was the great man here: he took the best place for himself; a dinner of four or five dishes was laid before him. When I asked for eggs, they brought me rotten ones; for butter they brought me ghee. The idle people of the village came all night and smoked till morning. It was very cold, there being a hoar frost."

Sept. 23.—"Our way to-day lay through a forest of firs; and the variety of prospect it afforded of hill and dale, wood and lawn, was beautiful and romantic. No mark of human workmanship was anywhere visible for miles, except where some trees had fallen by the stroke of the woodman. We saw, at last, a few huts in the thickest clumps, which was all we saw of the Curds, for fear of whom I was attended by ten armed horsemen. We frightened a company of villagers again to-day. They were bringing wood and grass from the forest, and on seeing us, drew up. One of our party advanced and fired: such a rash piece of sport I thought must have been followed by serious mischief, but all passed off very well. With the forest I was delighted; the clear streams in the valleys, the lofty trees crowning the summit of the hills, the smooth paths winding away and losing them-selves in the dark woods, and, above all, the solitude that reigned throughout, composed a scene which tended to harmonize and solemnize the mind. What displays of taste and magnificence are found occasionally on this ruined earth! Nothing was wanting to-day but the absence of the Turks; to avoid the sight and sound of whom I rode on. After a ride of nine hours and a-half we reached Mijingud, in the territory of Erzerum; and having resolved not to be annoyed in the same way as last night, I left the Tartar in the undisturbed possession of the post-house, and took up my quarters at an

Armenian's, where, in the stable-room, I expected to be
left alone; but a Georgian young man, on his way from
Ech-Miazin, going on pilgrimage to Moosk, where John the
Baptist is supposed to be buried, presumed on his assiduous
attentions to me, and contrived to get a place for himself
in the same room."

Sept. 24.—"A long and sultry march over many a
hill and vale. In the way, two hours from the last stage,
is a hot spring; the water fills a pool, having four
porches. The porches instantly reminded me of
Bethesda's pool : they were semi-circular arches, about
six feet deep, intended, seemingly, for shelter from the
sun. In them all the party undressed and bathed. The
Tartar, to enjoy himself more perfectly, had his calean to
smoke while up to his chin in water. We saw nothing
else on the road to-day, but a large and opulent family of
Armenians, men, women, and children, in carts and car-
riages, returning from a pilgrimage to Moosk. After
eleven hours and a half, including the hour spent at the
warm spring, we were overtaken by the dusk; so the
Tartar brought us to Oghoomra, where I was placed in
an Armenian's stable-room."

Sept. 25.—"Went round to Hussur-Quile, where we
changed horses. I was surprised to see so strong a fort
and so large a town. From thence we were five hours
and a-half reaching the entrance of Erzerum. All was
busy and moving in the streets and shops;—crowds passing along. Those who caught a sight of us were at a loss
to define me. My Persian attendants, and the lower part
of my dress, made me appear Persian ; but the rest of the
dress was new, for those only who had travelled knew it
to be European. They were not disposed, I thought, to
be civil ; but the two persons who preceded us kept all in

order. I felt myself in a Turkish town ; the red cap, and stateliness, and rich dress, and variety of turbans, was realized as I had seen it in pictures. There are here four thousand Armenian families, and but one church : there are scarcely any Catholics, and they have no church."

Sept. 29.—"Left Erzerum, with a Tartar and his son, at two in the afternoon. We moved to a village, where I was attacked with fever and ague : the Tartar's son was also taken ill, and obliged to return."

Sept. 30.—"Travelled first to Ashgula, where we changed horses, and from thence to Purnugaban, where we halted for the night. I took nothing all day but tea, and was rather better ; but headache and loss of appetite depressed my spirits ; yet my soul rests in Him who is ' as an anchor of the soul, sure and stedfast,' which, though not seen, keeps me fast."

Oct. 1.—"Marched over a mountainous tract : we were out from seven in the morning till eight at night. After sitting a little by the fire, I was near fainting from sickness. My depression of spirits led me to the throne of grace, as a sinful, abject worm. When I thought of myself and my transgressions, I could find no text so cheering as, 'My ways are not as your ways.' From the men who accompanied Sir William Ouseley to Constantinople, I learned that the plague was raging at Constantinople, and thousands dying every day. One of the Persians had died of it. They added, that the inhabitants of Tocat were flying from their town from the same cause. Thus I am passing inevitably into imminent danger. O Lord, thy will be done ! Living or dying, remember me !"

Oct. 2.—"Some hours before day, I sent to tell the Tartar I was ready, but Hassan Aga was for once riveted to his bed. However, at eight, having got strong horses, he set off at a great rate, and over the level ground he made us gallop as fast as the horses would go to Chifflick, where we arrived at sunset. I was lodged, at my request, in the stables of the post-house, not liking the scrutinizing impudence of the fellows who frequent the coffee-room. As soon as it began to grow a little cold, the ague came on, and then the fever : after which I had a sleep, which let me know too plainly the disorder of my frame. In the night, Hassan sent to summon me away, but I was quite unable to move. Finding me still in bed at the dawn, he began to storm furiously at my detaining him so long ; but I quietly let him spend his ire, ate my breakfast composedly, and set out at eight. He seemed determined to make up for the delay, for we flew over hill and dale to Sherean, where he changed horses. From thence we travelled all the rest of the day and all night ; it rained most of the time. Soon after sunset the ague came on again, which, in my wet state, was very trying ; I hardly knew how to keep my life in me. About that time there was a village at hand ; but Hassan had no mercy. At one in the morning we found two men under a wain, with a good fire ; they could not keep the rain out, but their fire was acceptable. I dried my lower extremities, allayed the fever by drinking a good deal of water, and went on. We had little rain, but the night was pitchy dark, so that I could not see the road under my horse's feet. However, God being mercifully pleased to alleviate my bodily suffering, I went on contentedly to the munzil, where we arrived at break of day. After sleeping three or four hours, I was visited by an Armenian merchant, for whom I had a letter. Hassan was in great fear of being arrested here ; the governor of the city had vowed to make an example of him for riding to death a horse belonging to a man of this place. He begged that I would shelter him in case of danger ; his being claimed by an Englishman, he said, would be a sufficient security. I found, however, that I had no occasion to interfere. He hurried me away from this place without delay, and galloped furiously towards a village, which, he said, was four hours distant ; which was all I could undertake in my present weak state ; but village after village did he pass, till night coming on, and no signs of another, I suspected that he was carrying me on to the munzil ; so I got off my horse, and sat upon the ground, and told him, 'I neither could nor would go any further.' He stormed, but I was immovable ; till, a light appearing at a distance, I mounted my horse, and made towards it, leaving him to follow or not, as he pleased. He brought in the party, but would not exert himself to get a place for me. They brought me to an open verandah, but Sergius told them I wanted a place in which to be alone. This seemed very offensive to them ; 'And why must he be alone ?' they asked : ascribing this desire of mine to pride, I suppose. Tempted, at last, by money, they brought me to a stable-room, and Hassan and a number of others planted themselves there with me. My fever here increased to a violent degree; the heat in my eyes and forehead was so great, that the fire almost made me frantic. I entreated that it might be put out, or that I might be carried out of doors. Neither was attended to : my servant, who from my sitting in that strange way on the ground believed me delirious, was deaf to all I said. At last I pushed my head in among the luggage, and lodged it on the damp ground, and slept."

Oct. 5.—"Preserving mercy made me see the light of

another morning. The sleep had refreshed me, but I was feeble and shaken; yet the merciless Hassan hurried me off. The munzil, however, not being distant, I reached it without much difficulty. I expected to have found it another strong fort at the end of the pass; but it is a poor little village within the jaws of the mountain. I was pretty well lodged, and felt tolerably well till a little after sunset, when the ague came on with a violence I had never before experienced: I felt as if in a palsy; my teeth chattering, and my whole frame violently shaken. Agar Hosyn and another Persian, on their way here from Constantinople, going to Abbas Mirza, whom I had just before been visiting, came hastily to render me assistance if they could. These Persians appear quite brotherly after the Turks. While they pitied me, Hassan sat in perfect indifference, ruminating on the further delay this was likely to occasion. The cold fit, after continuing two or three hours, was followed by a fever, which lasted the whole night, and prevented sleep."

Oct. 6.—" No horses being to be had, I had an unexpected repose. I sat in the orchard, and thought, with sweet comfort and peace, of my God; in solitude my company, my friend and comforter. Oh, when shall time give place to eternity! When shall appear that new heaven and new earth wherein dwelleth righteousness! There, there shall in nowise enter in anything that defileth: none of that wickedness which has made men worse than wild beasts,—none of those corruptions which add still more to the miseries of mortality, shall be seen or heard of any more."

Scarcely had Mr. Martyn breathed these aspirations after that state of blissful purity, for which he had attained

TOCAT.

Page 405.

such a measure of meetness,—when he was called to exchange a condition of pain, weakness, and suffering, for that everlasting "rest which remaineth for the people of God."

At Tocat, on the 16th of October, 1812, either falling a sacrifice to the plague, which then raged there, or, sinking under that disorder which, when he penned his last words, had so greatly reduced him, he surrendered his soul into the hands of his Redeemer.

The peculiar circumstances, as well as the particular period of his death, could not fail of greatly aggravating the affliction of his friends, who, amidst anxious hopes and fears, were expecting his arrival either in India or England. He had not completed the thirty-second year of a life of eminent activity and usefulness, and he died whilst hastening towards his native country, that, having there repaired his shattered health, he might again devote it to the glory of Christ, amongst the nations of the East. There was something, also, deeply affecting in the consideration, that where he sank into his grave, men were strangers to him and to his God. No friendly hand was stretched out,—no sympathizing voice heard at that time, when the tender offices of Christian affection are so soothing and so delightful; no human bosom was there, on which Mr. Martyn could recline his head in the hour of languishing. *Paucioribus lacrymis compositus es,*—was a sentiment to which the feelings of nature and friendship responded; yet the painful reflection could not be admitted,—*In novissimâ luce desideravêre aliquid oculi tui.* The Saviour, doubtless, was with His servant in his last conflict, and he with Him the instant it terminated.

So richly was the mind of Mr. Martyn endowed by the God of nature and of grace, that at no period could his death fail to be a subject of common lamentation to those who valued the interests of the Church of Christ.

"He was in our hearts," observed one of his friends in India,* "we honoured him;—we loved him;—we thanked God for him; we prayed for his longer continuance amongst us;—we rejoiced in the good he was doing:—we are sadly bereaved! Where such fervent piety, and extensive knowledge, and vigorous understanding, and classical taste, and unwearied application, were all united, what might not have been expected? I cannot dwell upon the subject without feeling very sad. I stand upon the walls of Jerusalem, and see the lamentable breach that has been made in them; but it is the Lord;—He gave, and He hath taken away."

"Mr. Martyn," remarks another of his friends,† in describing more particularly his intellectual endowments, "combined in himself certain valuable but distinct qualities, seldom found together in the same individual. The easy triumphs of a rapid genius over first difficulties never left him satisfied with present attainments. His mind, which naturally ranged over a wide field of human knowledge, lost nothing of depth in its expansiveness. He was one of those few persons whose reasoning faculty does not suffer from their imagination, nor their imagination from their reasoning faculty: both, in him, were fully exercised, and were of a very high order. His mathematical acquisitions clearly left him without a rival of his own age; and yet, to have known only the employments of his more free and unfettered moments, would have led to the conclusion that poetry and the classics were his predominant passion."

But the radiance of these talents, excellent as they

* The late Rev. T. Thomason.

† The Rev. C. J. Hoare, Archdeacon of Winchester.

were, was lost in the brightness of those Christian graces, by which he "shone as a light in the world, holding forth the word of life." In his faith there was a singular, a childlike simplicity:—great, consequently, was its energy, both in obeying Christ, and in suffering for His name's sake! By this, he could behold blossoms upon the rod, even when it was apparently dead; and in those events which, like the captain of the Lord's host seen by Joshua, presented at first a hostile aspect,—he could discern a favourable and a friendly countenance. Having listened to that tender and overwhelming interrogation of his Saviour, "Lovest thou me!" his love was fervently exercised towards God and man, at all times, and in all places. For it was not like the land-spring, which runs violently for a season, and then ceases; but resembled the fountain which flows with a perennial stream from the recesses of the rock. His fear of God, and tenderness of conscience, and watchfulness over his own heart, could scarcely be surpassed in this state of sinful infirmity. But it was his humility that was most remarkable:—this might be considered as the warp of which the entire texture of his piety was composed; and with this his other Christian graces were so intimately blended, as to beautify and adorn his whole demeanour. It was, in truth, the accordance and consent of various Christian attainments in Mr. Martyn, which were so striking. The *symmetry* of his stature in Christ, was as surprising as its *height*. That communion which he held with his God, and which caused his face to shine, was ever chastened, like the patriarch's of old, by the most awful reverence. The nearer the access with which he was favoured, the more deeply did he feel that he was but "sinful dust and ashes." No discordance could he discover between peace and penitence; no opposition between joy in God, and utter abasement before Him; and, truly, in this, as in every other respect, had he thoroughly imbibed the spirit of his own Church; which, in the midst of one of her sublimest hymns of praise, leads her members to prostrate themselves before their Redeemer in these words of humiliation: "Thou that takest away the sins of the world, have mercy upon us."

To be zealous without love; or to have that which is miscalled charity, without decision of character, is neither difficult nor uncommon. Mr. Martyn's zeal was tempered with love, and his love invigorated by zeal. He combined, also, ardour with prudence; gravity with cheerfulness; abstraction from the world with an enjoyment of its lawful gratifications. His extreme tenderness of conscience was devoid of scrupulosity; his activity in good works was joined to habits of serious contemplation; his religious affections, which were highly spiritualized, exceeded not the limits of the most cautious sobriety, and were so far from impairing his natural affections, that they raised and purified them.

Many sincere servants of Christ labour to attain heaven, but possess not any joyful hope of reaching it;—many vain hypocrites are confident of their salvation, without striving to enter in at the strait gate. With the Apostle, Mr. Martyn could say, "We are always confident; *wherefore* we labour," &c. Together with an assurance of his final and everlasting felicity, he had a dread of declension, and a fear of "losing the things he had wrought." He knew that the way to heaven was narrow, from the entrance to the end of it; but he was persuaded that Christ was with him, walking in the way, and that He would never leave him nor forsake him.

As these extraordinary and seemingly contradictory qualities were not imparted to him but by the Spirit of God, so they were not strengthened and matured but in the diligent use of the ordinary means of grace. Prayer and the Holy Scriptures were those wells of salvation, out of which he drew daily the living water. Truly did he "pray always, with all prayer and supplication in the Spirit, and watch thereunto with all perseverance." Being "transformed by the renewing of his mind," he was also ever "proving what was that good and acceptable and perfect will of God."

The Sabbath, that sacred portion of time, set apart for holy purposes in Paradise itself, was so employed by him as to prove frequently a paradise to his soul on earth; and it as certainly prepared him for an endless state of spiritual enjoyment hereafter.

By "daily weighing the Scriptures," with prayer, he "waxed riper and riper in his ministry," in the execution of which divine office there was in him an astonishing determination of soul for the glory of his Saviour, who "allowed him to be put in trust with the Gospel." Of the exceeding privileges of his holy function, and of its awful responsibility, he had the most vivid impression; and such was his jealousy of omitting any duty connected with it, that he deemed the work of translating the Scriptures themselves no justifiable plea for inattention to any of its more immediate and direct engagements. Reviewing frequently his ordination vows, in that affecting service in which they were originally made, he became more and more anxious to promote the honour of his Redeemer by preaching his Gospel. This, indeed, was the great end for which existence seemed desirable in his eyes; to effect which he spent much time in preparing his discourses for the pulpit; investigating the subject before him with profound meditation, and perpetual supplication to the Father of Lights. *Utilis lectio—utilis eruditio—sed magis unctio necessaria, quippe quæ docet de omnibus**—were the sentiments of his heart. When, therefore, he stood up and addressed his hearers on the entire depravity of man,—on the justification of the soul by faith in Jesus Christ,—on the regenerating and progressively sanctifying influences of the Spirit ;—when, "knowing the terrors of the Lord," he persuaded them to accept the offers of salvation ;—or when he besought them, by the mercies of God, to present their bodies to Him, as a living sacrifice,— he spake "with uncorruptness, gravity, sincerity, with sound words that could not be condemned ;" and none who knew their souls to be guilty, helpless, accountable, immortal, could listen to his preaching unmoved. In the delivery of his discourses, his natural manner was not good, there being a defect in his enunciation; this, however, was more than compensated by the solemnity, affection, and earnestness of his address. It should be added, also, that as practical subjects were discussed by him with constant reference to the peculiar doctrines of the Gospel, so likewise all doctrinal points were declared practically, with a view to self-application, rather than to disquisition. No one, as it regarded all doctrine, could enter more completely into the spirit of those words, both for himself and others ;—*Malo sentire compunctionem quàm scire ejus definitionem.*

With an intense anxiety to save souls, Mr. Martyn had an implicit reliance on that grace which alone can make men wise unto salvation. He was deeply conscious that it is "God that giveth the increase ;" and when he

* St. Bernard.

did not see, or thought he did not see, that increase, he meekly submitted to the Divine will, and patiently continued in well-doing. At such times, also, more particularly would he turn, with joyful thankfulness, to the contemplation of the successful labours of his brethren in the ministry; for he had no mean and unholy envy respecting them; nor had he what is so often allied to it, an arrogant or domineering temper towards his flock. His ambition was, to be a helper of their joy; he had no desire to have dominion over their faith. Too much had he of that beautiful part of a minister's character, a spirit which would sympathize with the poor and afflicted amongst his people, to court the appellation of Rabbi, or dogmatize with the air of a master of Israel. He was one of those *little ones*, of whom Christ affirms that whosoever receiveth them, receiveth Him. To no one, indeed, would he give occasion to despise him; but all the dignity to which he aspired was to be their servant, among whom he laboured for Jesus' sake. "A more perfect character," says one who bore the burden and heat of the day with him in India,* "I never met with, nor expect to see on earth. During the four years we were fellow-labourers in this country, I had no less than six opportunities of enjoying his company; and every opportunity only increased my love and veneration for him."

With respect to his labours, his own "works praise him in the gates," far above all human commendation.

By him, and by his means, part of the Liturgy of the Church of England, the Parables, and the whole of the New Testament, were translated into Hindostanee,—a language spoken from Delhi to Cape Comorin, and

* The Rev. D. Corrie: afterwards Bishop of Madras.

intelligible to many millions of immortal souls. By him, and by his means, also, the Psalms of David and the New Testament were rendered into Persian, the vernacular language of two hundred thousand who bear the Christian name, and known over one-fourth of the habitable globe. By him, also, the imposture of the prophet of Mecca was boldly exposed, and the truths of Christianity openly vindicated, in the very heart and centre of a Mohammedan empire.

If success be demanded, it is replied, that this is not the inquiry with Him "of whom are all things," either in this world, or in that which is to come. With Him the question is this:—What has been *aimed* at? what has been *intended* in singleness of heart?

God, however, has not left Mr. Martyn without witness, in the hearts of those who heard him in Europe and in Asia. Above forty adults and twenty children, of the Hindoos, have received Christian baptism; all of whom, with the exception of a single individual, were converted by the instrumentality of one man,* who was himself the fruit of Mr. Martyn's ministry at Cawnpore. At Shiraz a sensation has been excited, which, it is trusted, will not readily subside; and some Mohammedans of consequence there have declared their conviction of the truth of Christianity, —a conviction which Mr. Martyn was the means of imparting to their minds. But, when it is considered that the Persian and Hindostanee Scriptures are in wide and extensive circulation, who can ascertain the consequences which may have already followed, or foresee what may hereafter accrue from their dispersion? In this respect it is not perhaps too much to apply to Mr.

* Abdool Messeh.

Martyn those words, which once had an impious application :—

"Ex quo nunc etiam per magnos didita gentes,
Dulcia permulcent animos solatia vitæ."—LUCRETIUS.

Nor is the example which he has left behind him to be laid out of our account, in estimating the effects of his holy and devoted life. He, doubtless, forsook all for Christ. He loved not his life unto the death. He followed the steps of Zeigenbalg in the Old World, and of Brainerd in the New; and, whilst he walks with them in white, for he is worthy, he speaks, by his example, to us who are still on our warfare and pilgrimage upon earth. For surely, as long as England shall be celebrated for that pure and apostolical Church, of which he was so great an ornament; as long as India shall prize that which is more precious to her than all her gems and gold; the name of the subject of this Memoir, as a translator of the Scriptures and of the Liturgy, will not wholly be forgotten ; and, whilst some shall delight to gaze upon the splendid sepulchre of Xavier, and others choose rather to ponder over the granite stone which covers all that was mortal of Swartz, there will not be wanting those who will think of the humble and unfrequented grave of HENRY MARTYN, and be led to imitate those works of mercy, which have followed him into the world of light and love.

FINIS.

APPENDIX:

LETTERS TO MISS GRENFELL.

I.

Union, Falmouth, July 27, 1805.

. . . . As I was coming on board this morning, and reading Mr. Serle's Hymn you wrote out for me, a sudden gust of wind blew it into the sea. I made the boatmen immediately heave to, and recovered it, happily without any injury, except what it had received from the sea. I should have told you that the Morning Hymn, which I always kept carefully in my pocket-book, was one day stolen, with it and other valuable letters, from my rooms in College. It would be extremely gratifying to me to possess another copy of it, as it always reminded me most forcibly of the happy day on which we visited the aged saint. The fleet, it is said, will not sail for three weeks, but if you are willing to employ any of your time in providing me with this or any other MS. hymns, the sooner you write them the more certain I shall be of receiving them. Pardon me for thus intruding on your time; you will in no wise lose your reward. The encouragement conveyed in little compositions of this sort is more refreshing than a cup of cold water. The Lord of the harvest, who is sending forth me, who am most truly less than the least of all saints, will reward you for being willing to help forward even the meanest of His servants. The love which you bear to the cause of Christ, as well as motives of private friendship, will, I trust, induce you to commend me to God, and to the word of His grace, at those sacred moments when you approach the throne of our covenant God. To His gracious care I commend you. May you long live happy and holy, daily growing more meet for the inheritance of the saints in light.

I remain, with affectionate regard,

Yours most truly,

H. MARTYN

II.

Union, Falmouth, August 10, 1805.

MY DEAR MISS LYDIA,

It will, perhaps, be some satisfaction to yourself and your mother, to know that I was in time. Our ship was entangled in the chain, and was, by that means, the only one not under weigh when I arrived. It seems that most of the people on board had given me up, and did not mean to wait for me. I cannot but feel sensibly this instance of Divine mercy in thus preserving me from the great trouble that would have attended the loss of my passage. Mount's Bay will soon be in sight, and recal you all once more to my affectionate remembrance. . . . .

I bid you a long farewell. God ever bless you, and help you sometimes to intercede for me.

H. MARTYN.

III.

Serampore, July 30, 1806.

MY DEAREST LYDIA,

On a subject so intimately connected with my happiness and future ministry, as that on which I am now about to address you, I wish to assure you that I am not acting with precipitancy, or without much consideration and prayer, while I at last sit down to request you to come out to me to India.

May the Lord graciously direct His blind and erring creature, and not suffer the natural bias of his mind to lead him astray. You are acquainted with much of the conflict I have undergone on your account. It has been greater than you or Emma have imagined, and yet not so painful as I deserve to have found it, for having suffered my affections to fasten so inordinately on an earthly object.

Soon, however, after my final departure from Europe, God in great mercy gave me deliverance, and favoured me throughout the voyage with peace of mind, indifference about all worldly connections, and devotedness to no object upon earth but the work of Christ. I gave you up entirely—not the smallest expectation remained in my mind of ever seeing you again till we should meet in heaven : and the thought of this separation was the less painful from the consolatory persuasion that our own Father had so ordered it for our mutual good. I continued from that time to remember you in my prayers only as a Christian sister, though one very dear to me. On my arrival in this country I saw no reason at first for supposing that marriage was advisable for a missionary— or rather the subject did not offer itself to my mind. The Baptist missionaries indeed recommended it, and Mr. Crown ; but not knowing any proper person in this country, they were not very pressing upon the subject, and I accordingly gave no attention to it. After a very short experience and inquiry afterwards, my own opinions began to change, and when a few weeks ago we received your welcome letter, and others from Mr. Simeon and Colonel Sandys, both of whom spoke of you in reference to me, I considered it even as a call from God to satisfy myself fully concerning his will. From the account which Mr. Simeon received of you from Mr. Thomason, he seemed in his letter to me to regret that he had so strongly dissuaded me from thinking about you at the time of my leaving England. Colonel Sandys spoke in such terms of you, and of the advantages to result from your presence in this country, that Mr. B. became very earnest for me to endeavour to prevail upon you. Your letter to me perfectly delighted him, and induced him to say that you would be the greatest aid to the Mission I could possibly meet with. I knew my own heart too well not to be distrustful of it, especially as my affections were again awakened, and accordingly all my labour and prayer have been directed to check their influence, that I might see clearly the path of duty.

Though I dare not say that I am under no bias, yet from every view of the subject I have been able to take, after balancing the advantages and disadvantages that may ensue to the cause in which I am engaged, always in prayer for God's direction, my reason is fully convinced of the expediency, I had almost said the necessity of having you with me. It is possible that my reason may still be obscured by passion ; let it suffice however to say that now, with a safe conscience and the enjoyment of the Divine presence, I calmly and deliberately make the proposal to you—and blessed be God if it be not His will to permit it; still this step is not advancing beyond the limits of duty, because there is a variety of ways by which God can prevent it, without suffering any dishonour to his cause. If He shall forbid it, I think, that by his grace, I shall even then be contented, and rejoice in the pleasure of corresponding with you. Your letter dated December, 1805, was the first I received, and I found it so animating that I could not but reflect on the blessedness of having so dear a counsellor always near me. I can truly say, and God is my witness, that my principal desire in this affair is, that you may promote the kingdom of God in my own heart, and be the means of extending it to the heathen. My own earthly comfort and happiness are not worth a moment's notice. I would not, my dearest Lydia, influence you by any artifices or false representations. I can only say that if you have a desire of being instrumental in establishing the blessed Redeemer's kingdom among these poor people, and will condescend to do it by supporting the spirits and animating the zeal of a weak messenger of the Lord who is apt to grow very dispirited and languid, 'Come, and the Lord be with you!' It can be nothing but a sacrifice on your part, to leave your valuable friends to come to one who is utterly unworthy of you or any other of God's precious gifts—but you will have your reward, and I ask it not of you or of God for the sake of my own happiness, but only on account of the Gospel. If it be not calculated to promote it, may God in his mercy withhold it. For the satisfaction of your friends, I should say, that you will meet with no hardships. The voyage is very agreeable, and with the people and country of India I think you will be much pleased. The climate is very fine—the so much-dreaded heat is really nothing to those who will employ their minds in useful pursuits. Idleness will make people complain of everything. The natives are the most harmless and timid creatures I ever met with. The whole country is the land of plenty and peace. Were I a missionary among the Esquimaux or Boschemen I should never dream of introducing a female into such a scene of danger or hardship, especially one whose happiness is dearer to me than my own,—but here there is universal tranquillity,—though the multitudes are so great, that a missionary needs not go three miles from his house to find a congregation of many thousands. You would not be left in solitude if I were to make any distant excursion; because no chaplain is stationed where there is not a large English society. My salary is abundantly sufficient for the support of a married man; the house and number of people kept by each Company's servant being such as to need no increase for a family establishment. As I must make the supposition of your coming, though it may be perhaps a premature liberty, I should give you some directions. This letter will reach you about the latter end of the year,—it would be very desirable if you could be ready for the February fleet, because the voyage will be performed in far less time than at any other season. George will find out the best ship; one in which there is a lady of high rank in the service would be preferable. You are to be considered as coming as a visitor to Mr. Brown, who will write to you or to Colonel Sandys, who is best qualified to give you directions about the voyage. Should I be up the country on your arrival in Bengal, Mr. Brown will be at hand to receive you, and you will find yourself immediately at home. As it will highly expedite some of the plans which we have in agitation that you should know the language as soon as possible, take Gilchrist's Indian Stranger's Guide, and occasionally on the voyage learn some of the words.

If I had room I might enlarge on much that would be interesting to you. In my conversations with Marshman, the Baptist missionary, our hearts sometimes expand with delight and joy at the prospect of seeing all these nations of the East receive the doctrine of the Cross. He is a happy labourer : and I only wait, I trust, to know the language to open my mouth boldly and make known the mystery of the Gospel. My romantic notions are for the first time almost realized,—for in addition to the beauties of sylvan scenery may be seen the more delightful object of multitudes of simple people sitting in the shade, listening to the words of eternal life. Much as yet is not done; but I have seen many discover by their looks while Marshman was preaching, that their hearts were tenderly affected. My post is not yet determined; we expect however it will be Patna, a civil station, where I shall not be under military command. As you are so kindly anxious about my health, I am happy to say, that through mercy my health is far better than it ever was in England.

The people of Calcutta are very desirous of keeping me at the Mission Church, and offer to any Evangelical clergyman a chaplain's salary and a house besides.. I am of course deaf to such a proposal ; but it is strange that no one in England is *tempted* by such an inviting situation. I am actually going to mention it to cousin T. H. and Emma ;—not, as you may suppose, with much hope of success ; but I think that possibly the chapel at Dock may be too much for him, and he will have here a sphere of still greater importance. As this will be sent by the Overland Despatch, there is some danger of its not reaching you;—you will therefore receive a duplicate, and perhaps a triplicate, by the ships that will arrive in England a month or two after. I cannot write now to any of my friends. I will therefore trouble you, if you have opportunity, to say that I have received no letters since I left England, except one from each of these—cousin T. and Emma, Simeon, Sargent, Bates—of my own family I have heard nothing. Assure any of them whom you may see, of the continuance of my affectionate regard—especially dear Emma. I did not know that it was permitted me to write to you—or I fear she would not have found me so faithful a correspondent on the voyage. As I have heretofore addressed you through her, it is probable that I may be now disposed to address her through you—or what will be best of all, that we both of us address her in one letter from India. However you shall decide, my dearest Lydia, I *must* approve your determination, because with that spirit of simple looking to the Lord, which we both endeavour to maintain, we must not doubt that you will be divinely directed. Till I receive an answer to this, my prayers, you may be assured, will be constantly put up for you, that in this affair you may be under an especial guidance, and that in all your ways God may be abundantly glorified by you through Jesus Christ. You say in your letter that *frequently every day* you remember my worthless name before the throne of grace. This instance of extraordinary and undeserved kindness draws my heart toward you with a tenderness which I cannot describe. Dearest Lydia, in the sweet and fond expectation of your being given to me by God, and of the happiness which I humbly hope you

yourself might enjoy here, I find a pleasure in breathing
out my assurance of ardent love. I have now long loved
you most affectionately, and my attachment is more
strong, more pure, more heavenly, because I see in you
the image of Jesus Christ. I unwillingly conclude, by
bidding my beloved Lydia adieu.

H. MARTYN.

IV.

Serampore, Sept. 1, 1806.

MY DEAREST LYDIA,

With this you will receive the duplicate of the letter
I sent you a month ago by the Overland Despatch. May
it find you prepared to come! All the thoughts and
views which I have had of the subject since first addressing you, add tenfold confirmation to my first opinion;
and I trust that the blessed God will graciously make it
appear that I have been acting under a right direction,
by giving the precious gift to me and to the Church in
India. I sometimes regret that I had not obtained a
promise from you of following me, at the time of our last
parting at Gurlyn; as I am occasionally apt to be excessively impatient at the long delay. Many, many months
must elapse before I can see you, or even hear how you
shall determine. The instant your mind is made up, you
will send a letter by the Overland Despatch. George will
let you know how it is to be prepared, as the Company
have given some printed directions. It is a consolation
to me during this long suspense, that had I engaged with
you before my departure I should not have had such a
satisfactory conviction of it being the will of God. The
Commander-in-Chief is in doubt to which of the three
following stations he shall appoint me,—Benares, Patna,

or Moorshedabad; it will be the last most probably; this is only two days' journey from Calcutta; I shall take my departure in about six weeks. In the hour that remains, I must endeavour to write to my dear sister Emma, and to Sally. By the fleet which will sail hence in about two months, they will receive longer letters. You will then, I hope, have left England. I am very happy here in preparing for my delightful work; but I should be happier still if I were sufficiently fluent in the language to be actually employed; and happiest of all if my beloved Lydia were at my right hand, counselling and animating me. I am not very willing to end my letter to you; it is difficult not to prolong the enjoyment of speaking, as it were, to one who occupies so much of my sleeping and waking hours; but here, alas! I am aware of danger; and my dear Lydia will, I hope, pray that her unworthy friend may love no creature inordinately.

It will be base in me to depart in heart from a God of such love as I find him to be. Oh, that I could make some returns for the riches of his love! Swiftly fly the hours of life away, and then we shall be admitted to behold his glory. The ages of darkness are rolling fast away, and shall soon usher in the gospel period, when the whole world shall be filled with his glory. Oh, my beloved sister and friend, dear to me on every account, but dearest of all for having one heart and one soul with me in the cause of Jesus and the love of God, let us pray and rejoice, and rejoice and pray, that God may be glorified, and the dying Saviour see of the travail of his soul. May the God of hope fill us with all joy and peace in believing, that we may both of us abound in hope through the power of the Holy Ghost. Now, my dearest Lydia, I cannot say what I feel—I cannot pour out my soul—I could not if you were here; but I pray that you may love me, if it be the will of God; and I pray that God may make you more and more his child, and give me more and more love for all that is Godlike and holy.

I remain, with fervent affection,

Yours, in eternal bonds,

H. MARTYN.

V.

Serampore, Sept. 1806.

How earnestly do I long for the arrival of my dearest Lydia! Though it may prove at last no more than a waking dream that I ever expected to receive you in India, the hope is too pleasing not to be cherished till I am forbidden any longer to hope. Till I am assured of the contrary, I shall find a pleasure in addressing you as my own. If you are not to be mine, you will pardon me; but my expectations are greatly encouraged by the words you used when we parted at Gurlyn, that I had better *go out* free; implying, as I thought, that you would not be unwilling to follow me if I should see it to be the will of God to make the request. I was rejoiced also to see in your letter that you unite your name with mine, when you pray that God would keep us both in the path of duty; from this I infer that you are by no means *determined* to remain separate from me. You will not suppose, my dear Lydia, that I mention these little things to influence your conduct, or to implicate you in an engagement.—No, I acknowledge that you are perfectly free, and I have no doubt that you will act as the love and wisdom of our God shall direct. Your heart is far less interested in this business than mine, in all probability; and this on one account I do not regret, as you will be able to see more clearly the directions of God's providence. About a fortnight ago I sent you a letter accompanying the duplicate of the one sent overland in August. If these shall have arrived safe, you will perhaps have left England before this reaches it. But if not, let me entreat you not to delay a moment. Yet how will my dear sister Emma be able to part with you and George—but, above all, your *mother ?* I feel very much for you and for them, but I have no doubt at all about your health and happiness in this country.

The Commander-in-Chief has at last appointed me to the station of Dinapore, near Patna, and I shall accordingly take my departure for that place as soon as I can make the necessary preparations. It is not exactly the situation I wished for—though, in a temporal point of view, it is desirable enough. The air is good, the living cheap, the salary £1000 a year, and there is a large body of English troops there. But I should have preferred being near Benares, the heart of Hinduism. We rejoice to hear that two other brethren are arrived at Madras on their way to Bengal, sent, I trust, by the Lord, to co-operate in overturning the kingdom of Satan in these regions. They are Corrie and Parsons, both Bengal chaplains. Their stations will be Benares and Moorshedabad—one on one side of me, and the other on the other. There are also now ten Baptist missionaries at Serampore. Surely good is intended for this country !

Captain Wickes,—the good old Captain Wickes, who has brought out so many missionaries to India, is now here. He reminds me of Uncle S——. I have just been interrupted by the blaze of a funeral pile, within a hundred yards of my pagoda; I ran out, but the wretched woman had consigned herself to the flames before I reached the spot, and I saw only the remains of her and her husband. O Lord, how long shall it be? Oh! I shall have no rest in my spirit till my tongue is loosed to testify against the devil, and deliver the message of God to these his unhappy bond-slaves. I stammered out something to the wicked Brahmins about the judgments of God upon them for the murder they had just committed, but they said it was an act of her own free will. Some of the missionaries would have been there, but they are forbidden by the Governor-General to preach to the natives in the British territory. Unless this prohibition is revoked by an order from home, it will amount to a total suppression of the Mission.

I know of nothing else that will give you a further idea of the state of things here. The two ministers continue to oppose my doctrines with unabated virulence; but they think not that they fight against God. My own heart is at present cold and slothful. Oh that my soul did burn with love and zeal! Surely, were you here, I should act with more cheerfulness and activity with so bright a pattern before me. If Corrie brings me a letter from you, and the fleet is not sailed, which, however, is not likely, I shall write to you again. Colonel Sandys will receive a letter from me by this fleet. Continue to remember me in your prayers, as a weak brother. I shall always think of you as one to be loved and honoured.

H. MARTYN.

VI.

Dinapore, Oct. 24, 1807.

MY DEAR LYDIA,

Though my heart is bursting with grief and disappointment, I write not to blame you. The rectitude of your conduct secures you from censure. Permit me calmly to reply to your letter of March 5, which I have just received.

You condemn yourself for having given me, though unintentionally, encouragement to believe that my attachment was returned. Perhaps you have. I have read your former letters with feelings less sanguine since the receipt of the last, and I am still not surprised at the interpretation I put upon them. But why accuse yourself for having written in this strain? It has not increased my expectations, nor consequently embittered my disappointment. When I addressed you in my first letter on the subject, I was not induced to it by any appearances of regard you had expressed; neither at any subsequent period have my hopes of your consent been founded on a belief of your attachment to me. I knew that your conduct would be regulated, not by personal feelings, but by a sense of duty. And therefore you have nothing to blame yourself for on this head.

In your last letter you do not assign, among your reasons for refusal, a want of regard to me. In that case I could not in decency give you any further trouble. On the contrary, you say that "*present* circumstances seem to you to forbid my indulging expectations." As this leaves an opening, I presume to address you again; and till the answer arrives, must undergo another eighteen months of torturing suspense.

Alas, my rebellious heart! what a tempest agitates me! I knew not that I had made so little progress in a spirit of resignation to the Divine will. I am in my chastisement like the bullock unaccustomed to the yoke, like a wild bull in a net, full of the fury of the Lord, the rebuke of my God. The death of my late most beloved sister almost broke my heart; but I hoped it had softened me, and made me willing to suffer. But now my heart is as though destitute of the grace of God, full of misanthropic disgust with the world, and sometimes feeling resentment against yourself and Emma, and Mr. Simeon, and, in short, all whom I love and honour most. Sometimes in pride and anger resolving to write neither to you nor to any one else again. These are the motions of sin. My love and my better reason draw me to you again. * *

But now, with respect to your mother, I confess that the chief, and indeed only difficulty lies here. Considering that she is *your* mother, as I hoped she would be mine, and that her happiness depends so much on you; considering also that I am God's minister, which, amidst all the tumults of my soul I dare not forget, I falter in beginning to give advice which may prove contrary to the law of God. God forbid, therefore, that I should say, disobey your parents where the Divine law does not command you to disobey them; neither do I positively take upon myself to say that this is a case in which the law of God requires you to act in contradiction to them. I would rather suggest to your mother some considerations which justify me in attempting to deprive her of the company of a beloved child.

26. A Sabbath having intervened since the above was written, I find myself more tranquillized by the sacred exercises of the day. One passage of Scripture which you quote has been much on my mind, and I find it very appropriate and decisive,—that we are not to "make to ourselves crooked paths, which whoso walketh in shall not know peace." Let me say I must be therefore contented to wait till you feel that the way is clear. But I intended to justify myself to Mrs. Grenfell. Let her not suppose that I would make her, or any other of my fellow-

creatures miserable, that I might be happy. If there were no reason for your coming here, and the contest were only between Mrs. Grenfell and me, that is, between her happiness and mine, I would urge nothing further, but resign you to her. But I have considered that there are many things that might reconcile her to a separation from you (if indeed a separation is necessary, for if she would come along with you, I should rejoice the more). First, she does not depend on you alone for the comfort of her declining years. She is surrounded by friends. She has a greater number of sons and daughters honourably established in the world, than fall to the lot of most parents— all of whom would be happy in having her amongst them. Again, if a person worthy of your hand, and settled in England, were to offer himself, Mrs. G. would not have insuperable objections, though it *did* deprive her of her daughter. Nay, I sometimes think, perhaps arrogantly, that had I myself remained in England, and in possession of a competency, she would not have withheld her consent. Why then should my banishment from my native country in the service of mankind, be a reason with any for inflicting an additional wound, far more painful than a separation from my dearest relatives?

I have no claim upon Mrs. G. in any way, but let her only imagine a son of her own in my circumstances. If she feels it a sacrifice, let her remember that it is a sacrifice made to duty;—that your presence here would be of essential service to the Church of God, it is superfluous to attempt to prove. If you really believe of yourself as you speak, it is because you were never out of England.

Your mother cannot be so misinformed respecting India and the voyage to it, as to be apprehensive on account of the clime or passage, in these days, when multitudes of ladies every year, with constitutions as delicate as yours, go to and fro in perfect safety, and a vastly greater majority enjoy their health here than in England. With respect to my means, I need add nothing to what was said in my first letter. But alas! what is my affluence good for now? It never gave me pleasure, but when I thought you were to share it with me. Two days ago I was hastening on the alterations in my house and garden, supposing you were at hand; but now every object excites disgust. My wish upon the whole is, that if you perceive it would be your duty to come to India, were it not for your mother,—and of that you cannot doubt,—supposing, I mean, that your inclinations are indifferent, then you should make her acquainted with your thoughts, and let us leave it to God how He will determine her mind.

In the meantime, since I am forbidden to hope for the immediate pleasure of seeing you, my next request is for a mutual engagement. My own heart is engaged, I believe, indissolubly.

My reason for making a request which you will account bold, is that there can then be no possible objection to our correspondence, especially as I promise not to persuade you to leave your mother.

In the midst of my present sorrow I am constrained to remember yours. Your compassionate heart is pained by having been the cause of suffering to me. But grieve not for me, dearest Lydia. Next to the bliss of having you with me, my happiness is to know that you are happy. I shall have to groan long perhaps with a heavy heart; but if I am not hindered materially by it in the work of God, it will be for the benefit of my soul. You, sister beloved in the Lord, know much of the benefit of affliction. O may I have grace to follow you, though at a humble distance, in the path of patient suffering in which you have walked so long. Day and night I cease not to pray for you, though I fear my prayers are of little value.

But as an encouragement to you to pray, I cannot help transcribing a few words from my journal, written at the time you wrote your letter to me. (7th March.) "On the two last days (you wrote your letter on the 5th), felt no desire for a comfortable settlement in the world, scarcely any pleasure at the thought of Lydia's coming, except so far as her being sent might be for the good of my soul, and assistance in my work." How manifestly is there an omnipresent, all-seeing God, and how sure we may be that prayers for spiritual blessings are heard by our God and Father! Oh, let that endearing name quell every murmur! When I am sent for to different parts of the country to officiate at marriages, I sometimes think, amidst the festivity of the company, Why does all go so easily with them, and so hardly with me? They come together without difficulty, and I am balked and disconcerted almost every step I take, and condemned to wear away the time in uncertainty. Then I call to mind that to live without chastening is allowed to the spurious offspring; while to suffer is the privilege of the children of God.

Dearest Lydia, must I conclude? I could prolong my communion with you through many sheets; how many things have I to say to you, which I hoped to have communicated in person! But the more I write and the more I think of you, the more my affection warms, and I should feel it difficult to keep my pen from expressions that might not be acceptable to you.

Farewell! dearest, most beloved Lydia. Remember your faithful and ever affectionate,   H. MARTYN.

VII.

Cawnpore, March 30, 1810.

Since you kindly bid me, my beloved friend, to consider you in the place of that dear sister, whom it has pleased God in his wisdom to take from me, I gratefully accept the offer of a correspondence, which it has ever been the anxious wish of my heart to establish. Your kindness is the more acceptable, because it is shown in the day of affliction. Though I had heard of my dearest sister's illness, some months before I received the account of her death, and though the nature of her disorder was such as left me not a ray of hope, so that I was mercifully prepared for the event, still the certainty of it fills me with anguish. It is not that she has left me, for I never expected to see her more on earth. I have no doubt of meeting her in heaven, but I cannot bear to think of the pangs of dissolution she underwent, which have been unfortunately detailed to me with too much particularity. Would that I had never heard them, or could efface them from my remembrance! But, oh, may I learn what the Lord is teaching me by these repeated strokes. May I learn meekness and resignation. May the world always appear as vain as it does now, and my own continuance in it as short and uncertain. How frightful is the desolation which Death makes, and how appalling his visits when he enters one's family! I would rather never have been born, than be born and die, were it not for Jesus, the Prince of Life, the resurrection and the life. How inexpressibly precious is this Saviour, when eternity seems near! I hope often to communicate with you on these subjects, and in return for your kind and consolatory letters, to send you, from time to time, accounts of myself and my proceedings. Through you, I can hear of all my friends in the West. When I first heard of the loss I was likely to suffer, and began to reflect on my own friendless situation, you were much in my thoughts,— whether you would be silent on this occasion or no? whether you would persist in your resolution? Friends indeed I have, and brethren, blessed be God! but two brothers cannot supply the place of one sister. When month after month passed away, and no letter came from you, I almost abandoned the hope of ever hearing from you again. It only remained to wait the result of my last application through Emma. You have kindly anticipated my request, and, I need scarcely add, are more endeared to me than ever.

Of your illness, my dearest Lydia, I had heard nothing, and it was well for me that I did not.

Yours most affectionately,

H. MARTYN.

VIII.

Cawnpore, April 19, 1810.

I begin my correspondence with my beloved Lydia, not without a fear of its being soon to end. Shall I venture to tell you, that our family complaint has again made its appearance in me, with more unpleasant symptoms than it has ever yet done? However, God, who two years ago redeemed my life from destruction, may again, for his Church's sake, interpose for my deliverance. Though, alas! what am I, that my place should not instantly be supplied by far more efficient instruments? The symptoms I mentioned are chiefly a pain in the chest, occasioned, I suppose, by over-exertion the two last Sundays, and incapacitating me at present from all public duty and even from conversation. You were mistaken in supposing

that my former illness originated from study. Study
never makes me ill—scarcely ever fatigues me—but my
lungs! death is seated there; it is speaking that kills me.
May it give others life! "Death worketh in us, but life
in you." Nature intended me, as I should judge from
the structure of my frame, for a chamber-counsel, not for
a pleader at the bar. But the call of Jesus Christ bids
me cry aloud, and spare not. As His minister, I am a
debtor both to the Greek and the barbarian. How can I
be silent, when I have both ever before me, and my debt
not paid? You would suggest that energies more re-
strained will eventually be more efficient. I am aware
of this, and mean to act upon this principle in future, if
the resolution is not formed too late. But you know
how apt we are to outstep the bounds of prudence, when
there is no kind monitor at hand to warn us of the
consequences.

Had I been favoured with the one I wanted, I might
not now have had occasion to mourn. You smile at my
allusion, at least I hope so, for I am hardly in earnest.
I have long since ceased to repine at the decree that keeps
us as far asunder as the east is from the west, and yet am
far from regretting that I ever knew you. The remembrance of you calls forth the exercise of delightful affections, and has kept me from many a snare. How wise
and good is our God in all his dealings with his children!
Had I yielded to the suggestions of flesh and blood, and
remained in England, as I should have done, without the
effectual working of his power, I should without doubt
have sunk with my sisters into an early grave; whereas
here, to say the least, I may live a few years, so as to
accomplish a very important work. His keeping you
from me, appears also, at this season of bodily infirmity,

to be occasion of thankfulness. Death, I think, would be a less welcome visitor to me, if he came to take me from a wife, and that wife were you. Now if I die, I die unnoticed, involving none in calamity. Oh that I could trust Him for all that is to come, and love Him with that perfect love, which casteth out fear; for to say the truth, my confidence is sometimes shaken. To appear before the Judge of quick and dead is a much more awful thought in sickness than in health. Yet I dare not doubt the all-sufficiency of Jesus Christ; nor can I, with the utmost ingenuity of unbelief, resist the reasonings of St. Paul, all whose reasons seem to be drawn up on purpose to work into the mind the persuasion that God will glorify Himself by the salvation of sinners through Jesus Christ. I wish I could more enter into the meaning of this "chosen vessel." He seems to move in a world by himself, and sometimes to utter the unspeakable words, such as my natural understanding discerneth not; and when I turn to commentators, I find that I have passed out of the spiritual to the material world, and have got amongst men like myself. But soon, as he says, we shall no longer see as in a glass, by reflected rays, but see as we are seen, and know as we are known.

25th.—After another interval, I resume my pen. Through the mercy of God I am again quite well, but my mind is a good deal distressed at Sabat's conduct. I forbear writing what I think, in the hope that my fears may prove groundless; but indeed the children of the East are adepts in deceit. Their duplicity appears to me so disgusting at this moment, that I can only find relief from my growing misanthropy by remembering Him, who is the faithful and true witness; in whom all

the promises of God are yea and amen ; and by turning to the faithful in Europe—children that will not
lie. Where shall we find sincerity in a native of the
East ? Yesterday I dined in a private way with ——.
After one year's inspection of me, they begin to lose
their dread, and venture to invite me. Our conversation
was occasionally religious, but topics of this nature are so
new to fashionable people, and those upon which they
have thought so much less than on any other, that,
often from the shame of having nothing to say, they pass
on to other subjects where they can be more at home. I
was asked after dinner if I liked music. On my professing to be an admirer of harmony, cantos were performed
and songs sung. After a time I inquired if they had no
sacred music. It was now recollected, that they had
some of Handel's, but it could not be found. A promise
however was made, that next time I came, it should be
produced. Instead of it, the 145th Psalm-tune was
played, but none of the ladies could recollect enough of
the tune to sing it. I observed, that all our talents and
powers should be consecrated to the service of Him who
gave them. To this no reply was made, but the reproof
was felt. I asked the lady of the house if she read
poetry, and then proceeded to mention Cowper, whose
poems, it seems, were in the library; but the lady had
never heard of the book. This was produced, and
I read some passages. Poor people ! here a little,
and there a little, is a rule to be observed in speaking
to them.

26th.—From speaking to my men last night, and again
to-day conversing long with some natives, my chest is
again in pain, so much so that I can hardly speak.

Well! now I am taught, and will take more care in future. My sheet being full, I must bid you adieu. The Lord ever bless and keep you. Believe me to be, with the truest affection, Yours ever,

H. MARTYN.

IX.

Cawnpore, August 14, 1810.

With what delight do I sit down to begin a letter to my beloved Lydia! Yours of the fifth of February, which I received a few days ago, was written, I perceive, in considerable embarrassment. You thought it possible it might find me married, or about to be so. Let me begin, therefore, with assuring you, with more truth than Gehazi did his master, "Thy servant went no whither;" my heart has not strayed from Marazion, or Gurlyn, or wherever you are. Five long years have passed, and I am still faithful. Happy would it be if I could say that I had been equally true to my profession of love for Him who is fairer than ten thousand, and altogether lovely. Yet, to the praise of his grace, let me recollect that twice five years have passed away since I began to know Him, and I am still not gone from Him. On the contrary, time and experience have endeared the Lord to me more and more; so that I feel less inclination, and see less reason for leaving Him. What is there, alas! in the world, even were it everlasting?

I rejoice at the accounts you give me of your continued good health and labours of love. Though you are not so usefully employed as you might be in India, yet as that must not be, I contemplate with delight, your exertions at the other end of the world. May you be instrumental in bringing many sons and daughters to glory. What is

become of St. Hilary, and its fairy scenes? When I
think of Malachy, and the old man, and your sister, and
Josepha, &c., how some are dead, and the rest dispersed,
and their place occupied by strangers, it seems all like a
dream.

15th.—It is only little intervals of time that I can find
for writing; my visitors, about whom I shall write presently, taking up much of my leisure, from necessary
duty. Here follow some extracts from my journal.

*   *   *   *   *   *   *

Here my journal must close. I do not know whether
you understand from it how we go on. I must endeavour
to give you a clearer idea of it.

We all live here in bungalows, or thatched houses, on
a piece of ground inclosed. Next to mine is the church,
not yet opened for public worship; but which we make
use of at night with the men of the 53rd. Corrie lives
with me, and Miss Corrie with the Sherwoods. We
usually rise at daybreak, and breakfast at six. Immediately after breakfast we pray together, after which I
translate into Arabic with Sabat, who lives in a small
bungalow on my ground. We dine at twelve, and sit
recreating ourselves with talking a little about dear
friends in England. In the afternoon, I translate with
Mirza Fitrut into Hindostanee, and Corrie employs himself in teaching some native Christian boys whom he is
educating with great care, in hopes of their being fit for
the office of catechist. I have also a school on my
premises, for natives; but it is not well attended. There
are not above sixteen Hindoo boys in it at present; half
of them read the book of Genesis. At sunset we ride or
drive, and then meet at the church, where we often raise
the song of praise, with as much joy, through the grace

and presence of our Lord, as you do in England. At ten we are all asleep. Thus we go on. To the hardships of missionaries, we are strangers, yet not averse, I trust, to encounter them, when we are called. My work at present is evidently to translate; hereafter I may itinerate. Dear Corrie, I fear, never will,—he always suffers from moving about in the daytime. But I should have said something about my health, as I find my death was reported at Cambridge. I thank God, I am perfectly well, though not very strong in my lungs; they do not seem affected yet, but I cannot speak long without uneasiness. From the nature of my complaint, if it deserves the name, it is evident that England is the last place I should go to. I should go home only to find a grave. How shall I therefore ever see you more on this side of eternity? Well! be it so, since such is the will of God: we shall meet, through grace, in the realms of bliss.

I am truly sorry to see my paper fail. Write as often as possible, every three months at least. Tell me where you go, and whom you see, and what you read.

17th.—I am sorry to conclude with saying, that my yesterday's boasted health proved a mistake; I was seized with violent sickness in the night, but to-day am better. Continue to pray for me, and believe me to be

Your ever affectionate,

H. MARTYN.

X.

From the Ganges, Oct. 6, 1810.

MY DEAREST LYDIA,

Though I have had no letter from you very lately, nor have anything particular to say, yet having been days on the water without a person to speak to, tired also with reading and thinking, I mean to indulge myself with a little of what is always agreeable to me, and sometimes good for me: for, as my affection for you has something sacred in it, being founded on, or at least cemented by, an union of spirit in the Lord Jesus; so my separation also from you, produces a deadness to the world, at least for a time, which leaves a solemn impression as often as I think of it. Add to this, that as I must not indulge the hope of ever seeing you again in this world, I cannot think of you without thinking also of that world where we shall meet. You mention in one of your letters my coming to England, as that which may eventually prove a duty. You ought to have added, that in case I do come, you will consider it a duty not to let me come away again without you. But I am not likely to put you to the trial. Useless as I am here, I often think I should be still more so at home. Though my voice fails me, I can translate and converse. At home I should be nothing without being able to lift up my voice on high. I have just left my station, Cawnpore, in order to be silent six months. I have no cough, nor any sign of consumption, except that reading prayers, or preaching, or a slight cold, brings on pain in the chest. I am advised, therefore, to recruit my strength by rest. So I am come forth, with my face towards Calcutta, with an ulterior view to the sea. Nothing happened at Cawnpore after I wrote to you in September, but I must look to my journal.

I think of having my portrait taken in Calcutta, as I promised Mr. Simeon five years ago. Sabat's picture would also be a curiosity. Yesterday I carried Colonel Wood to dine with me at the Nabob Bahir Ali's. Sabat was there. The Colonel, who had been reading by the

way the account of his conversion in the Asiatic and
East Society Report which I had given him, eyed him
with no great complacency, and observed in French, that
Sabat might not understand him, " Il a l'air d'un sauvage."
Sabat's countenance is indeed terrible ; noble when he is
pleased, but with the look of an assassin when he is out
of humour. I have had more opportunities of knowing
Sabat than any man has had, and I cannot regard him
with that interest which the " Star in the East " is
calculated to excite in most people. Buchanan says, I
wrote (to whom I do not know) in terms of admiration
and affection about him. Affection I do feel for him,
but admiration, if I did once feel it, I am not conscious
of at present. I tremble for everything our dear friends
publish about our doings in India, lest shame come to us
and them.

November 5.—Calcutta.—A sheet full, like the preceding, I had written, but the moment that it is necessary to send off my letter, I cannot find it. That it does
not go on to you is of little consequence, but into whose
hands may it have fallen ? It is this that grieves me. It
was the continuance of my journal to Calcutta, where I
arrived the last day in October. Constant conversation
with dear friends here has brought on the pain in the
chest again, so that I do not attempt to preach. In two
or three weeks I shall embark for the Gulf of Persia,
where, if I live, I shall solace myself in my hours of
solitude with writing to you.

Farewell, beloved friend ; pray for me, as you do I am
sure, and doubt not of an unceasing interest in the heart
and prayers of your ever affectionate,

H. MARTYN.

XI.

At sea, Coast of Malabar, Feb. 4, 1811.

The last letter I wrote to you, my dearest Lydia, was dated November, 1810. I continued in Calcutta to the end of the year, preaching once a week, and reading the Word in some happy little companies, with whom I enjoyed that sweet communion, which all in this vale of tears have reason to be thankful for, but especially those whose lot is cast in a heathen land. On New Year's-day, at Mr. Brown's urgent request, I preached a sermon for the Bible Society, recommending an immediate attention to the state of the native Christians. At the time I left Calcutta they talked of forming an Auxiliary Society. Leaving Calcutta was so much like leaving England, that I went on board my boat without giving them notice, and so escaped the pain of bidding them farewell. In two days I met my ship at the mouth of the river, and we put to sea immediately. Our ship is commanded by a pupil of Swartz, and manned by Arabians, Abyssinians, and others. One of my fellow-passengers is Mr. Elphinstone, who was lately Ambassador at the Court of the King of Cabul, and is now going to be Resident at Poonah, the capital of the Mahratta Empire. So the group is rather interesting, and I am happy to say not averse to religious instruction,—I mean the Europeans. As for the Asiatics, they are in language, customs, and religion, as far removed from us as if they were inhabitants of another planet. I speak a little Arabic sometimes to the sailors, but their contempt of the Gospel, and attachment to their own superstition, make their conversion appear impossible. How stupendous that power which can make these people the followers of the Lamb, when they so nearly resemble Satan in pride and wickedness. The first part of the voyage I was without employment, and almost without thought, suffering as usual so much from sea-sickness, that I had not spirits to do anything but sit upon the poop, surveying the wide waste of waters blue. This continued all down the Bay of Bengal. At length in the neighbourhood of Ceylon we found smooth water, and came to an anchor off Columbo, the principal station in the island. The captain having proposed to his passengers that they should go ashore and refresh themselves with a walk in the Cinnamon-gardens, Mr. E. and myself availed ourselves of the offer, and went off to inhale the cinnamon breeze. The walk was delightful. The huts of the natives, who are (in that neighbourhood at least) most of them Protestants, are built in thick groves of cocoa-nut-tree, with openings here and there, discovering the sea. Everything bore the appearance of contentment. I contemplated them with delight, and was almost glad that I could not speak with them, lest further acquaintance should have dissipated the pleasing ideas their appearance gave birth to. In the gardens I cut off a piece of the bark for you. It will not be so fragrant as that which is properly prepared; but it will not have lost its fine smell, I hope, when it reaches you.

At Captain R.'s, the Chief Secretary to Government, we met a good part of the European society of Columbo. The party was like most mixed parties in England, where much is said that need not be remembered. The next day we stretched across the Gulf of Manaan, and soon came in sight of Cape Comorin, the great promontory of India. At a distance the green waves seemed to wash the foot of the mountain, but on a nearer approach little churches were seen, apparently on the beach, with a row of little huts on each side. Was it these maritime situations that recalled to my mind Perran Church and town in the way to Gurlyn; or that my thoughts wander too often on the beach to the east of Lamorran? You do not tell me whether you ever walk there, and imagine the billows that break at your feet, to have made their way from India. But why should I wish to know? Had I observed silence on that day and thenceforward, I should have spared you much trouble and myself much pain. Yet I am far from regretting that I spoke; since I am persuaded that all things will work together for good. I sometimes try to put such a number of things together as shall produce the greatest happiness possible, and I find that even in imagination I cannot satisfy myself. I set myself to see what is that "good for the sons of men, which they should do under heaven all the days of their life," and I find that Paradise is not here. Many things are delightful, some things are almost all one could wish: but yet in all beauty there is deformity; in the most perfect, something wanting; and there is no hope of its ever being otherwise. "That which is crooked cannot be made straight, and that which is wanting cannot be numbered." So that the expectation of happiness on earth seems chimerical to the last degree. In my schemes of happiness I place myself of course with you, blessed with great success in the ministry, and seeing all India turning to the Lord. Yet it is evident that with these joys there would be mingled many sorrows. The care of all the churches was a burden to the mighty mind of St. Paul. As for what we should be together, I judge of it from our friends. Are they quite beyond the vexations of common life? I think not—still I do not say that it is a question, whether they gained or lost by marrying. Their affections will live when ours (I should rather say mine) are dead.

Perhaps it may not be the effect of celibacy; but I certainly begin to feel a wonderful indifference to all but myself. From so seldom seeing a creature that cares for me, and never one that depends at all upon me, I begin to look round upon men with reciprocal apathy. It sometimes calls itself deadness to the world, but I much fear that it is deadness of heart. I am exempt from worldly cares myself, and therefore do not feel for others. Having got out of the stream into still water, I go round and round in my own little circle. This supposed deterioration you will ascribe to my humility; therefore I add, that Mr. Brown could not help remarking the difference between what I am and what I was; and observed on seeing my picture, which was taken at Calcutta for Mr. Simeon, and is thought a striking likeness, that it was not Martyn that arrived in India, but Martyn the recluse.

10.—To-day my affections seem to have revived a little. I have been often deceived in times past, and erroneously called animal spirits, joy in the Holy Ghost. Yet I trust that I can say with truth, "To them who believe, He is precious!" "Yes, thou art precious to my soul, my transport and my trust." No thought now is so sweet as that which those words suggest—"*In Christ.*" Our destinies thus inseparably united with those of the Son of God, what is too great to be expected? "All things are yours, for ye are Christ's!" We may ask what we will, and it shall be given to us. Now, why do I ever lose sight of Him, or fancy myself without Him, or try to do anything without Him? Break off a branch from a tree, and how long will it be before it withers? To-day, my beloved sister, I rejoice in you before the Lord, I rejoice in you as a member of the mystic body, I pray that your prayers for one who is unworthy of your remembrance may be heard, and bring down tenfold blessings on yourself. How good is the Lord in giving me grace to rejoice with His chosen, all over the earth; even with those who are at this moment going up with the voice of joy and praise, to tread His courts and sing His praise! There is not an object about me but is depressing. Yet my heart expands with delight at the presence of a gracious God, and the assurance that my separation from His people is only temporary. On the 7th we landed at Goa, the capital of the Portuguese possessions in the East. I reckoned much on my visit to Goa; expecting, from its being the residence of the Archbishop and many ecclesiastics, that I should obtain such information about the Christians in India as would render it superfluous to make inquiries elsewhere, but I was much disappointed. Perhaps it was owing to our being accompanied by several officers, English and Portuguese, that the Archbishop and his principal agents would not be seen; but so it was, that I scarcely met with a man who could make himself intelligible. We were shown what strangers are usually shown, the churches and monasteries, but I wanted to contemplate man, the only thing on earth almost that possesses any interest for me. I beheld the stupendous magnificence of their noble churches without emotion, except to regret that the Gospel was not preached in them. In one of the monasteries we 'w the tomb of Francis Xavier, the Apostle of India, most richly ornamented, as well as the room in which it stands, with paintings and figures in bronze, done in Italy. The Friar who showed us the tomb, happening to speak of the grace of God in the heart, without which, said he, as he held the sacramental wafer, the body of Christ profits nothing, I began a conversation with him, which, however, came to nothing.

We visited among many other places the convent of Nuns. After a long altercation with the lady-portress, we were admitted to the antechamber, in which was the grate, a window with iron bars, behind which the poor prisoners made their appearance. While my companions were purchasing their trinkets, I was employed in examining their countenances, which I did with great attention. In what possible way, thought I, can you support existence, if you do not find your happiness in God? They all looked ill and discontented, those at least whose countenances expressed anything. One sat by reading, as if nothing were going on. I asked to see the book, and it was handed through the grate. Finding that it was a Latin Prayerbook, I wrote in Latin something about the love of the world, which seclusion from it would not remove. The Inquisition is still existing at Goa. We were not admitted as far as Dr. Buchanan was, to the Hall of Examination; and that because he printed something about the Inquisitors, which came to their knowledge. The priest in waiting acknowledged that they had some prisoners within the walls, and defended the practice of imprisoning and chastising offenders, on the ground of its being conformable to the custom of the Primitive Church. We were told that when the officers of the Inquisition touch an individual, and beckon him away, he dares not resist; if he does not come out again, no one must ask about him; if he does, he must not tell what was done to him.

18. (Bombay.)—Thus far I am brought in safety. On this day I complete my 30th year. "Here I raise my Ebenezer; Hither by thy help I'm come." It is sweet to reflect that we shall at last reach our home. I am here amongst men who are indeed aliens to the commonwealth

of Israel, and without God in the world. I hear many
of those amongst whom I live, bring idle objections
against religion, such as I have answered a hundred
times. How insensible are men of the world to all
that God is doing! How unconscious of his purposes
concerning his Church! How incapable, seemingly, of
comprehending the existence of it! I feel the meaning
of St. Paul's words—"Hath abounded toward us in all
wisdom and prudence, having made known to us the
mystery of his will, that he would gather in one all things
in Christ." Well! let us bless the Lord—"All thy
children shall be taught of the Lord, and great shall
be the peace of thy children." In a few days I expect to
sail for the Gulf of Persia in one of the Company's sloops
of war.

Farewell, my beloved Lydia, and believe me to be
ever, Yours most affectionately,

H. MARTYN.

XII.

Muscat, April 22, 1811.

MY DEAREST LYDIA,

I am now in Arabia Felix; to judge from the aspect of
the country, it has few pretensions to the name, unless
burning barren rocks convey an idea of felicity; but
perhaps, as there is a promise in reserve for the sons of
Joktan, their land may one day be blest indeed.

We sailed from Bombay on Lady-day; and on the
morning of Easter saw the land of Mehran in Persia.
After another week's sail across the mouth of the Gulf,
we arrived here, and expect to proceed up the Gulf to
Bushire, as soon as we have taken in our water. You
will be happy to learn that the murderous pirates against

whom we were sent, having received notice of our approach, have all got out of the way; so that I am no longer liable to be shot in a battle, or decapitated after it, if it be lawful to judge from appearances. These pestilent Ishmaelites indeed, whose hand is against every man's, will escape, and the community suffer; but that selfish friendship of which you once confessed yourself guilty, will think only of the preservation of a friend. This last marine excursion has been the pleasantest I ever made, as I have been able to pursue my studies with less interruption than when ashore. My little congregation of forty or fifty Europeans does not try my strength on Sundays; and my two companions are men who read their Bible every day. In addition to all these comforts, I have to bless God for having kept me more than usually free from the sorrowful mind. We must not always say with Watts, "the sorrows of the mind be banished from this place;" but if freedom from trouble be offered us, we may choose it rather. I do not know anything more delightful than to meet with a Christian brother, where only strangers and foreigners were expected. This pleasure I enjoyed just before leaving Bombay; a ropemaker who had just come from England understood from my sermon that I was one he might speak to; so he came and opened his heart, and we rejoiced together. In this ship I find another of the household of faith. In another ship which accompanies us there are two Armenians who do nothing but read the Testament. One of them will, I hope, accompany me to Shiraz, in Persia, which is his native country.

We are likely to be detained here some days, but the ship that will carry our letters to India sails immediately, so that I can send but one letter to England, and one to

Calcutta. When will our correspondence be established ? I have been trying to effect it these six years, and it is only yet in train. Why there was no letter from you among those dated June and July, 1810, I cannot conjecture, except that you had not received any of mine, and would write no more. But I am not yet without hope that a letter in the beloved hand will yet overtake me somewhere. My kindest and most affectionate remembrances to all the Western circle. Is it because he is your brother that I love —— so much ? or because he is the last come into the number ? The angels love and wait upon the righteous who need no repentance ; but there is joy whenever another heir of salvation is born into the family. Read Eph. i. I cannot wish you all these spiritual blessings, since they are already all yours ; but I pray that we may have the spirit of wisdom and knowledge to know that they are ours. It is a chapter I keep in mind every day in prayer. We cannot believe too much or hope too much. Happy our eyes that they see, and our ears that they hear.

As it may be a year or more before I shall be back, you may direct one letter after receiving this, if it be not of a very old date, to Bombay; all after to Bengal, as usual. Believe me to be ever, my dearest Lydia,

Your most affectionate

H. MARTYN.

XIII.

Shiraz, June 23, 1811.

MY DEAREST LYDIA,

How continually I think of you, and indeed converse with you, it is impossible to say. But on the Lord's-day in particular, I find you much in my thoughts, because it is on that day that I look abroad, and take a view of the universal church, of which I observe that the saints in England form the most conspicuous part. On that day too, I indulge myself with a view of the past, and look over again those happy days, when, in company with those I loved, I went up to the house of God with a voice of praise. How then shall I fail to remember her who, of all that are dear to me, is the dearest? It is true that I cannot look back upon many days, nor even many hours passed with you;—would they had been more!— but we have insensibly become more acquainted with each other, so that, on my part at least, it may be said that separation has brought us nearer to one another. It was a momentary interview, but the love is lasting, everlasting. Whether we ever meet again or not, I am sure that you will continue to feel an interest in all that befals me.

After the death of my dear sister, you bid me consider that I had one sister left while you remained; and you cannot imagine how consolatory to my mind this assurance is. To know that there is one who is willing to think of me, and has leisure to do so, is soothing to a degree which none can know but those who have, like me, lost all their relations.

I sent you a letter from Muscat in Arabia, which I hope you received; for if not, report will again erase my name from the catalogue of the living, as I sent no other to Europe. Let me here say, with praise to our evergracious heavenly Father, that I am in perfect health; of my spirits I cannot say much; I fancy they would be better were ' the beloved Persis ' by my side. This name, which I once gave you, occurs to me at this moment, I suppose because I am in Persia, intrenched in one of its valleys, separated from Indian friends by chains of mountains and a roaring sea, among a people depraved beyond all belief, in the power of a tyrant guilty of every species of atrocity. Imagine a pale person seated on a Persian carpet, in a room without table or chair, with a pair of formidable mustachios, and habited as a Persian, and you see me.

26.—Here I expect to remain six months. The reason is this : I found on my arrival here, that our attempts at Persian translation in India were good for nothing; at the same time they proposed, with my assistance, to make a new translation. It was an offer I could not refuse, as they speak the purest dialect of the Persian. My host is a man of rank,—his name Jaffier Ali Khan, who tries to make the period of my captivity as agreeable as possible. His wife, for he has but one, never appears; parties of young ladies come to see her, but though they stay days in the house, he dare not go into the room where they are. Without intending a compliment to your sex, I must say that the society here, from the exclusion of females, is as dull as it can well be. Perhaps, however, to a stranger like myself, the most social circles would be insipid. I am visited by all the great and the learned; the former come out of respect to my country, the latter to my profession. The conversation with the latter is always upon religion, and it would be strange indeed, if with the armour of truth on the right hand and on the left, I were not able to combat with success, the upholders of such a system of absurdity and sin. As the Persians are a far more unprejudiced and inquisitive people than the Indians, and do not stand quite so much in awe of an Englishman as the timid natives of Hindostan, I hope they will learn something from me; the hope of this reconciles me to the necessity imposed on me of staying here ; about the translation I dare not be sanguine. The prevailing opinion concerning me is, that I have repaired to Shiraz in order to become a Mussulman. Others, more sagacious, say that I shall bring from India some more, under pretence of making them Mussulmans, but in reality to seize the place. They do not seem to have thought of my wish, to have them converted to my religion ; they have been so long accustomed to remain without proselytes to their own. I shall probably have very little to write about, for some months to come, and therefore I reserve the extracts of my journal since I last wrote to you, for some other opportunity;—besides that, the ambassador, with whose despatches this will go, is just leaving Shiraz.

July 2.—The Mohammedans now come in such num bers to visit me, that I am obliged, for the sake of my translation-work, to decline seeing them. To-day one of the apostate sons of Israel was brought by a party of them, to prove the Divine mission of Mahomet from the Hebrew Scriptures ; but with all his sophistry he proved nothing. I can almost say with St. Paul, I feel continual pity in my heart for them, and love them for their fathers' sake, and find a pleasure in praying for them. While speaking of the return of the Jews to Jerusalem, I observed that the "gospel of the kingdom must first be preached in all the world, and then shall the end come." He replied with a sneer, "And this event, I suppose you mean to say, is beginning to take place by your bringing the Gospel to Persia."

5.—I am so incessantly occupied with visitors and my work, that I have hardly a moment for myself. I have more and more reason to rejoice at my being sent here; there is such an extraordinary stir about religion throughout the city, that some good must come of it. I sometimes sigh for a little Christian communion, yet even from these Mohammedans I hear remarks that do me good ; to-day, for instance, my assistant observed, "How he loved those twelve persons ? " "Yes," said I, "and not those twelve only, but all those who shall believe in him;" as he said, "I pray not for these alone, but for all them who shall believe on me through their word." Even the enemy is constrained to wonder at the love of Christ. Shall not the objects of it say, What manner of love is this ?

I have learned that I may get letters from England much sooner than by way of India. Be so good as to direct to me to the care of Sir Gore Ouseley, Bart., Ambassador at Tehran, care of J. Morier, Esq., Constantinople, care of G. Moon, Esq., Malta. I have seen Europe newspapers of only four months' date, so that I am delightfully near you. May we live near one another in the unity of the Spirit, having one Lord, one hope, one God and Father. In your prayers for me, pray that utterance may be given me, that I may open my mouth boldly, to make known the mysteries of the Gospel. I often envy my Persian hearers the freedom and eloquence with which they speak to me. Were I but possessed of their powers, I sometimes think that I should win them all ; but the work is God's, and the faith of his people does not stand in the wisdom of men, but in the power of God. Remember me as usual with the most unfeigned affection to all my dear friends. This is now the seventh letter I send you, without having received an answer.

Farewell, yours

Ever most affectionately,

H. MARTYN

XIV.

A courier on his way to the capital, affords me the un-expected pleasure of addressing my most beloved friend. It is now six months since I left India, and in all that time I have not heard from thence. The dear friends there, happy in each other's society, do not enough call to mind my forlorn condition. Here I am still, beset by cavilling infidels, and making very little progress in my translation, and half disposed to give it up, and come away. My kind host, to relieve the tedium of being always within a walled town, pitched a tent for me in a garden a little distance, and there I lived amidst clusters of grapes, by the side of a clear stream; but nothing compensates for the loss of the excellent of the earth. It is my business, how-ever, as you will say, and ought to be my effort, to make saints, where I cannot find them. I do use the means in a certain way, but frigid reasoning with men of perverse minds, seldom brings men to Christ. However, as they require it, I reason, and accordingly challenged them to prove the Divine mission of their prophet. In consequence of this, a learned Arabic Treatise was written, by one who was considered as the most able man, and put it into my hands; copies of it were also given to the college and the learned. The writer of it said that if I could give a satis-factory answer to it, he would become a Christian, and at all events, would make my reply as public as I pleased. I did answer it, and after some faint efforts on his part to defend himself, he acknowledged the force of my argu-ments, but was afraid to let them be generally known. He then began to inquire about the Gospel, but was not satisfied with my statement. He required me to prove from the very beginning, the Divine mission of Moses, as well as of Christ; the truth of the Scriptures, &c. With very little hope that any good will come of it, I am now employed in drawing out the evidences of the truth; but oh, that I could converse and reason, and plead, with power from on high! How powerless are the best-directed arguments, till the Holy Ghost renders them effectual!

A few days ago I was on the eve of my departure for Ispahan, as I thought, and my translator had consented to accompany me as far as Bagdad; but just as we were setting out, news came that the Persians and Turks were fighting thereabouts, and that the road was in consequence impassable. I do not know what the Lord's purpose may be in keeping me here, but I trust it will be for the furtherance of the Gospel of Christ, and in that belief I abide contentedly.

My last letter to you was dated July. I desired you to direct to me at Tehran. As it is uncertain whether I shall pass anywhere near there, you had better direct to the care of S. Morier, Esq., Constantinople, and I can easily get your letters from thence.

I am happy to say that I am quite well, indeed never better; no returns of pain in the chest since I left India. May I soon receive the welcome news, that you also are well, and prospering even as your soul prospers. I read your letters incessantly, and try to find out something new, as I generally do, but I begin to look with pain at the distant date of the last. I cannot tell what to think, but I cast all my care upon Him who hath already done wonders for me, and am sure that, come what will, it shall be good, it shall be best. How sweet the privilege, that we may lie as little children before Him! I find that my wisdom is folly, and my care useless, so that I try to live on from day to day, happy in His love and care. May that

God who hath loved us, and given us everlasting consolation, and good hope through grace, bless, love, and keep my ever-dearest friend; and dwelling in the secret place of the Most High, and abiding under the shadow of the Almighty, may she enjoy that sweet tranquillity which the world cannot disturb. Dearest Lydia! pray for me, and believe me to be, ever most faithfully and affectionately yours,

H. MARTYN

XV.

Shiraz, October 21, 1811.

. . . . It is, I think, about a month since I wrote to you, and so little has occurred since, that I find scarcely anything in my journal, and nothing worth transcribing. This state of inactivity is becoming very irksome to me. I cannot get these Persians to work, and while they are idle, I am sitting here to no purpose. Sabat's laziness used to provoke me excessively, but Persians, I find, are as torpid as Arabs, when their salary does not depend on their exertions, and both very inferior to the feeble Indian, whom they affect to despise. My translator comes about sunrise, corrects a little, and is off, and I see no more of him for the day. Meanwhile I sit fretting, or should do so, as I did at first, were it not for a blessed employment which so beguiles the tediousness of the day, that I hardly perceive how it passes. It is the study of the Psalms in the Hebrew. I have long had it in contemplation, in the assurance, from the number of flat and obscure passages that occur in the translations, that the original has not been hitherto perfectly understood. I am delighted to find that many of the most unmeaning verses in our version turn out, on close examination, to contain a direct reference to the Lord our Saviour. The testimony of Jesus is indeed the spirit of prophecy. He is never lost sight of. Let them touch what subject they will, they must always let fall something about Him. Such should we be, looking always to Him. I have often attempted the eighty-fourth Psalm, endeared to me on many accounts, as you know, but have not yet succeeded. The glorious sixteenth Psalm I hope I have mastered. I write with the ardour of a student, communicating his discoveries, and describing his difficulties to a fellow-student.

• I think of you incessantly; too much, I fear, sometimes: yet the recollection of you is generally attended with an exercise of resignation to His will. In prayer I often feel what you described five years ago as having felt,—a particular pleasure in viewing you as with me before the Lord, and entreating our common Father to bless both His children. When I sit and muse, my spirit flies away to you, and attends you at Gurlyn, Penzance, Plymouth Dock, and sometimes with your brother in London. If you acknowledge a kindred feeling still, we are not separated, our spirits have met and blended. I still continue without intelligence from India; since last January I have heard nothing of any one person whom I love. My consolation is, that the Lord has you all under his care, and is carrying on His work in the world by your means; and that when I emerge, I shall find that some progress is made in India especially, the country I now regard as my own. Persia is, in many respects, a field ripe for the harvest. Vast numbers secretly hate and despise the superstition imposed on them, and as many of them as have heard the Gospel, approve it; but they dare not hazard their lives for the name of the Lord Jesus. I am sometimes asked whether the external ap-

pearance of Mohammedanism might not be retained with
Christianity; and whether I could not baptize them without their believing in the divinity of Christ? I tell
them, No.

Though I have complained above of the inactivity of
my translation, I have reason to bless the Lord that He
thus supplies Gibeonites for the help of His true Israel.
They are employed in a work, of the importance of which
they are unconscious, and are making provision for future
Persian saints, whose time is, I suppose, now near. "Roll
back, ye crowded years, your thick array!" Let the
long, long period of darkness and sin at last give way to
the brighter hours of light and liberty, which wait on the
wings of the Sun of Righteousness. Perhaps we witness
the dawn of the day of glory, and if not, the desire that
we feel, that Jesus may be glorified, and the nations acknowledge His sway, is the earnest of the Spirit, that
when He shall appear, we shall also appear with Him in
glory. Kind love to all the saints who are waiting His
coming.

Yours with true affection,

My ever dearest Lydia,

H. MARTYN.

It is now determined that we leave Shiraz in a week;
and as the road through Persia is impassable through the
commotions which are always disturbing some part or
other of this unhappy country, I must go back to Bushire.

XVI.

Tebriz, July 12, 181.

MY DEAREST LYDIA,

I have only time to say that I have received your letter of February 14. Shall I pain your heart by adding, that I am in such a state of sickness and pain, that I can hardly write to you? Let me rather observe, to obviate the gloomy apprehension my letters to Mr. Grant and Mr. Simeon may excite, that I am likely soon to be delivered from my fever. Whether I shall gain strength enough to go on, rests on our Heavenly Father, in whose hands are all my times. Oh, his precious grace! His eternal, unchanging love in Christ to my soul, never appeared more clear, more sweet, more strong. I ought to inform you that, in consequence of the state to which I am reduced by travelling so far overland, without having accomplished my journey, and the consequent impossibility of returning to India the same way, I have applied for leave to come on furlough to England. Perhaps you will be gratified by this intelligence; but oh, my dear Lydia, I must faithfully tell you, that the probability of my reaching England alive is but small; and this I say, that your expectations of seeing me again may be moderate, as mine are of seeing you. Why have you not written more about yourself? However, I am thankful for knowing that you are alive and well. I scarcely know how to desire you to direct. Perhaps Alexandria in Egypt will be the best place: another may be sent to Constantinople; for, though I shall not go there, I hope Mr. Morier will be kept informed of my movements. Kindest love to all the saints you usually mention.

Yours, ever most faithfully and affectionately,

H. MARTYN.

XVII.

Tebriz, Aug. 28, 1812.

I wrote to you last, my dear Lydia, in great disorder. My fever had approached nearly to delirium, and my debility was so great, that it seemed impossible I could withstand the power of disease many days. Yet it has pleased God to restore me to life and health again; not that I have recovered my former strength yet, but consider myself sufficiently restored to prosecute my journey. My daily prayer is, that my late chastisement may have its intended effect, and make me all the rest of my days more humble, and less self-confident. Self-confidence has often let me down fearful lengths, and would, without God's gracious interference, prove my endless perdition. I seem to be made to feel this evil of my heart more than any other at this time. In prayer, or when I write, or converse on the subject, Christ appears to me my life and strength; but at other times, I am as thoughtless and bold, as if I had all life and strength in myself. Such neglect on our part works a diminution of our joys; but the covenant, the covenant! stands fast with Him, for His people evermore. I mentioned my conversing sometimes on Divine subjects, for though it is long enough since I have seen a child of God, I am sometimes led on by the Persians to tell them all I know of the very recesses of the sanctuary, and these are the things that interest them. But to give an account of all my discussions with these mystic philosophers, must be reserved to the time of our meeting. Do I dream? that I venture to think and write of such an event as that! Is it possible that we shall ever meet again below? Though it is possible, I dare not indulge such a pleasing hope yet. I am still at a tremendous distance; and the countries I have to pass through, are many of them dangerous to the traveller, from the hordes of banditti, whom a feeble Government cannot chastise. In consequence of the bad state of the road between this and Aleppo, Sir Gore advises me to go first to Constantinople, and from thence to pass into Syria. In favour of this route, he urges, that by writing to two or three Turkish governors on the frontiers, he can secure me a safe passage at least half-way, and the latter half is probably not much infested. In three days, therefore, I intend setting my horse's head towards Constantinople, distant about thirteen hundred miles. Nothing, I think, will occasion any further detention here, if I can procure servants who know both Persian and Turkish; but should I be taken ill on the road, my case would be pitiable indeed. The Ambassador and his suite are still here; his, and Lady Ouseley's attentions to me, during my illness, have been unremitting. The Prince Abbas Mirza, the wisest of the king's sons, and heir to the throne, was here some time after my arrival; I much wished to present a copy of the Persian New Testament to him, but I could not rise from my bed. The book will, however, be given to him by the Ambassador. Public curiosity about the Gospel, now for the first time in the memory of the modern Persians, introduced into the country, is a good deal excited here, at Shiraz, and other places; so that, upon the whole, I am thankful for having been led hither, and detained; though my residence in this country has been attended with many unpleasant circumstances. The way of the kings of the east is preparing. Thus much may be said with safety, but little more. The Persians also will probably take the lead in the march to Zion, as they are ripe for a revolution in religion as well as politics.

Sabat, about whom you inquire so regularly, I have heard nothing of this long time. My friends in India have long since given me up as lost or gone out of reach, and if they wrote, they would probably not mention him, as he is far from being a favourite with any of them. ――――, who is himself of an impatient temper, cannot tolerate him ; indeed I am pronounced to be the only man in Bengal who could have lived with him so long. He is, to be sure, the most tormenting creature I ever yet chanced to deal with—peevish, proud, suspicious, greedy ; he used to give daily more and more distressing proofs of his never having received the saving grace of God. But of this you will say nothing ; while his interesting story is yet fresh in the memory of people, his failings had better not be mentioned. The poor Arab wrote me a querulous epistle from Calcutta, complaining that no one took notice of him, now that I was gone ; and then he proceeds to abuse his best friends. I have not yet written to reprove him for his unchristian sentiments, and when I do, I know it will be to no purpose, after all the private lectures I have given him. My course from Constantinople is so uncertain that I hardly know where to desire you to direct to me ; I believe Malta is the only place, for there I must stop in my way home. Soon we shall have occasion for pen and ink no more ; but I trust I shall shortly see thee face to face. Love to all the saints.

Believe me to be yours, ever
Most faithfully and affectionately,
H. Martyn.